EMPIRE AND EMANCIPATION

Scottish and Irish Catholics at the Atlantic Fringe, 1780–1850

S. Karly Kehoe

T0326936

Empire and Emancipation explores how the agency of Scottish and Irish Catholics redefined understandings of Britishness and British imperial identity in colonial landscapes. In highlighting the relationship of Scottish and Irish Catholics with the British Empire, S. Karly Kehoe starts an important and timely debate about Britain's colonizer constituencies.

The colonies of Nova Scotia, Cape Breton Island, Newfoundland, and Trinidad had some of the British Empire's earliest, largest, and most diverse Catholic populations. These were also colonial spaces where Catholics exerted significant influence. Given the extent to which Scottish and Irish Catholics were constrained at home by crippling legislation, long-established patterns of socio-economic exclusion, and increasing discrimination, the British Empire functioned as the main outlet for their ambition. Kehoe shows how they engaged with and benefitted from the security needs of an expanding empire, the aspirations of an emerging middle class, and Rome's desire to expand its influence in British territories.

Examining the experience of Scottish and Irish Catholics in these colonies exposes how the empire levelled the playing field for Britain's national groups and brokered a stronger and more coherent British identity. In highlighting specific aspects of the complex and multifaceted relationship between Catholicism and the British imperial state, Kehoe presents Britishness as an identity defined much more by civil engagement and loyalism than by religion. In this way, *Empire and Emancipation* furthers our understanding of Britain and Britishness in the Atlantic world.

S. KARLY KEHOE is Canada Research Chair in Atlantic Canada Communities at Saint Mary's University.

STUDIES IN ATLANTIC CANADA HISTORY

Editors: John G. Reid and Peter L. Twohig

This monograph series focuses on the history of Atlantic Canada, interpreting the scope of this field in a way that is deliberately inclusive and accommodating. As well as studies that deal wholly with any aspect of the history of the Atlantic region (or part thereof), the series extends to neighbouring geographical areas that are considered in conjunction with or in parallel with a portion of Atlantic Canada. Atlantic Canada's oceanic or global relationships are also included, and studies from any thematic or historiographical perspective are welcome.

For a list of books in the series, see page 289.

S. KARLY KEHOE

Empire and Emancipation

Scottish and Irish Catholics at the Atlantic Fringe, 1780–1850

UNIVERSITY OF TORONTO PRESS
Toronto Buffalo London

ISBN 978-1-4875-4107-1 (cloth)   ISBN 978-1-4875-4110-1 (EPUB)
ISBN 978-1-4875-4108-8 (paper)   ISBN 978-1-4875-4109-5 (PDF)

Library and Archives Canada Cataloguing in Publication

Title: Empire and emancipation : Scottish and Irish Catholics at the Atlantic
fringe, 1780–1850 / S. Karly Kehoe.
Names: Kehoe, S. Karly, author.
Series: Studies in Atlantic Canada history.
Description: Series statement: Studies in Atlantic Canada history |
Includes bibliographical references and index.
Identifiers: Canadiana (print) 20210334487 | Canadiana (ebook)
20210334509 | ISBN 9781487541071 (cloth) | ISBN 9781487541088 (paper) |
ISBN 9781487541101 (EPUB) | ISBN 9781487541095 (PDF)
Subjects: LCSH: Catholics – Atlantic Provinces – History – 18th century. |
LCSH: Catholics – Atlantic Provinces – History – 19th century. | LCSH:
Irish – Atlantic Provinces – History – 18th century. | LCSH: Irish –
Atlantic Provinces – History – 19th century. | LCSH: Scots – Atlantic
Provinces – History – 18th century. | LCSH: Scots – Atlantic Provinces –
History – 19th century.
Classification: LCC BX1422.A85 K44 2022 | DDC 282.71509/033 – dc23

We wish to acknowledge the land on which the University of Toronto
Press operates. This land is the traditional territory of the Wendat, the
Anishnaabeg, the Haudenosaunee, the Métis, and the Mississaugas of the
Credit First Nation.

This book has been published with the help of a grant from the Federation
for the Humanities and Social Sciences, through the Awards to Scholarly
Publications Program, using funds provided by the Social Sciences and
Humanities Research Council of Canada.

University of Toronto Press acknowledges the financial support of the
Government of Canada, the Canada Council for the Arts, and the Ontario Arts
Council, an agency of the Government of Ontario, for its publishing activities.

Canada Council   Conseil des Arts
for the Arts   du Canada

Funded by the   Financé par le
Government   gouvernement
of Canada   du Canada

for Lynn

Contents

Illustrations

Acknowledgments

This idea for this book emerged when I started reading the private journal of Richard Carr McClement in the Scottish Catholic Archives in Edinburgh, Scotland, in 2009. McClement was an Irish Catholic surgeon in the Royal Navy between 1857 and 1871. His journal was never supposed to leave the family; his son, Freddie, had taken it with him when he entered the Benedictine monastery at Fort Augustus in the Scottish Highlands in the 1880s. When the monastery closed in 1998, the journal and many other historical papers were transferred to Edinburgh.

Richard McClement recorded, with fascinating detail, the experiences that shaped his time in the navy. These included the enslaved people he saw and their Portuguese captors, the conditions in which the enslaved people were kept, and the inspections he was required to undertake as a medical professional when the Royal Navy captured a slaver off the West African coast. He also wrote about his responsibilities in various naval hospitals, including the one at Halifax, his sense of belonging within a growing naval medical community, and what it felt like to be either the only or one of the few Catholic officers on board. Like many naval officers, Richard's story became part of a much larger family tradition, but his stands out because the tradition started with him. Given prohibitions against joining the ranks of the officer class during the penal law era, a Catholic officer culture was in its infancy in the 1850s. When Richard's younger brother, Frederick, also became a naval surgeon, a family tradition, which continues to this day, was cemented. That each generation of this family has been sending men to sea since the middle of the nineteenth century is something I would never have known had Frederick's grandson, Chris McClement, not stumbled upon some of my work when researching his family's history. Sadly, Chris died of lung cancer in 2012, but his enthusiasm for this research was inspirational, and I would like to begin by thanking him, posthumously, for his friendship and curiosity.

Establishing a research context for this project would not have been possible without the support of a number of institutions and funding bodies. The visiting research fellowship that I received from the Beinecke Manuscript and Research Library at Yale University was pivotal because its collection of late eighteenth- and early to mid-nineteenth-century British and Irish material enabled me to form the argument about Catholicism's compatibility with the British constitution. I am also very grateful to the support and funding I was given by the Carnegie Trust for the Universities of Scotland, the Wellcome Trust, the Durham Residential Research Library, the Royal Society of Edinburgh, the Social Sciences and Humanities Research Council of Canada, and the Canada Research Chairs program.

I am fortunate to be surrounded by a fantastic and inspiring group of people. My conversations with Ciaran O'Neill, Mark McGowan, Ben Shepherd, Andrew Nicoll, Dara Price, Graeme Morton, John Reid, Michael Vance, Annie Tindley, Jim Hunter, Andrew Mackillop, Elaine McFarland, Mike Snape, James Kelly, Mark Doyle, Terry Murphy, Jerry Bannister, David Worthington, Jim MacPherson, and Elizabeth Ritchie were invaluable. A number of my Global Young Academy and Young Academy of Scotland friends have helped me to think about concepts and debates in new ways. Special thanks to Chris Dalglish, Eva Alisic, Jan-Christoph Heilinger, Teresa Stoepler, Jennifer Plaul, Saja Al Zoubi, Alaa Hamdon, and Moritz Reide. They are a phenomenal group of friends.

We all have our favourite places to work, to sit, and to reflect. For me, it has been Tinderbox on Byres Road in Glasgow and Dilly Dally on Quinpool in Halifax – these spaces kept me focused. Tess and Innes provided wonderful distractions, and my amazing people, Myles, Katie, Lynn, Rudy, Elaine, Rebecca, Billy, Bethsy, Iain, Christopher, and Alex gave me love, laughs, and, most importantly, reality checks.

EMPIRE AND EMANCIPATION

Scottish and Irish Catholics at the Atlantic Fringe,
1780–1850

Catholic Britons at the Atlantic Fringe

This is a large subject. It embraces not merely the peace of Ireland, but the ultimate security of the British Empire ... It is for man to do justice to man – to concede to each other equal, civil, and religious rights.

The Scotsman, 9 July 1829

The Scotsman, a conservative daily newspaper known for championing the views of the landed elites, was not a place where one would naturally look for a sympathetic view on the Catholic question. Yet in July 1829, shortly after Parliament passed the Roman Catholic Relief Act, its editors endorsed the extension of civil liberties to His Majesty's Roman Catholic subjects. This was not the first time that Britain's imperial security had been given as a reason for Catholic emancipation. Two previous governments, those under William Pitt the Younger and William Wyndham Grenville, had made similar cases, which resulted in their collapse, when each failed to convince an obstinate and deeply anti-Catholic king.

When the emancipation legislation finally came for the United Kingdom, it was the result of Daniel O'Connell's by-election win in Ireland and although met with much gratitude, many Catholics felt that it had taken far too long. For a significant number, the empire – that British space beyond the physical borders of the United Kingdom – had been a lifeline. The socio-economic exclusion that they had confronted since the Reformation meant that the empire had become *the* main outlet for their ambition. It enabled them to explore creative strategies for expanding the boundaries of their belonging and helped them to participate in defining the meaning of Britain and Britishness. The British Empire was where they proved themselves and where they showed their commitment as subjects and their loyalty as Britons.

This book challenges the presumption that Britain and its empire were Anglo-Saxon and Protestant spaces; it makes a strong case for Catholic Britons, those women and men who felt and acted every bit as British as their Protestant neighbours. In exploring some of the ways in which Scottish and Irish Catholics, in particular, engaged with the imperial state between ca. 1780 and 1850, it reveals how they were able to emerge as proactive respondents to a rapidly changing global dynamic and how this gave them more authority at home and in the empire. The decentred nature of the British maritime world is an important element that is brought into sharp relief as the mixture of Catholic experiences at the Atlantic fringe are encountered. The diversity of the Catholic experience highlighted across the book's six chapters offers a new perspective on the sea-based approach to the British Empire and exposes how, in the unfashionable edges of empire, the contribution of experimental religious diversity to Britain's imperial survival was most visible.

Geographically, the focus is on those Catholics who occupied the physical fringe of Britain's western Atlantic world – specifically, the northern territory of Newfoundland and the colonies of Nova Scotia and Cape Breton, the southern Caribbean territory of Trinidad, and, in between, Bermuda. Following the loss of the Thirteen Colonies and the rise of India, these holdings were pivotal to the safeguarding of Britain's imperial interests.[1] In acknowledging the "new importance" that these specific places took on in Britain's late eighteenth- and early nineteenth-century imperial strategy,[2] this concentration is also practical because these areas were where some of the empire's earliest, largest, and most diverse Catholic populations were located. Prince Edward Island (St. John's Island before 1798), which was located in the Gulf of St. Lawrence and sheltered from the open Atlantic by Nova Scotia and Cape Breton Island, also had a significant Scottish Highland Catholic population and so will appear at specific points in the discussion. New Brunswick, conversely, features rarely, because it was not at the geographic fringe, and, when compared to Nova Scotia, Cape Breton Island, and Prince Edward Island, the arrival and settlement of more substantial numbers of Scottish Highland and Irish Catholics happened there slightly later.[3] This mixture of colonies and territories enables us to encounter Catholics in places where they experienced different local structures – some of these places became long-term settlements while others existed as defence posts or were prized as economic assets. For those in the northern region, for example, the majority of Catholics were of Irish or Scottish origin, despite the presence of smaller numbers of Acadian and Indigenous Catholics. In Bermuda, they were predominantly Irish; while in Trinidad, most were French, Spanish, and

African, or of African descent, with English, Irish, and Scottish Catholics arriving in noticeable numbers only after Britain formally acquired the island in 1802.

Across all of these coastal spaces, Catholics were integral to community formation, and, over time, their presence changed understandings of what loyalty meant and perceptions of who could be loyal. Since the number of Irish and Scottish Highland Catholics were far greater in all of these places than their English and Welsh counterparts were, the focus will be primarily on them. Other Catholic groups – including the French, free people of colour, and enslaved people – are highlighted in various places throughout this book because of the important roles they played in extending Catholicism in Britain's northern Atlantic world. The book's concentration on Catholic Britons, however, means that the bulk of the attention is on the Irish and the Scots. Acadian, French, Indigenous peoples, and free people of colour were never perceived as equals, when it came to their citizenship – indeed, the latter group struggled even to achieve recognition as subjects. Enslaved people were confined to chattel status. What is highlighted throughout the book is the fact that the commitment of Irish and Scottish Catholics to delivering socio-economic stability in the overseas colonies translated into levels of civic and professional responsibility that were simply out of reach to their co-religionists back home.

The book's coverage of the period from about 1780 to 1850 means that the Catholic experience in the Thirteen Colonies has not been included. In no way does this suggest the insignificance of this experience; rather, it reflects my curiosity about parts of the British Atlantic during the second British Empire. The American Revolution had a major impact on Britain and Ireland's Catholic experience, not least because the need for troops prompted the first Catholic Relief Act in 1778. In the aftermath of America's secession, the story of Catholics in Britain's empire was influenced disproportionately by three main factors: the security needs of an expanding empire; the aspirations of an emerging Catholic middle class; and the desire by the Rome to expand its influence with the British imperial state. In exploring these points, I frame a nuanced and informed picture of what Britain and the empire actually meant to religious minorities such as Catholics in a specific selection of colonies and territories. Here, in the physical fringe, a process of negotiation and renegotiation, among a diverse range of collaborators, shaped the imperial state. Recognizing that the empire influenced almost every aspect of Britain's experience after the Act of Union in 1707, from political and economic discourses and notions of ethnicity and class to understandings of identity and religiosity, gives us a clearer picture of how the

British imperial state evolved. On one level, the state was an intangible and ongoing process of cooperation between London, the four nations of England, Ireland, Scotland, and Wales, and the British colonies; and yet, on another level, its methods of governance, politics, and economic systems were acutely tangible to those who interacted with them. I use 1850 as the other bookend because, by that time, the situation in Ireland had changed dramatically for a number of reasons – not least of which was the Famine. It was also in that year that the Catholic hierarchy was restored in England and so, while I do occasionally stray beyond this date in pursuit of a specific theme – such as in chapter 4, when I explore the nursing work of women religious and the mental health of military servicemen, or in chapter 5, when I frame an important discussion about the professionalization of women religious and their female students – it is not my intention to relocate the discussion beyond 1850s to any major extent.

The empire broadened the gaze of the British state and presented substantial opportunities to all four of Britain's national groups, which brokered a stronger and much more coherent British identity. Consequently, Britons naturally possessed dual (national and British), multiple (national, British, Catholic, Protestant), and even shifting (settler, traveller, soldier, merchant, priest, nun, teacher, minister) identities that were based on loyalty and allegiance.[4] This more inclusive picture of the British imperial state triggers new questions about the role that non-Protestants played in its development. Along with the general question of how migrant and minority agency informed politics within a global empire, other, more specific questions naturally arise. How have ethno-religious minorities contributed to the shaping of understandings of Britishness and British imperial identity? How have Catholics, and Irish and Scottish Catholics, in particular, participated in the construction of colonial civil landscapes? How did Catholic participation in these landscapes influence the shape of Britain's socioeconomic and political profile? All of these questions presume the imperial state to be an entity defined more by civil engagement and loyalism than by religious identity. Such a position contrasts sharply with Linda Colley's proposition that Protestantism was the glue that kept Britain together, and prompts a reappraisal of Jerry Bannister and Liam Riordan's claim that loyalism encompassed "dynamic conceptions of social order, Englishness and Britishness (as overlapping and divergent identities), Protestant Christianity, monarchy, commerce, and empire."[5] The problem with these positions is that both present loyalism and civil engagement as concepts that excluded Catholics, when neither actually did. As the following chapters reveal, loyalism and civil engagement created unprecedented opportunities for Catholics and other minority groups to participate in the process of colonialism and in the construction of the British imperial state. This is not to deny the persistence of either anti-Catholic or sectarian attitudes; rather, this book offers compelling evidence that these differences were set aside when the advantages of doing so were clear. Moreover, neither a Catholic identification with the British Empire nor a British dependence on Catholic Irish and Scots in building that empire was predicated on a denial of anti-Catholic or sectarian realities.

Empire and emancipation are the overarching themes of this book because they were interdependent in the Catholic context: the expansion and management of the British Empire required Catholic collaboration, and Catholics needed the platform that the empire provided to lobby for their emancipation. Closely connected with these themes are three other influential factors: national identity, imperial security, and minority agency. Each in its own way involved people and groups traditionally excluded from the British imperial narrative, and so illuminates new and unexplored dimensions. Alliances and partnerships formed in response to imperial need, and the fact that the British state reached out to Catholics as the French Revolution was pursuing a policy of "dechristianization" was no coincidence.[6] The British state was a collaboration of England, Scotland, Ireland, and Wales, and using the experience of minority groups to unpack its ethno-religious dimension exposes just how powerful and influential the state actually became. Similarly, in demonstrating that Britain and the empire actually had a Catholic past, we take an important step forward in constructing a more precise awareness of how imperial security, economic progress, and civil society functioned on the ground in colonial settings. This approach underscores the collaborative process that was empire building and connects with J.G.A. Pocock's broader observation about the purpose of the United Kingdom, the realm in which the British state existed:

> The British single kingdom – with its newly unified crown and parliament, its dual structures of laws and churches, its conquered annex in Ireland, its petty lordships in Man and the Channel islands not fully incorporated with either crown, its powerful trading corporations and its colonies in the Caribbean and the coast of continental America – had been created to safeguard its own stability and act as a power in Europe.[7]

This observation resonates with Barry Crosbie's reflections on the Irish in India: "Understanding them and their concerns," he points out, "means understanding the nineteenth-century Empire in its proper 'four nations' context."[8] Located within this statement is an awareness of the centrality of Britain's four nations to imperial discourse and a recognition of the agency of the individual. Agency, which refers to self-ascribed authority, enabled Catholics to engage with the political, economic, and socio-religious structures emerging throughout the colonies. It also underpinned the supportive relationships that many built with colonial officials, and the active roles they played in establishing the frameworks necessary for delivering law and order, good government, and economic stability.

When it came to defining citizenship and access to it, which many people in Britain and Ireland began to do from 1780, inspiration came from the United States, where newly created institutions offered exciting ideas about what else might be achieved.[9] In some ways, the question of citizenship links with the broader principle of reform, which saw people begin to question the value of age-old structures, to think more carefully about what they needed from an evolving state, and to consider the kind of values they wanted to promote. As Joanna Innes makes clear, reform was as much a feeling or an inclination as a movement, and it gave people the confidence to think about their world in new ways.[10]

Investigating the Catholic experience sharpens understandings of how one or more of Britain's constituent nations influenced the formation of British identity. *Empire and Emancipation*'s consideration of how Irish and Scottish Highland Catholics contributed to Britain's imperial program in ways that helped them to achieve civil equality emphasizes the fact that they did not have to stop being Catholic, Scottish, or Irish, to start being British. A four-nations lens integrates Irish Catholics within the British context without compromising their national integrity, and breaks down the myth that all Catholics in the United Kingdom or the British Empire were Irish or nationalist. Scottish Highland Catholics dominated in many parts of northeastern British North America, especially during the period under consideration here,[11] and despite having very little presence on the ground in these colonies, government officials in London and officials of the Catholic Church in Rome assigned vicars apostolic of the London District responsibility for a number of colonial missions. The initial shortage of male and female religious personnel certainly gave the Irish a numeric advantage, particularly from the 1840s, as Ireland's domestic seminaries and convents began to pump out missionaries, but the influence of Scottish and English Catholics was by no means insignificant. Prince Edward Island, while not a main focus here, will be intermittently highlighted as a prime example of Scottish Catholic influence and authority. The island acted as a springboard for the spread of Scottish Highland Catholics through Nova Scotia and Cape Breton Island as they moved in search of land they could own.[12] Trinidad, by contrast, shows just how far the reach of English Catholic authority could extend when called upon by the colonial office.

During the latter decades of the eighteenth century, when the British Empire was confronting serious threats to its stability, powerful debates started to take place about Catholicism's compatibility with the British constitution. As noted above, the conflicts that erupted between Britain and the American colonies and with France had a profound impact on the progress of Catholic emancipation, and they prompted a series of legislative developments that delivered Catholic relief by instalments. Catholic emancipation was a protracted process that was as dependent on international developments as it was on Irish protest. Events in France and in the Thirteen Colonies had inspired new thinking about the concepts of citizenship and reform, which put pressure on the British government to manage new expectations. One manifestation was an increasing toleration for Catholics. The first major shift occurred in the mid-eighteenth century, when Britain acquired, via the 1763 Treaty of Paris, a number of new colonies with large Catholic populations. Those in Quebec and in the Caribbean, for example, were predominantly French (with large Spanish populations in the latter) and gave their loyalty in exchange for freedom of worship and civil liberties. The loyalty of Quebec's French Catholic majority during the American Revolution is highlighted in the second chapter because it enabled Britain to withdraw from that conflict wounded, but not fatally so because it still had a North American empire. This collaboration with Catholics beyond the United Kingdom established a precedent for Catholics within it, and they grew more confident about their own positions as a result.[13]

Empire

In 1999, C.A. Bayly called for a deeper and more reflective consideration of the colonial experience. "The imperial history of the future," he said, "will have to take seriously the question of how far and in what ways, the imperial experience contributed to the making of national and regional identity in the British Isles itself."[14] Similarly, John Mackenzie noted that British imperialism gave countless peripheries the chance to construct their own "particular agendas and links with the metropolitan core, while being both influenced by and, in turn, influencing the Empire's development." Jennifer Ridden's contention that the empire was defined more by those on the spot than those in London connects with work on the Irish in India that explores the significance of sub-imperial culture.[15] The experiences of the Irish and Highland Scots in the empire are especially revealing because, while both possessed strong identities and were pivotal to the establishment of Britain's imperial authority, each confronted the confusing position of being subordinate at home but dominant abroad.[16] On the frontiers, where systems, processes, and institutions were being set up, both groups were essential in the organization of these new societies, which is why the claim that the empire was "nothing special, just ordinary, part of the world in which they [the British] lived," misses the mark when it comes to minority populations like Catholics.[17] The empire was enormously significant for them because it offered both an escape from the restrictions that had governed their lives at home and an opportunity to show their value to the British imperial process.

Interestingly, the foundations for Catholic participation had been established by the French, who had been either the European majority or a major population in places like Quebec, Grenada, St. Vincent, Dominica, and, later, Trinidad, prior to their acquisition by Britain. Although not a specific focus of this book because of its inland location, Quebec's influence was significant, and so that colony is referenced regularly : its Catholic hierarchy, which remained intact following the British conquest, had ecclesiastical responsibility for all of the northern Maritime colonies (which did not include Newfoundland). Its religious leadership also forged a fruitful relationship with British colonial officials, helping to deliver law and order in exchange for toleration; bishops saw to it that the wider French Catholic population, which numbered some 65,000 on the eve of the American Revolution, remained loyal.[18] These "new subjects," as they were called, cut a path for the Irish and Scottish Catholics who quickly spread throughout the empire as settlers, merchants, military servicemen, professionals, religious personnel, teachers, politicians, and community leaders. While these roles extended the boundaries of Catholic participation in Britain's imperial program, the rise of Protestant evangelicalism from the 1820s challenged the authority of the established churches of England and Scotland and fractured the exclusivity of their relationship with the state.[19] This view diverges from the argument that the "spirit of revived empire," which followed the Napoleonic Wars, was influenced by an overarching "Anglican providentialism."[20] The broader point, however, that religion was a major influence on Britain's imperial stage, rings true, but the ways in which British religiosity was articulated and expressed from multiple perspectives needs to be taken into account. The empire offered the opportunity for social and economic growth, alignment of an increasing number of sects, and, for English, Scottish, and Irish Catholics, expansion beyond Britain that enabled non-Anglicans to (re)define their own identities and connect with "the language of Britishness."[21]

This argument, that the survival of the empire required broad engagement, crystallizes with the experience of Irish and Scottish Catholics and aligns with the observation that, particularly after 1783, the empire's growing ethno-religious diversity was a source of strength.[22] Exploring the nexus between imperial security and the extension of rights to minority groups in Britain and the colonies illuminates the complexity of the empire-building enterprise and the collaboration it required. This was not unique to Britain – other powers had adopted similar approaches. Work on Jewish soldiers in late eighteenth-century France is particularly instructive in showing how imperial crises could prompt change.[23] Not only does it show how Jewish soldiers gained access to mainstream French society in ways that would have been unimaginable before the revolution, but also how this access transformed them into citizens "not just in principle but also in practice."[24] In many ways, Scottish and Irish Catholics experienced a similar shift in their status. The needs of the empire and the associated military conflicts gave them valuable options for negotiating expanded rights based on the loyalism they demonstrated through their service as British soldiers and sailors, by their acquisition of professional training, in their delivery of associated services, and with the work they undertook to build and extend colonial economies.[25] These activities certainly cut across class and gender lines, but what was most significant about them was how they enabled the emergence of an imperially networked and confident Catholic middle-class laity who assumed roles as community leaders and as shapers of colonial Catholic cultures.

Prior to the late 1830s, the number of priests and women religious available for the colonial missions was limited in the United Kingdom and, although their presence (particularly that of the Irish) and authority would grow exponentially after this period, the early efforts of an ambitious and pragmatic laity to embed a culture of Catholic loyalism, which was both calculated and not, was profound. Their goals aligned with a broader British imperial vision because they *were* British. The emphasis on ecclesiastical power structures over lay agency is facing increased scrutiny as researchers, such as Sarah Roddy, question the degree to which the Irish hierarchy, for example, actually understood and appreciated the reality of life for the vast majority of the Irish Catholic migrants on the ground.[26] It is telling, as the third chapter highlights, that the election of an Irish-descended Catholic, Laurence Kavanagh, to Nova Scotia's legislative assembly in 1820, seems to have received no mention in the papers of the Dublin clergy. In this respect and in others, the theme of empire adds a new dimension to the debate by showing just how invested the Catholic middle-class laity was in supporting the institutions, administrative systems, and policies of the British imperial state.

Emancipation

Emancipation is a virtuous word symbolizing freedom and justice. In the twentieth century, it described the struggle that women endured to win the right to vote and the closure of the final chapter on enfranchisement in the United Kingdom. Getting to that point, though, had been an epic battle with roots in the late eighteenth and early nineteenth centuries, when questions about emancipation represented a deliberate challenge to the parameters of political participation, equality, and property. In an examination of emancipation in the context of Black enslaved women, the concept's inclusivity is noted as having reflected people's "aspirations for autonomy in economic and personal life."[27] Debbie Lee echoes this, asserting that it also enabled a collective agency that saw people agitate for meaningful change.[28]

Although commonly associated with Black enslaved people, *emancipation* is a term that also held tremendous significance for Catholics and, while it underpinned each group's fight for freedom and equality under the law, major differences separated the enslaved African and Catholic experiences. The emancipation campaigns for Catholics and enslaved people were fundamentally different because the United Kingdom's Catholics were not slaves.[29] They had not been kidnapped en masse, transported across the ocean, and then sold. In fact, many Catholics, including both individuals and members of religious communities like the Jesuits, Capuchins, and Dominicans, colluded in the system of Black enslavement as enslavers and as Europeans ensconced in all levels of the economies that revolved around that system.[30] Where both campaigns aligned was in their fights against the injustices and restrictions that had been deliberately applied to them and not to others.

The concept of emancipation emerged at a time when there was a belief that an era of socio-economic improvement for the masses was dawning, and when there was a growing desire for freedom under the law, but how Catholics and enslaved people engaged with this, or the extent to which their engagement was permitted, was very different.[31] First, as Nini Rodgers explains, emancipation meant "relief" for Catholics and "abolition" for slaves.[32] This difference was fundamental and shaped the emancipation campaigns of each group. While Catholics in the United Kingdom were active and leading collaborators in the campaign to achieve civil equality, Black enslaved people, in spite of their various and powerful forms of resistance and testimony, did not have access to the political circles that would enable them to lead the formal campaign within Parliament to secure their freedom. The British state's need to secure its imperial interests provided the opportunity for a convergence because emancipation was, ultimately, a strategy designed to "avert the possibility of revolt and revolution."[33]

In the context of the United States and its civil war, an analysis of slave emancipation reveals how a domestic cotton crisis precipitated the emergence of a new global cotton empire.[34] This example is instructive, yet while this instance reveals how the end of slavery in the United States threw an entire economy into chaos, the emancipation to which I refer shows how the British state's decision to grant rights to Catholics preserved economic stability and extended its authority. Indeed, anti-Catholicism was "a more pronounced feature of eighteenth-century British discourse than hostility to Blacks,"[35] since the perceived power of Rome underpinned much of the anti-Catholic anxiety that permeated British society. In the 1780s, as the period of reform dawned, people did make connections between the emancipation of Catholics in the United Kingdom and that of enslaved people in the broader British Empire, but the discourse and rhetoric surrounding each was distinctive and focused. While the principles of dignity, freedom, and security under the laws of Great Britain were common,[36] the iconic "Am I not a brother and a man" refrain of the enslaved was fundamentally different from the "We are men and deserve to be free" refrain of the Catholic.[37] There was no question that Catholics were free people in contrast to those who were enslaved, because the latter were categorized as chattels. In addition to the exclusion experienced by the enslaved, even free people of colour were denied the most basic sense of belonging. Following the War of 1812, government officials in the United States argued that Black Britons would not qualify for the protections outlined in the treaty because they were not subjects.[38] Closer to home, perceptions also differed as people sought to prioritize the emancipation of Catholics over that of enslaved people, and while some thought it "disgraceful, unwise and absurd" to require Catholics to argue for their freedom alongside enslaved people, others admitted elements of a common struggle.[39]

The Catholic dimension was complicated by the relationship among the four nations, since Catholics occupied inherently different positions in each one, which affected how and when emancipation, via relief, was delivered. In England, for example, emancipation represented the opportunity to assimilate more completely with mainstream British society; in Scotland, where Catholics were driven underground, it complemented the upwardly mobile and newly emerging elites' use of marriage and property to climb the social ladder by removing a major obstacle to their respectability.[40] In Ireland, by contrast, Catholics were the majority and so, for them, emancipation symbolized full political integration and a means to an end.[41] When the emancipation legislation finally came in 1829, it represented religious equality under the law and gave Catholics access to the highest offices in the land (apart from the Crown) and to Parliament as members. Moreover, it enhanced their strong position in many colonies, where they were already integral to the civil society and working to extend Britain's imperial authority.

Chapter Overview

For much of the eighteenth century, being a Catholic in the United Kingdom meant having to accept the suspension of the civil liberties and sense of belonging that others took for granted. Among other restrictions, Catholics could not join the armed services, inherit land, or go to school, and they were forbidden from becoming a child's legal guardian. Yet, as Britain's imperial interests expanded, the practical value of the restrictions imposed on Catholics were questioned by a growing number of political and colonial elites who recognized the need to reach out to Catholics to shore up support for the empire. One of the things this book does is interweave major themes with the histories of selected colonies to highlight instances where they benefit from more detailed treatments. Thus, the first chapter, "Catholics, Colonies, and the Imperial State," considers the changing perceptions of Catholics. It examines the meaning of Britishness within a four-nations context and looks at how Catholics engaged with and participated in shaping this identity. It then considers the diversity of Catholic identity and the significance of Rome to get a deeper sense of how Catholics functioned locally in Britain and the role that Rome played in fostering collaboration among English, Scottish, and Irish Catholics in a way that more firmly supported Britain's imperial program. It also explores the concept of loyalism to reveal its inherent inclusivity.

Chapter 2, "Imperial Security and Catholic Relief," concentrates on the era of emancipation, the period between the late 1770s and 1829, and considers how, in the context of major conflicts abroad and pressures for reform at home, defining the place of Catholics and Catholicism in British society became an inescapable issue. Although much of the impetus for change came from a pragmatic and increasingly ambitious

Catholic middle class – largely, but not exclusively, Irish – external pressures were pivotal. One of the bravest governing strategies adopted in the last quarter of the eighteenth century was the reconfiguration of Catholicism as a faith that was compatible with the British constitution. In spite of the persistent and often vicious anti-Catholic rhetoric of the popular press, toward the end of the eighteenth century the debate about Catholics turned to points of law and civil participation and away from concerns about theology. Although the Quebec Act of 1774 was deeply unpopular at home, it ensured the loyalty of the Catholics in that distant colony as Britain waged war with the Thirteen Colonies between 1775 and 1783. The path toward emancipation for Catholics in the colonies and territories selected for this book was broken by the imperial state's need to accommodate the extremely large Catholic populations in both Quebec and Grenada. At home, some opinions began to shift on account of the plight of Catholic refugees from France in the mid-1790s and the participation of thousands of Irish and Scottish Highland Catholics in major military campaigns. In terms of the wider Atlantic context, Britain's constitution functioned as an imperial safeguard because of the accommodation it offered Catholics.

As administrative structures improved and communities took shape abroad, Catholics became embedded in the political and civil affairs of the colonies in which they lived. The third chapter, "Colonial Catholics and Constitutional Change: Developments in Cape Breton Island and Nova Scotia," focuses on the extent to which the successful management of the settler colonies depended on a mutually supportive relationship between the Catholic Church and British colonial officials. Specifically, the need to cultivate a sense of loyalty among settlers in Nova Scotia and Cape Breton Island is considered and linked with the Catholic pursuance of the civil and political roles that induced emancipation. It reveals how the lack of a resident Catholic clergy – or any real church infrastructure before the early 1820s, for that matter – saw an ambitious and pragmatic Catholic laity, many of whom were Irish-descended entrepreneurs, take responsibility for engaging with Britain's imperial program.

The acquisition of new territories in the Caribbean and in northeastern British North America, through major military campaigns, meant that Britain's military commitments expanded dramatically in the last quarter of the eighteenth and early nineteenth centuries, in spite of the loss of the American colonies. Chapter 4, "Engaging with Imperial Traditions: Military Mobilization and Slavery," highlights two different but connected themes. While Britain's military conflicts and the management needs of the empire led to a rise in the number of Catholic servicemen and to the emergence of a formal and informal Catholic chaplaincy, the acquisition of territory in the Caribbean forced Britain to engage directly with the Catholic dimension of slavery. The sea and battlefield became neutral spaces for Britain's Catholic subjects and while creed mattered in the armed services, a willingness to defend Crown and country mattered more. Similarly, in the context of slavery, the chapter reveals that the economic motivations of white Europeans were the same regardless of religious affiliation and that Catholics were as committed as Protestants to preserving the institution of African enslavement.

Chapter 5, "Enabling Ambition through Education," explores colonial and Irish educational culture in order to consider the professionalization of Catholics. The most effective way of extending the reach of the Catholic Church and the imperial state into colonial society was through education, and, over the course of the nineteenth century, an extensive program of church and school building was introduced across Britain and its colonies. Specifically, the focus of this chapter will be on the development of higher education and training for the Catholic middle class – female and male. As educational provision and access to it expanded, Catholics were effective in using it to improve their prospects and to reinforce their roles in broader British society. The chapter begins with a consideration of how the anti-clerical shift in revolutionary France led to the reintroduction of the religious life in Britain and how the new religious personnel, who arrived as refugees, influenced the development of Catholic education. It then moves on to discuss the professionalization of young women by scanning the rise of female religious congregations, which offered one of the very few safe spaces for Catholic women's intellectual pursuits. The male dimension of education is explored with reference to the importance of university education. This discussion highlights the proliferation of Catholic universities in the Canadian Maritimes as a way of demonstrating the progress that their agency delivered.

The final chapter, "The Decline of Lay Authority: Ecclesiastical Reorganization and Imperial Power in Trinidad and Newfoundland," investigates how a broader desire to circumvent anti-Catholicism sharpened the Catholic Church's ability to renegotiate the boundaries of its civic partnerships. This chapter reveals how the Catholic leadership's anxiety to ensure authority over the laity prompted a process of ecclesiastical expansion and a push by the Catholic leadership in Britain and Rome to assume responsibility for imperial collaboration. This chapter explores the relationship that emerged between the laity, the clergy, and the colonial administrators in Newfoundland and Trinidad.

While Trinidad had to face unique challenges as a slave, and then a post-slavery, society, both it and Newfoundland experienced profound ethno-religious tensions among the Irish and other Catholic or Protestant groups; indeed, the influence of Quebec is noted as having loomed large over Newfoundland. In exploring these points, the chapter highlights some of the main strategies employed by the Catholic Church to manage colonial relationships on the ground and cement itself as a partner of the imperial state.

This book and the research underpinning it offer an important and overdue update to our thinking about the British imperial process and the people who engaged with it. It broadens our sense of what Britishness meant by exploring the significance of Britain's largest minority group – Catholics at the Atlantic's fringe – during a period of substantial and transformative change.

PART I

Identity, Catholic Relief, and Imperial Security

Chapter One

Catholics, Colonies, and the Imperial State

> Here lies the body
> Alex'r Beaton
> Son of Finlay Beaton
> Coal Mines. Born in the
> Braes of Lochaber
> N: Britain
> Who departed this life
> July 4th 1831
> Aged 34 years
> May he rest in peace
> Amen

Following the loss of the thirteen American colonies, Nova Scotia emerged as one of Britain's most valued colonial possessions. Stationed at the entrance to the St. Lawrence River, on the east coast of what would become Canada, Nova Scotia was perched on the edge of the open Atlantic. It was Britain's eyes and ears on the eastern seaboard of North America, mediating trade with the Caribbean and accommodating the headquarters of the Royal Navy's Atlantic station at Halifax from 1758 until 1819. Nova Scotia's strategic importance to an imperial state recovering from dramatic territorial loss was significant, but so was the fact that it and its neighbouring Atlantic colonies and territories – namely, Prince Edward Island, Cape Breton, and Newfoundland – were being populated by a growing number of Irish and Scottish Highland Catholics. The presence of these people throws up important questions about an empire frequently perceived as Protestant.

Alexander Beaton, from whose tombstone the above inscription comes, was a Highland Scot, who had likely arrived in Cape Breton

via Prince Edward Island around 1800. While he had little choice about
whether or not to emigrate from Britain, a consequence of both his age
and the sweeping land-management changes that were displacing numerous settlements across the Highlands, he did get to choose how he
would be remembered. Alexander Beaton was a Catholic from North
Britain, who died at Mabou Coal Mines on Cape Breton Island in the
province of Nova Scotia in 1831, two years after Catholic emancipation
became a reality in Britain and Ireland.[1] Beaton and countless other
Scottish and Irish Catholic folk, many distinguished by neither wealth
nor influence, represented the intrinsic and deeply rooted connections
between Catholicism and the British Empire. Despite having a sizeable
presence in Britain and its empire, Catholics were perceived consistently
as peripheral to both empire and state – unable or unwilling to belong.

Catholicism in the United Kingdom during the period under investigation here was extremely complex – and even this is an under-
statement. Internal, national distinctions based on culture, tradition,
language, and politics meant that it endured fluctuation and schism
at home and abroad. In the latter part of the eighteenth century, the
toleration of Catholics and Catholicism was fiercely debated and one
that was influenced heavily by the rapidly changing international climate. Efforts to expand the rights of Catholics formally began in the
late 1770s, with the introduction of relief legislation, but conflicting priorities, coupled with the fact that not all Catholics had felt the impact
of the penal laws in the same ways, meant that the implementation of
relief across the four nations of the United Kingdom was unequal and
slow. In Ireland, the local influence, church ties, family networks, and
lease speculations of Catholic middlemen (mostly outside of Ulster)
positioned them as de facto power brokers at a grassroots level.[2] In
London, the Irish Catholic community benefited from business and
class ties that gave them significant freedoms and access to numerous
opportunities.[3] England's major recusant families, such as the Throckmortons, faced the perpetual threat of "arrest and harassment" but used
marriage alliances and educational opportunities abroad to retain their
status, land, and influence. Although many Protestants had begun to
view marriage in terms of emotional attachment and individual choice
by the early eighteenth century, the major Catholic families of England
continued to use it to cement the alliances necessary to preserve their
faith.[4] As in Scotland, elite Catholic women in England were intrinsic to the preservation of national Catholic traditions, and while the
Scots did not establish a Continental convent culture like their English
counterparts, both groups of women possessed and asserted authority
over Catholic culture.[5] Essentially, the late eighteenth-century Catholic

Figure 1. Mabou Catholic church and convent (with permission
of Nova Scotia Archives)

Relief Acts were the precursors to full emancipation in 1829, in that
they represented the loosening and then the outright repeal of various
elements of the crippling penal legislation that had been imposed upon
the majority of Catholics following the Revolution of 1688–89.

As noted in the introduction, for much of the eighteenth century, being a Catholic in the United Kingdom meant having to accept the suspension of the civil liberties and sense of belonging that the majority
took for granted. Yet, as Britain's imperial interests expanded or came
under threat, the practical value of these restrictions was increasingly
questioned by members of the political elite, who recognized the value
of shoring up support for the empire at home by bringing in previously excluded minority populations. This chapter lays the foundation
for the rest of the book by examining three important themes that influenced and shaped the relationship that Catholics had with Britain
and its empire. First, it considers the meaning of Britishness within a
four-nations context and explores how Catholics engaged with this and
collaborated in shaping its development. Second, it examines the diversity of Catholic identity and the significance of Rome to provide an
overview of how Catholics functioned locally. Rome, particularly the

Sacred Congregation *de Propaganda Fide*, fostered greater collaboration among Britain's national Catholic groups (often unintentionally) and in supporting the British state's imperial program. Finally, Catholic loyalism is discussed as a way of highlighting loyalism's inclusive nature and of demonstrating how minority groups like Catholics engaged with it. Loyalism was "motivationally complex" and a more appropriate gauge of Britishness than was religious identity.[6]

Perceptions of Britishness

The rise of Irish nationalist agitation from the late eighteenth century enhanced perceptions of Catholics as deviant subjects not to be trusted. By then, however, a broader debate was taking place, and important thinkers such as Thomas Macaulay, the essayist and Whig politician, were openly questioning the logic of such opinions. Macaulay's position was that agitation in Ireland was due to the length of time it had taken for the British state to grant Catholics the "liberties of subjects," and not to any inherent disloyalty.[7] The situation for Catholics abroad was very different. Not only were they able to achieve recognition as eager and willing participants in the expansion and stabilization of the empire, but they also demonstrated an instinctive commitment to British ideals and values by engaging with colonial replicas of Britain's civic and political institutions. Catholics in Quebec, Nova Scotia, Grenada, and Bermuda, for example, strengthened positive perceptions of Catholicism when they exhibited loyalty and endorsed an overarching sense of Britishness through military service, educational institutions, print media, and politics. All of this activity boosted their confidence over time, and, by the 1850s, they felt comfortable enough to join their fellow Britons in calling for the support of government against "rebellious" populations.

Across Britain and its empire, Catholics were, by the middle of the nineteenth century, building churches, schools, and communities; they were serving as soldiers and sailors in the armed services; and they were becoming adept and skilled civil servants and politicians. Understanding how they got to this point necessitates a deeper investigation of their relationship with Britain and Britishness – two concepts evolving rapidly and by no means set in stone. While the influence of Rome helped to align the United Kingdom's various Catholic traditions with the ambitions of the imperial state over the course of the century, the development of a British identity among colonial Catholics on the ground was a process led by an ambitious and pragmatic laity beginning in the last quarter of the eighteenth century. The ubiquity of Irish and Scottish Highland Catholics in the armed services, coupled with the activities of an emerging business class and the growing desire of its members for political collaboration, enabled a deeper engagement with an Anglo-Christian British Empire through social and political networks, church policy, and a burgeoning Catholic associational culture. Evolving understandings of Britishness, across all groups and sects, were central to Catholic activities, and yet scholars have rarely considered this. Recognizing that Britishness was (and remains) a much more complex and inclusive concept than is often assumed allows us to take another look at, and to be open to new understandings of, its "multiple meanings" and consequences, particularly when it comes to religious minorities.[8]

Much of the scholarship that engages with the meaning of *British* and *Britishness*, including this book, has been influenced, in one way or another, by J.G.A. Pocock's seminal article, "British History: A Plea for a New Subject," which makes a case for England being at the centre of a community of cultures. The implication appears to be that the self-perception of the Scottish, Irish, and Welsh has been fundamentally influenced by the "official [and] unofficial, public [and] private, conscious [and] unconscious" structures introduced through their contact with the centre (England).[9] In terms of the formation of the British state, Britain's union with Ireland was the "logical extension" of England's integrationist policy, which began with Wales in the middle of the sixteenth century.[10] In many ways, it was the empire, more than anything, that illuminated core elements of what it was to be "British," and so, while it is right to underscore the importance of "political allegiance," economic allegiance through imperial activity was foundational.[11] Notwithstanding these components, the contention that England was always prepared to cut loose its "colonies" – which included Scotland, Ireland, and Wales – to protect itself sits uncomfortably with four-nations scholars who are justifiably uneasy with the suggestion that Ireland and the Irish and Scotland and the Scots faced a perpetual threat of exclusion from the parliamentary unions that created the United Kingdom of Great Britain and Ireland. This "lopsidedness" is correctable if Britain is understood as a "union of multiple identities" wherein national identities were enhanced and strengthened.[12] There are benefits to approaching the idea of Britain in this way. First, it allows us to recognize Britain as a working state with an identity that was neither fixed nor stagnant. Second, it permits a more flexible framework for understanding how each nation connected with the British state and how their peoples functioned abroad as part of an expanding ethnically and religiously diverse British diaspora.

Linda Colley provided the chief platform for discussing what being British and being a Briton actually mean. Her enormously influential book, *Britons*, which argues that Protestantism was the glue that held Britain together, prompted a flurry of research that is maturing our thinking about the union and identity.[13] Some of this work, however, casts light on why conceptualizing the terms *British* and *Briton* within a common Protestant framework cannot work. Protestantism could unify, but tensions between the Church of England and the Church of Scotland could be equally disruptive.[14] A study of the relationship between the Scottish Highlands, the army, and the British Empire, shows that established Protestantism did not achieve "anything like complete control" in Britain, since there was no such thing as a "common Protestantism" binding England and Scotland.[15] Nor was there such a thing in England itself, as the establishment of the Church of England led to more, not fewer, divisions among Protestants in England, because people felt compelled to push against the teachings and structures they could not endorse.[16] Similarly, the doctrinal differences dividing Scottish Presbyterians prevented the Church of Scotland from becoming wholly representative. Moderate and evangelical Presbyterians, for example, constructed different versions of Scotland's religious past to achieve legitimacy.[17] This influenced how Scots perceived Britain and suggests that the dominant voice of Presbyterian Scotland was not necessarily unionist.[18] The Scottish situation is complicated further by the fact that Episcopalians and Catholics, groups with their own distinctions and allegiances, were actually the majority populations in many parts of northern Scotland.[19]

The elephant in the room, as ever, is Ireland. The Irish, precariously positioned as part colony, part colonizer, and predominantly Catholic, do not fit the theory and were all but excluded from Colley's important discussion. What is becoming increasingly obvious, particularly as more research is undertaken in British, American, Italian, and Canadian archives, is that, even before Ireland's parliamentary union with Britain, many Catholic and Protestant Irish saw themselves, or attempted to characterize themselves, as British for financial, diplomatic, political, and/or personal reasons – not unlike the Scots, and probably not unlike the English or the Welsh. A detailed study of Irish Catholic networks in eighteenth-century London, for example, demonstrates just how absorbed they were in aristocratic, gentry, merchant, and professional networks and reveals the extent to which class solidarity "overrode confessional or political divisions."[20] An anonymous newspaper clipping about Britons, of 1781, from the Archives of *Propaganda Fide* in Rome illustrates this wider point:

> Consult yourselves, consult your religion – you cannot be indifferent, unfeeling, when the dangers of war surround and threaten this kingdom, and with the rest of whose members, you are melted together, and

compose the same, social indivisible body. However divided we may be in religious opinions, we are but one people, we have but one King, one country – this country – to this gracious King you owe every duty that the loyal and faithful subject can perform.[21]

It is not known if the author of this statement was Catholic or Protestant and, in many ways, it does not matter, because it was written before Ireland's parliamentary union with Britain, when the four nations were united under one Crown, and when many Irish, from across the denominational spectrum, were identifying as loyal subjects.[22] For much of the eighteenth century, national identity was an understood but fluid concept, as people used what they needed to achieve a particular result. Both Scots and the Irish, to denote a claim to a common set of shared political and legal values, for example, used the term *Englishness* throughout the eighteenth century; it was not about an allegiance to or identification with a specific location of birth, and it did not preclude pre-existing national identities.[23] An instructive essay on Protestant identities in Ireland asserts that the "fractured Protestant interest" would, over the course of the eighteenth century, thwart any semblance of unity among the various sects.[24] Although some argue that Englishness "facilitated the easy Anglicization of the eighteenth-century Atlantic world,"[25] one should not assume that everyone was able to access it in the same way or that it superseded or displaced the more local identities of Scottish (itself divided between Highland and Lowland), Irish, and Welsh. The English of Ireland were constantly reminded of the ways in which they differed from the "metropolitan English."[26] Identities were strong because of accepted boundaries. In the sixteenth century, Scots from across the political and religious spectrum had agreed that there had been an independent monarchy in Scotland since ancient times.[27] Territorial boundaries defined where the four nations were located, but the distinct identities within these boundaries were obvious to the people who lived within and outside of them long before and long after the Reformation. Work on Irish medical professionals, for example, emphasizes the centrality of an enduring and defining sense of Irishness to the lives of those who lived and worked outside of Ireland.[28]

Further distinctions about how Britain was understood at local levels emerge in relation to language. While it is right to be critical of studies that fail to take into account the ways in which Irish and Gaelic speakers understood their relationship with Britain,[29] the tendency to overlook the extent to which class informed perceptions of Britain and Britishness in Ireland and the Scottish Highlands has also been limiting.

Engagement with the empire was pivotal and facilitated the creation of important cultural tools. The publication of the first Gaelic dictionary in 1828, for example, was made possible by upper- and middling-rank Gaels or people of Highland descent who were temporarily located in the Caribbean but plugged in to the massive merchant networks of London, Bristol, and/or Glasgow.[30] While this book may not engage with Irish or Gaelic sources in a way that would satisfy everyone, its focus on the broader Catholic dimension and the ways in which it builds a better awareness of how that faith and its followers endured fluctuation and schism does address a major deficiency in the historiography.

A critical turning point for the ideas of *Britain* and *British* came in 1603. James VI and I – the son of Mary, Queen of Scots, and her murdered second husband, Henry Stewart, Lord Darnley – had been king of Scotland for thirty-six years before the union of the English and Scottish Crowns. It brought the people of Scotland, England, Wales, and Ireland together under a regal union, but it did not fundamentally change their base identifications or allegiances. The parliamentary unions were different. They opened up the empire to the Scots and the Irish and altered the socio-religious dynamic. While they did contribute to the development of ideas about Britishness, it was not in the way many might expect. The 1707 union of England and Wales with Scotland cast Britishness as an experience of national and imperial belonging, whereas the one with Ireland, which happened almost a century later, in 1801, saw imperial security trump religious grouping. Suddenly, Britain's population was at least one-quarter Catholic, and a significant number of Catholics, be they Scottish, Irish, English, or Welsh, believed themselves to be Britons because of what that label entitled them to – just like their non-Catholic neighbours. Yet because Catholicism was not accommodated in 1801 in the same way that Presbyterianism had been in 1707, and because the king had declared that anyone who pressed for further concessions for Catholics was his "personal enemy," it is easy to see why many contemporaries and subsequent commentators have been convinced of the "Protestant nature of Britishness."[31]

Anti-Catholicism certainly anchored a Protestant identity, but it was not a sentiment held by everyone.[32] The belief that the identities of the indigenous Scottish, English, and Welsh Catholics, as well as many Irish, were suspended or consigned to the fringes of Britishness falls apart in the context of the British Empire, where they represented a significant proportion of the settling populations and showed themselves to be innately supportive of advancing an overarching British identity.[33] The unique structure of the British state had important implications for imperial culture. That Britain was a constituency of

four nations influenced the social, political, and religious development of British North America, because it attracted settlers from all
four but "disproportionately from Ireland and Scotland."[34] The idea
that people could have more than one identity was particularly ap-
parent in the British North American colonies, where migrants arrived
already in possession of dual identities. Even Canada's first prime
minister, Sir John A. Macdonald, a Glasgow-born Scot of Highland
descent, described himself as Canadian and British. What emigration
and colonial settlement offered to the Scots and Irish was the breath-
ing room they needed to form deeper and more collaborative relationships with the centre state.

It was the second British Empire, the one that emerged after the loss
of the Thirteen Colonies that "forge[d] a sense of Britishness"[35] that
included Catholics. It confirmed that Britons from across the religious
spectrum possessed dual and shifting identities that enabled them to
claim a place in the nation, state, or empire, as and when needed.[36] An
interesting illustration of this comes from a report of the Highland Society of London in 1813. Devoted to enhancing and promoting a distinct regional identity that was based on ties to a location, language, and
kin networks, this society engaged with an overarching British imperial
identity. Its membership, comprising mainly aristocrats, leading businessmen, and professionals, was based on Highland birth or descent and
included both Catholics and Protestants, though the latter dominated. It
was felt that Britain's national distinctions strengthened the empire:

> That it is in the interest of the United Kingdom to keep alive those national,
> or what, perhaps, may now more properly be called local distinctions
> of English, Scotch, Irish and Welsh, I think can be proved by reasoning
> founded upon the first law of nature – I mean self-love ... I humbly con-
> ceive that the glory of the British Empire may be upheld under the united
> flag, by keeping alive in its inhabitants the local distinction of English,
> Scotch, Irish and Welsh, thereby creating a generous emulation between
> them, which, under the direction of one free and paternal government,
> many promote the good and glory of the whole.[37]

This is just one example, but it shows that approaching the idea of Britain and British from the perspective of multiple identities allows for
a deeper understanding of how those perceived as minorities or peripheries (e.g., Scottish Highlanders and Irish Catholics) were actually
pivotal in shaping the identity of the imperial state. As this quotation
suggests, the survival and flourishing of national identity *after* the loss
of national autonomy, which was exchanged for economic and political

improvement, underscore the importance of civil society in this process. Civil society was a crucial outlet offering national populations options for retaining and redefining their characters and for preserving and/or renegotiating their authority and identity by incorporating those people and groups previously excluded.[38] This extended beyond Catholics and was indicative of a broader socio-political eclipse that confronted authority structures in Britain and the empire. Fundamentally, civil society opened the floor to the "rational discussion and reasoned discourse and arguments" that would prove a "capacity for political citizenship; the demand for middle-class men to be enfranchised."[39]

In many ways, *British* represented one of a number of interconnected identities, but it was complicated and could provoke crisis, when access to its presumed or expected civil liberties was unequal. The legal restrictions in force against Catholics until 1829 had resulted in political, economic, and social crises in Ireland, where the majority of the island's population faced political exclusion.[40] The consequences of this exclusion were obvious to some, as will be shown, but not to others. What is required now is a serious re-evaluation of the role that the colonies and their populations played in the socio-religious and political development of Britain itself. After all, British imperialism was "an interactive process in which peripheries constructed their own particular agendas and links with the metropolitan core, while being both influenced by and, in turn, influencing the Empire's development."[41]

Scholars tend to agree that the empire, which worked to level the playing field among Britain's national groups, facilitated the emergence of a stronger and more coherent British identity throughout colonial society.[42] The problem, though, is that few have recognized the implications that this had for religious identities as old authority structures were either reworked or abandoned. Britishness, as an identity in the colonial context, was broadly conceived and was able to work with numerous distinctions. In some cases that meant a loss of status, but in others it meant the opposite, and a prime example was the decline of Anglican hegemony and the rise of Catholicism, Presbyterianism, and Methodism. Anglicanism did not dominate in many colonies because it could not compete with the large and often overwhelming populations from the other Christian churches.[43] In Upper Canada, for example, the imposition of a more "democratic church polity" by diverse settler populations saw a prerogative asserted over religious culture that suited local needs.[44] Such needs, of course, were influenced by concerns about commerce, security, and the broader process of socio-cultural colonial development.

What empire highlighted was that Scottishness, Irishness, Englishness, and Welshness could and did co-exist relatively easily with a form of Britishness that was responsive both to local circumstances and to the need for "negotiation and renegotiation," as and when required.[45] Even to Irish Catholics – a group often perceived as being wholly opposed to the British state and to Ireland's place within it on account of the growth of Irish nationalism among some following the 1798 rebellion – Britishness could be a natural identity that did not mean a suspension of either their Irishness or their Catholicism. Revisionist work on Irish political activity, new research on military service, social networks, and Catholic education, and studies investigating the wider evolution of a Christian British Empire are updating the discourse surrounding the relationship between national identity, religiosity, Britishness, loyalism, and professional ambition.[46] In relation to Canada, the point is made that "many of these people left the British Isles defining themselves as English, Irish, Scottish, or Welsh ... Their experiences in British North America provided an impetus to further assimilation into a British identity, as they were forced to live together with people other than those of their own nation and were no longer exposed solely to a narrowly national perception of their homeland."[47] British migrants were the "engine of empire," and, by establishing themselves and their families abroad, they demonstrated significant agency.[48] They had no real desire to cut ties with their homeland, but their needs did change as their communities evolved. In the process of defining their new settlements, communities, and nations, multiple identities became absolute necessities, and so it was in this context, in environments where social, political, and religious structures were being formed, that Catholics found a solid platform for civil inclusion. Thus, the overarching Britishness that existed in the nineteenth century and was exhibited by myriad faiths had emerged over time through the imperial activities of many Britons, Catholics included, from distinct national traditions.

Catholic Identities and the Significance of Rome

England's diverse Catholic community numbered approximately 80,000 by the end of the eighteenth century, with the overall British population being around 10 million.[49] They had survived since the revolution of 1688–89 by walking a political tightrope and reaching out to friends on the Continent. Toward the end of the eighteenth century, some of their lay leaders, who were becoming more confident and aware of their own socio-economic influence, began to connect with the political discourse associated with the emerging culture of popular dissent.[50] In Scotland, where Catholicism had existed almost completely underground since the Reformation, adherents adopted a quiet and conservative approach in an effort to preserve what was left of their traditions. Indigenous Scottish Catholics there were intensely hostile to outsiders, especially the Irish.[51] It was a very different story in Ireland, where the hierarchy of the Catholic Church had never been completely abolished. The Irish were much more confident in expressing their faith and in pressing for increased recognition under the law; the dominance they began to exercise over Catholicism in Britain after 1801 frustrated their English, Welsh, and Scottish co-religionists. The Maynooth Grant, for example, caused them numerous headaches because it had so inflamed anti-Catholic sentiment among Scottish evangelicals that sympathetic Whig politicians were pushed aside.[52] Irish frustration was chronic, peaking at moments of turmoil and discord such as the Famine, the Fenian crisis, and, later, the land wars of the 1880s.[53]

In the Catholic world, just as in other worlds, feelings of vulnerability in the face of more dominant groups were difficult to avoid, particularly in mission territories like Britain, the Dutch Republic, and Switzerland, where Catholicism was not embedded as the established church. Both Britain and the Dutch Republic "received a missionary status from the outside [i.e., Rome], contrasting with their strong indigenous convictions of continuity and feelings of authenticity. Finally, each, within the framework of its own state, was confronted with a massive yet socially and politically marginalised Catholic majority in a separate political territory – the Generality Lands of the Dutch Republic, and Ireland for the British Crown."[54]

Many of the cultural differences that existed among Catholics in the four nations were brought into sharp relief during periods of intense political debate, such as that surrounding Catholic relief and emancipation. On these issues, Scottish and English Catholics viewed the Irish approach as antagonistic, presumptuous, and potentially explosive, though it is important to bear in mind that obtaining emancipation in Ireland was more about realizing "a greater degree of democratic control over the political process" than about nationalism.[55] While there was significant support for the emancipation of English Catholics because it was seen as just for a loyal population, there was far less support for the emancipation of Irish Catholics, whose loyalty was perceived as being clouded by broader questions about race, national identity, and class.[56]

That anti-Catholicism was often conflated with anti-Irishness in the nineteenth century infuriated Scottish and English Catholics, as they had been trying to draw distinctions between each other and the Irish for centuries.[57] In the late twelfth century, Scotland had fought for and won distinct status with *Cum universi*, the papal bull of 1192, which declared the existence of *Scotticana ecclesia* and effectively quashed any claims

York thought it had over lands to the north.[58] From this point, Scotland became a "special daughter" of Rome, whose protection continued up to and beyond the Reformation. Following the Reformation, there were other, unique challenges to confront. As adherents of an outlawed faith in their home country, English, Irish, and Scottish Catholics scrambled to establish Continental colleges, which were boarding schools and seminaries run by religious orders and designed to feed their local missions with educated elites and priests. The Scots, arguably the most vulnerable on account of their small population, were also the most obstinate, particularly when it came to working with other national groups. They took exception to the proposal to establish one overarching British college in Rome, seeing a merger of the three existing national colleges as tantamount to an English takeover of religious culture and instruction.[59] Around the same time in the eighteenth century, wandering Irish missionaries were practically chased out of the Scottish Highlands by local priests who feared their influence.[60] The English had their own issues with the Irish, particularly in the nineteenth century. The diaries of William Poynter, a Hampshire native, who served as vicar apostolic of the London District between 1815 and 1824, reveal his deep frustration with some of his Rome-based Irish colleagues. Writing in early 1815, he reflected upon a frank conversation with a Roman cardinal wherein he had complained about the English Catholics being "sacrificed" for the Irish. In fact, the tensions between the Irish and English clergy in Rome were so acute in that era that Scots College had to be used as neutral territory for meetings.[61] Poynter was even called a "vile apostate" and a "mock doctor and perverted wretch" who was prepared to barter the purity of Irish Catholicism for the state sanctioning of Catholic bishops.[62] William Petre, one of Britain's unofficial agents in Rome, shared Poynter's frustration and worried that the pope's knowledge of Irish affairs was "heavily influenced by the anti-English attitudes of the Irish bishops."[63] In a letter to Thomas Sherburne, a priest at England's Ushaw College, in 1818, Robert Gradwell, the newly installed rector of the English College in Rome, was scathing of the Irish there: "All of the channels from Ireland have been for some years so poisonous; the Irish send such flaming characters of worthless persons, that in the characters of men from that Island Rome can scarcely form a just opinion without a miracle."[64]

Yet, the door could, and did, swing both ways. Over the course of the nineteenth century, English influence in Rome expanded significantly, thanks in part to the Cisalpine Movement, which formed in the early 1790s, and the Oxford Movement, which was at its height between the mid-1830s and the mid-1840s and was opposed to evangelicalism in the Church of England.[65] In 1860, when Nicholas Cardinal Wiseman, the Ushaw College–educated archbishop of Westminster, was in the Italian capital to deliver an address to Pope Pius IX, Tobias Kirby, rector of the Irish College, refused to attend, citing a busy schedule; secretly, though, he feared the effect that Wiseman's anti-Irish attitudes would have on the minds of Roman officials.[66]

These internal tensions could be set aside, though, when confronting Roman attempts to assert or assume control over activities that would have a direct influence in shaping religious culture back in the United Kingdom or in its colonies. When it suited them or when it was required, the Catholic leaders of the United Kingdom used the British umbrella to protect their collective interests. The archives of the Archdiocese of Westminster holds a series of letters about the efforts undertaken by Scotland, England, and Ireland's most senior Catholic leaders to have "national" superiors rather than Italian ones placed in charge of their Roman colleges. Writing to his English counterpart in 1783, George Hay, vicar apostolic of Scotland's Lowland District, suggested collaborating to ensure the selection of their own countrymen. His strategy, which advocated involving the British Court as a way of getting officials in Rome to pay attention, emphasized a demonstration of their loyalty to Britain:

> I have sent you the above [overview of situation] that you many have time to consider what further steps are to be taken in case the request [to remove the Italians] is not granted; and if it is not, it will be to no purpose for you or the English vicars to apply anymore to the cardinals on that head … Let the application be made in the name of Catholics of the British Dominions, & let it come from the Court, & then it will be regarded. It will not be difficult to make the Court enter into your views, nay you may make a great merit with them for asking their interposition; it will show them how much you are attached to your Country … As for a joint application to his Holiness I have no objection and shall chearfully [sic] concur for our common good in anything that shall be thought conducive thereto, & if necessary shall wait upon you at London any time you shall appoint. In the meantime I have sent a very strong letter to His Holiness about six weeks ago, wherein I told him several truths which I thought very necessary for him to know.[67]

What Hay actually told the pope, and whether or not his "truths" were taken under advisement, is unknown, but the fact that the bishops worked together on this and identified as British is revealing in the sense of belonging that it suggests. Aside from these periodic and pragmatic collaborations, and notwithstanding the use of the British umbrella when required, significant tensions connected with political status endured because each had a "totally different" relationship with government.[68] Irish Catholics saw emancipation as a "right and as the only possible way to remedy the restrictive political and economic position in which they found themselves," whereas English, Welsh, and Scottish Catholics viewed it as a "privilege or a reward granted ... in exchange for unending expressions of their loyalty to the Protestant establishment."[69]

At the turn of the nineteenth century, the Catholic Church was not yet the universal church that it is today. Even by the 1830s, Catholicism, as a faith, continued to exist very much according to national custom, tradition, prerogative, and practice.[70] Yet the almost complete destruction of clerical authority in France during the Revolutionary era, the subsequent rise of Rome, as well as the mass migration of Catholics to Britain's colonies were doing much to change perceptions of Catholics. Moreover, there was unprecedented sympathy for what many of the religious personnel in France had experienced in 1793–94. As Catholic immigrants from Scotland and Ireland began to scatter across Britain's overseas colonies, the Catholic identities that emerged in those places tended to complement and enhance an overarching sense of Britishness and imperial purpose.[71] How Rome approached the British imperial state at this time, and vice versa, was also influential. The series of wars, revolutions, and rebellions that took place between 1756 and 1815, as well as the authority that Britain acquired over territories in the Caribbean and in North America, notwithstanding the loss of the Thirteen Colonies, had a tremendous influence over how the Catholic Church interacted with secular temporal governments, particularly with those of non-Catholic states.

This level of change amounted to what has been described as a "political earthquake," as the church adopted more moderate and compromising approaches to international relations to ensure productive relationships.[72] The revolutionary charge that had been lit first in America and then in France was equally concerning to Britain and Rome; their mutual fear of popular radicalism had the unintended consequence of pushing them into closer collaboration. This was required when issues surrounding Continental politics emerged. In 1814, for instance, when Rome sought to restore the Papal States, Cardinal Consalvi, Rome's secretary of state, was dispatched to London to secure Britain's support. There, Consalvi met with the foreign secretary, Viscount Castlereagh, and the Prince Regent, who agreed to lend their support, since it was in Britain's interest to have Europe divided into as many small powers as possible and to have Rome's support for the abolition of the slave trade.[73] By no means did the suspicions between the two powers disappear, but what emerged was a more manageable relationship based on mutual dependence, since the security and prosperity of each were dependent, at least in part, on the other.

Far from alienating Catholicism or undermining its progress, the British Empire actually supported its expansion and consolidation. The centralizing nature of the church, complemented by a deeply hierarchical order, extended the authority of the British state by involving Catholics in the process of British colonialism.[74] This involvement was of enormous benefit to Britain and in a distant colony like Quebec, for instance, where the Catholic Church exercised significant authority over a large population, and British officials collaborated with church leaders to install new governmental structures that included Catholics.[75] This collaboration would be replicated in Trinidad, where the Catholic body was mostly French, Spanish, and African. Such cooperation enhanced Britain's value in the eyes of the Catholic leadership because it demonstrated how it could keep local bishops in check when Rome could not. Equally important, in Quebec, it enabled British officials to exploit the loyalties of a largely Gallican priesthood. Gallicanism, a tradition rooted in France, challenged the ultimate authority of Rome by deferring to local bishops and/or temporal leaders; the independence and authority of the French church had never sat well with Roman officials. In their eyes, British colonial officials, who had no interest in competing with them for spiritual or doctrinal clout, were often preferable to the French clerics, who had become too comfortable with their presumed power over the colonial faithful.

During the mid-to-late eighteenth century, as British officials struggled to establish their authority over a number of newly acquired colonies, the Gallican tradition was helpful, but it became less workable in the nineteenth century, as Britain looked to Rome for assistance in managing increasingly dispersed colonial Catholic populations. After the 1830s, the white-settler colonies were transitioning from frontiers to more established and stable societies, and the Catholic Church in Europe was on the road to recovery after the devastating effects of the French Revolution. In the Caribbean, the colonies and territories under Britain's jurisdiction were transitioning from slavery to apprenticeship to freedom. As a consequence, Gallicanism was being swept aside by an increasingly powerful ultramontane agenda, which prioritized the prerogative of Rome.[76] Ultramontanism, which prioritized the primacy of the Holy See over national interests, emerged strongly following the French Revolution as a way to mitigate radicalism. This shift was tremendously advantageous to both Britain and Rome. On one level, Rome's attempts to erode the strong Gallican influence of the French church throughout the Atlantic colonies had been boosted by Britain's increasing emphasis on Anglicization. On another level, as Rome's authority expanded, with Britain's permission and, in many instances, with its money, the Catholic culture of the colonial world enabled government officials to better manage rapidly expanding Catholic populations.[77]

Although British officials could not be seen to be having any direct relationship with Rome on account of *praemunire* – a law introduced by Henry VIII that forbade the exchange of diplomats and that remained on the statute books – as well as the persistent culture of anti-Catholicism, cautious cooperation had been happening at high levels. Relations between London and Rome improved as lines of direct, albeit unofficial, communication reopened or expanded through members of the Royal Family, such as George III's son, Prince Edward, the aristocracy, and through the exchange of pseudo ambassadors.[78] In Rome, for example, one of London's first men-on-the-spot was John Hippisley, an "ambitious barrister" and political operative, who had spent considerable periods of time in Rome since the late 1770s. His counterpart in London, Charles Erskine, was the son of a Jacobite exile of noble blood, who had been taken under the wing of Henry Benedict, Cardinal Duke of York, after the death of his parents in Rome.[79] Benedict, or Henry Stuart, was the son of the "Old Pretender," James VIII and III, and brother of the "Young Pretender," Charles Edward Stuart. Having trained his protégé in the art of high-level diplomacy, Benedict saw to it that Erskine would serve as an unofficial apostolic envoy to London's Court of St. James's in the 1790s and early 1800s.

This kind of activity helped to consolidate and enhance the authority of an increasingly powerful colonial church leadership and an imperial state, which had to assert its authority from a great distance, over numerous Catholic communities that were ethnically, culturally, and racially diverse. In the Caribbean, the Catholic population included tens of thousands of enslaved people who, from a relatively early stage, were expected to be the focus of Catholic missionaries. In his pastoral letter of 1770, Richard Challoner, the vicar apostolic of the London District between 1758 and 1781, whose spiritual jurisdiction included Catholics in Britain's Caribbean possessions, showed a particular concern for the salvation of the enslaved:

> [Readers are] strictly obliged to take to heart the instruction and salvation of the poor negroes, who are detained in slavery amongst you. Your non-compliance with this obligation would be of dreadful consequences to thousands of these poor souls, whose blood would most certainly cry to heaven for vengeance against those by whose unchristian cruelty they should be thus given up to Satan, and suffered to die in their ignorance and sins.[80]

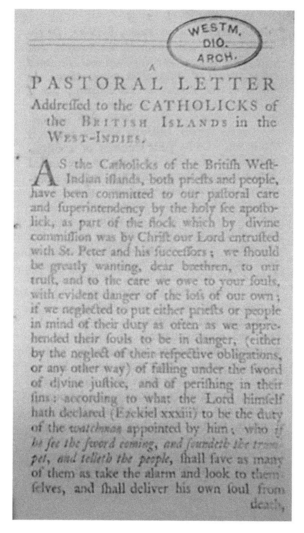

Figure 2. Image of "A Pastoral Letter Addressed to the Catholicks of the British Islands in the West-Indies" (with permission of the Westminster Diocesan Archives)

The role of the Catholic Church in stabilizing new colonial settlements by imposing authority, structure, and Christianity made it an important imperial ally, particularly when there was a distinct lack of unity among the various Protestant sects. The civil societies, political structures, and institutions that emerged abroad had significant Catholic input and, since taking a share of the responsibility for imposing Britain's authority was a rather natural role for the church, mitigated

the risk of popular sovereignty by promoting the authority of a central-
ized hierarchy. Moreover, it was an easy sell to those British and Irish
Catholics at home and abroad who already felt a belonging to Britain's
expanding imperial program.

Catholic Loyalism

The expansion of Catholics' participation in colonial development tes-
tified to their efforts to have their sense of loyalty, subjecthood, and
claims to citizenship recognized. As Britain was battling for its imperial
life in America in 1781, Catholics in Britain and Ireland were beginning
to have their identity and sense of loyalty validated at official levels. An
anonymous Irish newspaper clipping aimed at Catholics stressed unity
and obedience to the Crown:

> As subjects, my dear brethren, you are members of the great political body
> which forms this kingdom. Innumerable bonds of mutual dependency,
> mutual necessity, good offices and friendship, connect you with the other
> members of every persuasion, belonging to this political body. The same
> laws indiscriminately protect the property, the lives of all against foreign
> invasion and domestic plunder. Not one temporal advantage or blessing
> do we enjoy, which is not derived to us from our quality as subjects, seated
> under the shelf of the lawful dominion and civil authority.[81]

Seventeen years later, as yet another war with France was underway
and rebellion raged in Ireland, these sentiments were repeated in
Catholic chapels up and down the country. The vicars apostolic committed themselves, their priests, and their followers to protecting and
securing the peace and authority of Britain. Concerned that the conduct
of Catholics in Ireland was having a direct bearing on perceptions of
Catholics in Scotland and England, Scotland's vicar apostolic, George
Hay, stressed the loyalty of Ireland's Catholic religious leaders and
elites in his 1798 *Pastoral Address*: "Happy we are indeed to see the firm
and steady conduct of the Catholic Bishops of that country, in guard-
ing their people against the fatal seduction; and the public declarations
which they and the Catholic gentry made, of their loyalty and adher-
ence to the Government."[82]

Although the Reformation may have stopped Catholics from participating in official civic life until the late eighteenth century, it did not stop
them from *belonging* to the nations in which they and their families, for
countless generations, had been born and raised. The empire provided
the platform they needed to engage with the ambitions of the state and to
demonstrate their value as collaborators in the imperial program. Their

allegiance, like everyone else's, was motivated partly by economics, but also by a sense of belonging and a commitment to a shared crown. The process of bringing together the peoples of what would become the United Kingdom of Britain and Ireland within a constitutional structure had begun with the union of the Crowns in 1603. From this point, a British identity based on an amalgamation of distinct peoples with different languages, traditions, and customs began to take shape; it was developed further with the equalization of access to empire by the parliamentary unions of 1707 (England and Wales with Scotland) and 1801 (Britain and Ireland). What helped to cement the relationship between Britain's constituent nations was loyalism. Defined as a commitment to protecting and enhancing the interests of the British Crown and the imperial state, *loyalism* was an inherently inclusive concept that had a profound influence on the shape of Catholic identity at home and abroad. That scholars have overlooked this and have characterized the British Empire as an entity that existed in opposition to Roman Catholicism meant that loyalism, as a central tenet of Britishness, has been consistently misappropriated and underestimated.

In reality, loyalism was a broad and inclusive concept, and one that offered space to Britain's religious minorities. Not only did it transcend religious identity and extend far beyond a Protestant and English framework, but it invited the collaboration of other religious and ethnic groups, such as Catholics, Scots, and Irish. As Rafferty rightly emphasizes, building a "Protestant empire for a Protestant people" was neither "possible nor practical."[83] That loyalism was not the sole preserve of Protestants was revealed, most alarmingly, during the American Revolution, when the imperial state was taught an important and perhaps surprising lesson – that Catholics – French ones, for that matter – were capable of being loyal when English and Scottish Protestants were not. While more will be said on this in the following chapter, having been granted freedom of worship and under heavy pressure from church authorities, Quebec's Catholics refused to side with the seceding American colonists during the Revolutionary War. This show of loyalty convinced many of Britain's political elites that concessions to Catholics were beneficial and in the best interests of imperial security and that a union with Ireland and its Catholic majority was feasible. In Ireland itself, many Protestants joined with their Catholic brethren in calling for Catholic relief because they believed it was right and the only way to ensure greater national prosperity.[84] The eighteenth century had been a hard one for Ireland; unlike Scotland, which had skilfully exploited the economic opportunities of empire at every turn, its socio-economic development had stagnated by comparison.

While Catholic loyalty did not really differ from that of the Protestant majority, the perception that Catholics, especially Irish Catholics, were disloyal was very strong.[85] The complex nature of Catholicism's relationship with the British constitution, a central feature of the next chapter, was enhanced by colourful anti-Catholic rhetoric. A good example is Jacobitism. Cast as a Catholic scourge, the reality was that about three-quarters of Jacobites were Episcopalian, who, on account of their loyalty to the House of Stuart, refused to swear oaths of allegiance to the Hanoverian throne. The 1715 and 1745 rebellions saw Jacobite opposition to the Hanoverian dynasty characterized as treacherous expressions of disloyalty, despite the fact that the movement was neither republican nor anti-union. Even if the Catholic Stuart, James the Old Pretender (or VIII and III), did return to the throne, he had no intention of overturning the authority of Protestantism or of "returning the three kingdoms to Rome"; rather, the Church of England would be secured and, in the opinion of two Catholic theologians, "It will never be in the King's power to change these laws without a Parliament."[86]

And there is one more point. In a study of two of Canada's best-known heroines, Laura Secord and Madeleine de Verchères, Colin M. Coates and Cecilia Morgan depict loyalism as a gendered concept that was inherently male and "associated with political decision-making, a sphere from which women were officially excluded."[87] This important observation raises questions about loyalism's ethno-religious and cultural associations that may help us to become more comfortable with seeing Catholic loyalism as a pivotal dimension of Britain's imperial experience, an experience that was shared broadly, as the sections on women religious that follow in chapters 4 and 5 illustrate. Loyalism was a complex, contoured, and "ambiguous political ideal."[88] An excerpt from a newspaper article on Catholic loyalty from 1857 is illustrative of a wider Catholic perspective:

> To the heartless mendacity of those political mendicants, who with mock patriotism on their lips to disguise their selfish, their sneaking parasitism, accuse Catholics of disloyalty, we have but to point out the earnest language, the soul stirring exhortations of the Catholic Hierarchy who wielded the destinies of the Church in the British Empire. Anyone who peruses their pastoral letters, their appeals to their several flocks must indeed be blind, if he does not recognise therein the purest patriotism and loyalty with which reasons and religion combined can inspire in the heart of man.[89]

Thus, the British Empire was more closely aligned with commerce and perceptions of liberty than with any sort of an imagined Protestant collective or "mythical unity."[90] Loyalism was a concept in Britain that was appropriated by myriad traditions and groups and, contrary to popular perception, Catholic loyalism was not a new phenomenon; in the imperial context, Catholics acted no differently than their non-Catholic neighbours. The business of expanding the empire and exploiting its opportunities was a collective enterprise that engaged increasing numbers of Britons, including many Highland and Lowland Scots and Protestant and Catholic Irish, throughout British North America and the Caribbean from the early eighteenth century.[91]

While empire highlighted the sense of belonging that existed among the United Kingdom's minorities, it also revealed that a commitment to Britain was predicated upon pre-existing national attachments that could not be erased. The attachment to the British Empire by Catholics and all other religious groups was based on a range of complex reasons; in the Catholic context, it was evidenced by consistent military service, increasingly collaborative relationships between colonial officials and church authorities, the evolution of a Catholic associational culture, an enhanced commitment to civic responsibility, and an expanding engagement with political processes. In spite of this, distinctions between the religious cultures of Britain and Ireland's Catholics, which included discipline, "matters relating to liturgy, clerical education and dress, and the observance of religious feast days," were significant.[92] At a colonial level, the nature of settlement and the fact that the colonies were far more religiously mixed meant that these differences were more easily absorbed. Catholics understood, helped to implement, and engaged with colonial civil societies and political infrastructures that were inherently British, and this activity abroad boosted the confidence of their co-religionists back home. It was a complex situation on one level but a liberating one on another, since Catholics learned quickly how to use their dominant positions abroad to press for civic and religious equality under the law. The following chapter develops further the points that have been introduced here by focusing on Catholic relief, which became part of the growing discussion about reform involving many groups, ranging from non-conformists and the labouring poor to abolitionists and radicals, in calling for more widespread socio-economic and political change.

Chapter Two

Imperial Security and Catholic Relief

What began to bring many influential Catholics and non-Catholics together from the 1760s was a deeper engagement with the meaning and purpose of the British constitution. Ireland's influence over Catholic affairs and the determination of an increasingly active laity, largely in Ireland, but also in England and Scotland, facilitated a process of socio-economic reform that pushed the issue of Catholic emancipation onto the political agenda and prompted debates about Catholic loyalty and citizenship.[1] The ever-present threat of France and the need to find a way of integrating Ireland more effectively in the imperial program encouraged this discussion. How far the process of constitutional engagement was influenced by the progress of Britain as an imperial state and its calculated approach to Catholics, both the "new subjects," who came with acquired territories, and those within the United Kingdom itself, is a question that needs to be considered. This chapter explores the framework within which colonial Catholics operated and is therefore focused on the political debates that raged and the resulting legislative change to show how Catholicism was reconsidered as an integral component of the process of empire building.

The era of emancipation, from the late 1770s to 1829, was characterized by an emerging and increasingly ambitious Catholic laity, who were intent on joining Britain's public and professional life. Their agenda for inclusion required an engagement with the civil processes of the state, but it made local church leaders uneasy about the prospect of having their influence further subverted.[2] That such ambition and tensions between a Catholic laity and clergy existed at all was an important sign of life in a church that had been all but crushed by the sixteenth-century Reformation and by the devastating penal legislation that followed. Notwithstanding the array of Continental colleges that had been established in France, Spain, Portugal, Germany, and Italy by the English, the Scots, and the Irish, it was the Irish who led the charge for extending civil equality at a domestic level because they were the only ones capable to doing so: in spite of efforts to eradicate Catholicism and its hierarchy in Ireland, both had survived. Its growing economy presented Catholics with the opportunity to acquire more social and political influence, but, as noted in the previous chapter, this dominance frustrated English and Scottish Catholics because their socio-religious cultures were markedly different, and they had every intention of maintaining their autonomy.[3] Beyond that was their belief that keeping a low profile would lead to toleration and economic prosperity.[4]

Meaningful and noticeable change for Catholics started in the 1770s, as Britain looked to gather as much support as it could muster to protect its territories. The acquisition of Quebec and a number of islands in the Caribbean following Britain's defeat of France during the Seven Years' War, coupled with the fact that these regions had significant Catholic populations, forced Britain to engage with Catholics in a way that would support imperial planning. Quebec forced a radical rethinking of colonial management in terms of safeguarding economic stability, recognition of pre-existing laws, and awareness of local governance practice.[5] Earlier, English interaction with Irish Catholic planters and merchants in Barbados and Montserrat during the second half of the seventeenth century provided some vital instruction. However, increased wartime cooperation between Irish and Dutch merchants added to the introduction of new French and enslaved Catholic populations across many more islands, which presented an entirely new set of challenges.[6] In addition to this were changes taking place among Catholics at home: Britain's expanding empire and the growing concerns about how to ensure its security were coupled with an expanding Catholic middle class, led by the Irish, who began to challenge the tradition of socio-political exclusion by making use of the range of opportunities that empire offered. They were influenced by the broader discussions taking place around them about reform and the growing desire by many in Britain and Ireland to make society more responsible, accountable, and just, and to enable a broader culture of improvement to take hold. At this point, the discussions were not yet about parliamentary reform, but rather an "indeterminate force of reform" that was being used by myriad groups to bring about change.[7]

While Catholics from across the United Kingdom were experiencing change and were engaging, to varying degrees, with imperial activities, those from Scotland and England were less intent on securing immediate legislative change, and it was this position that caused the most friction with their Irish counterparts. These contrasting priorities, which were reinforced by the Continental colleges, those institutions established across Europe following the Reformation to educate and train the next generation of Catholic elites and priests, reflected the inherent diversity of Catholic culture in the United Kingdom. Catholics in the United Kingdom, like Protestants, came from distinct national traditions that had very different relationships with both the Crown and, as it developed, the central British state. In England and Wales, for example, a minority Catholic base had been maintained by the landowning families through kin networks, business interests, and, in some areas such as the northeast, political influence.[8] In spite of this, it was really only toward the end of the eighteenth century, as an active lay base expanded, that the direction shifted toward securing greater inclusion in Britain's political process.[9] In Scotland, Catholicism had been so reduced by the strength of Presbyterianism that surviving pockets were barely recognizable from one side of the nation to the other. In contrast to the traditions of the western Highlands and Islands, where unique local practices had developed on account of extreme isolation and the lack of clergy, Catholics in northeast and southwest Scotland had developed underground, conservative, and extremely localized identities.[10] Ireland was a completely different story, since Catholics there were not underground and had developed a far more entrepreneurial outlook.[11] This was especially the case in the southwest of Ireland, where families, in spite of numerous obstacles, found ways of sending their children into the professions and the church and of exploiting European and Caribbean trade markets.[12] Diversity within Catholic culture was not unique to these three kingdoms: it was a fact of Catholic life across Europe, as language, custom, kinship, national prejudice, and economics were contested within and across national boundaries.[13]

The persistence of such strong national traditions in Britain was both liberating and restrictive because, although it allowed Catholics to share a sense of national identity with their non-Catholic neighbours, the existing tensions between national traditions became a significant factor in delaying full emancipation.[14] In fact, Catholics in England, Ireland, and Scotland were so different that they were likelier to make common cause with other minority groups than with each other. The Continental colleges offer a unique perspective on this diversity and merit more concentrated attention than can be devoted here because even though the various colleges communicated and, in some instances, collaborated with each other, their aim was to preserve and protect distinctive national traditions.[15] Another issue alluded to above was the tension that arose between the laity and the clergy. Many local church leaders reacted negatively to attempts by a frustrated laity to bring about an extension of rights for Catholics, fearing that it would undermine their authority and, in the long run, make them more vulnerable to Rome's intervention and control. Rome's growing interest in the affairs of Britain and Ireland worried those who had managed to circumvent its influence over the appointment of vicars apostolic (bishops), but a greater torment for many of Britain's senior clergy was the growing power of the laity. The leaders' desire to keep a low profile and to avoid unwanted interference clashed with the aims of an increasingly ambitious and pragmatic laity, who sought greater social integration and equality.[16] The fiery vicar apostolic of England's Midland District, John Milner, frequently attacked Charles Butler, an English Catholic lawyer and lay spokesman, because the latter had a public profile, had little time for church authority, and was intent on seeing Catholics in public office.[17] Milner also criticized Richard B. Sheridan when he learned that the member of Parliament was thinking about supporting a bill that would prohibit monastic institutions in Britain: "The present bill is of the most oppressive nature with respect to the families in question & the Catholics in general. It invades the secrets of conscience."[18] That such a debate even emerged was due to the significant number of male and female religious who found themselves in Britain after fleeing persecution in France.[19] In the end, Sheridan opposed the bill, and it was defeated, but the episode pointed to changing times for Catholics and to the ways in which concerns beyond Britain's shores were beginning to shape broader questions about the place of Catholics in British society.[20] Developments on the Continent were extremely important to reviving Catholicism in Britain, but it was the acquisition of colonies with majority Catholic populations on the other side of the Atlantic Ocean in the 1760s that proved constitutionally transformative. The relief legislation that was introduced incrementally between 1778 and 1793 gave the laity important traction by removing some of the most prejudicial laws in force against them. Emboldened by their new freedoms, Catholics engaged, in growing numbers, with the task of imperial defence and colonial expansion.

The Significance of Quebec and the Caribbean

Catholicism's compatibility with the British constitution was first tested in Quebec, a far off, fur-rich, and heavily forested inland North American colony, and in Grenada, a Caribbean sugar island acquired by Britain through the Treaty of Paris at the conclusion of the Seven Years' War in 1763. In many ways, Quebec was more significant. In addition to the Cree, Huron, Mohawk, and Ojibwa people who lived there, Quebec had a well-established French settler population that was almost entirely Catholic, and their presence forced a reappraisal of Britain's imperial strategy.[21] Conscious of the fact that Britain's troubles with France were hardly finished and that those with America were just beginning, British officials regarded Quebec as a possession with the potential to concentrate metropolitan power and to extend civil jurisdiction. Accomplishing this required securing the loyalty of the colony's Catholics.[22] Quebec's pre-existing governing structures, which were influenced heavily by its powerful Catholic leadership, meant that a pathway had already been established for the relatively swift centralization of British authority. This was in stark contrast to colonies further east, where the slow pace of settlement had kept authority structures embryonic for a long time, in spite of the establishment of legislative apparatus in Nova Scotia in 1758.[23]

Grenada, which signified Grenada, the Grenadines, Dominica, St. Vincent, and Tobago for the purposes of colonial administration, presented an entirely different situation. The attention of Britain's expanding merchant community was much more focused on India and on the sugar- and cotton-producing colonies of the West Indies than it was on Quebec.[24] In their opinion, the northern colony required too much investment for too little gain; in no way could fur come close to generating the profits that sugar could, and so the planter interest in the West Indies was far less willing to give accommodations to the existing Catholic population. Yet Quebec did have its sympathizers, those in London and Quebec who wanted to support the "infant commerce to and from that part of the world."[25] Earlier, in the Caribbean, Irish Catholics also had their advocates. In the late seventeenth century, following the accession of William and Mary, as Catholic lands were being confiscated in Ireland, and in spite of the widespread fear of Irish treachery, the Irish Catholics of Montserrat received special status. Colonial officials there extended "some toleration and allowance" to the resident Irish Catholics because few posed any kind of threat, and these merchants and landowners "enjoy their estates and Livelyhoods as quietly and happily as the English subjects."[26]

In the 1760s, the imperial government, through the secretary of state for the southern department, worked to protect Britain's imperial interests and enhance its security by pursuing a policy of religious toleration in Quebec and Grenada. Although this policy was undermined in Grenada by an aggressive, inherently greedy, and predominantly xenophobic gang of Scottish planters and would ultimately collapse – with tragic results – it was successful in Quebec.[27] The reason why it worked in one place and not the other came down to the nature of the colonial economies, perceptions of race, and settlement. The Caribbean was perceived solely as profit generating and so lacked a permanent British settler class; moreover, Grenada's landowning class was dominated by French-speaking free people of colour. During and after the Revolutionary War, British North America's more mixed economy and strong tradition of permanent white settlement helped Quebec become an important buffer against the Americans. In the eyes of London and many prospective emigrants, British North America offered greater long-term stability and security than did the Caribbean islands. Additionally, settlers in British North America wanted limited government interference so that they might create their own new societies, whereas those in the Caribbean, conscious of their own transience, relied on government to protect their economic interests.[28] Thus, the pre-existing populations and the type of migrants that each region attracted were fundamentally different, in terms of both their aspirations and their motivations, and these differences influenced the shape of colonial development in each society and the extent to which Catholicism was tolerated.

In the context of Britain's ongoing conflict with France, Quebec's strategic importance was recognized early on by the more astute members of Britain's political establishment, who wanted to use it to bring about the "economic ruin" of its arch-rival through the creation of a British-dominated "seaborne Atlantic Empire."[29] Realizing this ambition required the collaboration of a local population and an evolution of new thinking and new legislation.[30] Not only would Catholicism need to be reconfigured as a faith that had the potential to be compatible with the British constitution, but innovative legislation to that effect would need to be introduced. The Royal Proclamation of 1763 permitted Catholics to sit as members of Quebec's legislative council and secured protection for French civil law alongside English criminal law,[31] but the loyalty of the *Canadiens* would be cultivated by greater religious toleration introduced through landmark legislation. There were no clear precedents to guide British colonial officials in how to navigate Quebec's religious issue, and so the period between 1763 and 1774 was one of "trial and error."[32] Even Article IV of the Treaty of Paris, which was meant to protect freedom of worship for Catholics in Quebec and Grenada, caused confusion and forced legal experts to "apply their brains" to Quebec's "particularities."[33]

When it was introduced, the Quebec Act, which has been described as the "historical barometer of [one of] the most sensitive issues within the British Atlantic empire," was a transformative piece of legislation.[34] Passed in London in June 1774, it legalized freedom of worship for Catholics in Quebec and formally recognized their church as part of the colony's governing structure. This legislation was *the* major turning point for Catholicism's relationship with the British state, and the fact that the process began outside of Britain should not dilute its importance. While critics in Britain and in the American colonies saw it as an attempt to subvert the British constitution, in reality its purpose was to safeguard it and offer added protection to the empire. The Catholic leadership of Quebec certainly viewed it this way and argued that opposition to the Crown was "outmoded, self-indulgent and ultimately counter-productive."[35] The need to safeguard its imperial interests led to a reconstruction of the boundaries of Britishness as an identity and to the realization that what would keep Britain together was not Protestantism but, rather, a strong empire fuelled by loyalty and a responsive economy.

In high political circles, the Quebec Act passed without much debate, but on the streets and in the coffee houses, the affairs of this far-off francophone colony were hotly debated as people questioned notions of citizenship and rights in the empire. Most of the attacks were politically motivated, opportunistic, and designed to take advantage of the engrained anti-Catholic sentiment that feared a return to papal tyranny,[36] but there was also genuine disbelief that the government had gone so far as to establish a legislative precedent for the civil inclusion of Catholics. As the "hottest political potato in British domestic politics," debates about the constitution were bound to attract attention, given the major consequences that any revised understanding of it would provoke.[37] Anti-Catholicism was sustained in the eighteenth century by sermons, thanksgiving services, folk tales, pamphlets, almanacs, satirical prints, and even by demonstrations in which the pope was burned in effigy,[38] but the press also stoked the national campaigns, and publications such as *Gentleman's Magazine*, the *Morning Chronicle and London Advertiser*, and the *Caledonian Mercury* were hostile, carrying story after story about the egregious threat Catholicism posed to the constitution. If anything, these kinds of responses from English- and Scottish-based publications simply reinforced the metropole's disconnection from the realities of colonial life.[39] Complex discussions about Catholicism's relationship with the state were also happening in Ireland in newspapers such as the *Hibernian Journal*. In many ways, its press became a vehicle for "promoting a vision of Catholic loyalty to the Hanoverian state" and gave Catholics of all stripes the opportunity to speak for themselves.[40]

The government's firm resolve to move things forward received support from high-ranking figures such as Thomas Lord Lyttelton, the chief justice of Ireland, appointed in 1775; Edmund Burke, a politician of intimidating intellect; and Richard B. Sheridan, an anti-union radical politician who eventually secured a seat on the Privy Council. Lyttleton defended the bill because, although it allowed Quebec's Catholics to express religious and cultural difference, it made them subject to British law and "separated them from the state of Rome."[41] Moreover, one important safeguard had been implemented to limit the influence of the Catholic Church over the legislative affairs of the colony: Quebec was not given a legislative assembly – its people had to accept a London-appointed lieutenant governor and council.[42] Still, opponents paid scant attention to these protections and continued to see the Quebec Act, and the 1791 Constitutional Act, which organized the provinces of Upper and Lower Canada and installed a formal legal relationship between Britain and Canada, as legislation that paved the way for Catholicism to achieve the "same footing as Anglicanism and Scottish Presbyterianism."[43] Of course, Catholicism was not placed on the same footing as these Protestant churches, but the 1774 legislation did give Quebec's Catholics a level of legal recognition and civic standing that was far beyond the reach of their co-religionists in the United Kingdom. The ability of Quebec's Catholics to support British rule stemmed from the theological ethos that had been developing in the colony since the seventeenth century. The Gallican tradition, which emphasized the prerogative of local state governments over that of Rome, was promoted most strongly by the Sulpicians, a male religious order founded in Paris that was dedicated to the training of priests. Present in Quebec since the middle of the seventeenth century, the Sulpician influence had made it easier for the colonial clergy to "recognise the British conquerors and also to demand recognition of their legitimacy from the populace."[44] Any attachment to France was "quickly sacrificed" to ensure the protection and preservation of "local" Catholicism and a culture that included, as one of its pillars, an Augustinian-influenced Catholicism unique to Quebec.[45]

That the Quebec Act did not extend to the neighbouring colonies of New Brunswick, Prince Edward Island, or Nova Scotia confirmed Quebec's special status and the influence that its Catholic majority had on imperial policy. Rather than clarifying the status of Catholics to the east, this legislation confused the situation. Even when the penal laws, which had restricted the right of Catholics to own land, enter into military service, receive an education, act as guardians for children, and inherit property, started to be repealed in the United Kingdom in 1778, there was little clarity on what parts of the legislation could or should apply to the colonies. Consequently, colonial administrators tended to err on the side of caution. When pressed for a decision, Nova Scotia's governing council upheld the restrictions, first established in 1757 and 1758, that limited voting rights and membership of the legislative assembly to Protestants.[46] Initially, this caused little concern because Catholics were so few in number. The 1767 census, which should be used with caution and seen as indicative only, stated that 2,146 of the colony's 13,374 people were Catholic and that in Halifax, the capital, just 667 of its 3,022 residents were Catholic. Even such numbers were too high for one enumerator, who complained that "far too many [of them were] Irish papists."[47]

Rapid population growth in northeastern British North America began from the early 1770s, as the socio-economic change taking hold in Britain and Ireland prompted an emigration surge from the Scottish Highlands and Ireland. The Maritime colonies were a prime destination, and, as Catholic settlers spread throughout the region, many from an initial base in Prince Edward Island, their faith achieved a legitimacy there that had not been achieved at home.[48] An important factor was that the local colonial administrators could see the need for religious toleration.[49] While permanent European settlement made religious toleration a pressing issue in British North America, it was also supported in many of the Caribbean colonies because of the proximity of French- and Spanish-governed territories and the opportunities these offered to Irish Catholics to circumvent British restrictions. Orla Power's work on St. Croix, for example, details how they moved, with relative ease, between colonial spheres and forged social and economic relationships with other European partners.[50] In Britain's Caribbean territories, such as Grenada, religious toleration was often undermined by members of a British planter class who had little interest in accommodating the French Catholics whose lands they wanted. Yet the centrality of the French and of free persons of colour to Britain's retention of its colonies in this region was indicative of an evolving strategy of imperial security. Regardless of their personal feelings about granting concessions to French Catholics, the commissioners responsible for surveying and selling off parcels of land on the ceded islands recognized the necessity of such concessions and warned the Lords of Treasury of the consequences of a failure to grant them:

> It would be a step very prejudicial to the settlement of this island to oblige so many persons to desert it. As from its situation in case of a future war if well settled and inhabited, it would probably enable us greatly to obstruct the commerce of the French in the West Indies, and we likewise were of opinion that most of the estates now inhabited by the French if abandoned by them, would not be speedily bought by British subjects, as few of them are fit for sugar plantation and in general very laborious.[51]

Carriacou, a tiny island among the Grenadines, "possessed the most ethnically diverse set of Caribbean landholders during the eighteenth century," including many Highland Scots, but it escaped the religious tensions that engulfed Grenada.[52] Although the anti-Catholic attitudes of the Scottish planters in particular sparked Grenada's Fedon Rising, a bloody conflict that resulted in the murder of many of the island's leading planters, the underlying racial tensions within the enslaver class (white British and francophone free persons of colour) had also been a significant factor.[53] Privy Council records reveal that the island's Catholic population was so aggrieved by their lack of representation on the council and in the assembly in 1790, and by the fact that they had been "dispossessed by force of the Churches heretofore confined to the exercise of their Religion," that they petitioned London to recall the terms of the 1763 treaty, which ceded Grenada and the Grenadines to Britain, and to provide for Catholics there the same liberties as those in Quebec.[54] While the Fedon Rebellion was a setback for the ruling elites, it revealed the surprising flexibility of Britain's constitution when the needs of empire shifted. Colonial officials had to be able to respond quickly when they encountered new situations and so needed to be able to employ creative strategies, such as Catholic relief, when it came to building imperial security.

Further north, in the Maritime colonies, where the Acadians and Mi'kmaq represented virtually no threat to the growing British settler population, in spite of fears to the contrary by British governors, who remained apprehensive about Mi'kmaw military power, a climate of toleration was taking hold. Writing to a fellow priest, John Geddes, in Scotland from his perch at Prince Edward Island's Savage Harbour, Angus MacEachern explained that "every religion is tolerated here without being subject to pay any sallery to the Church of England clergy. My father bought 100 acres and paid 160£ sterling for them."[55] Reports of such toleration boosted the confidence of those engaged in pressing for further reforms at home. The Quebec Act and the Constitution Act of 1791 inspired new approaches to political participation, first in the imperial context, but eventually in Britain itself. That one group of Catholic subjects in the British Empire had the freedom to "profess the worship of their religion according to the rites of the Romish Church, as far as the laws of Great Britain permit[ed]," encouraged others to wade deeper into a serious and more informed debate about the extension of civil liberties to religious minorities in Britain.[56] Thus, between 1778 and 1793, Catholics in Britain and Ireland benefited from the introduction of relief legislation that provided them with new ways of overcoming some of the most persistent restrictions facing them, such as their exclusion from military service and schooling.

The issue of imperial security was intrinsic to this debate, and the first major challenge came in 1775, when the Thirteen Colonies revolted.

It was a humiliating rupture that exposed Britain's vulnerability. Ireland's precarious position as part of the United Kingdom, but separate from Britain, did not help. The anxiety that British ministers felt about Ireland's desire to break away was unfounded, since it overlooked the desire for partnership. In fact, "for the Protestant population ... an often prickly sense of their kingdom's rights and grievances coincided with a well-developed sense of its place in the Hanoverian dominions and its resulting share in a heritage of British liberties and price in British imperial power."[57] As serious discussions began about how Ireland might be more fully integrated into Britain's constitutional fold, the opinions of Britain and Ireland's political elites, by the early 1790s, began to converge on the idea of a parliamentary union.[58] Not everyone was convinced, and there was a genuine fear about the damage that England's fundamental lack of understanding of Ireland and its people would do.[59] Yet, as politicians in both places began to accept the possibility of a union, their engagement with the legal status of Catholics became unavoidable.[60] In the 1790s, redefining that status was much easier in a colonial context than in a domestic one, but, as Britain entered an era of revolution abroad and reform at home,[61] the need to deliver imperial security at a time when the international climate was inherently unstable meant that something had to give. The Quebec Act was not coincidental, but rather marked the beginning of a protracted process of extending relief to Catholics at home and abroad.

Catholic Relief

As the prospect of war with the American colonies and with France loomed, the fact that Ireland and the Scottish Highlands offered a reservoir of soldiers and sailors was a welcome relief. Neither the army nor the navy had recovered from the crippling casualties sustained during the Seven Years' War, and so they were unprepared for another major conflict. Although "discreet" lobbying for Catholic relief was undertaken by high-ranking Irish Catholics in London as early as the 1730s, a relaxation of the penal laws in England, Wales, and Ireland became a reality only from 1778, when the first Relief Act was passed.[62] This legislation, which was augmented by additional acts in 1782 and in the early 1790s, paved the way for substantial Catholic military service and returned to Catholics the right to buy land, attend school, act as legal guardians, sit on juries, attend Mass, and act as barristers and solicitors.[63] The ferocity of anti-Catholic opinion in Scotland delayed relief legislation there until 1793, just as Britain entered its final major war with France.[64] That year's legislation also introduced an important difference between Irish and English Catholics, in that the former were permitted to serve as domestic officers, whereas Catholics could still not be commissioned as officers in England.[65] The opening up of military service gave Britain's imperial forces a much-needed boost, as Catholics from the four nations, but especially from Ireland and Scotland, flooded into the services. Imperial security became the catalyst for far-reaching and genuinely transformative legislative change at home.

Relieving Catholics of many of the civil disabilities in place against them was part of the broader process of reform being advocated at this time by an emerging middle class. As their frustration with the landed elites' political monopoly grew, vital "cross-fertilisation" occurred as "religious poetry, devotional tracts and political pamphlets" were written and exchanged.[66] People, politicians, and literary figures were absorbed by the growing range of material. In the literary realm, for example, individuals such as Charlotte Smith, Felicia Hemans, and, a little later, Percy Bysshe Shelley, the Romantic poet and husband of *Frankenstein* author, Mary Shelley, had been spurred by the spirit of reform and used their craft to comment on the extension of rights to Catholics. While many still had problems with Catholicism, they were committed to reform. Shelley, for instance, was critical both of the Irish and of Catholicism, but opposed what he saw as the "persecution against those whose religious opinions differed from the Establishment." For people like him, those who wanted "global reform," the process needed to start at home.[67] Such sentiments extended across the religious landscape, and, although reform was the dominant view of Dissenters, many within the Church of England also wanted corrections.[68] Numerous societies, including the Friends of the People, the London Corresponding Society, and the Catholic Committee, sprung up or resurfaced as advocates for socio-religious reform.

The Catholic question, which revolved around how to deal with Catholics in the United Kingdom and the calls for the removal of disabilities against them, arose as a natural consequence of the growing culture of dissent and engaged people across the length and breadth of Britain and Ireland. It was also a debate that enhanced understandings of what Britain was starting to represent to all its people and forced a discussion about what the state needed to provide for them. Support for those Catholics participating in the discussions came from unlikely places. Reporting on Edinburgh's political news in 1782, a priest named MacPherson (first name unknown) informed George Hay, the vicar apostolic of Scotland's Lowland District (1778–1805) and Scotland's most senior Catholic cleric, that the town's clubs and societies were pushing for dramatic governmental reform: "Through the streets at night" he said, "*no king, no aristocrats* is openly cried … I must not forget to tell you that all the clubs and associations express the greatest sympathy for the R. Catholic sufferings in Britain and Ireland."[69] Radical sentiments indeed in a town notorious for anti-Catholicism and one that had witnessed the infamous Gordon Riots just two years earlier.

In Britain, one of the most outspoken proponents of Catholic relief and complete emancipation in England was Sir John Coxe Hippisley, a social climber and Anglican MP for the "pugnaciously anti-Catholic constituency" of Sudbury. Having spent extended periods of time in Italy, he had also acted as Britain's pseudo ambassador to Rome at various points between 1792 and his death in 1825.[70] In addition to using speeches and pamphlets at home to convince parliamentary colleagues of the necessity of relief, Hippisley also impressed upon the rectors of Rome's Scottish, Irish, and English colleges the need to ensure that their young charges, the seminarians who would serve the missions of the "British dominions," understood their roles in safeguarding Britain's civil constitution and in promoting allegiance to the Crown.[71] Although Roman intervention and influence was a constant worry, the reopening of the English College, under the rectorship of Robert Gradwell, in 1818 after its 1798 closure was an important development influenced by the demise of Napoleonic France and the expansion of Britain into a range of new territories.

Ireland's inclusion in Hippisley's instruction to the colleges implies a more comprehensive awareness of what Britain was coming to represent. The shared Crown, integrated merchant class, and interdependent political culture meant that it was easier to assume a common cause than not. Astute diplomatic operatives like Hippisley and Charles Erskine, a Rome-based Scottish priest of Jacobite parentage who acted as Rome's unofficial papal envoy in London at the end of the eighteenth century,[72] understood these inherent connections and succeeded in navigating the rocky political terrain to build more cordial links between London and Rome. They and many others recognized that improved relations would not only serve Britain's imperial agenda by promoting stronger commercial ties with continental markets, but that they would also ensure a balance of power in Europe. Desperate to find a way of salvaging its influence on the Continent and in need of new ways to expand its influence beyond Europe, Rome had as much to gain as Britain did and looked to overseas colonies as an opportunity.[73]

Such developments were critical because, for the first time since the Reformation, there was a feeling among many Catholics that the time to begin participating in the public debates about their place in British society had finally arrived. The problem was the lack of a unified voice; participation was channelled through specific organizations that tended to be divided along lay, clerical, or national lines. In Ireland, a growing number of Catholic professionals, who believed that the political climate was ripe for change, began to participate in Britain's civil processes through organizations focused on securing Catholic relief.[74] In 1771, *The Humble Address, and Petition of the Roman Catholics of Ireland*, signed by thirty-seven nobles and gentry, and "above three hundred other respectable persons," was presented to Ireland's lord lieutenant. In addition to highlighting their growing frustration with the lack of opportunity for sustained or long-term improvement, it revealed the depth of their discouragement with the inheritance restrictions that undermined a culture of "industry":

> Whilst the endeavours of our Industry are thus discouraged, no less we humbly apprehend, to the Detriment of the national Prosperity, and the Diminution of your Majesty's Revenue, that to our particular Ruin, there are a set of Men, who instead of occupying any honest Occupation in the Common Wealth make it their Employment to pry into our miserable Property, to drag us into the Courts, and to compel us to confess on our Oaths, and under Penalties of Perjury, whether we have in any instance, acquired a property in the smallest Degree exceeding what the Rigour of the Law has admitted ... By the Laws now in force in the kingdom, a Son, however, undutiful of profligate, shall, merely by Merit of confirming to the Established Religion, deprive the Roman Catholic Father of the free and full possession of his Estate.[75]

English Catholics shared similar frustrations, and in a memorial to the Earl of Shelbourne on the eve of the Gordon Riots, Charles Lord Stourton, Robert Edward Lord Petre, John Courtenay Throckmorton, Thomas Stapleton, and Thomas Thorngold, an extremely influential group of elite men, declared with frustration that "the Roman Catholics of England are as good subjects as those of Ireland or any persons of any description in any country whatsoever."[76] The desire of these and others to be seen as "useful citizens to our Country, and Subjects as profitable as we are loyal to your Majesty," was underpinned by a sense of loyalty, "which all our Sufferings have not been able to abate."[77] Undoubtedly, "practical and public protests of loyalty" were just as important for Catholics in Britain and Ireland as they were for those in a distant colony like Quebec, where the Catholic leadership made a point of assuring government officials of Catholic loyalty.[78]

The Catholic committees were early expressions of Catholic associational culture. Founded in the late 1750s, Ireland's Catholic Committee was a "middle/upper class organisation ... at pains to disassociate itself from the activities of the Whiteboys."[79] Its aim was to keep the issue of Catholic relief in the public eye, but Connolly's assessment is that it was "unimpressive": after an initial burst of activity, it stagnated for the next couple of decades until the late 1770s, when it was resuscitated to press for Catholic relief.[80] Given the comparative paucity of Catholic leadership in Ulster, the committee struggled to gain a strong following there, and the region's absence from its early campaigns was conspicuous.[81] Moreover, its rather conservative and protracted approach to change frustrated people like John Keogh, an ambitious Dublin merchant and member of the town's United Irish Society, which was led by the charismatic Theobald Wolfe Tone, who wanted to break the control exerted by Ireland's Catholic elite.[82] England's Catholic Committee, founded in 1778 and comprising gentry and aristocrats, emerged from a different set of priorities. Specifically, its members wanted the national bishops to break free from Roman influence, but the desire to limit Ireland's growing influence on church politics was also a motivating factor in its establishment.[83] Members of England's first Catholic Committee, led by lawyer William Sheldon, wanted a way of defining Catholic "political capacity" in the face of an "ambivalent" clergy.[84] By 1788, the group had focused on obtaining specific freedoms that would place them on the same footing as Protestant Dissenters. They agreed "that the chief object of the Application now intended to be made by the English Catholics for Relief is, to obtain the Repeal of all the Statutes of Recusancy; of all the statutes which disable them from serving in the navy and army or from practising Law or Physic; and all the Statutes which prevent their enjoying their property."[85] There was no Catholic Committee in Scotland. Its laity was comparatively weak and constantly confronted a pervasive and vicious culture of anti-Catholicism. Nevertheless, and notwithstanding the differences between the English and Irish organizations, which continued to widen after the parliamentary union,[86] the fact that these organizations existed at all represented an important first step for Catholics in learning how to assert their British citizenship before it was formally extended to them. The desire to reassess notions of citizenship was part of a socio-political awakening with significant repercussions for religious minorities. As a movement, Dissent was a social leveller, and the challenges it posed to provincial elites after 1783 meant that the existing status quo could be legitimately contested.[87] One of the most effective ways this was done was through pamphleteering,[88] and a plethora of organs sprang up as a consequence between the late 1770s and 1810. While the Dissenting movement did encourage more activity from the Church of England, it also convinced many of the need to argue for the removal of the political disabilities in place against

Catholics and Dissenters so that a "policy of imperial assimilation could develop."[89] From the 1790s, the arguments in favour of Catholic relief and emancipation became more sophisticated, and the debates began to concentrate on constitutional as opposed to theological arguments.

Ireland and the Irish were often at the centre of these debates, especially as the prospect of expanding the union became more of a reality and there was growing concern over how Ireland's restricted access to the empire impeded development. A growing middle tier, which was dominated by Catholics and Dissenting Protestants, was frustrated with an out-of-touch class of governing elites who remained unconvinced that Ireland's security and long-term prosperity required civil and religious liberty. The penal laws, increasingly regarded as vindictive and outdated, were blamed for thwarting meaningful economic growth and social improvement.[90] All of these arguments were predicated on expanded understandings of Britain and Britishness. In 1792, a year before it dissolved itself on account of a government crackdown on "representative assemblies,"[91] the General Committee of Roman Catholics of Ireland questioned the value of liberty if the majority of the Irish population remained subject to unequal laws. It argued that the constitution's emphasis on liberty actually made room for Catholics and that, to deny this, to be "excommunicat[ed] from the liberties of our country taints the source and impairs the essence of those very liberties."[92] Catholic exclusion cast serious doubt on the principle of equality: "We are not conspirators against Church or State. We do not grudge to Protestants the advantage of constitutional rights. We desire to partake in them as benefits, in which the acquisition of one man is not the determinant of another – free and common benefits. The constitution is large enough for us all."[93] This position was echoed by Edmund Burke. In a printed letter to his countryman Sir Hercules Langrishe, a long-time Irish politician who endorsed, for the most part, the idea of Catholic relief, Burke questioned the purpose and durability of the constitution if it was not going to work for all of Ireland's citizens. "Our constitution," Burke explained, "is not made for great, general and proscriptive exclusions; sooner or later, it will destroy them or they will destroy the constitution."[94] In his opinion, "ecclesiastical allegiance, social order, and clear thought" were interdependent; Christianity, as opposed to any one sect, needed to be promoted as a unifying force.[95] Instinctively, he pointed to the political management of Quebec as proof that extending civil rights to Catholics safeguarded Britain and its empire. He noted that,

> in that system the Canadian Catholics were far from being deprived of the
> advantages or distinctions, of any kind which they enjoyed under their

former monarchy. It is true, that some people, and amongst them one eminent divine, predicted at that time, that by this step we should lose our dominions in America. He foretold that the Pope would send his indulgences thither; that the Canadians would fall in with France; declare their independence, and draw or force our colonies into the same design. The independence happened according to his prediction, but in directly the reverse order. All our English Protestant colonies revolted. They joined themselves to France; and it so happened that Popish Canada was the only place which preserved its fidelity; the only place in which France got no footing, the only peopled colony which now remains to Great Britain.[96]

Burke's linking of Catholic emancipation with imperial security exposed just how high the stakes actually were and just how dominating a role the empire was playing in domestic politics and in thinking about reform. Burke, and figures like him, did not call for parliamentary reform; rather they sought to curb corruption, greed, and "royal influence."[97] While he advocated the evolution of social prosperity through equal access to the "common advantages," an impetus for change was also driven by the actions of settlers.[98] The loyalism demonstrated by colonial Catholics helped to reshape elite political opinion, which increasingly began to press the necessity of Catholic relief and complete emancipation. Given Britain's imperial strains with America and France, their motives were pragmatic, but the willingness of a growing number of non-Catholic political elites to consider the meaning of the constitution for imperial purposes indicated an increasingly popular belief that denying citizenship based on religion was an untenable position.

As noted in the previous chapter, loyalty, and whether or not a Catholic's ultimate allegiance could be to the king rather than to the pope, was a primary consideration. Increasingly, *Britain* and *British* were defined more in terms of a loyalty to the Crown (the institution of the monarchy and not necessarily the person on the throne), and to a pragmatic commitment to growing an empire, than to an attachment to any particular faith or denomination. A precursor to this ideological debate was Jacobitism. The majority of its Episcopalian and Catholic supporters felt that they were acting in the best interests of the Crown; the same can be said of the motives of William of Orange's supporters, whose efforts to push James VII and II into exile had inspired Jacobitism in the first place. By the end of the eighteenth century, the needs of the empire meant that the idea of Britishness was being aligned with constitutional loyalism. Among the political elite, there was an emerging notion that Catholic loyalty to the Crown was possible, but this development sat alongside more hardened views, which saw the Crown as an important defence against "popery." Change would come, but it would come slowly.[99]

Despite its inherently conservative and British character, government propagandists portrayed Jacobitism as a "savage," "disloyal," and "enemy within" movement.[100] This negative legacy was most damaging to Catholics, and so the Catholic leadership and laity tried to reframe their image with expressions of loyalty. Most Catholics across the British Isles were already living with loyalty in their everyday lives simply by going about their business like everyone else, but they were conscious of the fact that they needed to do more to prove it. In Scotland, where the confiscation of Highland estates had been widespread and crippling to many families, a gathering of Highland Catholic gentry resolved to raise a Catholic regiment "for his Majesty's service" in the spring of 1794. The linking of their heritage with the region's tradition of militarism was highly symbolic, both for them and for the government, in that it represented an invocation of a shared yet contentious past of protection and pacification.[101] And even though their request to raise this regiment was denied, the canny Lord Advocate, Henry Dundas, acknowledged that "His Majesty views with much approbation this proof of loyalty and attachments to his person and Government, which has been manifested by his Catholic subjects in Scotland."[102] The Glengarry Fencibles, a predominantly Highland Catholic regiment, were founded a few months after Dundas became secretary of state for war in 1794.[103]

Ireland and Parliamentary Union

The loss of so many of the American colonies had shaken British confidence and highlighted the presence of national fault lines that had the potential to upset the security of the union. While empire and the profits it generated had kept Scotland in the union, it would be naive to assume that this had led to the formation of a "one-nation" identity. Ireland added another significant complication. An underlying issue was Britain's inability to realize the full potential of its empire because the "home" country was vulnerable. For much of the eighteenth century, right up until 1815, Britain was at war, and this had a defining influence on domestic arrangements. In 1707, Scotland and England united in a parliamentary union, thus completing the state structure that had begun over a century earlier with the union of their Crowns. The union of 1707 was prompted by the desire to secure the Hanoverian and, ultimately, Protestant succession, thereby preventing the possibility of a European Catholic alliance and the erosion of what had previously been England's empire. Securing the British Empire had also been the impetus of the next union – that between Britain and Ireland – in 1801. Arranged to fend off Napoleon's France, to placate Ireland's Protestant Ascendancy, and to tame the island's Catholics, the 1801 union re-established a sense of political stability in a climate of pan-European instability, and this allowed Britain's empire to grow.[104] The series of unions, which ultimately created the United Kingdom of Great Britain and Ireland, were responses to crises rather than examples of long-term planning, and the results were mixed. The failure to grant full emancipation to Catholics, which had been promised as a condition of union with Ireland, meant that many of the gains experienced by Catholics in the previous three decades were effectively "put on ice," and relations between that island and the British state became strained.[105] The delay, due "as much to casual evasion as to visceral opposition and contempt," stemmed from the fact that the vast majority of British politicians involved with Ireland made little or no attempt to acquire or build any kind of foundational understanding of it.[106] It did not help that they continued to view Ireland and its people, both Catholics and Protestants, as "primitive, barbaric, corrupt, violent, unreliable, dangerous and badly in need of Anglo-Saxon discipline."[107] Inevitable fractures and ruptures emerged from the second decade of the nineteenth century and carried on throughout that century, incorporating the campaign for repeal and bolstering sectarian tension.[108]

The problem was that, rather than being given, Catholic emancipation had to be taken; George III's opposition was so vociferous that the measure could not be passed until 1829, after his death, when Daniel O'Connell's election as MP for County Clare in 1828 forced the issue.[109] Following the union, in the lead-up to 1829, three Catholic relief bills had been introduced to Parliament; all were introduced by Irishmen, and all failed.[110] Hostility to full equality was relatively widespread, as many non-Catholics feared that it would open the door to Roman influence and undermine the authority of the Crown and Parliament. To the king and his supporters, such as John Fitzgibbon, Lord Earl of Clare, who gave a speech opposing concessions to Catholics in the House of Lords, and Henry Petty-Fitzmaurice, Lord Kerry, who thought Catholic priests guilty of inciting "demons of every sort,"[111] a parliamentary union with Ireland to secure the British state was one thing, but the extension of full civil liberties to a people still widely perceived as spiritually corrupt and politically subversive was quite another.

Political opposition to Catholic emancipation was influenced by the fear that it would undermine the security of the British union, since Catholic MPs, empowered by a growing number of Catholic voters, would press for Irish independence as soon as they got the chance.[112] On another level, though, opposition stemmed from the belief that

Catholics were incapable of abandoning Rome for London. Ernst Augustus I of Hanover, Duke of Cumberland and later king of Hanover, was the fifth son of George III and a staunch opponent of Catholic emancipation, unlike his younger brother, Augustus Frederick, Duke of Sussex, who, like many other influential politicians and members of the aristocracy and landed elite, made frequent visits to Rome and requested audiences with the pope.[113] The elder brother believed that Catholic emancipation contravened the Coronation Oath, which obliged the monarch to swear to maintain the "Laws of God the true Profession of the Gospell and the Protestant Reformed Religion Established by Law" and to "Preserve unto the Bishops and Clergy of this Realme and to the Churches committed to their Charge all such Rights and Priviledges as by Law."[114] In 1807, when he was made grand master of the Orange Lodge, an anonymous pamphlet, *The Patriot King*, signed by "A Foe to Bigotry," was dedicated to him. Not simply an expression of anti-Catholicism, the document sought to demonstrate the threat that Rome's influence posed to constitutional security:

> With respect to the Papists ... that there could be no fair objection to their participating in a general toleration, provided their non-conformity was founded *only* on a difference of opinion in religion; and their principles did not extend to a subversion of the Civil Government: – but while they acknowledge a foreign power, superior to the sovereignty of the kingdom, they cannot complain, if the laws of that kingdom will not permit them an unlimited participation, and treat them on the footing of Protestant subjects.[115]

Two years earlier, John Milner, the outspoken, controversial, and long-serving vicar apostolic of England's Midland District from 1803 until 1826, had stressed that Catholics' acknowledgment of the pope was strictly spiritual. He was affronted by the oaths that Catholics were expected to swear, declaring them to be "stupidly ignorant" and "malicious." Catholicism, he argued, like the Dissenting traditions, would not undermine the authority of the Crown.[116] Clearly the arguments both for and against Catholic emancipation were involving more civil than theological considerations; by the early nineteenth century, theological arguments were beginning to fall out of favour with imperially minded political elites. There remained, however, one major stumbling block, and it was in Ireland.

The Protestant Ascendency was bitterly opposed to Catholic emancipation: it feared a loss of authenticity and superiority if Catholics, who were Ireland's majority population, were granted equal rights under the law.[117] Since the British government needed the Irish Parliament to ratify the union for the sake of the empire and effectively write itself out of existence, it agreed to grant titles, positions (clerical and political), and compensation to members of Ireland's Protestant establishment to ensure the bill's passing.[118] Those Catholic clerics who had managed to steward Catholic support for the union were rewarded too. Dublin's archbishop, John Thomas Troy, whose *Pastoral Address on the Duties of Christian Citizens* "provoked outrage" among those opposed to conceiving of Catholics as citizens, and who had continually emphasized the need for loyalty among his labouring-class co-religionists, received "generous compensation" for the Catholic property that had been destroyed by Orangemen during the 1798 rebellion.[119] Notwithstanding this, union with Ireland forced a debate about the meaning of the constitution and of Catholics' relationship with it.

The debate about Catholicism's compatibility with the British constitution, as revealed in countless printed pamphlets and letters, occurred within the context of a deeper consideration of the expansion of the state structure and a reconfiguration of Britain's relationship with Ireland. The issues were not inherently theological, but the relationship between Catholic identity and Britishness was at the fore as a matter of civil participation and social justice. And, while it was true that the union hardened sectarian tensions among some in Ireland, it was also true that many Catholics possessed or took on dual Irish and British identities. Britain's character, as a collaboration of four nations, meant that such dual identities were accommodated relatively easily, since understandings of Britishness were predicated upon national conditions as opposed to those of the centre state. Catholics, a numerous body, could no longer be excluded from the process of defining what Britishness meant at home or abroad.

While the unions of 1707 and 1801 were forged in response to concerns for the empire, the nature and timing of each were inherently different and led to distinct outcomes. Considering the unions of Ireland and Scotland together is useful as long as their fundamental differences are understood. Ireland was a dependent, rather than an independent, kingdom,[120] and it was never going to be a partner in the empire in the same way that Scotland had been. The Irish had been involved in the slave-based plantation economy of the Caribbean and had even dominated aspects of the provisioning trade, but the unrestricted West Indian profit-spinning that had brought the Scots so much wealth as plantation owners, merchants, and bankers was drawing to a close by the time Ireland arrived in 1800–1, for a start.[121] Beyond that was the fact that the 1707 dynamic had already solidified, and Ireland would only ever be seen as a necessary, but not necessarily wanted, junior partner. Between 1801 and 1830, the character of the union was "intrusive and coercive," and very little thought had been given to the actual structures required to facilitate Ireland's inclusion.[122] Apart from the island becoming off-limits to France, questions about the role that Ireland was going to play in this new super-state and how the Irish nation would be accommodated within Britain had no clear answers. Many believed that an important starting point was to extend equal rights to all of Ireland's people as a way of levelling the economic playing field; civil equality, not just in Ireland but across the four nations, would lead to greater cooperation and a more resilient empire, but, as indicated already, this was easier said than done. The problem boiled down to "the complete lack of post-union administrative innovation" and the "deliberate ignorance" about Ireland and Irish affairs.[123]

Writing in 1801, the Irish barrister John Joseph Dillon reasoned that if the "national appellations of the Irish and the Scots were not invidiously contrasted with that of the Englishman," the British Empire would be far more powerful. He was annoyed that Catholic emancipation had not been introduced with the passing of the Act of Union and believed that "we proceed still further, extending the cause of weakness, and refining on the principle of disunion, by our local factions of Protestant and Catholic."[124] In his opinion, which was shared by others, achieving real economic growth and stability required Catholic emancipation, since keeping the majority of Ireland's population in a state of civil uncertainty endangered nation, state, and imperial security.[125] Henry Augustus Dillon-Lee, 13th Viscount Dillon, a young MP from Ireland, agreed, and declared the remaining penal laws obsolete. He wanted attention focused on the improvement of the lower orders and for educated Catholics to be allowed to become "engaged with British issues on British territory," as it made little sense for Catholic freeholders to be able to vote, but for their landlords to be excluded from Parliament.[126]

Four years later, in 1805, these sentiments were echoed by John Milner, who questioned the value of alienating a "high spirited and gallant people, who already fight half the battles of the empire by sea and land ... merely because they adhere to the religion of their and our ancestors," at a time when the Napoleonic Wars were intensifying.[127] Exclusion on the basis of religion had become an untenable position in imperial politics: the British Empire could not afford such divisions. The positioning of empire as a central feature of the emancipation debate demonstrates the extent to which Catholics were invested in the broader imperial program.[128] It was what enabled them to access mainstream British society because, in the empire, there was no question that Catholics were Britons.

Aware that their loyalty to the Crown and state continued to be under intense scrutiny, Catholics made repeated attempts to emphasize their commitment to imperial defence. By the first decade of the nineteenth century, and thanks to previous relief legislation, the army and navy were benefiting from significant numbers of Irish and Scottish Highland Catholic servicemen.[129] Recognition of the consistency of their commitment to Britain's armed forces, and of the fact that they had no problem fighting their fellow Catholics to defend Britain and the empire, informed the debate, and numerous pamphlets emphasized Britain's reliance on Catholics in the armed services. One in particular argued for the compatibility of Catholicism with the Coronation Oath and stated that "if any of your Protestant acquaintances ... are disposed to censure this practice, let them say: We are able to fight our own battles, without the numerous and hardy sailors and soldiers of the sister island."[130]

Indeed, disproving Catholic loyalty became difficult, as prominent Irish Catholic lawyers such as John Joseph Dillon and Denys Scully, who had worked with Pitt to try to secure Catholic emancipation, produced mountains of evidence detailing military service as proof of Catholics' commitment to king and country. That Catholic soldiers and sailors willingly opposed their French co-religionists was stressed to show how the interests of the state trumped those of religion: "Do not our Sailors ..., mostly Irish, beat them [the French] to a jelly wherever they meet them? Do they not, at every opportunity, land in open boats upon hostile shores, spike their guns, storm their batteries, and ever conquer Frenchmen, even upon French ground?"[131] While Dillon praised Irish Catholics for "maintaining with their blood the glory and prosperity of the Empire," Scully poured scorn on "shrivelled French Fops, who feed upon garlic, chicken broth, frogs, rats, and other vermin, who wear rings in their ears, and muffs on their delicate hands."[132] An uncharacteristically diplomatic Milner reminded people that the extension of civil rights to Quebec's Catholics had enhanced imperial security by generating loyalty at a time when the empire's survival was at risk. In his reply to *Considerations on the Coronation Oath*, a tract written by the Oxford lawyer John Reeves to defend the king's opposition to Catholic emancipation, Milner pointed out that "the first act in favour of Catholics was the Quebec Act, by which the religion in question was legally established in that extensive and important part of his Majesty's dominions, and I believe few people will dispute with me that it was owing to this wise and conciliating conducts of the Legislature, that Canada continued firm in its allegiance, when the neighbouring Protestant Colonies, by common consent shook it off."[133]

As criticisms levelled against Catholics by those who feared the loss of influence continued unabated, they were met by counter-arguments that undermined the position that the 1798 rebellion in Ireland had been the result of a popish plot: many Catholic militia, noblemen, gentlemen, and farmers had tried to suppress it. In fact, very few of the pamphleteers and tract writers opposed to Catholic emancipation used the rebellion as evidence against its introduction, since it had been led by Ulster Presbyterians who wanted self-determination.[134] This is not to suggest that there had not been significant Catholic involvement – there had been – but it is difficult to know just how far radicalism, as opposed to self-interest, motivated this involvement. At the end of the day, Catholics sought acceptance as members, as opposed to enemies, of the state.[135]

Seven years after the 1801 union, and despite Catholics receiving credit for their loyal military service, emancipation remained a long way off. Attempts in 1805 to persuade the House of Commons to support a petition that would see "all the liberties & privileges of British subjects/of the Catholics of Ireland" restored failed when Pitt, who was "favourable to the principle of the petition," declined to introduce it and indicated his intention to oppose it should come before Parliament at that time.[136] For many, the worry was not that the Catholics *would* cause problems, but that they *might*: "It is possible the Catholics would not make a bad use of the power demanded, BUT SUPPOSE THEY SHOULD."[137] These lingering worries reveal the inherent lack of understanding that many opponents had about how Catholics and Catholicism existed or should exist within the United Kingdom. A genuine distance existed between Britain's Catholic communities and Rome, not unlike that which separated Rome from other Catholic communities across Europe, but this fact was not appreciated (deliberately or not) by opponents of emancipation in Britain. The Catholics of England, Scotland, and Ireland had always favoured national priorities over Roman ones, and this custom would continue even as ultramontanism gathered force and as the relationship between London and Rome improved.[138]

These national priorities, however, meant a distinct lack of Catholic unity in the United Kingdom, which complicated the progress of emancipation. The differences were most obvious in the ways in which Catholics engaged with political debates: "In Ireland, the Catholics, by far the majority, looked upon further emancipation as a right and as the only possible way to remedy the restrictive political and economic position ... 'The English Catholics, few in number and without even the potential for political power which the Irish Catholics had, viewed emancipation as a privilege or a reward' for their loyalty to the Protestant state."[139] As the vicars apostolic of England, Scotland, and Ireland worked together to assert their authority in the face of Roman interference and more general anti-Catholic opposition, a degree of unity was achieved. During the Napoleonic Wars, they sometimes jointly but often separately waded into debates about the position of Catholics in Britain and Ireland. Their message was that Catholics were loyal subjects, but they recognized that opinions about Irish Catholics influenced how non-Catholics perceived all of them, and this prompted those in Scotland and England to go out of their way to stress the loyalty of their Irish brethren. While their military commitment had been helpful in building a broader awareness of their loyalty and dependability as subjects, Catholics also benefited from changing perceptions of Britishness, as this extract from an 1812 tract entitled *An Appeal against the Roman Catholic Claims* reveals: "They [Catholics] have also not been backward in menacing us with the number of Roman Catholics which compose our Army and Navy, – and pointing at the acts of bravery by which we are to be overawed into more than unconditional submission to their moderate expectations. To admit that they are as brave as they are stated to be, is only to admit that they are Britons."[140] Notwithstanding the fundamental critique inherent in this source, the acknowledgment of Catholics as Britons was an important turning point for how Catholicism was perceived in British society. During the conflict of 1812, the French Catholics of Quebec once again stood with the British Crown against the Americans, but there was restlessness among them as they recognized the precariousness of their status until Catholic emancipation was delivered.[141] In an 1812 statement to his fellow parliamentarians, Henry Grattan, an Anglo-Irish nationalist MP and "parliamentary champion of Catholics,"[142] warned that the futures of both Britain and its empire were at stake as long as the issue of emancipation remained unresolved: "The day you finally ascertain the disqualification of the Catholic, you pronounce the doom of Great Britain. It is just it should be so; the king who takes away the liberty of his subjects, loses his crown; the people who take away the liberty of their fellow-subjects, lose their empire."[143] It was no coincidence that this speech was delivered when it was. In 1812, the United States declared war on Britain and, although the conflict was perceived in Britain as more of a skirmish than a major conflict, it had the potential to ignite a much bigger fire.[144] Britain's impressment of sailors, the seizure of American vessels, and heavy trade restrictions were antagonistic, but they were issues easily dealt with. What was less easy to tackle was the ferocity of anti-British opinion in the United States.[145] Given the influence that such subversive sentiments might have on settlers in, say, Upper and Lower Canada, or further east in the coastal Maritime colonies, significant consideration was given to finding ways of consolidating support for Britain's imperial interests. In addition to the soldier settlement schemes, such as those introduced in the Ottawa Valley and led by Scottish Highlanders,[146] recognizing Catholic loyalty, in a manner similar to what had been done in Quebec, became a necessity. Although figures such as Grattan worked to convince sceptics of the necessity of granting further concessions to Catholics as a way of safeguarding and preserving imperial integrity,[147] still others, with the help of populist publishers such as John Joseph Stockdale, countered that it was concessions that had lost them America in the first place.[148] In the end, however, Grattan's opinion and concerns for the survival of the empire carried more weight.

Moving from partial relief, which had started in 1778, to full emancipation was a defining process for Catholics. It demonstrated a growing confidence among the wider Catholic body but also connected them with other reform-minded individuals who believed in the principles of religious toleration and civil equality. *The Scotsman* printed a series of pro-emancipation commentaries as a way of showing, or attempting to show, a growing preference for full emancipation. Echoing the sentiments of the evangelical churchman Thomas Chalmers, one anonymous contributor advanced that "we, the Protestants, have acknowledged ourselves in error by the mere fact of repealing four-fifths of the old disqualifying statutes. Let us then complete the good work we have begun, and blot out the last remaining shred of a code of persecution, of which as a while, the most rancorous bigot would now be ashamed."[149]

These public condemnations existed alongside private ones. A poem penned at some point in the early 1830s by the Catholic convert Josiah Spode IV of the Spode pottery family hailed the 1829 emancipation legislation as a sign of freedom and justice:

> *On the Catholic Emancipation*
> Peruse the public journals, you will see,
> The Bill is pass'd – the Catholics are free!
> Emancipation, late each bosom fir'd,
> And has at length my humble pen inspir'd;
> Would I had pow'r & talent to describe,
> Th' effects which it produced on ev'ry tribe,
> Opinions various as the colour'd bow
> In rich & poor appear'd, in high & low.
> Some judg'd it wrong to offer such a Bill

Whilst others further'd it with all their will;
These Requisitions sign'd for conscience's sake
Those, begg'd the King concessions not to make;
Whilst one exclaims "The Lords will cast it out,"
Another cries "it will be brought about!"
"or else and insurrection must decide,"
"For Catholics not more will be deny'd."
An Eldon here, is seen though aged quite,
T'oppose the Bill with all his pow'r & might:
While there, and Chalmers, equally renown'd,
Amongst its strongest favourers is found;
A pious few, remote from public sight,
In frequent earnest prayers to God unite,
That he his true religion would protect,
And King, & Ministers himself direct,
Thus, they from earthly rulers, wrest the sword,
And place it in the hands of Heav'n's great Lord.
The Bill at length is pass'd – But oh! a Bill,
Of more importance is impressing still;
For all "Emancipation" greatly need,
From sin & Satan's slav'ry to be freed.
To Heav'n's high court "petitions" we must send,
And Jesus will his people's cause befriend;
He'll not "cast out" but hear our humble pray'r,
The liberty of children, we shall share;
His death has out adoption made secure,
He with his blood, has sealed his promise sure.[150]

Given his conversion, Spode's sympathy was understandable, but he was by no means alone, and the list of non-Catholic supporters was long and distinguished. Supporters of Catholic emancipation included, in addition to the literary figures mentioned above, Thomas Chalmers, perhaps the best-known evangelical of the nineteenth century; Zachary Macaulay, slavery abolitionist and former governor of Sierra Leone; Sydney Smith, Church of England clergyman, reformer, and co-founder of the *Edinburgh Review*; and Henry Thomas Cockburn, Lord Cockburn, a well-known Scottish judge who was later appointed to the court of session.

An expanded understanding of the concept of citizenship had allowed Catholic grievances to blend with a broader collection of issues that had inspired calls for reform, but the issue of imperial security was never far away. Securing Catholic emancipation in British North

America was easier to achieve, not simply because it was important to keep American territorial encroachment at bay, but because colonial development required significant settler input. As the following chapter shows, the socio-economic roles that settlers were required to play if these new societies were to flourish as British colonial holdings meant that Catholics were at a distinct advantage. The mass outmigration of Catholics, particularly from Ireland and northern Scotland after 1770, was a consequence of socio-economic dislocation at home and a growing awareness of the fact that many of the colonies offered better options. Those along the eastern coast of what would become Canada were important destinations for many of the early Scottish and Irish Catholic migrants. These immigrants exploited a range of opportunities, and many became extremely successful at negotiating spaces for themselves within the political and civil fabric of newly emerging societies. Not only were they able to establish an important foothold in colonial society, but they also came to exert significant influence over the strategies of the imperial state.

Chapter Three

Colonial Catholics and Constitutional Change: Developments in Cape Breton Island and Nova Scotia

At the end of the eighteenth century, colonial Catholics, like their counterparts in Ireland and the Scottish Highlands, were becoming increasingly aware of their military and economic value to the British imperial state. This awareness encouraged a political consciousness that informed the development of the civil structures in their new societies. Unlike in Ireland, where sectarian tension would increase in the decades immediately following the Act of Union in 1801,[1] what characterized the Catholic experience in northeastern British North America in the period before 1830 was significant cooperation with their Protestant brethren. In the coastal Maritime colonies – those spaces that would evolve into Canada's Maritime provinces – Catholicism went from being a "small, almost homogeneous community proscribed by law," where ecclesiastical protocol was virtually non-existent, to a church "much larger and more diverse in its membership, fully emancipated, and governed by its own bishops."[2] This transformation was intrinsically linked with imperial stability.

On guard against a retributive France keen to reclaim what it had lost in the Seven Years' War, and rocked by the secession of the American colonies in 1783, British North America emerged as the lynchpin of Britain's new imperial strategy. Central to this strategy, as noted in the previous chapter, was the establishment of a loyal settler base. In the case of Quebec, where Catholics had been the majority in a population of approximately 65,000 at the point of the Conquest, this was achieved with the Quebec Act of 1774. The situation in the Maritimes was entirely different. Notwithstanding the fact that the Anglican Church had been established in Nova Scotia, albeit without the ability to collect tithes, there was no formal, overarching church structure, and the region's growing population comprised people from different religious and ethnic backgrounds. In the early 1770s, the region's non-Indigenous

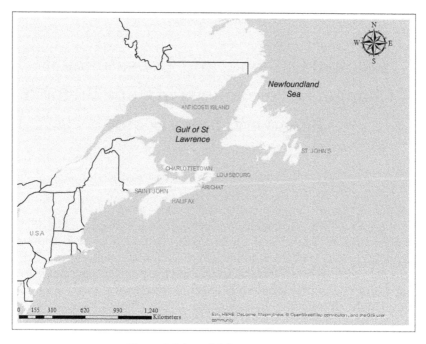

Figure 3. Map of Atlantic Canada

population included Anglicans, Methodists, Baptists, Presbyterians, and Catholics. This diversity continued to expand so that, by 1806, the 100,000 or so people in Nova Scotia, Prince Edward Island, and New Brunswick were widely distributed and representative of Britain's main Christian sects.[3] Such diversity meant that it was impossible for politics to be dominated by the agenda of any one church; as a result, Catholics confronted far less hostility than their co-religionists continued to face in Britain. That these colonies were at a significant distance from London and that the United States posed a persistent threat encouraged British planners to seek to "accommodate their empire to the Catholics of North America."[4]

This chapter considers how the successful management of the settler colonies that became the Canadian Maritimes, especially Nova Scotia and Cape Breton, depended on a mutually supportive relationship between the Catholic Church and the British state. Colonial officials were pivotal to this process, but so too was an ambitious and pragmatic laity. The earliest years of Catholic development in these colonies had been led by an expanding Irish Catholic middle class, who had gradually acquired a voice in the political and civil affairs of the region. The support that they received from their non-Catholic business partners, family members, and friends enabled them to take active roles in colonial development – communities took shape and administrative structures improved as a consequence of greater cooperation. Catholics integrated into every level of emerging civil life, and this involvement was aided by the paucity of resident clergy and a lack of official church structures. At this critical juncture, a pragmatic laity confronted virtually no clerical interference. They were also encouraged by colonial administrators appointed by London to cultivate a sense of loyalty among the settler population. Although Scottish Highland Catholics arrived in large numbers, their exposure to intense anti-Catholic hostility at home had forged an intensely exclusive and conservative culture, and so it was the early activism of the Irish that set a precedent for progressive church development in the Maritimes.

Catholic Settlement and Jurisdiction

In the early 1770s, the majority of Catholics in British North America were concentrated in Quebec and lived according to the rules of a deeply embedded French Catholic tradition. Further east, the Catholic culture that would start to emerge was distinct. Initially, the Catholic population in the coastal colonies had been largely Acadian – the local French-speaking population – who had remained (mostly) neutral during the rising tensions between Britain and France, and the Mi'kmaq – the region's Indigenous population.[5] As the eighteenth century progressed, the Acadian community struggled to rebuild following the *Grand Dérangement*, the expulsion of most Acadians by the British authorities between 1755 and 1762. The arrival of so many Scottish Highland, Irish, and Loyalist settlers began to change the region's Catholic dynamic. By the early 1790s, settlements of say 100 or 200 Scottish, Irish, and Loyalist families were emerging in Halifax and in southwestern Nova Scotia, across Prince Edward Island, in what became eastern New Brunswick, and on Cape Breton's Isle Madame.[6] Highland settlement started on Prince Edward Island in 1770, with the first large-scale Catholic wave in 1772 on the northern shore, and then in eastern Nova Scotia in 1773, but this movement was temporarily interrupted by the American Revolution.[7] In Nova Scotia's capital, Halifax, an Irish presence had been known since the town's foundation in 1749, and, although Scottish Catholic settlements remained relatively small elsewhere until the turn of the nineteenth century, numbers in Cape Breton had been growing due to steady migration, particularly from

Newfoundland, since the 1760s.[8] The end of the American Revolution brought more Catholics, in the form of Loyalist refugees. The total Loyalist migration amounted to around 35,000, and, while the vast majority were Protestant, there were a number of Catholics and Quakers among them.[9] It is estimated that by 1816 there were approximately 15,500 Catholics in Nova Scotia and Cape Breton alone, and that by 1828 their numbers had reached 40,000.[10] By 1828, in New Brunswick and Prince Edward Island, continued Irish and Scottish Highland settlement saw Catholic populations grow to 21,500 and 12,500, respectively.[11] These rising numbers meant that Catholics were poised to play a significant role in colonial development. More than that, though, was the part that the Irish would play as English-speaking Catholics in a territory hitherto dominated by a French Catholicism. Between 1780 and 1830, an ambitious and assertive Catholic laity used their money and growing influence to press for legislative change and to recruit willing clergy.[12]

Britain's governing structure was reflected in Nova Scotia when a lieutenant governor, legislative council, and a legislative assembly were installed in embryonic form in the 1750s. These structures established a constitutional precedent that was eventually replicated in other Maritime colonies: Nova Scotia was granted a legislative assembly in 1758, Prince Edward Island and New Brunswick received theirs in 1773 and 1784, respectively. The anomaly was Newfoundland, and, although more will be said of Newfoundland in the final chapter, it is worth highlighting some of its unique qualities here. To start with, Newfoundland gained an assembly only in 1832, the same year that Britain's Great Reform Act was passed. Situated at the extreme edge of the continent, this island, thanks to the bountiful Grand Banks, was the most lucrative seasonal fishery in the world.[13] Unlike in Nova Scotia or New Brunswick, which also had strong fisheries but were very close to the United States, there was no real desire by the imperial government to establish a stable settler society in Newfoundland.[14] Its population was small and, for a long time, largely seasonal. Rum, molasses, and sugar shipped up from the Caribbean, and salt cod shipped back down, were the major commodities.[15] Growth came slowly to Newfoundland, a territory whose primary function was to provide a crop of cod in times of peace and sailors for the Royal Navy in times of war.[16] Importantly, there was a Catholic presence from an early stage, due, in large part, to the significant number of Irish who worked there.[17] Unlike New Brunswick, Nova Scotia, Cape Breton, and Prince Edward Island, whose ecclesiastical management fell to the bishop of Quebec before Halifax was established as a vicariate in 1817, Newfoundland, like the islands in the Caribbean, was under the jurisdiction of a very reluctant vicar apostolic of London until 1784, when Rome granted the colony ecclesiastical independence, and James Louis O'Donnell, an Irish Franciscan, took charge.[18] James Talbot, bishop of the London District, had been trying, unsuccessfully, to shed responsibility for various colonies, and so was likely pleased with the new arrangement.[19] O'Donnell was consecrated bishop of Newfoundland in 1796, becoming the first bishop in North America outside of Quebec.[20] Having been "unanimously" invited by "all the Roman Catholick Inhabitants & Merchants" before being confirmed by London or Rome, the fact that he could speak Irish in a colony where "7/8ths" of its Catholics were from Ireland was an important consideration for his ecclesiastical superiors:

> His conduct has been exceptionally irreproachable & regular; He is well informed, & long experienced in the duties of his sacred ministry – a zealous and popular preacher in both the English & the Irish language; (& this latter I beg leave to observe to your lordship, is indispensably necessary, to render a missionary useful in Newfoundland, as most of those, upon whom his labours are to be employ'd speak nothing else).[21]

Island colonies and territories often served different economic and political purposes than mainland ones, which influenced how Catholic culture emerged in these places. While the Irish clergy were deeply invested in Newfoundland because of the dominating presence of the Irish people there, it was a different story in the Maritime colonies. Quebec was meant to be responsible for them, but a shortage of priests and a lack of any real desire by those in Quebec to move east meant that the French bishops had very little understanding of the society that was emerging to the east of them. Moreover, at this time, Rome understood very little about the state of Catholicism in North America beyond its two principal dioceses of Quebec and Baltimore and believed, wrongly, that all territory under the jurisdiction of Quebec was French and everything under Baltimore was English. It is hardly surprising, then, that the situation became more complicated after the secession of the Thirteen Colonies. Despite administering its mission territories through the Sacred Congregation *de Propaganda Fide*, a body established in 1622, Rome achieved a clear picture of what was going on in North American only after the church structures became more formally established in these colonies.

Joseph-Octave Plessis, who held the post of bishop of Quebec between 1801 and his death in 1825, was, like his predecessors Jean Olivier Briand and Louis-Philippe Mariauchau d'Esgly, as much a diplomat as a churchman. Described as "stocky, assertive, energetic and charming," Plessis cultivated good relations with the province's colonial officials, with London, and with Rome.[22] While British officials would have preferred an Anglo-Catholic identity in British North America, Britain had benefited enormously from Quebec's loyalty. In 1812, as Britain fought a war on two fronts (France and the United States), Plessis was given a seat on Quebec's legislative council; yet, while this strengthened Franco-Catholic culture in Quebec, it did little to advance understandings of the needs of the Anglo- and Gaelic-Catholic communities that were expanding rapidly in the Maritimes.[23]

The Establishment of Maritime Catholic Culture

Although the Catholic population of the Maritimes had been rising steadily, one of the factors inhibiting the emergence of a more unified Catholicism was language – the newcomers were English and Gaelic speakers as opposed to French speakers. What is more, there were significant historic tensions separating these language groups.[24] Although under the political jurisdiction of Britain, these settlers were, as noted above, under the ecclesiastical authority of Quebec. The unbridled growth of Scottish Highland and Irish Catholics in the region, coupled with Quebec's lack of attention to them – a point noted regularly in the correspondence that passed between Scottish priests based in the Maritimes and their colleagues at the Scots College in Rome – left a leadership vacuum that was filled by a growing middle-class Catholic laity.[25] Plessis was concerned by this and so, when he assumed the leadership of the Diocese of Quebec, which made him responsible for the Catholics in Upper Canada, New Brunswick, Prince Edward Island, Nova Scotia, Cape Breton Island, and the mission at Red River in what would later become Manitoba, he set about planning its reorganization to extend the church's official influence. Already well aware of what was lacking on the ground, the laity in Nova Scotia and Cape Breton had taken it upon themselves to make contact with the Quebec-based, Irish-born cleric Edmund Burke.[26]

Serious attention to the changing demography of the coastal colonies began only when Burke, who was originally from County Kildare and who had been ordained in Paris before moving to Quebec in 1786, took notice. In political circles, he was seen as having a deep loyalty to Britain, and this won him important and influential allies, including John Graves Simcoe, the governor of Upper Canada between 1791 and 1798.[27] Burke had been instrumental in asserting British authority in Raisin River (near Detroit) in 1775, a mission technically sitting in American territory, but one that was torn between the dioceses of Baltimore and Quebec. His value to both Rome and London as someone able to break the spiritual monopoly of the French Catholics was recognized in 1801, when he was named vicar general of Nova Scotia. He had lobbied, behind the back of the bishop of Quebec, for Kingston in Upper Canada and Halifax in Nova Scotia, regions with significant British Catholic settlement, to have more independence from Quebec. His continued efforts in this regard led to his appointment as vicar apostolic of Nova Scotia in 1817.[28] One year later, Alexander Macdonell, the Scottish Highland priest who had helped protect the border between Upper Canada and the United States by settling disbanded soldiers in the Eastern Townships, was named vicar apostolic of Kingston.[29]

Plessis was not unaware of the problems Burke identified in the Maritimes; indeed, he embarked upon a tour of the region in 1811–12 to get a better sense of the state of Catholicism there.[30] Notwithstanding Burke's attention, the lack of resident priests, significant cultural differences separating the settling groups, and the geographic isolation of many communities had led to a diversity of religious practice that was barely recognizable to a bishop raised in the relative comfort and sophistication of Quebec Catholicism. For Plessis, the trip confirmed the impossibility of uniting the various traditions under one central, French-speaking diocese. While quick to acknowledge the kindness of those he had met and admiring their spiritual commitment under challenging circumstances, he was vexed by the unorthodox and often dismal customs he encountered. He was scathing of the Scots especially and, when visiting a congregation in Prince Edward Island, remarked that "only a priest brought up in Scotland would ever think of celebrating the Sacred Mysteries with the trash that is found therein." He went on: "When they came to a strange land, they brought their customs with them and it is almost impossible to make them understand that the respect due to religion, in a diocese where entire freedom of worship prevails, requires of them something more in the way of exterior propriety. Singing is as rare in their churches as ceremonies and vestments."[31] While pointing the finger at their Calvinist tendencies, he admitted that their customs had been formed in Scotland, where intense anti-Catholicism meant that they either kept their heads down and blended in or risked serious consequences. In the archives of England's Ushaw College, correspondence from Father Andrew Scott, the proactive Banffshire-born, Glasgow-based priest, described the harshness of Catholic practice in those parts of the Highlands from which these settlers came – Glencoe, Badenoch, Glengarry, Knoydart, Morar, and Eigg:

In every one of these missions, the chapels, 50 or 60 years ago were built of dry stone walls about 8 feet high and thatched with turf and heath. Part of the walls have fallen down, and nearly half of the roofs are blown away.

The people are exposed to wind and rain while in the chapel, if chapels they be called. There are now neither doors nor windows in them, and the roofs being half uncovered there is no possibility of getting candles to burn during the time of the mass but by putting candles in a lantern. Years ago, the people were more able to do something for themselves than they are now. The most substantial among them have gone to America, and the most of the proprietors are great bigots and very inimical to our religion.[32]

This explanation notwithstanding, Plessis's sympathy had its limits. At Port Hood, a fishing and trading village on Cape Breton's west coast, he found both the ruinous state of the chapel and the people's conduct during Mass disgraceful: "If this chapel was indecent because of its shape, it was more so because of the multitude of dogs within it, and the babbling and bawling of perhaps more than forty children in their mothers' arms; several mothers spanked their children noisily, to prevent them from crying, but the remedy only made them cry louder."[33] Given what they were used to in Scotland, the settlers would not have shared his opinion. Nevertheless, the tour convinced Plessis of the need for reorganization and additional priests. He was concerned that so many Catholics, which included upwards of 800 Gaelic-speaking families in the vicinity of Port Hood alone, had no access to regular religious instruction. This was something that the leading Catholic laymen already knew, which was why they had started recruiting clergy on their own. This aligns with what is revealed by research on the Irish abroad and indicates that such lay agency was far more common than often assumed.[34]

The lack of clerical leadership in Nova Scotia had propelled a number of the colony's leading merchants and traders to the forefront of community development. Prior to the Napoleonic Wars, a significant proportion of these individuals were Irish who had either migrated directly from Ireland or indirectly from Newfoundland. They saw empire as the best way to achieve their goals of financial security and political influence and, in many cases, to escape the pervasive anti-Catholic prejudice and restrictions at home. The entrepreneurial drive of the colonists from Britain and Ireland played a definitive role in the direction of Maritime Catholicism. Political enfranchisement was critical and, because there was significant cooperation between Catholic and Protestant Irish in the Maritimes, an embryonic associational culture emerged to support those efforts. In Nova Scotia, the Charitable Irish Society, which included Irish of both religious persuasions, demonstrated Irish authority in philanthropic and business arenas.[35] It showcased Irish leadership as proactive merchants and traders focused on bringing economic stability in the region. At this juncture of colonial and imperial necessity, Catholics in Nova Scotia were able to acquire a level of political influence that was quite simply out of reach for those Catholics across the Atlantic in Britain and Ireland.

The Charitable Irish Society of Halifax was founded in 1786, inspired by the network of charitable societies of various sorts spreading across Ireland. Charitable societies emerged in Ireland primarily because Poor Law provision, such as that on offer in England and Scotland, was largely absent, and the number of people in need was rising.[36] Halifax faced a similar situation, and its growing Irish merchant community wanted to access respectability by demonstrating charitable activism. The society was non-denominational, and membership was open to "Irishmen or the sons of Irishmen" (until 1795, when the constitution was updated to read that "Irishmen or the sons of *Irishmen* and *Irishwomen*" could become members).[37] Father William Phelan, an Irishborn priest, described Halifax as a town "larger than Cork, but not so large as Kilkenny," and noted that he had "received more dinner invitations from Protestant & Cath. than I could accept for a month. I have been from house to house with them every day since I came."[38] Members of the Society also included many Irish from Cape Breton. Its events, such as annual St. Patrick's Day dinners, included local dignitaries, government and military officials, and members of the other national societies as invited guests. The incorporation of national saints and military symbolism into the decorations for events showed an engagement with a version of Britain and its empire that was inclusive and nationally rooted:

> The room was decorated with great elegance and the whole has the best effect. At the heart of the room was a portrait of St Patrick, on the right that of St George and on the left, a painting of St Andrew in transparency. A beautiful and brilliant device in variegated lamps ornamented the lower part of the room, representing the Harp with Erin Go Bragh and the colours of the battalion of militia to which the members of the society belong, were suspended carefully from the columns.[39]

Throughout the nineteenth century, the society's members were invited to events organized by the other societies, such as the 1864 celebration procession that the St. George Society organized in honour of William Shakespeare, which also included the North British Society and the Highland Society; some years later, all of these societies even shared a meeting room.[40] The process of cooperation was strong from an early stage, and there did not seem to be any question that Ireland and the Irish were anything but a vital component of Britain.

The empire played a critical role in enhancing such perceptions, particularly from the late eighteenth century, as Irish networks expanded and became embedded within the civil structures of Halifax and Nova Scotia more broadly. The activities of those in Halifax are representative of a broader dialogue taking place about Ireland's relationship with Britain. While the members of the Charitable Irish Society possessed strong Irish identities, they did not see these as being incompatible with a British one. Meetings were regularly held in the British Coffee House, and, in times of crisis, the Society endeavoured to demonstrate a firm commitment to "king, country and constitution." Its minutes focus on members and on the petitions they received for support from the poor and distressed; they contain no mention of religion or politics, apart from one reference to politics in May 1798:

> The Charitable Irish Society impressed with an opinion that it is the duty of all individuals who enjoy the happiness of the British Government to express their sentiments on the present occasion and to join their fellow subjects in declaring that it is their unanimous determination to support their King, country and constitution, with their lives and fortunes, have thought proper to subscribe again, to enable them as a society to express those sentiments which they have already individually declared by their subscription. The Society therefore do give the sums annexed to their names towards supporting the present, just and necessary war in which our country is engaged.[41]

The activity of the Charitable Irish Society reveals something about the ambition of the middle-class Irish and demonstrates that, in the imperial setting, they were far less concerned with religious differentiation than with accessing the prosperity that an alignment with the British Empire offered. Armed with political and economic influence, Catholics in the Maritimes, but especially in Nova Scotia and Cape Breton, began to press for civil and religious equality at a relatively early stage.[42] A critical difference between these colonial Catholics and those back in Britain was that those in British North America received indirect support from their Presbyterian neighbours, who pushed against the presumed authority of the Church of England. This opposition eroded Anglicanism's authority and helped to build a closer relationship between Catholicism and the British state.[43] The Catholic Church and Catholics in general, who became "one of the most influential groups in contemporary Canada," were important allies for colonial officials concerned that the dominance of Presbyterian Dissenters would weaken Britain's influence.[44] In Newfoundland, the growing popularity of Methodism among the governing elite challenged Anglican dominance, and in Nova Scotia, the antagonism that existed between Presbyterians and the Anglican establishment, particularly in the realm of higher education, created a space wherein Catholics could become political allies.[45]

Since Catholic missionaries in British North America, unlike their Dissenting brethren, had, for the most part, no wish to conduct "constitutional experiments" that would extend democratic input, it is understandable that neither popular sovereignty nor monarchical opposition was tolerated.[46] Endorsing royal absolutism was relatively straightforward and made it easier to convince colonial administrators of the church's inherent value as an institution capable of exerting a significant degree of social control over a rapidly expanding Catholic population. While this social control would only really get going after 1830, as the emancipation legislation sunk in and the Catholic Church began to consolidate its authority and reclaim control from the laity, the period before emancipation saw Britain adopt a comparatively liberal attitude toward Catholics in British North America. The imperial state's desire to cement its authority in a region that was vulnerable to American incursion had important implications for Catholic political agency. Accessing the emerging political structures was accomplished with relative ease, as the following section, which focuses on the election of a Catholic merchant from Cape Breton to Nova Scotia's legislative assembly in 1820, reveals.

The Politicization of Enterprising Catholics

The island of Cape Breton, which sits to the northeast of mainland Nova Scotia, had been, for most of the first half of the eighteenth century, the seat of one of France's most powerful colonial fortresses. Louisbourg, a major French defence and fishing centre, had a population of almost 4,000 people (1,250 soldiers and 2,690 civilians) in 1757, though it fell to 1,766 the next year after a British siege.[47] It was a fortress built to guard the entrance to the St. Lawrence River and, through that, access to Quebec, which was the heart of France's power in North America. The whole island, which included Louisbourg and the prosperous trading and fishing village of Arichat on the tiny island of Isle Madame just off Cape Breton's southeast coast, was turned over to the British with the Treaty of Paris in 1763. At that point, Cape Breton was annexed to the larger colony of Nova Scotia until 1784, when it was given autonomy after a Loyalist, Abraham Cuyler, managed to convince the British government that the island could support itself. Promising an influx

Figure 4. Louisbourg (with permission of Beinecke
Rare Book and Manuscript Library)

of Loyalist settlers, he planned the exploitation of Cape Breton's rich
coal deposits, but neither happened.[48] Apart from Arichat, which had
a population of 1,000 by 1801 and continued to thrive on account of its
position as a fishing, trading, and customs hub, prospects for the rest
of island were limited; Louisbourg fell into rapid decline and became
little more than a memory of French power, while the Loyalist-founded
administrative centre of Sydney experienced only slow and limited
growth.[49] After a thirty-six-year interlude, Cape Breton was re-annexed
to Nova Scotia in 1820.

While Cape Breton's position as a viable colony was tenuous, this
change in colonial boundaries was not simply the result of a broken
Loyalist promise. The end of the Napoleonic Wars brought a post-war
depression that forced Britain to re-evaluate how its rapidly evolving
colonial holdings functioned and the purposes they served. The imposition of more robust governing structures in British North America was part of a strategy to fend off both the ideological and military
threat posed by the United States. Strategic settlement plans, road construction, and canal building were all intended to improve the lines of
communication and defence within and between the colonies. In Upper and Lower Canada, for example, boundary lines were drawn and
settlements of ex-soldiers from disbanded Highland regiments were
established in areas deemed vulnerable to possible American attack. In

Figure 5. Arichat (with permission of Nova Scotia Archives)

Lower Canada, the Catholic Church was further incorporated into legislative affairs. Further east, Nova Scotia and Cape Breton Island were united and plans to direct foreign investment into coal mining in Cape Breton and in Pictou on mainland Nova Scotia were initiated.[50] There was opposition to this consolidation, but the business elites, many of whom were Irish, were largely in favour, viewing it as an opportunity for economic growth.

As noted above, Cape Breton had been attracting an increasing number of Newfoundland Irish since the 1760s, and their focus was on extending commercial enterprise. They built useful relationships with colonial officials anxious to facilitate a culture of entrepreneurship as a way of enhancing socio-economic development and settler loyalty. The Kavanaghs were one family of particular note, arriving in Louisbourg from Newfoundland in the early 1760s. In 1767, they were granted a licence by the Crown for 500 acres of land, and by the early 1770s, in addition to their significant interest in the fishery, they owned almost half of all the cattle, horses, sheep, and pigs in the entire town and employed 59 per cent of its people.[51] These Irish Catholic trading merchants had deep connections to Britain and the West Indies and dealt in fish, livestock, tobacco, molasses, sugar, and textiles;

they also imported rum and wine (legally and illegally), products they deemed necessary for "carrying on the fishery in [such an] Intemperate climate."[52] Their economic success won them valuable political allies, and, since the government was keen to promote business and the fishery, William Legge, second Earl of Dartmouth and secretary of state for the American colonies between 1772 and 1775, dismissed a complaint made about their monopolistic business practices because they had been "very much recommended, by some of the principal merchants here [London] trading to Nova Scotia."[53] That these Irish Catholics had advocates within the highest political circles was part of a wider trend focused on strengthening colonial stability and the imperial economy following the Seven Years' War and in advance of the war with the Thirteen Colonies. The Kavanaghs suffered a major setback in 1774 when the patriarch, Laurence Kavanagh Sr., died in a shipwreck en route to Halifax. Following this tragedy, the family moved south along the coast to St. Peter's, a small settlement with a sheltered harbour close to Arichat, where they were able to maintain, and even grow, their economic and political influence.

The links between the Irish in Cape Breton and Nova Scotia were extensive long before re-annexation, with families like the Kavanaghs sharing reciprocal trade arrangements, family ties, and, often, a religious identity with their Irish brethren in Halifax.[54] Together, they formed a growing community of entrepreneurs who collaborated to develop new opportunities and to acquire greater rights. As early as 1781, Halifax's "small but rising Irish Catholic middle class," which included members of Cape Breton families, was active in calling for Catholic relief. That year, they submitted a petition to the legislative assembly requesting the repeal of statutes imposed in 1758 and 1759 that outlawed priests and prohibited Catholics from holding title to land other than grants given by the Crown.[55] The signatories, John Mullowny and John McDaniel, who petitioned "on behalf of themselves and others," followed up the petition with a letter that stressed the existing legislation's negative impact on the colony's economic growth. Specifically, they criticized the restrictions surrounding land ownership and inheritance, which discouraged Catholics "from becoming settlers and cultivating Lands in this country," and asked that specific sections of the acts in question be suspended "for one year, or until His Majesty's pleasure herein is known."[56] Like their co-religionists in Britain and Ireland, the petitioners viewed these laws as redundant, and, notably, so did the colony's legislative assembly. After a year of waiting on the non-elected legislative council to make a decision, but with the knowledge of the fact that toleration for Catholics in Britain was expanding with the second Relief Act, which lifted the ban on priests and granted Catholics the right to inherit or acquire land by deed, the Halifax cohort again pressed for relief.

Their willingness to lobby for change testifies to the broader claims that settlers were making to their rights as colonial citizens and British subjects.[57] They believed that altering legislation in Nova Scotia was wholly justifiable since a British subject was a British subject whether at home or abroad. In Nova Scotia, the development of a stable and sustainable economy required collective enterprise. Land cultivation and the exploitation of resources for the purposes of food production and trade, for example, needed widespread participation and so, despite the province's assembly and colonial officials seeing the benefit of removing restrictions on Catholics in the colonies, London dragged its feet, which brought renewed pleas to the lieutenant governor:

> That your Petitioners did on the 3rd day of July last make application by Petition to your honour's predecessor in the government of this province praying a relaxation or repeal of certain grievous laws which in the policy of former times might seem necessary to be and were enacted against your petitioners, but of late in the great wisdom and humanity of our most Gracious Sovereign and his faithful Lords and Commons have been deemed injurious and oppressive. That Your honour's Petitioners then and now considering themselves included in the General Grace Extended to His Majesty's Subjects professing the Roman Catholic Religion in all other of His Majesty's Dominions were the more embolden humbly to make the aforesaid requisition.[58]

In 1783 the rights given to Catholics in Ireland, England, and Wales were extended to those in Nova Scotia.[59] Thanking the colony's new lieutenant governor, Sir Andrew Snape Hamond, the petitioners wrote:

> Permit us to return our unfeigned and most humble thanks for the same and to assure your honour, that we are sensible of the benefits we may enjoy in future (by being altho' a circumscribed degree upon the footing of the People professing our Religion in his Majesty's Kingdoms of Great Britain and Ireland) that we shall at all times be ready to lay down our lives and fortunes in defence of His Majesty's Person and Government in support of our most Excellent Constitution.[60]

The timing of this legislation in Britain and Nova Scotia was no coincidence. The war in America had gone badly, and Britain suffered a devastating blow with the loss of the Thirteen Colonies, and any extension of rights to Catholics at this time was part of that broader context. More than ever, Britain needed the support and loyalty of its Catholics.

Achieving Emancipation

The Kavanaghs weathered the American Revolution well, and Laurence Jr., the son who succeeded his father, worked with his mother, Margaret Farrell, to manage the family business and extend the family's influence across Cape Breton.[61] Their wealth and political influence brought Laurence increased civic responsibilities, and by 1813, during the last stage of Britain's wars with France and the United States, he was in charge of the 2nd Regiment of the Cape Breton Militia.[62] His impact upon constitutional change, however, came when Cape Breton was re-annexed to Nova Scotia in 1820: the island was given two seats in the province's legislative assembly and he, a Catholic, was elected to one of them. Richard John Uniacke, an Irish-descended Protestant, was elected to the other.[63]

Kavanagh's economic influence was as important as his religious background, and, given the significant Catholic population on the island, his election was a powerful statement about minority agency in the colonial world. Although based in St. Peter's, he was a landowner in Margaree and so was elected as a member for Inverness, a district on the other side of the island with many Scottish Highlanders and Irish Catholics. The painting used as the cover image for this book shows the view he would have had from his land. As a justice of the peace, Kavanagh was called upon to settle property and trespassing disputes in villages such as Margaree, which was a mix of Acadian, Scottish Highland, Irish, and Loyalist settlers. In one case, a Miles McDaniel, a fellow Catholic, who also became a justice of the peace, asked Kavanagh to provide a no-trespassing public notice that he could post on his land.[64] Given his identity as a figure of immense local influence, Kavanagh had the profile required for politics, and, in the context of imperial governance, his election was a wake-up call for the Colonial Office about the growing significance of local agency. Fundamentally, the election of this Irish-descended Catholic from a small, frontier trading outpost in a coastal periphery was about to play a major role in imperial politics that would have a knock-on effect for Britain.

Kavanagh's election occurred eight years before Daniel O'Connell's by-election win forced the issue of Catholic emancipation in Britain and eleven years before Robert George Throckmorton became England's first Catholic MP. It was a major turning point, though, and served as a reminder to Britain's colonial governing circles that imperial security would come at a price and that Catholics, a rapidly expanding and essential settler-colonist group, were critical to the empire's survival.[65] Like other religious minorities, the preparedness of many Catholics to go where they could access opportunities off-limits to them at home was hugely symbolic and revealed the extent to which Britain's imperial program could, did, and needed to include them. The increasing political involvement that Catholics were achieving was indicative of colonial requirements and local conditions being prioritized and of the metropole's need to adjust accordingly. In the case of Kavanagh's election, the Colonial Office was forced to recognize that, in the colonies at least, Catholics were seen as perfectly capable of representing their neighbours in an elected assembly. Yet, the fact that Kavanagh was permitted to stand as a candidate at all raises important questions about colonial agency and the extent to which fears about the level of opposition to Cape Breton's re-annexation to Nova Scotia, in the face of a growing threat from the United States, were used as political leverage. Permitting Cape Breton some leeway with respect to its elected representatives seemed a small price to pay, but what cannot be discounted is the possibility that colonial officials may have simply overlooked this island.[66]

While Kavanagh's actual election had been relatively straightforward, the process of getting him into his seat in the legislative assembly without requiring him to renounce the core principles of his Catholicism required careful handling and a change in the law. Accomplishing this task fell to the assembly's reform-minded members, who were led by the former president of Halifax's Charitable Irish Society and Kavanagh's fellow Cape Breton member, Richard John Uniacke.[67] Catholics in Nova Scotia were at a distinct advantage because, unlike in Ireland, where Dublin Castle followed a policy of "resisting the question" of Catholic emancipation, there was a willingness to do whatever was needed to ensure the success of the colony.[68] That Protestant and Catholic Irish in the province collaborated to support community development and extend entrepreneurship aided the process and ensured that colonial officials did not fear Catholic emancipation in the same way their political colleagues in Britain and Ireland did. Beyond the assembly, Nova Scotia's lieutenant governor, Sir James Kempt, also needed to be brought on side; luckily, he was amenable from an early stage.

Prior to arriving in Nova Scotia in 1820 to mediate Cape Breton's re-annexation to Nova Scotia, Kempt, a Scot, had had an illustrious military career that had spanned Europe and British North America and peaked at the Battle of Waterloo, where he commanded the 8th Brigade. When he turned his attention to the colonial service, his first post was as lieutenant governor of the garrison at Fort William, Scotland. This was followed by a stint at Portsmouth, England, before he succeeded his good friend Lord Dalhousie in Nova Scotia after the latter moved on to Quebec.[69] Unlike Dalhousie, who was not popular with locals, Kempt was tactful, diplomatic, and likable.[70] Even the Catholic priests thought so, with one remarking that he had an "excellent disposition."[71] Writing to Aeneas (Angus) Macdonald, rector of Scots College in Rome between 1827 and 1834, Aeneas MacEachern, a Scottish Highland priest in Prince Edward Island who became the bishop there and acted as a kind of mentor to priests across the Maritimes, described Kempt as civil and helpful. He was particularly grateful to him for providing introductions to other colonial officials such as New Brunswick's lieutenant governor, Sir Howard Douglas.[72]

In Nova Scotia, Kempt's approach was conciliatory, and his sensitivity to local issues convinced many of the province's political elite that he was someone with whom they could work. Although he ruffled a few feathers when he refused to attend the Charitable Irish Society's annual St. Patrick's Day dinner in 1822, they were comforted by the fact that he had declined invitations from all of the national societies.[73] Nevertheless, with the aid of local officials, he brought Nova Scotia and Cape Breton together, arranged the management of mineral rights with London's General Mining Association, and tried to introduce non-denominational higher education, though in this he was thwarted by the "abominable obstinacy" of the archbishop of Canterbury, who vetoed a union between the newly established non-denominational Dalhousie College and the Anglican King's College.[74] Kempt's role in the Kavanagh case was perhaps the most delicate of his tenure, since his first duty was to advise London of the best way forward for the colony's development and, on this point, it was a duty that required him to innovate.

On 25 February 1822, a resolution introduced in the assembly proposing that Kavanagh be allowed to take his seat by only swearing the state oaths was defeated by a vote of 17 to 13. In the same sitting, the assembly then passed a bill "to remove certain disabilities, which H. M. subjects, professing the Popish religion, now labor under in this province," but it was rejected by the legislative council.[75] It was not that the council opposed such a resolution – on the contrary, it agreed with the assembly that restrictions should be lifted – but it worried whether "such a subject should be at all agitated in this colony, before the mother country has decided so important a question."[76] That Nova Scotia's legislative assembly was pushing against and contesting the authority of the non-elected council was something that was happening more often in the colonies.[77]

In a letter to the secretary of state for war and the colonies, the Earl of Bathurst, Kempt attached an address prepared by the members of the assembly expressing their desire to see Catholics admitted with just the common state oaths; they felt that the additional oaths required of Catholics – against popery and the doctrine of transubstantiation – were provocative and unnecessary. Crucially, Bathurst's background in strategic and imperial defence, which included devising the plan for the settlement in Upper Canada of disbanded Highland soldiers, many of whom were Catholics, meant that he could see the value of Catholic emancipation.[78] Kempt was similarly inclined, sympathetic even, but, as lieutenant governor, he was conscious of protocol and had refused to admit Kavanagh until royal permission was granted. But in his letter to Bathurst, he pressed for Kavanagh's admission: "It may be necessary for me further to add, that I agree with the opinion expressed by His Majesty's Council that no evil is to be apprehended in this Province from the admission of Catholics into the Legislature provided that they take all the oaths provided in the Royal Instructions except the declaration against Transubstantiation."[79]

Bathurst moved the case through the necessary channels and was able to reply to Kempt less than two months later with the announcement of a landmark decision: the king had granted the assembly's request "to admit Mr. Kavanagh to take his seat in the Assembly on taking the State oaths and to dispense with his making the declaration against Popery and Transubstantiation."[80] On 3 April 1823, Kavanagh was sworn in by the Honourable Judge J. Stewart of the supreme court of Halifax and officially took his seat in the assembly as one of Cape Breton's two elected members.[81] The *Proceedings* of the house recorded the event thus:

> Resolved, That this House, grateful to His Majesty for relieving His Majesty's Roman Catholic subjects from the disability they were heretofore under from fitting in this House, do admit the said Laurence Kavanagh to take his seat; and will, in future, permit Roman Catholics, who may be duly elected, and shall be qualified to hold a seat in this House, to take such seat, without making the Declaration against Popery and Transubstantiation, and that a Committee be appointed to wait upon His Excellency the Lieutenant Governor, and communicate to him this resolution of the House.[82]

This resolution set an important precedent for civil equality in the British Empire and was evidence of an awareness that colonial prosperity and imperial security needed religious tolerance; later, this would be enshrined in the British North America Act of 1867.

While the practicalities and legal issues were dealt with at the highest political levels, the case generated significant public interest. In terms of the broader Catholic response, there was tremendous gratitude expressed to members such as Uniacke for their efforts to speak on behalf of their Catholic neighbours, but also concern to ensure that the oaths required "as tests of eligibility" did not mislead people about the tenets of Catholicism. A petition received by the house of assembly in 1827 acknowledged the great debt owed by Catholics to the members while it challenged the wording of some aspects. The petition, signed by 647 men from across Nova Scotia, stressed that, although Catholics might pray to saints, for example, to enable the "House to intercede with his Majesty," they do not presume to challenge the king's authority.[83]

While there was some opposition to Kavanagh's election by individuals such as John Inglis, the Anglican bishop of Halifax, who was appalled that a Catholic had been admitted to the assembly, such anxiety does not appear to have been widespread, since most people were united by a fundamental concern about civil equality. In a society with a diverse religious base, there was a natural inclination toward opposing perceived domination by any one sect or group. This growing tolerance was highlighted in the local press, which followed these developments closely. After being criticized for printing a letter questioning the legality of "so novel and dangerous experiment," the *Acadian Recorder*, a Halifax weekly newspaper, explained that it was "sincerely desirous of seeing the Roman Catholic representative from Cape Breton ... assume his seat."[84] Its editors argued that change was necessary to ensure equality and the economic viability of the province. In this respect, they echoed an opinion that had also been expressed in Ireland in the late eighteenth and early nineteenth centuries, when the focus of its emerging middle class had been on economic progress and social development through religious inclusion.[85] When Kavanagh died at his home in St. Peter's in August 1830, the Halifax paper described him as a "worthy man."[86]

Although Catholics elected to the Nova Scotia assembly no longer had to swear the oath against popery and transubstantiation after 1823, this dispensation did not apply to the wider population, since the king did not remove the remaining disabilities. On 26 February 1826, Richard Uniacke introduced a resolution to establish a committee "to prepare an Address to his Majesty, begging of him to dispense with the oath now used as a qualification for office."[87] The resolution drew support from both the assembly and council and passed unanimously. The statements of those who publicly spoke in favour of it emphasized the inherent differences between the status of Catholics in Britain and those in the colonies. One advocate was Sir Brenton Halliburton, a politically moderate Anglican of Loyalist stock and member of Halifax's social elite set to become the province's chief justice.[88] Appointed to the legislative council in 1816, he had significant political experience. He reflected that, "in this province Catholics and Protestants unite in social circles; form friendships of an enduring nature, and mourn each other in death; while in the mother country the most rancorous feelings agitate the hearts of each."[89] Alexander Stewart, a newly elected assembly member for Cumberland and proponent of Catholic emancipation, agreed, arguing that, although opposition to such a resolution in the House of Lords made it a difficult topic in England, "such was not the case in the colonies."[90] While relations between Catholics and Protestants in Britain were certainly more complex than these statements suggest, the fact that these commentators saw Nova Scotia's situation as entirely different from Britain's suggests that local needs were eclipsing the prejudices of the mother country.

In Nova Scotia, the proposed committee was duly formed, and, in March 1827, its address imploring the Crown to remove the remaining disabilities was read to the assembly before being sent to London. It emphasized Catholic loyalty and the necessity of civil equality for the future progress of the province:

> We have been the witnesses of their [Catholics'] civil conduct, and it is but a testimony due to truth when we say that they evince as zealous a disposition for the maintenance of your Majesty's Government as any other denomination of your Majesty's loyal subjects ... How auspicious for the future interests of the Province such a condition is, we feel that we shall best consult our own prosperity by using every method in our power to insure its continuance.[91]

Such sentiments were not restricted to the public arena. In the same month, Thomas Chandler Haliburton, himself an Anglican member of the legislative assembly (no relation to Sir Breton Halliburton), wrote to Abbé Jean-Mande Sigogne, the Catholic priest credited with getting him elected as representative for Annapolis County, to report that "an application had been made to remove all test oaths from Roman Catholics, and I could assure you it gave me sincere pleasure to raise my feeble voice in its favour." Haliburton, a prolific author who served as a supreme court judge in Nova Scotia before moving to England and, in 1859, getting elected to the House of Commons as the member for Launceston in east Cornwall, went on to explain that, "as a stranger, I was favoured with unanimous support of all your people, in a manner so cordial and so friendly that I shall feel most happy when any occasion offers to testify most hearty acknowledgement of a kindness shown to me when I stood in need of it."[92]

Beyond sheer gratitude as a reason for supporting this change, many Nova Scotians stressed the commitment that Catholics had made to imperial defence and reminded their political colleagues in Britain of "those spots in Canada, whose sods cover the remains of heroes, who fell in repelling those foreign invaders, who did not expect, and were not prepared to resist their valour."[93] This statement refers to the War of 1812 and reveals the kernel of an emerging Canadian nation that extended from Nova Scotia to Upper Canada. This assertion from the colonies gave Catholics in the United Kingdom encouragement and a legal precedent for an extension of Catholic rights.

Times were changing, in terms of both imperial authority and perceptions of citizenship. The campaign for Catholic emancipation used language similar to that employed for the emancipation of enslaved Africans throughout the British Empire and the fight for parliamentary and electoral reform in Britain. Unsurprisingly, developments in Nova Scotia and the eventual granting of complete Catholic emancipation by the legislative assembly on 17 April 1827, two years before Britain, were followed intently by those Catholics elsewhere still pressing for emancipation.[94] The news of what had occurred in Nova Scotia was greeted with enthusiasm by organizations such as the British Catholic Association (BCA). The BCA's Defence Committee, which was responsible for pamphleteering to promote the cause of Catholic emancipation, published a report entitled *State of the Catholics in Nova Scotia*.[95] Frustrated by the lack of movement on the emancipation question in Britain, the BCA used colonial examples to push its own cause.

The fact that emancipation legislation was being approved by the king for Nova Scotia while any debate on the issue by cabinet in London was still being avoided, and any development of government policy on it consequently delayed, testifies to the inherent agency of colonial populations and to the political elite's awareness of the link between imperial security and the provision of mechanisms that would help colonial societies to become socially and economically stable.[96] It also demonstrates the extent to which the political system in Britain was hamstrung. Confronting the Catholic question could be political suicide for a British MP, eliminating any chance of re-election unless he had unusually deep pockets. In British North America, where Catholics represented a significant and growing proportion of the electorate and business community, this was not the case.

That the situation for settlers and for the consolidation of settler societies in British North America was fundamentally different had come into clearer focus through the process of achieving Catholic emancipation. Years later, when looking back on the progress of Catholics in

Figure 6. Laurence Kavanagh House, ca. 1910 (with permission of John William Coffey)

Nova Scotia, Sir Nicholas Meagher, supreme court justice for Nova Scotia between 1890 and 1916, observed that people had more important things to worry about than what church their neighbour attended: "The people, through lack of newspapers, and by reason of their arduous struggles with forest, and sea, to gain a living were largely mind-free from political affairs, and whatever the dispositions of Protestants, respecting their Catholic neighbours, and their religion, many have been, their relations were, it is believed, neighbourly."[97]

Laurence Kavanagh's election opened the door for further Catholic participation in Nova Scotia's politics, and it was no coincidence that another Catholic to be elected to the legislative assembly was Lawrence O'Connor Doyle, Kavanagh's cousin and a protégé of Richard Uniacke. Under Uniacke's tutelage – and influenced, no doubt, by Doyle's school days at Stonyhurst, a Jesuit boarding school in Lancashire, England, between 1815 and 1821 – Doyle had become a fiery young lawyer and politician.[98] After his petition for enrolment as an attorney in Nova Scotia's supreme court was approved in April 1828, he became the province's first Catholic lawyer. He also served as president of the Charitable Irish Society three times.[99] Doyle represented the second phase of Catholic political activism in Nova Scotia; after practising law on his own from 1828 to 1833, he was elected to the assembly in 1833 and remained there until 1855. His tenure was clouded once, in 1848, when his election to a Halifax seat was plagued by questions about his status as a forty-shilling freeholder; he submitted evidence of having acquired a hundred acres of land on the Musquodoboit River in Halifax County in April 1847.[100]

Described by one biographer as "the most humorous debater in the House" and an advocate of responsible government, Doyle died in New York in late October 1864.[101] Other Catholics, such as Peter Smyth, an immensely wealthy Irish-born merchant and landowner in Port Hood, Cape Breton, would follow Doyle into politics. In addition to being a member of the legislative assembly, Smyth was also appointed to the legislative council in 1867 – the year of Canadian Confederation. Like Kavanagh, Smyth commanded the local militia and was a tough businessman.[102] Prior to his election, he had served as captain of the 1st Battalion, 3rd Regiment of the Cape Breton Militia and was later appointed lieutenant colonel unattached.[103] These distinctions did not endear him to the people of his community. They despised him because, as a merchant, he had accumulated much of his land and wealth by seizing the property of anyone unable to pay the debts they had accumulated in his shop. In addition to holding a rich cache of indenture documents relating to Smyth's property acquisition, the Chestico Archives and Museum in Port Hood also holds a copy of a Gaelic poem (with the English translation) that had been written by a local bard whose brother's property was confiscated by Smyth:

> Oran Pheadair
> A mhic a bh'ann an Eirinn
> Ou bheil thu an deidh air mo chur an call,
> Gun d'thug thu ionnsuidh le cunntas breugach
> A runn do chieich's isd sinan dram.
> Mar is leif dhuit no rinn thu dh'eugrachl
> An am dhuit cirigh bho'n eallach throm,
> Mu'n teid do thilgail an aite peundail
> An priosa eighin gu uirseach ann.
> Ged tha thu earbsach air lagh 'a'phrovince'

Le Sam'is Domhnull is do chas no laimh,
Gun d'this me tairgsinn dhuitmar bu choir dhomh
Gum paigh an corr anns no bh'anns an t'suim.
Ach tha thu gorach, a'cosg do storas
A ghleidh thug rob aima bheil me mall,
Gum faic thu Eirinn 'ro' tholl do thoine,
Mu'm faight thu coir airna bheil me'n geall. ...

O, son of a miller, you who came from Ireland
You have me at a loss.
You gave an indication with the countless deceits
That your clerks made over the drink.
If you can realise all your devious work
It's time you straightened from your crooked position,
Before you are thrown in the place of pain,
That prison of suffering without any ease.
You have the Law of the province backing you
With Sam and Donald having your brief in hand.
I made you an offer, as I should have,
That I'd say you the sum without any argument.
You are crazy to be squandering your money
You won't have a mite,
And you'll see Ireland through your rear end
Before you receive any more than was owed.[104]

To the locals, this was Peter Smyth, and unflattering stories about him still circulate in Inverness County today.

The growing confidence of Catholics in Nova Scotia and the United Kingdom, aided by the emancipation legislation, had a knock-on effect in the other Maritime provinces, as was commented upon in correspondence between Prince Edward Island and Rome. In 1830, Aeneas MacEachern explained that "our assembly having been dissolved lately, we have already some Catholic subjects returned for the new general assembly. Such is the consequence of the Emancipation Act. We live on the best terms with our Protestant neighbours."[105] In 1831, seven of the eighteen members of Prince Edward Island's legislative assembly were Catholic; two of them were Hugh and Angus Macdonald, sons of a Scottish Highland immigrant.[106]

The political integration of Catholics, from the earliest stages of the development of the Maritime colonies, meant that anti-Catholicism became more of a peripheral experience there, at least before the 1840s. In a book that considers the relationship that Rome had with both the

British and Canadian governments, Roberto Perin suggests that a "tradition of religious tolerance had well-established historical roots" and
that, far from being a marginal population, in major centres like Halifax,
Saint John, Charlottetown, Chatham, and Sydney, Catholics represented
between 30 and 42 per cent of the population by the beginning of the
twentieth century.[107] In 1831, Catholics in Nova Scotia and Cape Breton
Island numbered around 50,000. Prior to 1840, the serious gap in religious provision had enabled the Catholic laity to take responsibility for
establishing a political presence in the Maritimes. That Catholics were
fully integrated into the civic and political life of many colonies by the
late nineteenth century says much about the success of their early efforts.

In 1829, as emancipation legislation was finally being passed for
Britain and Ireland, and Maritime papers such as the *Acadian Recorder*
and the *Nova Scotian* gave full reports of the progress of the legislation
through both Houses of Parliament in London,[108] Catholicism, in this
region of the empire, as well as in the United Kingdom itself, was enter-
ing a new phase of development. There was a proliferation of missions
and dioceses in Prince Edward Island and New Brunswick, while Cape
Breton was united with the vicariate of Nova Scotia. Political change
led to the empowerment of the institutional church, which led to the
authority of the laity, once the bedrock of Catholic identity in these
provinces, being supplanted by that of a clergy whose focus was on
church expansion and community consolidation. The expansion of a
church infrastructure, which included the recruitment of religious communities, the provision of support for a ballooning number of Catholics
in the British Army and Royal Navy, the establishment of social welfare
agencies, and the emergence of a system of church-run education at
multiple levels, secured the place of Catholics within the fabric of British citizenry at home and abroad.

PART II

Service, Education, and Political Influence

Chapter Four

Engaging with Imperial Traditions: Military Mobilization and Slavery

Eighteenth-century military conquests gave Britain a range of new responsibilities that needed accommodation within a wider imperial agenda that included retaining existing territories, securing new ones, and disrupting French power or eliminating it entirely. One of the responsibilities revolved around the rise in the number of soldiers and sailors as Britain's military capabilities consolidated and its army and navy expanded. Following the first Catholic Relief Act of 1778, which coincided with Britain's need for manpower on account of the American War of Independence, Catholic representation in the army and navy increased dramatically. Encompassing policies, ideologies, emotional commitments, and aspirations, Britain's tradition of military mobilization was concentrated on running war machinery capable of delivering imperial dominance. For Catholics, enlistment symbolized a formal reconnection with a tradition that had excluded them for almost a century.

The direct participation of Catholics in the armed services was noticeable everywhere, but especially in British North America, where the reach of settler Catholic populations had extended rapidly. Their presence and the emergence of a renewed Catholic military culture testify to the expanded role that minority populations like Catholics were playing in the empire. It was not that creed no longer mattered in the armed services, because it did, as Gavin Daly shows, but the willingness to demonstrate loyalty by defending Crown and country mattered more.[1] The army and navy emerged as neutral spaces wherein Catholics could demonstrate a commitment to defending the empire while making a claim to citizenship. Their activity, which included soldering, sailing, chaplaincy, and, in the case of women religious, front-line nursing, changed how the structures of the state interacted with them at home and abroad, because it bound them more firmly to Britain's imperial program.

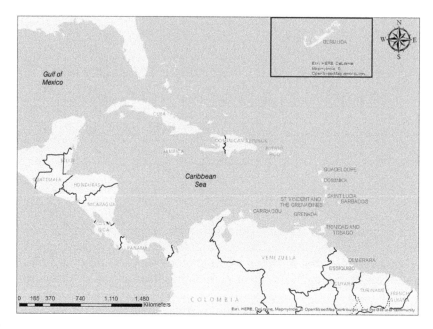

Figure 7. Map of the Caribbean

Beyond a rise in the actual number of service personnel, Britain's military conquests also resulted in a sharp increase in the number of Catholic civilians under the state's jurisdiction between 1765 and 1815. A regular flashpoint in Britain's eighteenth-century wars with France was the Caribbean. Sugar, cotton, and a range of other products from this region had become staples in European households, and keeping up with the public's ever-growing demand for them meant acquiring new territory for exploitation. Although the acquisition of Quebec, Île Royale (Cape Breton), and Île St-Jean (Prince Edward Island) had placed tens of thousands of French and Indigenous Catholics under Britain's jurisdiction, the scenario in the Caribbean was different: the Catholics there were a far more diverse lot and included a significant number of enslaved people.

Britain's relationship with Caribbean plantations and African slavery began in the seventeenth century with the acquisition of Barbados (1627), Jamaica (1655), and Bermuda (1684).[2] The interconnectedness of the Atlantic economy meant that most of Britain's colonies were touched by the labour of enslaved Africans, and this only intensified after 1765, when Britain acquired the islands of Dominica, Grenada and the Grenadines, St. Vincent, and Tobago. In 1802, Britain also gained Trinidad from Spain and, twelve years later, took control of Berbice, Demerara, and Essequibo from the Dutch. As planters, merchants, labourers, indentured servants, and tradespeople, Irish and Scottish Catholics were present in all of these places, but it was the other Catholic groups, specifically the French, Spanish, free people of colour, and the enslaved, who represented the largest segments of the Catholic populations. In some colonies, Catholics were even the majority, which threw up unique challenges for Britain's colonial officials.[3] One of the most significant challenges was how to maintain law and order on islands where enslaved Catholics were numerous. In part, this was accomplished, as this chapter will show, with a fundamental change in the nature of the relationship between the British government and the Roman Catholic Church. Military mobilization and slavery facilitated a growth in the number of Catholics (British, Irish, free and enslaved people of colour, and Indigenous peoples) under the state's direction, and their presence enabled a more direct intervention in securing imperial stability and in progressing the wealth of the United Kingdom's constituent nations.

Catholics in the Armed Services

The wars that Britain fought between the mid-1770s and 1815 offered Catholics the chance to prove their worth as subjects by enlisting in the army or navy. Given the number of troops required to win land and sea battles, the government adopted a creative approach to dealing with the recruitment crisis caused by the Seven Years' War.[4] With the supply of eligible young men exhausted, the government looked to previously excluded groups – Scottish Highland and Irish Catholics and enslaved people. Starting in 1778, when Britain was in the middle of a war with the American colonists and approaching the start of another one with France, government officials, with the support of Parliament, took the pragmatic step of offering Catholics a measure of relief and some enslaved people their freedom in exchange for military service.

Enacted to incapacitate the military capabilities of Catholics, the penal laws had failed to stop some from maintaining links with Britain's military services. At the elite level, centuries-old links were maintained, whereas non-elites simply disguised their religion or enlisted with Continental allies.[5] When the Relief Acts of 1778 and 1793 came into force, the floodgates officially opened to Catholic military enlistment. Precise numbers for the army are unknown, but Michael Snape suggests that Catholics represented a significant proportion of the army's 400,000 men by 1814.[6] Estimates for the Royal Navy are even sketchier, but there is no question that Catholics had also been a major boost to that service, which numbered roughly 142,000 sailors and marines in 1813.[7] Scottish and Irish sailors frequently joined or were impressed into the navy in the Caribbean and in Newfoundland because of the seafaring experience they had acquired on inter-island or north–south merchant-trading trips.[8] Free Black people were also impressed or recruited into the service with increasing regularity, as were a number of enslaved Catholics, much to the outrage of their enslavers.[9] The British government effectively became the largest "owner" of people in the entire empire when it appropriated roughly 13,000 enslaved people to "man its Caribbean forces."[10]

Regardless of their religious background, young men in Britain and Ireland joined the military for a variety of reasons, including loyalism, an escape from uncertain futures, the opportunity to see the world, a need for adventure, a family or community tradition of military service, a desire to "impress fair damsels," and, in the case of the enslaved, to become free.[11] The majority of Catholic soldiers and sailors came from the labouring classes of Ireland and the Scottish Highlands. Highland Scots were renowned for their military prowess. One of the earliest Scottish Catholic–dominated regiments, the Glengarry Fencibles, had acquired the moniker "Devil's Bloodhounds" during Ireland's 1798 rebellion, "on account of their dress and of their habit of climbing and traversing the mountains."[12] Scotland's exclusion from all pre-1793 relief legislation meant that the ability of its Catholics to engage in military service was much more restricted. The Irish faced no comparable obstacles, and, by 1830, they (both Catholics and Protestants) outnumbered the Scots in the army and represented an overwhelming 42.2 per cent of Britain's total non-commissioned officers and regular troops.[13] No religious breakdown for 1830 exists, but, in 1868, Catholics represented over 28 per cent of British Army personnel.[14]

The prospect of employment was a key motivator, but the desire to claim a space in the imperial program also compelled minority groups to enlist. Work on Jewish soldiers in the French army offers important corroboration, by exposing how imperial agendas redefined understandings of citizenship and how religious minorities used military service to acquire social capital. In the case of France, Jewish soldiers received access to "particular honors and privileges unavailable to most other members of their communities," military service "reinforce[d] [their] integration into French society."[15] In Ireland's case, this sense of integration had a direct influence on the parliamentary union.[16] The role that military service played in offering Catholics (particularly Irish Catholics) the opportunity to forge meaningful connections with British society and the colonial world is clear.[17] Ultimately, Britain's tradition of military mobilization afforded Catholics a platform for reconstructing their image as loyal subjects. As an act of loyalty, military service was one of the main tools that former Jacobites, for example, had to transform their image from "menace[s] at home" to heroes abroad.[18] Indeed, the significance of the 1778 Relief Act was considerable for Catholics who had much to prove with their military service, though there was probably little difference between what motived young, labouring-class Englishmen, Irishmen, Scotsmen, and Welshmen to join the armed services.

Elite Catholics differed in their motivations: they tended to view military service as a way of reclaiming the social influence that they had lost.[19] To them, it was much more a fundamental obligation, based on tradition, that compelled them to serve Britain and its European allies, but they faced considerable resistance from a governing class who wanted to control and limit their influence. In Ireland, where there was a competing Continental military tradition emanating from the early seventeenth-century migration of the "Wild Geese" to Spain and later to France, the efforts of late eighteenth-century elites to raise regiments in support of Britain's wars were unsuccessful.[20] Yet, the prohibition of Catholics from having any direct involvement did not stop influential Catholic landowners from trying to raise regiments. Lord Trimleston, from County Meath, for example, tried to at least six times to raise a regiment to support "either the Elector of Hanover (i.e., George III) or the King of Portugal."[21] Their English and Scottish counterparts made similar attempts but also encountered stiff opposition. In 1788, under the auspices of the Catholic Committee, English petitioners' requests for permission to serve as officers in the army and navy were denied.[22] Six years later, a group of influential Scottish Catholic Highlanders, whose families and friends had seen their assets and influence erode dramatically following the battle of Culloden, asked if they could raise regiments in defence of Crown and country, but Henry Dundas, Scotland's astute political manager who went on to serve as secretary of state for home affairs from 1791 until July 1794, refused. Interestingly, the Glengarry Fencibles, comprised largely of Catholics, were founded a few months after he took over as secretary of state for war.[23]

The penal laws had been devastating for the Catholic elites, and so being able to connect with Britain's military tradition was deemed an essential part of their social recovery. Yet the obstacles in their path took their toll and added to their already significant frustrations with the limitations of the Relief Acts. Only in 1817, when parliament passed the Annual Indemnity Act, which classed Catholics as Dissenters, was the position of Catholic officers clarified.[24] The Irish had been in a different category from the English and Scots because, although the 1793 Catholic Relief Act allowed them to command regiments in Ireland, they were restricted from leading colonial troops.[25] Given that Ireland had not yet entered the British parliamentary union, this limitation was understandable, but it reinforced Ireland's precarious position in relation to Britain and its inferior status in the eyes of King George III. It was a "strange inconsistency" that exasperated the Irish Catholic gentry.[26] They resented their exclusion "from office, commissions in the British army and even the purchase or mortgage" of land, and appealed to Ireland's lord lieutenant, John Russell, 6th Duke of Bedford, to the prime minister, William Wyndham Grenville, 1st Baron Grenville, and to the entire cabinet for redress.[27] Persuaded that "no measure could more effectually promote the general interests of the Empire," Grenville was sympathetic.[28] His view had little effect on a king whose madness had rendered him unfit to rule by 1807 and who refused to entertain any notion of Catholic emancipation.[29] Grenville's government collapsed later that year because of the impasse.

Servicemen, Chaplains, and the Catholic Experience

While the elites struggled to find suitable roles, the number of regular Catholic troops and sailors had become so large that the war office took the step of permitting Catholic soldiers in Ireland to attend Mass in 1793, though this was not granted beyond Ireland until 1806 and, even then, permission was dependent upon a sympathetic commanding officer.[30] Another important development was the appointment in 1793 of Alexander Macdonell, a Highland Scot, as the army's first Catholic chaplain. A respected priest, who had trained at the Scots colleges in Paris and Valladolid, Macdonell was a diplomat of extraordinary skill who took every opportunity to highlight Catholic loyalty. His appointment as bishop of Kingston, Upper Canada, in 1826, which made him British North America's first bishop with ordinary jurisdiction outside of Quebec, was a testament to his influence.[31] He worked well with colonial officials but, like the majority of the Scottish Catholic clergy at the time, he was extremely cautious of the Irish, whose religious culture contrasted sharply with his own.[32] In 1831, he expressed concern that the growing number of Irish in Upper Canada was impeding his overworked priests' ability to provide adequate spiritual support to the soldiers among them, who, according to his own estimation, numbered roughly three-quarters of the 75,000 soldiers who had arrived that year.[33] Macdonell's own census in 1828 put the total number of Catholics in Upper Canada between 40,000 and 50,000, with "only about a dozen priests to assist them."[34] While Scottish priests in places like Upper Canada begged their Roman contacts to put pressure on Irish bishops to halt emigration, it was the Irish-born priests, rather than the soldiers or the bulk of the civilian population, who made them anxious.[35] Most of the Irish-descended priests had relatively positive relationships with the Scots, but the belief that those of Irish birth had been radicalized and sought a repeal of the union (and many did) caused friction.[36]

As I have shown elsewhere, embedded within Scottish Catholic culture was a deep mistrust of the Irish, which affected how the two groups interacted in colonial settings.[37] A run-in that Macdonell had with a priest named William O'Grady in the 1830s is a prime example. O'Grady, originally from County Cork, had spent time in "the Brazils" before surfacing in Upper Canada at the start of the decade. He clashed almost immediately with Macdonell, who accused him of possessing radical ideologies and of challenging his authority by "organis[ing] a formidable faction of Irish bullies and drum hands, the very dregs of the population of this town who assemble in mobs."[38] It took considerable effort, including sending a report to Rome, but Macdonell eventually forced him out. Anxious about the negative impression that O'Grady may have made on Sir John Colborne, Upper Canada's lieutenant governor, Macdonell stressed to Colborne that he had "given in one month more substantial proofs of [his] loyalty to [his] King and country, than Mr O'Grady has in all his lifetime."[39] Macdonell emphasized loyalty again in an address to the inhabitants (Catholic and Protestant) of Upper Canada's Glengarry County following the rebellion of 1837–38, when he commended their "distinguished" and "powerful" contribution to the defence of the British Empire.[40]

Priests like O'Grady were drifters, figures who popped up frequently in colonies that struggled to attract and retain missionaries because of the lack of strong structures and adequate resources. Fathers Anthony O'Hannan and William Phelan were two others who shuffled between colonies in an effort to escape bad reputations and scandal. In their case, however, neither excelled at keeping his head down. Phelan fled to Nova Scotia from Ireland in the late 1780s under a cloud of about £300 of debt, and it was not long before people there started complaining of the outrageous fees he was demanding for marriages, baptisms, and burials. He scurried down to the United States in 1794 and died not long after.[41] O'Hannan surfaced in Grenada in the late 1820s, after leaving the United States under a cloud of numerous rape and seduction allegations. In Grenada, the vicar general of the vicariate, Guillaume Le Goff, knew nothing of this and, desperate for clergy, gave him charge of St. George's Church. Before long, O'Hannan fell out with both the newly installed vicar apostolic of the West Indies, Daniel McDonnell, and Grenada's governor, Andrew Houston. Branded an "agitator," O'Hannan had disappeared from the island around 1835 and is thought to have died within a few years.[42] The frequent appearance of priests such as O'Grady, Phelan, and O'Hannan in colonies with large concentrations of troops convinced government and church authorities of the need for more effective collaboration to ensure order and good behaviour.

The appointment of more Catholic chaplains was a major turning point for Britain's armed services and was symbolic of a formal recognition of Catholicism as part of its military tradition. However small, and notwithstanding the fact that many officiating clergymen went unpaid, the state's investment in a Catholic chaplaincy also confirmed that Catholics were recognized as occupying a significant section of the services. While some scholars argue that the promotion of a "Christian" identity within the army came only after Crimea in the 1850s,[43] this process actually started as soon as the number of Catholics in the service began to rise. Part of the reason for this change was the Catholic leadership's concerns over spiritual intervention, potential conversion to Protestantism, and apostasy. In 1798, Edmund Burke, the French-educated priest of Irish descent who served in Quebec before moving on to Nova Scotia in 1801, reported that commanding officers were forcing Catholic soldiers to attend Protestant services and that many men were dying without last rites.[44] He and others were also concerned about the preponderance of nominal Catholicism because, although some Catholic soldiers had permission to attend Mass as part of a broader agenda to improve the "living and serving" conditions for soldiers from the early nineteenth century, it is likely that many commanding officers did little to promote it.[45] Moreover, the fact that many troops preferred cabarets and pubs to Mass distressed Burke, who received regular reports about the "très mauvais Catholiques" stationed in and around Upper Canada's Niagara region.[46]

Providing adequate support for Catholic and Dissenting servicemen while maintaining Anglican hegemony of both services was a complex endeavour that compelled cooperation among church leaders, military officials, and colonial administrators. Achieving this balance required an awareness of the three power dynamics that were constantly at play: the military officials, who wanted to preserve the command structure; the Catholic priests, who wanted to prevent conversions to Protestantism; and the government, which wanted a strong, united, and respectable fighting force. Priorities often clashed, but there was agreement that the image of British soldiers and sailors as representatives of the imperial state needed reshaping.[47] Increasingly, both church and government officials came to be of the opinion that chaplains were integral to transforming the morally corrupt image of British troops.

Myriad challenges confronted the Catholic chaplains, including unequal pay, insufficient travel support, hostility from commanding officers, fatigue, exhaustion, illness, and even death.[48] The dearth of chaplains also put tremendous pressure on a small pool of already exhausted local missionaries, since government officials did what they could to avoid paying non-Anglican chaplains.[49] Father T. O'Mealy, the officiating clergyman for the army and navy at Sheerness in Kent, requested a government stipend in 1822 but that petition was likely denied, as internal notes about his request highlighted the rejection of a similar request six years earlier by a priest who visited sick and dying sailors and soldiers at Haslar Hospital at Gosport, Hampshire.[50] Inadequate provision was a persistent theme. In Jamaica, for example, where many of the estimated 8,000 Catholics were army troops, a chaplain was assigned to the camp barracks near Kingston in the early 1840s, but "at the other stations throughout the island [troops] are wholly destitute of spiritual consolation. Their average number is 1,000."[51] Ten years later and much further north, Newfoundland's bishop John Thomas Mullock wrote to Downing Street requesting support for the "maintenance of a Roman Catholic clergyman for the spiritual instruction of the Roman Catholic soldiers" there.[52] The secretary at war responded with a promise of 10 shillings a week for a chaplain to visit sick soldiers at the garrison hospital, "so long as their numbers exceed one hundred."[53]

Despite these limitations, the army had better provision than the navy. The first permanent Catholic army chaplains, nineteen in total, were named on 5 November 1858, though none served in Ireland, because Cardinal Paul Cullen refused to accept anyone who was not hand-picked by himself. Less than a decade later, the *Irish Catholic Directory* recorded eighteen chaplains serving at Dublin, Fermoy, Aldershot, Woolwich, Greenwich, and Plymouth, as well as Gibraltar, China, and Halifax.[54] In the Royal Navy, Catholic sailors went much longer without spiritual instruction, as only Anglican chaplains were allowed to sail. The paucity of naval chaplains led one priest to complain that the "only Spiritual provision made for Catholics in the Navy was the appointment, in the year 1854, of three or four Catholic chaplains at the principal naval stations of the united kingdom."[55] Another reflected that, because Catholic chaplains did not receive commissions, they had no recognized position and were refused facilities "for seeing the Catholic sailors on board their own ships for religious instruction or for preparation for the sacraments."[56] Unfortunately, a systematic list of British army and naval chaplains equivalent to Dom Aidan Henry Germain's American list does not exist, and so information is more sketchy.[57] In most cases, rather than formal appointments, the norm was to rely upon the good will of local clergy or officiating clergymen, as those assigned to the garrisons or ports were known in Catholic circles. Edmund Burke was one of them and found his duties utterly exhausting. Not only was he responsible for Halifax's rapidly increasing civilian congregation, but he was also acting as chaplain to the military hospital and to "plus de la moitié de la garrison," which included Irish, Scottish, and German Catholic soldiers and sailors.[58]

A culture of anti-Catholicism was rife in both services. Orange Lodges, for example, operated openly in the army until 1822, despite a ban during the Napoleonic Wars, when a desire to curb sectarian tensions and the swearing of secret oaths prompted their suppression. Recovering personal testimony from rank-and-file Catholic soldiers about the prejudice they encountered in the early nineteenth century is difficult, due to low literacy rates at the time, but enough evidence exists to show that religious toleration was complicated for Catholics and Dissenters, despite government directives to the contrary.[59] The absence of chaplains or local officiating clergymen also meant that sailors and troops lacked advocates to challenge the tendency of commanding officers to reject requests to attend Mass. Yet one supporter, and an extremely powerful one, was Henry George, 3rd Earl Grey. Appointed secretary at war in 1835, he and some of his colleagues, including Sir John MacDonald, adjutant general at the Horse Guards, worked to enable separate services for Catholic soldiers serving in Ireland. Writing to General Charles Grey in 1836, 3rd Earl Grey explained that separate services would allow the War Office to "turn off" a priest who "misbehaves," and he directed that, "as it would be inconvenient to give any order on the subject from headquarters the way of doing it would be for Blakeney privately to let commanding officers know that where they can make satisfactory arrangements for the performance of separate services for adequate numbers of men, their applications to the W.O. [War Office] to sanction the expense will be favourable entertained."[60] Only in 1835, after persistent complaints by chaplains and other Catholic officials, was a general order issued to all troops explaining their rights, but even then, Catholics struggled to get permission to attend Mass.[61] Dissenters faced similar challenges, and there was very little recourse if a commanding officer said no.

Substantial pressure was put on troops to attend Church of England services, and refusals often led to punishments, some severe, as Charles O'Neil, an Irishman from County Louth, discovered. The son of a carpenter and one of four brothers in a family of eleven children, O'Neil had enlisted in the British Army during the Napoleonic Wars. In a memoir published many years after he left the army, he described a violent incident at Gibraltar in 1811, which left him recovering in the barracks hospital for at least three weeks. After enlisting for the third time (he had already deserted twice) and refusing to attend Anglican services because, he said, "there was one of [his] own denomination in the place," he was sentenced to 300 lashes.[62] Stripped from the waist up and strapped to a wooden triangle strong enough to support his weight, he was whipped with a cat-o'-nine tails to a count of 300 in front of his unit.[63] While in hospital, he managed to write to the Duke of York to inform him of what had happened and "soon after, [that gentleman] sent an order that the soldiers should be permitted to attend church where they pleased."[64] In the decades that followed, physical punishments for refusing to attend Church of England services waned, but life as a Catholic in the services remained difficult and was often very lonely. According to one naval chaplain, those "attached to the African squadron and its sanatorium at the island of Ascension" were among the most vulnerable, because they were "deprived of every opportunity of attending their religious duties, whether in health or sickness."[65]

Officers were expected to be models of Victorian morality, but the Catholics among them faced unique challenges. The private diaries of two Irish Catholic naval officers, who served during the 1850s, 1860s, and 1870s, highlight the loneliness some experienced during extended periods at sea, when they had no access to chaplains.[66] One of them, Richard Carr McClement, often found himself the only Catholic officer on board and declared himself a "solitary owl" on Sundays.[67] Catholic servicemen were not without advocates, though, and from an early stage a number of people fought on their behalf to improve conditions. Sir Harry Calvert (c. 1763–1826), who, as adjutant general, held one of the most senior posts in the British Army, was described as a humanitarian because he was well known for the improvements he made to the provision of health care, including for mental health, in the army. In promoting a culture of "evangelical nondenominational religion" among soldiers, he believed, as others did, that freedom of worship enhanced discipline.[68] In non-military circles, a number of MPs made similar arguments, with some even flagging the militias as a special case and arguing that they deserved the right to attend Catholic Mass, just like regular troops.[69] The Act to Permit the Interchange of the British and Irish Militias Respectively (1811), was one result.

As the number of Catholics in the services increased, calls to appoint more chaplains became louder, and, following Catholic Emancipation in 1829, Catholic chaplains, officiating clergymen, and bishops were less intimidated about pushing for greater access to Catholic service personnel. Published statements such as *State of Catholics in the Navy* and *Catholics in the British Navy* helped raise awareness of sailors' lack of access to priests, putting pressure on government officials to expand support.[70] Yet tensions remained, and, even in cases where a priest did gain access, one wrong move could see it swiftly withdrawn. This was what happened to Bermuda's Reverend Thomas Lyons, who, in addition to being the local priest to a small group of resident Catholics, served as chaplain to the island's soldiers, sailors, and convicts. When he married two civilians on-board a convict hulk, the colony's governor between 1846 and 1854, Sir Charles Elliot, immediately barred him for unauthorized use of government property and conducting the wedding without permission.[71] While Elliot admitted that he was sorry to revoke Lyons's privileges because they had enjoyed a good relationship, Elliot's refusal to reinstate him forced the cleric to beg his superiors to intercede with the colonial office. According to Lyons, Elliot was a man of "a liberal good disposition," if an occasional "Blunderer," and the priest blamed the "malicious designing of a most inveterate enemy – the Protestant convict chaplain Parson *Mantach for the governor's heavy-handedness."*[72] The secretary of state reinstated Lyons, after ruling that, although the priest's decision to perform a marriage ceremony had been a "serious impropriety," it was due to a "want of reflection" rather than anything more sinister.[73]

Marriages were sensitive subjects that often led to clashes between Catholic priests and Protestant ministers. In Newfoundland, for example, Methodist clerics could be obstructive when it came to stamping their authority on colonial religious culture and, in one case, an unnamed minister attempted to invalidate the Catholic re-solemnization of two marriages between soldiers and local women. The minister petitioned the lieutenant governor, Sir John Harvey, for an annulment, since the second set of ceremonies had occurred when neither soldier had been granted leave. An irritated Harvey dismissed the request as nothing more than a petty grievance.[74] The minister was likely giving vent to frustrations over the growing influence of the Catholic Church and, more specifically, to the passing of the colony's education act in the spring of 1843.[75] Burials could be equally contentious. In the 1850s, there was considerable angst in Bermuda when Church of England ministers tried to prevent the burial of non-Anglican Christian soldiers and sailors in the garrison graveyards on Ireland and St. George's Islands. Governor Elliot insisted to the Admiralty that *all* British Christian servicemen should be buried in Crown graveyards and warned of "the ill consequences which would not fail to arise if this subject were to grow into heated discussion amongst a body of soldiers and their ministers following different forms of Christianity."[76]

The scarcity of chaplains was felt acutely by sick and dying servicemen. Remarking on their desperate state as he passed through the "Bermudas" on his way to Britain in 1842, William Clancy, vicar apostolic of British Guiana and a notorious drunkard who had a strong preference for wine, reported that "several hundred of Catholics [were] without a chapel, or a priest." When he arrived, the "major of the 20th regiment" directed him to the hospital, where "upwards of sixty persons, young & old in hospital begged to have their confessions heard" and two received last rites.[77] Robert Higgs, a Catholic layman in Bermuda, opined in 1843: "Good God! What a lamentable thing to think of the poor creatures who have lately died of the Fever, being stretched on the bed of death, calling in vain for the assistance of a Catholic clergyman in their last moments. What a pity it is that a Catholic should ever become a soldier in the British Service where he is denied religious liberty."[78]

Bermuda was a set of small islands situated almost equidistant from Britain's north Atlantic and Caribbean colonies. A haven for smugglers moving goods to and from the United States, it had also become, ironically, a convict depot and the headquarters of the Royal Navy's North American Atlantic Station after the latter's transfer from Halifax in 1819.[79] Like the islands of Ascension and Saint Helena in the south Atlantic, Bermuda was strategically important as a stopping place where troops could rest and ships could resupply. Although the bishop of Halifax in Nova Scotia was responsible for Bermuda's Catholics from 1817, Rome needed to remind Halifax of its responsibility in 1843. Before 1820, the number of Catholics in the archipelago was miniscule, but it grew dramatically as the number of service personnel and convicts increased.[80] Halifax struggled to take care of its own needs, let alone those of Bermuda, and so it was only in 1858, as fears grew over the latter's increasingly restless convict population, that plans for a chapel on St. George's Island were approved. James Rogers, a native of County Donegal and one of two priests assigned to Bermuda, warned of a convict uprising if more support did not materialize and pointed to the murder of a guard, and the two prisoners who tried to protect him, as evidence.[81]

When it came to Bermuda's convict population and the soldiers who guarded them, colonial officials wanted Catholic chaplains on the ground. Governor Elliot, who was not predisposed to favour the Church of England if it put colonial stability at risk, lobbied hard for an additional Catholic chaplain. He informed the secretary of state, Henry

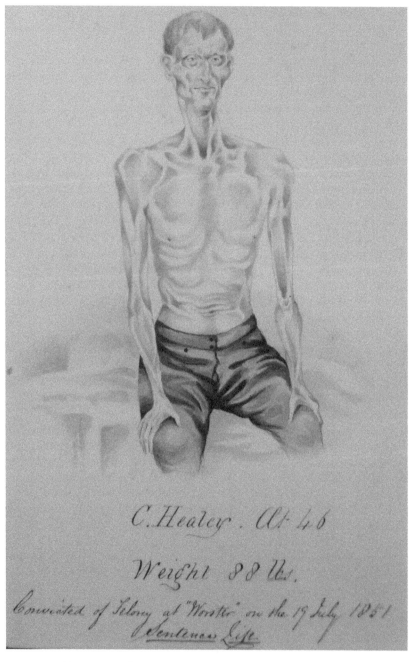

C. Healey . At 46

Weight 88 lbs.

Convicted of Felony at "Worster" on the 19 July 1851
Sentence Life

Figure 8. *Irish Convict*, C. Healy (Royal Naval Historical
Branch, uncatalogued drawings)

Pelham Fiennes Pelham-Clinton, 5th Duke of Newcastle-under-Lyme, that over half of the convicts on Bermuda's Boaz Island were Catholic and in need of more support. He opposed appointing a second Church of England minister, deeming it unnecessary and more likely than not to inflame tensions.[82]

Anti-Catholicism was endemic across the services, but the lack of spiritual provision was an issue confronting all Nonconformists.[83] Further research on the experience of Church of Scotland (Presbyterian) servicemen is needed because, although they belonged to one of Britain's two established churches, they faced persistent discrimination and were regularly denied recognition.[84] In spite of this, the army was more forward-looking than any other service and, by 1850, could be credited with having been "one of the most religiously tolerant institutions of the British state." Overall, on an everyday level, Catholic soldiers and sailors tended to integrate well with their Protestant brethren of a similar rank.[85] Military service provided a powerful bond, and it was likely that many Protestants who served alongside Catholics went away with a "very different impression" of Catholicism than the one they possessed when they had first joined.[86] The shared experience of war undoubtedly increased religious tolerance among the troops because camaraderie was (and remains) a unifying force.

An important turning point came with the war in the Crimea. This was the first major conflict followed by the press, and the coverage forced a dramatic shift in the wider British public's perceptions of soldiers.[87] The stories that flowed back to the British public were harrowing: men dying on bloody battlefields or in makeshift hospitals without the comfort of a clergyman to deliver last rites. The lack of spiritual assistance for Catholic soldiers on the front formed part of the broader critique aimed at the elites whom many in Britain blamed for the atrocities experienced by British and Irish soldiers. While the *Lancet* led the charge on the medical front, attacking the incompetence of those directing the surgeons,[88] Frederick Lucas, the London-born MP for County Meath and founder of the *Tablet*, argued in the House of Commons that, if Catholics were "hazarding their lives on behalf of their country," then they deserved proper spiritual assistance.[89] He pointed out that they received less spiritual support than Protestant convicts, even though they represented at least a third of the army and a quarter of the navy.[90]

Crimea was a conflict that had particular significance for Catholic women. For the first time, the public saw images of women religious nursing injured and dying soldiers and providing spiritual direction. Britons were as shocked by the reality of war as they were by the sheer incompetence of the army's aristocratic leadership. That the Crimea brought the "imaginative associations between medical and military forms of heroic masculinity" into focus, and prompted a "valorization of grassroots sacrifice," created space for considerations of minority groups like Catholics who shared in the sacrifice and brutality of a badly managed war.[91] Women religious also played a leading role in the feminization of this badly managed war, since the presence of nursing sisters gave rise to a more gendered awareness of war: the Crimea fused Victorian ideals of womanhood with those of military masculinity.

The Sisters of Mercy established the roots of this feminization in the early 1830s. Founded in Dublin by Catherine McAuley, the "Mercies" were a congregation of active women religious whose mission included caring for the sick. The decision to include nursing work as part of the Mercy mission was influenced by McAuley's maternal uncle, William Armstrong. The director of Apothecary's Hall in Dublin between 1794 and 1819, Armstrong was a formidable figure in Ireland's emerging medical profession and an important role model for Catherine and her brother, James, who, after converting to Protestantism, studied medicine at Trinity College, Dublin.[92] The Sisters of Mercy acquired valuable nursing experience during the cholera and typhus outbreaks of the 1830s and 1840s, which informed the future training of the congregation's wider membership.[93] Crimea was a pivotal moment for the entire congregation: their willingness to travel to the front to care for injured and dying soldiers changed perceptions about what Catholic sisters did. The Mercy sisters – who were different from nuns, in that they were not enclosed and took simple vows of poverty, chastity, and obedience – went to the Crimea in 1854 from convents in London, Dublin, Kinsale, Cork, Carlow, and Liverpool. Some of them recorded their experiences in poems and diaries.[94] *Lines on the Eastern Mission of the Sisters of Mercy* includes a poem by Mother Mary Joseph Croke, which describes how the sisters coped,[95] and some diary entries that describe the plight of the soldiers:

> The first day the General Hospital opened 200 patients were admitted who had come from the Crimea. Most of these were so prostrate as to be unable to aid themselves. It was necessary to cut and comb their overgrown hair and beards, wash their faces and even feed them like babies. Many a time the poor fellows burst into tears on being spoken to and exclaimed, "Oh, it is long since I heard a kind word."[96]

According to one estimate, over 59,600 Irish served in the Crimea, and it is likely that a number of these soldiers' mothers knew one or more of the sisters nursing on the front.[97] These women were not chaplains in the technical sense, but they were as much spiritual advisers as they were nurses when they worked alongside their male counterparts. The "Catholic soldiers," wrote Sister M. Aloysius Doyle, a native of County Kildare, "had every consolation of our holy religion, the chaplains were untiring, they were late and early in the wards. Of course, we were free to say prayers for them, and, whenever we could, a word of instruction or consolation."[98] Doyle entered the Mercy community at Carlow in 1849 and became the superintendent of female nursing at the English general hospitals in Turkey. What she is describing is ministry work and although the sisters were expressly prohibited from discussing religion with Protestant patients by the War Office, they admitted that sometimes it could not be helped. The hospital beds were so close together that "it was impossible for a nun to talk about religion to a Catholic without the man in the next bed hearing what she said."[99]

The Sisters of Mercy in Crimea were only one example of how women religious engaged with Britain's imperial traditions. By the 1850s, many new communities of sisters began to spread rapidly throughout the empire. The first wave tended to focus on education, as the next chapter highlights, but, from mid-century – and in addition to those who undertook nursing or care work in response to acute need in places where no other services were available – a growing number concentrated on health-care provision.[100] As British soldiers and sailors travelled around the world, their encounters with women religious became increasingly frequent. This contact could be uncomfortable for those who were unable to fathom the idea of unmarried women living in convents beyond the gaze of men. Anathema to mainstream Victorian culture, this life path, which revolved around self-organizing and highly independent female-only communities, gave rise to salacious rumours and a colourful literary culture intent on sexualizing chaste women.[101] Catherine McAuley confronted significant resistance from those who perceived her "behaviour [to be] inappropriate for a woman."[102] Yet, this resistance failed to stop the spread of female congregations and communities. Moreover, for many Catholic servicemen, the presence of women religious was welcome.[103]

It was really only with the Crimean War that the British public actually began to see the extent of the Catholic participation in the military tradition. When the conflict ended in 1856, Britons mourned together. England's Catholic hierarchy emphasized the Catholic sacrifice to priests and congregations across the land: "You, dearly beloved, have shared with your fellow subjects the anxieties of war. Your brothers, your children, your kin, and your friends have been in every trench, and in every field, in every hospital, and in every storm. The blood of your families has been poured out as freely as that of any others."[104]

Following this conflict, health became an important focus in the armed services, and legislative developments such as the 1858 Medical Act established clearer guidelines for training and practical improvements including regular reporting. The work of army and naval surgeons looked a lot like general practice work due to their civilian officer status,[105] but the Catholics among them had the added responsibility of acting as pseudo-chaplains. Alcoholism and depression plagued both services, but the pressure on Catholic naval surgeons to deal with these illnesses was arguably greater because the Royal Navy excluded Catholic chaplains from its vessels.

The lack of access that Catholic and Dissenting sailors had to their own clergymen affected their mental health. Richard McClement, an Irish Catholic surgeon about whom I have written elsewhere, was usually the highest-ranking Catholic on board his ships, and so it fell to him to treat and to pray with dying sailors, to officiate at their burials, and to deal with incidents of acute mental distress.[106] In this, McClement was not alone, and one of his colleagues, Alexander Crosbie, another Irish Catholic surgeon, wrote about these challenges. His notes on the tragic case of Thomas Watts, a twenty-year-old sailor on the H.M.S. *Shannon*, who was discovered "in his hammock rotating the end of a gun, and kicking out with his legs," is illustrative of some of what they encountered:

> From the 14th to the 21st May he showed occasional vagaries, once jumping overboard, and thrice passing faeces on deck. Singing and talking to himself occasionally. From the 21st to the 28th he remained much quieter and talked very little to himself ... There appears a meaning and definite purpose that he has a strong dislike to return to his ship. Was sent to hospital on the 28th May, and returned on board on the 11th June, having shown in the interim no indication of insanity. On the night of his return he again commenced his vagaries, and jumped overboard in a nude state the next morning (12th June). Since that time he has been perfectly quiet, – in irons for security.[107]

Suicides in the services were common and recorded carefully when medical reports became standard practice in the 1850s. At Ascension, Richard McClement attributed two cases (a marine private who cut his throat, and a master in charge of stores who shot himself) to alcohol withdrawal.[108] At Bermuda, he recorded the resuscitation of a drunken sailor who attempted to kill himself by walking off the edge of a wharf.[109] In 1861, another surgeon logged three suicides at Bermuda – two men hanged themselves and a third cut his throat.[110] That

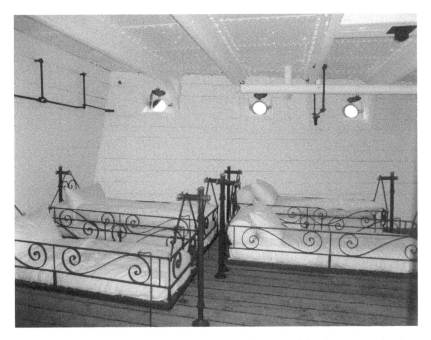

Figure 9. Portsmouth ship hospital ward (photograph by S. Karly Kehoe)

same year in Halifax, naval surgeons recorded the death of a young Irish Catholic gunner, Peter Convery, who hanged himself, while in the cells for some unknown crime, by "fasten[ing] a small leather waist belt to an iron grating."[111]

At relatively isolated stations like Halifax and Bermuda, rates of alcoholism and depression were high. Dismal landscapes and the lack of any kind of entertainment were contributing factors. John Mitchell, a Young Irelander and leading voice of the *Nation* Ireland's leading nationalist newspaper, was one of Bermuda's highest-profile prisoners, after being sentenced to fourteen years' transportation in 1848.[112] Although the subject of two failed rescue plots before his transfer to Tasmania in the spring of 1849, he was in Bermuda long enough to get a sense of its bleakness. "The land," he wrote, "not under wood is of a brownish green colour, and of a most naked and arid, hungry and thirsty visage"; "not one single stream, not one spring, or well gushes, trickles or bubbles."[113] A surgeon who blamed the landscape's dullness for the endemic depression and alcoholism that wreaked havoc on the men posted there authenticates Mitchell's description: "There is something connected with such stations as this," he observed, "that has a great tendency to demoralize the soldier ... The total absence of all places of amusement ... drive[s] him to the spirit shop where he too often abandons himself to excess."[114] Given their role among sick, injured, and dying seamen, Catholic naval surgeons took on responsibilities normally reserved for priests and chaplains.[115] They, like nursing sisters, were essential to the military's support system and acquired significant social authority as a result.

Slavery and Catholic Colonialism

The presence of British army personnel overseas led to deeper and more extensive links between the colonies and Christian missionaries from the four nations.[116] In many Caribbean colonies and in Quebec, a significant proportion of these missionaries were Catholic. As the previous section revealed, the growing number of Catholic soldiers and sailors spreading throughout the northern colonies and the Caribbean gave the Catholic Church a foothold in Britain's Christian mission, as women religious, chaplains, missionary clergy, and even surgeons expanded the Anglo- (and Gaelic) Catholic colonial infrastructure. Unpacking the complex relationship between the Catholic Church and the British government in the Caribbean requires an acknowledgement of earlier European Catholic missionary activity. Grenada, St. Vincent, Dominica, Montserrat, and Trinidad had existing and very large Catholic populations because of the colonial foundations established there by France and Spain. Rather than excluding these populations, Britain's colonial officials sought accommodation to ensure good government and law and order.

From the earliest stages of France's plantation economy, Catholic missionaries had sought conversions among the enslaved Africans, the majority of whom came from the Gold Coast, the Bight of Benin, and west-central Africa. Sue Peabody's work on the French Antilles reveals that many enslaved people were receptive to baptism because it gave them an affinity with a belief culture that emphasized spiritual powers and fed their desire for a sense of spiritual equality with those who enslaved them.[117] There is an obvious connection with Vincent Brown's observations about how the enslaved used ritual and the supernatural to transgress the boundaries of slavery as defined by their enslavers.[118] From the seventeenth to the mid-eighteenth century, male religious orders, namely, the Capuchins, Dominicans, and Jesuits, spearheaded the French Catholic Caribbean missions to enslaved people. Originally, these orders intended to convert the local Carib population, but their failure on that front saw them turn their attention to the enslaved Africans. These religious orders were also the "owners" of enslaved people; they did not advocate freedom, but rather emphasized how the enslaved should "live their lives consistent with Catholic teaching."[119]

The French planters initially accepted the activities of the missionaries, but their toleration declined as the focus on increasing sugar profits and expanding the shipments of people from West Africa intensified. By the time Britain assumed control of the ceded islands in the mid-1760s, the exodus of Catholic religious personnel had already started, but for those who were still there, their position, if difficult before, became untenable. British commissioners concentrated on appropriating their property: in 1765, the Jesuits in St. Vincent had their 143 uncleared acres, 547 cleared acres, and "valuable buildings" seized.[120] The resulting vacuum in religious instruction led to a rise in Catholic folk practices among the enslaved people. The adoption of such practices was not unlike what emerged in many parts of the Scottish Highlands and Islands following the Reformation, when Catholic priests no longer had regular access to the people living there, and what the Mi'kmaq of Cape Breton experienced, when the missionary priest Pierre Maillard was captured by the British and returned to France in 1745.[121]

It was often the case in the Caribbean that the European country that ended up in possession of a particular colony or territory was not the original colonizer. When colonies were transferred from France to Britain, religious practice on the ground became more complicated.[122] For the European portion of such societies, changes included the loss of privilege and increased restrictions on sacraments such as marriage and baptism; for the enslaved people, it could mean being subjected to post-mortem desecrations by British planters.[123] Religious allegiance was an important part of the colonizing process. Protestant and Catholic Europeans faced discrimination if, in following economic opportunities, they ended up on an island or territory held by a crown that was aligned with a different church and so while anti-Catholicism was a defining feature of the British territories, Protestants living under the jurisdiction of France or Spain confronted equally egregious prejudices. In Spanish territories, for example, Protestantism was the minority faith and completely outlawed. In fact, when compared with British colonies, life for a Protestant in a Spanish territory was even more circumscribed. In those territories, all "long-term foreign visitors" were required to swear an oath of Catholicity, and it was only in 1869 that a declaration of religious tolerance was introduced.[124] Like Catholics in eighteenth-century Britain before the Relief Acts, Protestants who wanted to retain their faith in French or Spanish Caribbean colonies had to "settle for private home services, services aboard British or American ships, and illegal private services held by a sojourning clergyman."[125]

Despite coming from theologically distinct traditions, the Europeans active in the Caribbean shared a desire for personal enrichment at the expense of enslaved Africans and their descendants. That Catholic missionaries were enslavers from an early period well into the nineteenth century is no surprise, especially since Rome's position on the subject of African enslavement was ambiguous. Pope Eugene IV's *Sicut Dudum* and Pope Paul III's *Sublimus Dei* discussed only the specific cases of the inhabitants of the Canary Islands and the "Indians of the west and south" (Caribs). The enslavement of these latter groups was condemned because it undermined their conversion to Catholicism, but neither apostolic letter mentioned Africans. This distinction is important.[126] During the height of the transatlantic slave trade in the eighteenth century, the Holy See failed to single out or criticize directly France or Spain, perhaps because there were French and Spanish Catholic missionaries working for conversions among their colonial enslaved African populations. Only in 1839, a year after slavery was finally abolished in the British Empire (apprenticeship should still be considered a phase of slavery), did Rome, with Pope Gregory XVI's *In Supremo Apostolatus*, actually condemn it and forbid "any Ecclesiastic or lay person from presuming to defend as permissible this traffic in Blacks."[127]

While some of the Spanish colonies gave the impression of a tradition of converting enslaved people to Catholicism and of permitting manumission, at local levels it was more complicated and often not what was actually happening.[128] Slavery increased dramatically in Spanish territories during the nineteenth century as efforts to maximize sugar profits accelerated. Richard Robert Madden, an Irish Catholic anti-slavery activist who served as stipendiary magistrate in Jamaica during its transition from enslavement to apprenticeship, confirmed this. Madden, who had also worked as commissioner for liberated Africans in Cuba and as special commissioner of inquiry into the administrations of the British settlements on the west coast of Africa, observed that the spiritual welfare of the enslaved was of little concern to the planters who continued to deliver "brutal discipline."[129]

In addition to the French and Spanish, Irish Catholics had also had an extended presence in the Caribbean, and many of their communities in Montserrat and Barbados predated Britain's union with Ireland by over 150 years. Nini Rodgers, Hilary Beckles, and others have catalogued Catholic Ireland's long and varied history with the Caribbean and a variety of European powers such as the French, Spanish, and Dutch. They point out that, while many were there as indentured servants, free labourers, and plantation owners, there were also surgeons, missionaries, traders, innkeepers, and a host of other occupations.[130] In Ireland itself, many more were connected to the plantation economy through the provisioning trade of salted beef, butter, pork, and coarse linen, and by their work as deck hands, sailors, and even as slave-ship captains.[131] French, Dutch, and Spanish plantations facilitated the re-establishment and growth of an Irish Catholic merchant class, who, despite being officially excluded from England's and, after 1707, Britain's colonies, found ways of building successful networks along the coasts of western Europe.[132] The *Code Noir*, introduced in 1685 by the French government to give instruction on how enslaved people were to be treated, including directions for their baptisms, education, and food provision, enabled Irish merchants to construct deeper and more robust links with France's Caribbean.[133] Irish salt beef became an important commodity and a growing number of the merchants providing it were Catholic. In Brittany, Irish salt beef dominated the export trade to the West Indies.[134] The French were important early customers, but, by the 1680s, the Irish were responsible for exporting over half of the food to the British West Indies, and they continued to supply this market throughout the eighteenth century.[135]

Caribbean products such as sugar, cotton, rum, and salt were major profit-spinners for British planters and merchants, but the economies of the northern Atlantic colonies depended on being able to exchange these products for timber and salt fish. Sugar dominated the West Indian trade, but salt and the brutal business of harvesting it underpinned the entire northern cod fishery, which not only fed populations in the Caribbean but also reached deep into the heart of Catholic Europe.[136] An awareness of these and other economies inspired many Irish to look beyond their own island for ways of building more expansive networks that would allow them to exploit these and other colonial economic systems that the Royal Navy and the British Army were charged with defending.[137] The British Caribbean's pervasive and pre-existing Catholic history had a profound influence on how London and Rome approached Catholicism in the region. While Britain introduced legislation aimed at increasing toleration, provided financial support for chaplains and church building, and attempted to appoint colonial governors capable of working with Catholics, the Holy See directed missionaries to the colonies with large Catholic populations and installed vicars apostolic to manage evolving and expanding church structures.

Although the relationship between London and Rome had been evolving since the late eighteenth century, a more recognizable alliance between the two could be felt in the Caribbean between the late 1810s and the late 1840s. We see clear evidence of this in a letter to the rector of Lisbon's English College, Edmund Winstanley, wherein William Fryer, a London-based priest with old ties to the college, noted that the establishment of the vicariate apostolic of the West Indies was "a new thing, in which the Pope & this government are both united."[138] A colony's economic and defensive value influenced how London and Rome approached it, but an important concern for both was leadership. As will be seen in the final chapter, the desire to install a British ethos played a major role in shaping the communications that passed between British colonial officials and those of the Sacred Congregation *de Propaganda Fide* surrounding potential candidates for senior clerical positions in British territories. In 1781, Rome had given Richard Talbot, vicar apostolic of the London District, responsibility for Catholics in Britain's Caribbean and North American colonies.[139] Trinidad was a comparatively recent acquisition when placed alongside Britain's other Catholic colonies, but it became the focal point for Catholicism in the British Caribbean because of the sheer size of its Catholic population, which included enslaved people, free people of colour, French, Spanish, and Irish.[140] In 1817, the Holy See placed responsibility for Catholics in Jamaica, St. Christopher, Montserrat, Antigua, Grenada, Barbados, Tobago, Trinidad, and other islands with the vicar apostolic of the West Indies based in Port of Spain.[141] This arrangement remained in place until 1850, when Rome established the archdiocese of the Port of Spain as a way of consolidating ecclesiastical responsibility for the entire region.[142]

In a manner similar to Quebec, colonial officials sought to provide an atmosphere of relative religious accommodation on Trinidad.[143] The management of Catholics there differed markedly from other territories like Bermuda and Newfoundland, and a major factor was that the vast majority of its Catholics were civilian, non-British, and non-white. Another factor was that there had been no British institutions there before the Treaty of Amiens in 1803.[144] The clear preference in Trinidad for English or English-born clergy to lead its Catholic community, which will be discussed in chapter 6, was in stark contrast to the above colonies, where clerical leads were Scottish, French, or Irish. The challenge facing colonial administrators and the bishops of the London District was in finding English priests willing to take on a mission like Trinidad, which was at a significant distance from Britain and notorious for its difficult climate, chronic lack of resources, and range of deadly tropical diseases.[145]

Chapter Five

Enabling Ambition through Education

The emergence of teaching and the religious life for women and medicine for men as bona fide professions afforded young middle-class Catholics the opportunity to acquire the professional acumen and qualifications that enabled them to move, with relative ease, throughout the empire and become active partners in its development. As time went on, neither profession would end up being the exclusive preserve of one sex, but in the period considered here, there was a clear divide.[1] One of the most important consequences of the colonial enterprise was Catholic participation in shaping the character and values of new settlements.[2]

Following the Catholic emancipation legislation of 1829, an emphasis for church leaders and lay Catholics alike was on improving the socio-economic lot of Catholics and on expanding the Catholic middle class in ways that linked it more effectively with civil society, which helped the church provide more support to the state in controlling rapidly expanding Catholic populations at home and abroad.[3] Education was critical to both goals. The energy invested by a growing cadre of religious personnel over the nineteenth century to ensure that Catholics would eventually have access to the whole range of educational opportunities – from infant and parish schools, Sunday schools, and boarding schools to seminaries, teacher-training colleges, and universities – was significant. In addition to preventing conversions to Protestantism, it helped create a cohesive and devout community. The effects were numerous: it enhanced the reputation of the Catholic Church in the eyes of the state, addressed the ambitions of the new moneyed elite, served an aristocracy slowly waking up to a new era, and satisfied an energetic convert class that was used to having significant power and influence.

The fact that the British state was increasingly interested in consolidating its authority over education made all this feasible, but it was in Ireland, where education became a preoccupation of both government and the church, that change was most noticeable. That nation saw significant developments from 1829, including the establishment of the National Education Board for Ireland in 1831, but calls for a national and united education system had actually started a decade earlier.[4] These developments contrasted sharply with what was happening across the Irish Sea: state efforts to gain incremental control over elementary education were confined to grants until education boards comparable to Ireland's emerged in England and Wales in 1870 and in Scotland in 1872. Ireland was the nation with the Catholic majority, and the desire to organize education there stemmed from the need to "accommodate the educational aspirations of the emerging catholic nation, while also cementing it to the legislative union comprising the interests of presbyterians and anglicans."[5] Education policy for Ireland, however, was a two-way street: it was as much a reflection of the state's desire to subvert Catholic influence as it was a confirmation of a desire by the church and an upwardly mobile laity to be recognized as loyal subjects and citizens. The new Catholic educational dawn that broke first in England with elite education was followed closely by a middle-class charge in Ireland.[6]

The shaping of Catholic educational ambition became a transnational enterprise very quickly, as rapidly expanding armies of religious personnel took responsibility for delivering the bulk of Catholic teaching at home and abroad. The foundation established by the Continental colleges of the sixteenth, seventeenth, and eighteenth centuries supported an expanding of college and university provisions that catered to young men eager for careers in the empire. Having started out as seminaries to grow a "local" priesthood, they evolved in ways that satisfied the needs of an increasingly ambitious middle class. What needs unpacking is how the transition to a broad-based education system happened, when, prior to the nineteenth century, the only Catholics with any access to schooling were the elites, and most of them had beaten a path to the Continent to circumvent the penal laws that excluded them at home. This normalized pattern of "strategic educational migration" defined the patrician Catholic experience, but extending it beyond that class was a massive undertaking.[7] Confronting the stigma associated with a poorly educated population and overcoming the inherent lack of confidence that such a culture of intellectual darkness had enshrined were significant challenges. Yet France's revolution had sparked a new era for the Catholic Church, and the changes were especially profound in the realm of education.

Since elementary schooling, which was extremely important to Catholic aspirations and community consolidation, already has been much studied, the focus here is on higher education and training provision for the growing Catholic middle class – specifically, the training of those poised to implement the elementary school system or to use it to advance their own professional development. This discussion reflects the gendered nature of nineteenth-century education, where education and training of women and men was structured according to sex. The first section of this chapter discusses how the dramatic anticlerical shift that occurred in France during the last decade of the eighteenth century led to the reintroduction of Catholic religious life in Britain and prompted the emergence of a domestic culture of Catholic education. Next, I examine the professionalization of young women, linking the rise of female religious congregations with the new opportunities for religious and teacher training that offered a safe space for women whose futures did not include marriage and/or motherhood. The teaching congregations highlighted were either the first or among the first to arrive in a particular mission and by no means represent an exhaustive list. The unique learning environment that these international congregations created shaped the aspirations of their students, many of whom would go on to direct further educational development in Britain and the colonies. Finally, the importance of university education to the aspirations of young men is considered, highlighting the medical training offered at the Queen's University in Ireland to those keen to carve out professional careers abroad.

The Beginning of a Culture Shift

The French Revolution and the violent events of 1793, which saw religious personnel and the religious life openly attacked in France, were the early catalysts of a broad Catholic culture shift that would be felt across Britain. The persistent rise of Catholic migration from Ireland to mainland Britain following the 1801 Act of Union augmented this shift. The catastrophic events in France shook the tired, comfortable, and somewhat complacent old Scottish and English Catholics from insularity and catapulted many into immediate action. The indiscriminate sacking of convents and monasteries in 1793, the theft of enormous sums of money that had been funnelled to France for safekeeping, and the destruction of irreplaceable religious archives had shocked the old elites, who feared a more widespread breakdown of the social hierarchy. This dramatic anti-clerical pivot, which saw more than 4,500 Catholic refugees from France arrive in Britain in 1794, prompted a flurry of humanitarianism, as Britons from all sects leapt to their defence, providing shelter, aid, and money. Another shock came in 1798, when a

French invasion of Rome forced the pope into exile. The consequences of these events were dramatic for Catholicism's profile in the United Kingdom. Not only had the British public come to see French Catholics as victims of tyranny and as people in desperate need of support, but their presence prompted the reintroduction of Catholic education in Britain. Almost overnight, Catholic Britons stopped sending their children to the Continent for schooling and instead started sending them to the schools set up by the French *émigré* and returning British and Irish religious. From the early nineteenth century, the religious life expanded rapidly in Britain as growing student bodies led to new vocations, with women, in particular, embracing the new opportunities.

The progress of Catholic education in Britain was determined by the number of religious communities springing up, with the bulk being born out of Irish, French, or Belgian congregations. Until the 1840s, the main beneficiaries were the children of the elites, but, after this point, much more emphasis was placed on the schooling of poorer children throughout the United Kingdom and the overseas colonies.[8] While many communities of religious personnel (female and male) and the secular clergy established new mission or parish schools, Sunday schools, and boarding schools, others founded seminaries, colleges, and universities. The rapid expansion of the Catholic diaspora called for new strategies to deal with constant requests for colonial missionaries who could not only run missions but also establish schools, seminaries, convents, and colleges. Just like the other Christian churches, the Catholic Church struggled to provide the human and financial resources needed for the colonial missions, but women religious, particularly those from Ireland and France, gave it a distinct advantage.[9] Quite simply, the women who entered religious life became an army whose vows of poverty, chastity, and obedience made them an exceptional, motivated, and highly exploitable resource. Male congregations, such as the Jesuits, the Marist Brothers, the Christian Brothers, and the Benedictines, also made valuable contributions to the church's educational mission, but their numbers paled in comparison to their female colleagues.

Inspiration came from mainland Europe. French women religious saw education as a way of "re-Christianizing" a society recovering from the mass upheaval of the revolution. Such perceptions stirred women across the United Kingdom to engage with teaching as a profession, and the only way that many could do this in the early years was to enter the religious life.[10] Women religious, who were unaffected (directly) by marriage and motherhood, became the primary architects of Catholic education.[11] They became teachers, teacher-trainers, administrators, managers, and policy makers, and their influence and presence extended across Britain, Ireland, and the empire in places like Canada, Australia, Jamaica, and India.[12] Their influence was profound, as they had the responsibility for training waves of lay women, whose presence in classrooms became ubiquitous by the end of the nineteenth century.

How women religious got to the point of having a monopoly over Catholic female education is remarkable, given the circumstances. Although the relief legislation that passed for Catholics in 1791 removed restrictions to education, their exclusion had inhibited the intellectual development of the wider Catholic community. Moreover, the slow emergence of Catholic education in England and Scotland prior to 1850 meant that developments thereafter aligned with or followed what was happening in the colonies. The only significant difference was related to elite education. In that realm, Britain and Ireland's advantage was that fewer elites – those "highly integrated into the governing structure ... as landlords, professionals, businessmen, county officers, civil servants, or members of religious orders" – emigrated, because they did not need to.[13]

Catholic boarding schools, such as those run by the Sisters of the Congregation of Notre-Dame, had been operating in Quebec since the middle of the seventeenth century. They were the first "canonically erected order of 'active' sisters in the French world," and their founder, Marguerite Bourgeoys, had been an extremely powerful force in the development of Catholicism in the French colony. Yet colonial officials in the adjacent colonies were uncomfortable with the prospect of any extension of this culture beyond Quebec.[14] Halifax's vicar apostolic, Edmund Burke, had his 1802 proposal to establish a boy's college flatly refused by Nova Scotia's lieutenant governor, Sir John Wentworth, who was a staunch proponent of the "civilizing" influences of Anglicanism and distrustful of a Catholic priesthood.[15] This position was untenable by the 1820s, but it was only after mid-century that the Catholic elite population of British North America was sufficient enough to support their own schools. Prior to this time, parents with means sent their children, both male and female, to England or Scotland. Records for Scotland's convent boarding schools reveal that a number of their students and postulants had been sent there from various colonies. Edinburgh's St Margaret's Convent School, which was run by the ultra-elite Ursulines of Jesus, had students from the West Indies, India, Ceylon, Australia, and even from regions beyond Britain's control such as the United States and South America, in addition to those from the home nations.[16]

The most prestigious Catholic schools were in England. These included Stonyhurst (Jesuit) and Oscott College (secular) for young men and the Bar Convent at York (Institute of the Blessed Virgin Mary) and New Hall in Essex (Canonesses of the Holy Sepulchre) for young

Figure 10. Marguerite Bourgeoys (photograph by S. Karly Kehoe)

women. Originally founded in France in 1593 to provide a Catholic education for English recusants, Stonyhurst was re-established in Lancashire, England, in 1794, following the Jesuits' departure from France. Oscott College, on the other hand, while having been established by English Catholic gentry with "Cisalpine leanings," who wanted to keep episcopal control to an absolute minimum, ended up being jointly managed by the gentry and the local bishops.[17] While the majority of the most affluent families in Ireland sent their children to schools in England, there were also some elite institutions in Ireland, with Clongowes and Tullabeg being considered the most prestigious. Both were Jesuit schools for young men and the "products both of Jesuit tradition *and* the marketplace of their time."[18] These Irish institutions were seen as progressive, intuitive, and socially networked, which suited those families who "shared many of the racial and cultural assumptions of the European upper classes and whose experiences placed them squarely within the interlinked processes of defining the empire at home and abroad."[19] In many ways, these Irish schools replicated the English public schools in providing students with an exclusive education that connected them, through social, sporting, and religious networks, with the empire. As will be shown below, the situation was somewhat different for girls and young women.

The Role of Female Religious Congregations

Although there were communities that catered exclusively to the daughters of the elites, the majority of teaching communities had rules and constitutions requiring both convent boarding schools and parish schools. Under this two-tiered system, the tuition fees they earned from the former enabled them to run the schools that served girls and young women from labouring backgrounds. The first wave of Catholic education for girls in the United Kingdom focused exclusively on elite education, although this changed as the number of women religious grew and their ability to assume a greater share of the responsibility for mission schools increased. Like Stonyhurst, New Hall had been established in England in 1799 by religious who had fled France. By contrast, York's Bar Convent, which was run by the Institute of the Blessed Virgin Mary, was home-grown, dating back to 1686. Taking responsibility for the "spiritual and devotional training of young women," the school boarded a number of girls from Catholic elite families, mostly from the north of England, but also from London, Ireland, and Scotland. Scottish pupils began attending the school in 1741. From then until 1886, at least sixty-five Scottish-born pupils were enrolled, in addition to the

ten "Spanish Gordons," who were young women of Scottish Catholic descent in Spain.[20] The school had also been favoured by Ireland's
wealthy Catholics since the early eighteenth century.[21]

York emerged as an educational hub for Catholic women and provided both boarding and day schools. The influence of the Bar Convent
on the lives of its students was formative, but it was also central to the
growth of Catholicism in the United Kingdom and the British Empire
more broadly, since a number of its pupils stayed on and became nuns
themselves.[22] The school also emerged as an important focal point for
the wider patrician Catholic community, which had no other meeting
place, and placed the nuns at the centre of a British Catholic world – a
position that afforded them significant autonomy and authority.[23] While
offering a relatively local option for Catholic schooling, it also trained
the next generation of women religious and congregational founders,
such as Mary Aikenhead, who started the Irish Sisters of Charity in
1815, and Frances (Teresa) Ball, who established the Loretos in Ireland
in 1821. Both had gone to York from Ireland for their novitiate, with
the plan of founding new congregations back in Ireland. Each had a
mammoth influence over the development of Catholic education and
social welfare at home, throughout Britain's colonies, and across the
wider world. The establishment of these new congregations was only
the beginning – a plethora of new foundations soon spread from one
end of the empire to the other.

By the beginning of the nineteenth century, twenty-four convents
had been founded in England, with the majority (eighteen) set up
during the tumultuous years of 1794 and 1795 by orders that had fled
Belgium and France.[24] The influence of France was profound – not
only had French women religious come to Britain and established the
convents and boarding schools that would help establish the roots of
a more refined culture of female Catholicity, but a significant proportion of Britain and Ireland's first generation of local women religious
were trained by these French sisters. That the convents offered a unique
form of higher education for women is important, but they also marked
the beginning of a "new phase" for the religious life. Congregational
growth was so rapid that, by 1900, eighty congregations (and thirteen
orders) were operating in England and Wales, with the majority (56 per
cent) being in London and the Midlands.[25] It was a similar situation in
Scotland, with two of its most influential teaching congregations, the
Ursulines of Jesus and the Franciscan Sisters of the Immaculate Conception, coming from France. The Franciscan Sisters, who were established in Glasgow in 1847 by two French nuns, founded twelve more
communities in Scotland during the nineteenth century, as well as one

in Ireland, one in Jamaica, and another in England (the latter two eventually became independent congregations). They later established additional communities in Nigeria, Kenya, and the United States.[26] While the deep links between Scotland and Jamaica are receiving increased attention on account of the Scots' extensive involvement with slavery, the educational links, such as those forged by the Franciscan Sisters, need more research. It was relatively common for the children (white and mixed-race) of Scottish planters and merchants (and English and Irish ones as well) in Jamaica to be sent "home" for schooling at one of the academies or boarding schools. Although very common during the eighteenth century, it was a tradition that continued after the abolition of slavery.[27]

This movement for education of Catholic girls connected with the broader educational program pushed by a growing Catholic middle class intent on building upon the foundation that emancipation provided. The migration of Catholic daughters and sons to the religious life enabled them to guide the development of a system of transnational Catholic education that eventually extended to all classes and touched every corner of Britain's expanding empire. The marked expansion of the religious life among women coincided with efforts by Rome to extend the reach of Catholic education. The emergence of education as a policy area for church officials put significant pressure on the bishops, as it fell to them to implement and deliver new systems. Many were completely unprepared for the enormity of the task and would have failed had it not been for their female colleagues – a fact often overlooked in the history of the Catholic Church. In the colonies, the nature of civil society as a work in progress, at least until the last quarter of the nineteenth century, meant that a Catholic education system encompassing all levels, from elementary to university, extended the authority of the church and the British government simultaneously.

In those colonies that would eventually make up Canada, the religious personnel, female and male, charged with extending education became active imperial agents. The Institute of the Blessed Virgin Mary (the Lorettos), which was founded in Toronto in 1847 by sisters from Ireland's Rathfarnham convent, had an enormous influence over Catholic education in that city.[28] In the Caribbean colonies, Catholic priests and sisters laboured alongside other missionaries from the Presbyterian, Anglican, Wesleyan, and Moravian churches to transform the children of former enslaved people into loyal subjects. As early as 1836, the Sisters of St. Joseph of Cluny, a French congregation highlighted in the following chapter, were operating a convent school at Port of Spain in Trinidad that was aimed specifically at the daughters of the upper middle class. According to a Colonial Office report, the school "was organized upon a plan of superior boarding schools in the mother country. From the high character of the ladies conducting the female institution, it appears to have gained the confidence of that class of colonists for whose benefit it was more particularly intended."[29]

Following the Catholic emancipation legislation of 1829, a more complete system of Catholic education, one that went from the primary level right through to university, was devised and prioritized by Britain and Ireland's Catholic leadership. The result was a relatively comprehensive system that included middle-class boarding schools, infant and parish schools, seminaries, colleges, and universities, all of which promoted a common educational agenda across a range of students. The organizational structure of the religious congregations made the development of this system possible, since sisters, nuns, and brothers in one region were intimately connected by shared vows, a common congregational ethos, and Rome-approved rules, to members of the same congregation in another. This meant that a school run by the Sisters of Charity in Scotland would be recognizable to a pupil from a Sisters of Charity school in Nova Scotia, Ireland, or Australia. The transnational quality of societies, congregations, and mixed orders such as the Jesuits, the Sisters of Mercy, the Marist Brothers, the Sulpicians, the Loretos, the Sisters of the Sacred Heart, the Vincentian Fathers, the Franciscan Sisters of the Immaculate Conception, the Ursulines of Jesus, the Brothers of the Christian Schools, the Sisters of St. Joseph, the Sisters of Notre Dame, and many, many more, ensured a shared Catholic educational experience for pupils throughout the United Kingdom and the empire.[30]

This list includes both female and male congregations, but it was the influence of women that really took off. They dominated the educational and social welfare arena because of a few specific factors. First, the majority of the pioneer congregations in Britain and Ireland focused on teaching, and this inspired many of the pupils under their instruction to join them. This growth in personnel allowed for the expansion of both domestic and colonial missions. Second, local priests, who were desperate to corral their growing congregations in an effort to fend off Protestant proselytizers and to achieve some semblance of control over ballooning populations, focused their attention on recruiting from teaching congregations. It was only once schools were established that parish priests and bishops began recruiting sisters with other specialisms, such as nursing, caring for the poor, caring for the elderly, and palliative care.[31] The paucity of communities during a mission's pioneering years saw teaching sisters also undertake nursing alongside other works of charity to alleviate suffering during periods of acute

distress. That they possessed spiritual authority was comforting to people.[32] Third, the religious life was one of the few career paths open to
women, and it appealed to those who had a religious vocation or who
wanted to avoid marriage and/or motherhood.

The training that women religious received exceeded by far what
lay women could expect, at least until the late 1850s, when training
colleges, such as that run by the Sisters of Notre Dame de Namur in
Liverpool, started to open. At a time when women were formally excluded from the institutions of higher education, teaching communities
offered women an extended connection to a culture of education that
was otherwise off limits. The fact that Catholic women could choose
the religious life, either as choir sisters or, if they lacked a dowry, as
lay sisters, and embrace a spiritual mission instead of marriage and
motherhood gave them a distinct professional advantage over lay and
non-Catholic women. Unlike governesses, for example, where training
was associated with "an acquired skill rather than with intellectual"
development, women religious (choir sisters) could access some semblance of an intellectual life. And while there was significant pressure
on middle- and upper-class women to demonstrate their accomplish-
ments rather than their intellectual capacity, women religious could,
and did, demonstrate both.[33]

The transnational character of religious communities, their profes-
sionalism, and their cost-effectiveness meant that their value was virtually incalculable to an expanding world church whose missions had
limited financial resources.[34] Their influence was further enhanced by
a willingness of religious personnel to go where lay women and men
either could not or would not go: urban settings, where poverty and
deadly diseases, such as cholera and typhus raged, and colonial frontiers, where harsh weather, untamed landscapes, warfare, and a lack of
basic necessities threatened daily existence. Religious personnel were
put on the front lines and paid a high the price for their service. In Toronto, for example, when the pioneering sisters of the Institute of the
Blessed Virgin Mary arrived in the late 1840s, they had not been properly informed about what to expect in terms of weather conditions and
so arrived without winter clothing. Sister Mary Gertrude Fleming, a
native of Dublin, underwent a leg amputation due to gangrene from
severe frostbite before dying at the age of twenty-nine; many others
suffered from serious illness, such as typhus and tuberculosis, which
often led to desertions from the religious life and to death.[35] Tropical
climates were equally dangerous: in 1838, for example, the Port of Spain
convent of the Sisters of St. Joseph of Cluny was temporarily closed due
to an outbreak of yellow fever.[36] In Jamaica, the Franciscan Sisters of

the Immaculate Conception and the Sisters of Mercy also experienced a range of diseases. Although Mother Veronica Cordier, the Franciscan founder, survived a deadly typhus outbreak in Glasgow, she suffered in the Caribbean. Not long after making a foundation in Jamaica, she was forced to return to France because of blood poisoning.[37] The outbreak of typhoid among the Sisters of Mercy just three months after their arrival in Jamaica, caused by poor sanitation, almost ended their mission when it claimed the life of the community's founder, Mother Winifred Furlong. Tuberculosis and fevers were extremely common and often deadly. Many of the pioneering sisters were grossly unprepared for the conditions in the colonial missions.[38] As a consequence some fell out with the priests who, in their desperate search for sisters, recruited them under false pretences. There was no love lost between Furlong and the priest who brought the congregation to Jamaica: "The foundation was sent out too quickly – Father Chandlery was a great cheat. His first letter was false from beginning to end. He knew nothing of what he was writing. My indignation rises when I think of him. I may just add here we have not yet been able to have anything like Community life."[39]

In some colonies, language was also an issue for teaching sisters. The annals of the Mercy community in Jamaica provide a rather humorous description of the first few days of school for the newly arrived sisters. Apart from finding their thick black habits absolutely suffocating in the extreme heat, the sisters struggled to communicate with their pupils, who had developed their own coping strategy:

> Teacher and scholar seemed to be at cross purposes, for neither understood the other's language or ways. The major portion of the pupils solved the problem – at least to their own satisfaction by rising superior to any grasping desire for knowledge. While a few struggled to master the intricate elements of the English language, the greater number calmly steered out of the strong sea of learning and anchored into the haven of sleep.[40]

Yet, in spite of the risks sisters undoubtedly took, their decision to dedicate their lives to the mission of their congregations enabled them to emerge as the church's most effective means of consolidating Catholic communities across the empire. They shared in Britain's broader "civilizing" Christian mission and became an extremely powerful force in the process.

As noted above, when a new community arrived at a mission, the pattern was to set up a convent boarding school and a mission school as soon as possible. The Congregation de Notre Dame (CND), renown for teaching excellence, had made a foundation in Montreal in the seventeenth century and then went on to found a number of other North American communities. After a couple of attempts in the eighteenth century to establish a solid foundation at Louisbourg on Cape Breton Island failed due to tensions and war between Britain and France, the sisters finally succeeded in Arichat, Cape Breton, in 1856.[41] When the sisters arrived in this prominent fishing and trading port, which had been the centre of Catholic power in the Maritimes from the 1760s until the official rise of Halifax a century later, they set up a convent boarding school and a parish school almost immediately. The curriculum of the boarding school looked very similar to what was offered at other CND schools in Britain; it included French and English, writing, arithmetic, bookkeeping, algebra, geometry, geography, ancient history, rhetoric, botany, philosophy, chemistry, music, drawing, painting, and needlework.[42] The option of bookkeeping, in a village dominated by Irish Catholic trading merchants, indicates female involvement in the management of family businesses. Provision was more limited in the parish schools, with little offered beyond the three Rs. The CND mission in Arichat had been so successful that the sisters expanded to West Arichat (1863), Pictou (1880), and Antigonish (1883).[43] While West Arichat was a comparatively poor village and could support the community only until 1894 (when it merged with neighbouring Arichat), the sisters in Antigonish were immensely successful and founded Mount Saint Bernard College in 1886. This college was incorporated into St. Francis Xavier University in 1894 and became the first Catholic college in North America to award degrees to women.[44]

The foundation of communities like CND benefited from local support. Peter Smyth, the wealthy but unpopular Cape Breton merchant and landowner who was mentioned at the end of chapter 3, left $18,000 to the Catholic Church in his will, and while $4,000 was for the completion of the chapel at Port Hood, a significant amount was earmarked for education. In addition to leaving $1,000 to support aging priests and another $1,000 to clear some of the debt of Antigonish's St. Ninian's Cathedral, he bequeathed $4,000 for a Catholic boys' school, $4,000 for a Catholic girls' school run by women religious, and $4,000 to the college of St. Francis Xavier.[45] The sisters at Mount Saint Bernard benefited from his generosity, as did their pupils and trainees.

In addition to being a testament to Catholic female intellectual ambition, Mount Saint Bernard College also represented the growing "compartmentalization" of professions within the religious life.[46] As the number of religious communities multiplied, their skills specialized, and communities began to focus on one level of education, such as elementary or secondary education, higher education, and teacher training.

Teacher training emerged within convents before colleges formally opened. Many women religious received their "theoretical and practical on-the-job training" from experienced religious.[47] Gradually, as congregations became more established, training took place in religious-run colleges and, to a limited extent, universities. It was from this point that lay women were incorporated into the education system.[48] The Sisters of Notre Dame de Namur, which prioritized teacher training, had been founded in France in 1804 by Julie Billiart and Françoise Blin de Bourdon. It opened its Liverpool college in 1856. Sister Mary of St. Francis, the daughter of Lord Stafford, entered the Liverpool community after the death of her husband and used her significant wealth to fund the college's establishment.[49] In 1894, the congregation opened a teacher-training college in Scotland, at Glasgow's Dowanhill, and by 1903 the first batch of students enrolled at the University of Glasgow, reflecting the evolving relationship between the college and the university.

The growing provision of, and access to, university classes stemmed from the changing needs of Catholic women. Middle- and upper-class Catholic families were acutely aware of what their daughters needed to prosper in a rapidly changing world. Parents pushed for more practical subjects that would give them more opportunities at home and abroad. A single-sex environment remained the preferred option, but new subjects, such as bookkeeping, were introduced more widely to help them keep pace with economic changes. In England, for example, the focus of female education had been on religion and refinement until parents started to demand that their daughters be prepared for the local examinations for Oxford and Cambridge. The Sisters of Notre Dame de Namur responded by adding advanced science, shorthand, typing, art, music, and French to their curriculum.[50] University of Glasgow graduates acquired degrees in philosophy, logic, English, natural philosophy, political economy, geology, mathematics, and chemistry.[51] Others went on to become women religious themselves, either within the Notre Dame de Namur congregation or with one of the many others that had sprung up.[52]

It is estimated that, between 1800 and 1880, some four hundred congregations, comprising around 200,000 women, were founded in France in an attempt to "re-Christianize French culture and society."[53] Aside from those who fled to Britain in the 1790s, there were many more who migrated to communities in Britain's colonies. Religious congregations were not restricted by national boundaries, and sisters went or were sent where they were needed. Internally, however, national identities were strong, and understanding these influences is imperative when assessing the congregations' ability to extend Britain's imperial influence. Thus, although many communities had obvious French roots and were shaped by them, the infusion of sisters from the four nations ensured the transmission of Britain and Ireland's cultural authority.[54]

Ethnic tensions within communities were extremely common. It was often the case that sisters from one group or tradition closed ranks to ensure the promotion of a particular ethos and identity to the students, postulants, and novices under their direction.[55] The rising number of British and Irish women religious at home and abroad transformed the communities they joined into indispensable tools of imperialism that consolidated Catholic communities and gave women the authority to inform and direct educational and, as a consequence, social development.

Higher Education in Ireland and the Empire

The importance of Irish universities cannot be underestimated when examining the role of Catholics in the development of the British Empire. Not only were these institutions intrinsic to imperial management, providing a significant proportion of "the intellectual capital needed to consolidate and govern such diverse territories," but they also prepared the personnel needed for the creation of a transnational body of Irish Catholic professionals.[56] Attending university and obtaining the requisite diplomas and degrees enabled young Catholic men to access a range of professions that had traditionally been largely, if not entirely, out of reach. In becoming physicians and surgeons, lawyers, engineers, civil servants, and officers in the armed services, Catholics engaged more directly with middle-class British citizenship on multiple levels. All of these professions helped build a broader sense of Catholic achievement and established pathways to social acceptance as Britons, but it was medicine that stood out as particularly influential.

During the nineteenth century, the ranks of most professions in the United Kingdom were filled largely by non-Catholics. This is not too surprising, given the educational restrictions imposed on Catholics during the penal era and the lingering psychological effects of such exclusion even after 1829. While efforts were underway to expand elementary and secondary schooling provision for girls by training women as teachers and as members of transnational religious congregations, Catholic men were seeking access to higher education. As confidence in their ability to participate more directly in mainstream society increased, their desire to attend college and university grew. Higher education became an increasingly popular route to both respectability and a professional career for Catholic middle-class men. In Ireland, this trend was particularly noticeable: despite an overall population decline of 21 per cent between 1851 and 1881, student numbers at Irish universities grew by

23 per cent.[57] Medicine had always been a popular choice, with many young men travelling to Scotland for training – between 1776 and 1825, just under one-third of students (958 of 3,194), who received medical degrees from the Universities of Edinburgh and Glasgow were Irish.[58] While it is unlikely that many were Catholic, some were: we know this thanks to a letter found in the papers of Lisbon College, which explains that sons of Scottish and English Catholics elites went to Paris for medical training in the late eighteenth century because they preferred it to Edinburgh for surgical training and midwifery.[59] As noted in the previous chapter, Irish doctors began to flood the armed services after mid-century; the civil service witnessed similar growth, as a plethora of young Irish engineers and junior colonial administrators sought admission. Whether they knew it or not, the Catholics among them were advancing the rebranding of Catholicism as an essential component of British imperialism.

Irish Catholic elites tended to send their sons to university in England, Scotland, or, if they remained in Ireland, to Trinity College. While these young men tended to avoid careers in medicine and the foreign and domestic civil service, their middle-class counterparts did not.[60] The expansion of domestic higher education provision from the mid-1840s was fuelled by a rush from the latter group in Ireland. Medical schools were extremely popular and proved a rich source of doctors for the military. The Irish represented over 50 per cent of all army surgeons in 1858 and, while a precise denominational breakdown is not known, if figures for the Royal Navy are anything to go by, an increasing number of surgeons would have been Catholic.[61] Catholic doctors had comparatively fewer job prospects at home than their Protestant counterparts and so took opportunities where they could find them. Obtaining a medical degree was pragmatic because it offered Catholics financial security, independence, and respectability. Beyond these things, though, was a recognition of the fact that medicine was a profession that created a space for social mobility and movement into the social circles that had previously been off-limits. Its reputation as a profession "free of many residual sanctions against Catholics" that were still widespread elsewhere made it a particularly attractive choice.[62]

In the late 1840s, the opening of the Queen's Colleges in Cork, Galway, and Belfast, which together formed the Queen's University, got the ball rolling for Catholic medics. Modelled on the English red brick universities, these colleges were intended to stimulate the "improvement" of Ireland's social condition by expanding its middle class through the delivery of a non-sectarian and "more vocational" training.[63] This emphasis was noted in the annual president's report: "The collegiate scheme established by your Majesty has solved the problem of combining the various denominations for mental culture, without interference with religious convictions, and of providing, at the same time, for the young man, if under age, that spiritual instruction of which his parents approve, or, if above age, which his own choice and position may dictate."[64]

Practical education in Ireland had actually started at Trinity College, when a chair in civil engineering was established in 1841, but its pioneering efforts were soon followed and expanded upon by the Queen's University, which offered modern languages, pure and applied sciences, and, perhaps most significantly for Catholics, medicine.[65] Adequate facilities took time to develop. In Belfast, for example, students had access to an anatomical museum to supplement lectures, but space was cramped, and students complained about the mile they had to walk between the museum and the dissecting room before a purpose-built facility was constructed on college grounds in 1863.[66] In spite of growing pains, the opening of these colleges was a major turning point for Catholic aspirations. The prospect of professional recognition appealed to the increasingly ambitious and pragmatic Catholic middle class, eager to secure careers in the empire. The results were obvious: by 1860, Catholics represented approximately 51 per cent of the student bodies at Galway and Cork; the number was lower in Belfast, which reflected Ulster's Protestant-dominated population and small Catholic middle class.

As entry qualifications for the armed services evolved to meet the growing need for trained professionals, the number of Catholic surgeons serving as civilian officers (surgeons were civilian rather than military officers) increased dramatically. By 1900, some 124 of the 892 surgeons who had served or were serving in the navy had received their diplomas from the Royal College of Surgeons in Ireland, but this figure underestimates the total number of Irish, since those Irishmen who had received their diplomas outside of Ireland were not included in the count.[67] Economic considerations were an obvious motivator in serving as surgeons in the armed services, but so was loyalty to the Crown and to the empire. Many Irish, like many Scots, English, and Welsh, saw their relationship with the empire in practical terms – as exciting, necessary, and potentially deeply transformative for themselves and their families. The introduction of exams for admission to the Indian Civil Service (1854) and the army, naval, and Indian Medical Service (1857) opened up a whole new world to those who, on account of their religion or socio-economic background, lacked many of the connections normally required for entry into these fields.[68]

While Catholics from across the United Kingdom focused their attention on these services, the most noticeable impact was on the prospects

of those from Ireland. Not only was the number of Irish Catholics working in various services across the empire greater than that of Scots and
English combined, but Ireland's late entry into the parliamentary union
meant that the socio-economic needs of its people were more acute. The
growing importance of the imperial services repositioned the authority
of the universities and enabled them to assume responsibility for training that emphasized the importance of practical education to a maturing empire. It was a responsibility that the universities took seriously:
engaging with Britain's broader imperial agenda, which included the
"taming" of Ireland, was perceived as a duty. Such sentiments were expressed in various president's reports, and the 1864 report for Queen's
College Belfast stated confidently its desire to become one of the best
in the empire.[69]

During the second half of the nineteenth century, young men were
spoiled for choice. Those wishing to build careers outside of the priesthood had the option of Queen's University and Trinity, whereas those
keen to train as priests had Maynooth or, after 1842, All Hallows,
though the latter was criticized as having "little to recommend it in
terms of teaching, facilities, or prestige" and for cultivating "excessive
Irishness."[70] The Queen's Colleges at Cork, Galway, and Belfast played
important roles in professionalizing Ireland's Catholics. A great irri-
tant to the Catholic hierarchy because they were not church-run, these
institutions prompted the introduction of new educational initiatives,
including the Catholic University. The consistent rise in the number
of Catholic students in the colleges after 1849 testifies to the increased
emphasis on professional training, but also to the willingness of many
Catholic students to ignore the Irish hierarchy's instructions to boycott
the Queen's University and Trinity College. Embroiled in an internal
struggle over the rise of ultramontanism, Ireland's Catholic Church was
bitterly divided over the issue of university provision.[71] Daniel Murray,
archbishop of Dublin between 1823 and 1852, had been supportive of
the Queen's University, but others, including his powerful ultramontane successor, Paul Cullen, who was appointed archbishop of Armagh
and "primate of all Ireland" in 1849 before serving as archbishop of
Dublin from 1852 to 1878, were vehemently opposed. Cullen accused
the colleges of jeopardizing the faith of Catholic students by failing to
ensure a more equal proportion of staff and by failing to employ state-
funded Catholic chaplains.[72]

The broader ecclesiastical context shaping the church's agenda in Ireland and in Britain's other Catholic churches was the growing power
of an ultramontane lobby, which was committed to imposing a more
Rome-centred structure. Establishing and expanding a system of

Catholic education across the four nations was an important component of the agenda of this lobby. In Ireland, the non-denominational education offered by the Queen's University was deemed a threat to this agenda, and so, in 1850 – the year that the Catholic Hierarchy was restored in England – the Queen's University was officially condemned by the Irish Catholic Hierarchy, with Cullen declaring its mixed education premise as the "fatal source of indifferentism to religion."[73] Cullen and his supporters argued that the drive for mixed education was being led by "enemies of the faith," who wanted nothing more than to promote Protestant proselytism.[74] Such opinions attracted significant criticism from figures such as J.E. Cairnes, a leading Irish economist and a professor of jurisprudence and political economy at Queen's College Galway. He argued passionately that Ireland's post-famine recovery required mixed education to undermine the deeply entrenched culture of religious bigotry and to open up higher education to those "three-fourths of the youth" to whom it had been previously denied.[75] Britain's leading Catholic intellectual, John Henry Newman, sided with Cullen. A former fellow of Oriel College, Oxford, Newman had converted to Catholicism in 1845 and spearheaded the campaign to create a Catholic Oxbridge in Ireland. When the Catholic University for Ireland was established, he was named rector. Approved by Rome in 1852, the university opened in 1854, after the publication of *Optime Noscitis, On the proposed Catholic University of Ireland*, which outlined Rome's great "annoyance" that in-fighting among the Irish clergy was delaying progress.[76]

The Catholic University had major support from some in British North America, but it is important to recognize that many of its supporters, such as Nova Scotia's bishop, William Walsh, owed their ecclesiastical careers to Cullen. Writing to an old student friend and long-time correspondent, Tobias Kirby, a confidant of Cullen's and the man in line for the post of rector of Rome's Irish College, Walsh praised the university initiative, which prompted an enthusiastic reply from Kirby:

> Glory be to Halifax! I have just read your magnificent letter on the C. University; and I need hardly tell you that all with whom I have spoken on the subject are delighted with it. The Primate is exceedingly well pleased with it. And thinks that it will do a great deal of good in spreading throughout all the Americas that sacred fire which St. Patrick lit up in Ireland, and symbolized by that of Tara. Glory be to Halifax![77]

The Catholic world was expanding rapidly, and Irish priests were running missions across the empire. The "sacred fire" of St Patrick, though, brought little comfort to those Scottish and English Catholics

who resented the growing authority of the Irish.[78] In fact, the possibility
of creating a single Catholic college or university in Nova Scotia was
struck down by the Scots, who feared "the Irish characteristic of wishing
to domineer would break out within the College walls – that they would
be apt thus to consider us poor uncircumcised Scotch as of a caste inferior to themselves."[79] Another problem was the failure of some clergy to
appreciate the importance of university education to Catholic youths.
When calls were made for a Catholic university in England, Henry Augustus Rawes, a convert to Catholicism, who was ordained in 1857 and
was an original member of Cardinals Wiseman and Manning's Oblates
of St Charles, was deeply critical: "I know of nothing that is indispensable for Catholic youths except the faith and morals of the Church ... The
Church is the best judge of what is necessary or advantageous for her
children. And (to anticipate what I shall say afterwards) there is, in Dublin, a Catholic University for those who speak the English tongue."[80]
The problem was that this sort of opinion contrasted sharply with the
ambitions of a rising Catholic middle class eager to build careers for
themselves and to secure futures for their children. The intellectual
value of Ireland's Catholic University was considerable, and a lot of
energy was invested in giving it credibility, though with only partial
success: although it had faculties of theology, law, medicine, philosophy,
natural science, and mathematics, medicine was its only real success.

That medicine played such an important role in improving the intellectual culture of Britain's and Ireland's Catholics was something
that Newman understood, and he wanted to use it to gain a greater
degree of social influence over the labouring poor. In emphasizing the
need for more Catholic doctors, he criticized their low numbers in the
Dublin hospitals:

> The medical establishments have been simply in the hands of the Protestants
> ... I understand that at this time out of all the Dublin hospitals, only three
> have any Catholic practitioner in them at all, and that even in these three,
> the Catholic Officials do not exceed the number of Protestants. On the other
> hand out of sixty-two medical officers altogether in the various hospitals, the
> Catholics do not exceed the number of ten. Again out of five medical schools
> in Dublin ... [and] out of forty-nine lecturers only two are Catholics.[81]

The Catholic University was not endowed but, instead, relied on diocesan collections and other donations – practically all of the first enrolments were wealthy foreign students. It was an institution that ultimately
failed, being absorbed by University College Dublin in 1909, but that it
managed to survive as long as it did stemmed from its ability to engage

with external institutions and recruit outstanding and highly respected staff for its chairs in Anatomy and Physiology, Pathological Anatomy, and Theory and Practice of Surgery.[82] It also benefited from its base in Apothecaries' Hall, which was an excellent facility on Dublin's Cecilia Street. Its weaknesses, however, were its distance from the support mechanisms of the state and its failure to receive permission to award the class certificates that students needed to sit the exams of the various licensing bodies (the Royal College of Surgeons, the King and Queen's College of Physicians, and Trinity College all awarded these certificates).

Newman's preoccupation with establishing an Irish Catholic Oxbridge meant that he had failed to understand the complexities of Irish society and to see what many young, middle-class Catholics had long understood – that practical training, linked with Britain's imperial program and provided by institutions like the Queen's University, had the potential to improve their career prospects dramatically and help the nation recover from the catastrophic effects of the Famine. It was for these reasons, in spite of the hierarchy's ban on Catholics attending the Queen's Colleges and their labelling the institution a "Satanic scheme," that Catholic students continued to enrol in the colleges.[83] The *Irish Catholic Directory*'s robust defence of the university in 1864 suggests the hierarchy was struggling to convince people of its value: "The number of matriculated Catholic students in Cork College in February last was 86. Were not these institutions justly banned by the Church, it ought to be ten times that number." This argument was not exactly convincing, especially since it failed to mention that Catholics had also been enrolling, and would continue to enrol, in the other colleges at Galway and Belfast.[84]

Assuming that "Catholics would follow blindly advice from the altar" was not a useful approach.[85] The colleges' president's reports between 1849 and 1869 noted that at least 132 Catholics had chosen to enter the three colleges, but such numbers constituted only the tip of the iceberg, since Queen's College Belfast alone had enrolled at least 214 Catholic students by 1881. This number might seem low, considering that the total number of students at that college was 3,625, but given the lack of tradition of higher education achievement among Catholics, it was significant. Nor were Catholics the smallest group at Belfast since there had been 2,231 Presbyterians, 755 from the Church of Ireland, 158 Methodists, and 267 from other, smaller churches. Ultimately, the number of Catholics symbolized the appeal of imperially networked and practically based higher education to ambitious young men eager to establish themselves as professionals outside of Ireland.[86]

It was also clear that the Catholic students enrolling with the Queen's University favoured medicine, and records from the 1850s suggests that they did pretty well, winning a number of prizes and scholarships, including some of the prestigious senior scholarships: three of the ten senior scholarships in 1853–54 were awarded to Catholics (of the remaining seven, two went to Methodists and five to students from the Church of Ireland), one was awarded to a Catholic in 1855–56, and one in 1856–57.[87] Richard Carr McClement, the Catholic naval surgeon mentioned in chapter 4, enrolled at Queen's College Belfast in 1854. He won a number of distinctions, and, when he did not receive the senior scholarship in Therapeutics and Pathology in 1857, despite being shortlisted, he appealed the decision.[88] McClement was a typical Catholic medical student in that he had an eye on a career in the army, navy, or Indian Medical Service, and he had deliberately chosen the Queen's University because of the accredited training it offered. His younger brother, Frederick, and many others, including Sir Anthony McDonnell, who, after attending Queen's College Galway, entered the Indian Civil Service before serving as lieutenant governor of Bengal, did the same thing. The decisions that these young men made about their education shows how they saw their futures as being connected with Britain's imperial program, and their Catholicity as being defined by their own ambitions rather than those of their church.

The example of the McClement brothers is instructive because, although they studied in Ireland when the Catholic University and its medical school were operating, neither chose to attend that institution. Location and cost may have been factors, with Queen's College Belfast being closer to their home and therefore cheaper, but these were unlikely to have been the dominant reasons, since both men elected to take their diplomas outside of Ireland: Richard took his at the Royal College of Surgeons in London and Frederick's was from Edinburgh's Royal College of Surgeons. Their career decisions, like those of many of their medical colleagues, were made on professional grounds rather than religious ones. [89]

Enrolments in the Catholic University's medical school jumped in 1885, when the Education Endowments (Ireland) Act was passed. This legislation gave the Catholic University a share of state funding, which enabled it to extract itself from total episcopal control and appear more like a national university that could appeal to a broader and increasingly ambitious student body. Previous attempts to access state funding had failed, in spite of pressure being exerted by influential Catholics in the colonies. In Canada, for example, Catholic leaders had emphasized the influence that the institution would have on professionalization, but their reasons for supporting it were complex. While Halifax's archbishop William Walsh, out of loyalty to Cullen, threw his support behind the institution in the early phase of its development, John Joseph Lynch, bishop of Toronto between 1860 and 1870 and archbishop between 1870 and his death in 1888, saw it as a way to curb the unbridled and disruptive effects of widespread Irish immigration to Canada. Eager to distance himself and his city from Ireland's more radical elements, and believing that a petition from the Canadians would "carry immense weight" in London, Lynch lobbied for the Catholic University in Ireland to be granted a charter similar to the one given to Quebec's Université Laval, which started as a seminary.[90] The Université Laval, which had its roots in the seventeenth-century Séminaire de Quebec, received a Royal Charter in 1852 and was authorized by Rome to grant degrees in theology the following year. It continued to operate very much like a seminary and was run by priests who did not envision creating an "intellectual clergy."[91] To British officials, filling Quebec with priests by way of a university charter was one thing, particularly given the pivotal role they had played in supporting the British against American incursions and in setting up a progressive social welfare and educational system, but supporting such as institution in Ireland, where the majority of clerics outside of the upper echelons were widely mistrusted and believed to possess nationalist sympathies, was something entirely different.

The petition that the Canadians sent to the queen about the Irish Catholic University was received by Downing Street in March 1879. It displayed the constructive and inherently collaborative relationship that existed in Canada between Catholics and the state.[92] In emphasizing the loyalty of Canada's Catholics to the Crown and their commitment to working with government to build a successful nation, the petition threw the benefits that Canada's Catholics took for granted into sharp relief: "That on comparison between the government of Ireland and that of Canada your Majesty's Irish subjects are saddened at the thought that the Roman Catholics of Ireland do not enjoy the educational privileges which are freely granted to your Majesty's Catholic subjects in Canada."[93]

The 1867 British North America Act had woven Catholicism into the fabric of the Canadian nation by guaranteeing provision for Catholic education, but, beyond the realm of constitutional politics, Canadian petitioners were also interested in consolidating the authority of the church over the wider Catholic body. The Canadian bishops' close relationship with government (both Canadian and British) enabled them to collaborate with the state on an extensive system of Catholic education that stretched from the primary level through to university, to counter what both the church and state viewed as emerging "socialistic and revolutionary principles, which are calculated to undermine the throne, as well as the altar."[94] These religious leaders saw themselves as being intrinsic to Canada's emerging civil society and social order. In their opinion and that of legislators who worked with them, serious issues surrounding the rise of "radical" ideologies could be dealt with only "by placing education under the blessed and saving influences of religion, which is the unfailing prop of civil order[,] the firm foundation of the social fabric of the unshaken support of lawful authority."[95] There was a strong and productive relationship between Lynch, an Irishman notorious for his opposition to Irish immigration to Canada, and high-ranking government officials such as Lord Dufferin, another Irishman, whose great love of tobogganing and friendly relations with Canadian Catholic leaders endeared him as the country's third governor general between 1872 and 1878. Similarly, the support of John A. Macdonald, a Scottish Presbyterian immigrant and Canada's first prime minister, was crucial in giving these Roman Catholic leaders the confidence to lobby the Crown.[96]

That this kind of relationship between the state and the Catholic clergy was lacking in Ireland meant that Catholics there remained at a distinct disadvantage, and so took opportunities where they could find them. Medicine opened a lot of doors. The Catholic University's Medical School did overtake Queen's College Galway in enrolments between 1860 and 1880, but it did not overtake the other colleges before 1900; yet the fact that it did, eventually, overtake them highlights the cultural importance of the medical profession to Catholic aspirations.[97] The choices that Richard and Frederick McClement made about their education differed little from those of their fellow Irish students, both Catholic and Protestant. That the majority of all Irish medical students between 1860 and 1880 were enrolled in the colleges of the Queen's University testifies to the rising ambitions of Ireland's middle class as a whole – and to the fact that most could not rely on family or friends to secure admission to the older, more established institutions like Trinity College.[98]

To the Catholic leadership in Ireland and elsewhere, the Catholic University symbolized an opportunity to assert Irish Catholicism at home and abroad. This was emphasized in the opening address of the 1863–64 academic year, when the institution's rector, Monsignor Bartholomew Woodlock, reminded his audience of the university's important role in establishing a distinctly Irish brand of imperial Catholicism:

> As far as this Empire is concerned, from her chiefly must go forth Catholic apologists, Catholic orators, Catholics magistrates, Catholic soldiers, Catholic statesmen. God grant that the day may not be distant when, in the sister countries of England and Scotland, Catholicity may resume at least a part of

Figure 11. Lord Dufferin and party on the toboggan slide at Rideau Hall
(with permission from Library and Archives Canada)

its old splendour, and may rule over the hearts of the people; but, humanly speaking, this will not be for many a weary day, and the strength which numbers can give to our holy religion in the Empire of Great Britain and Ireland, must chiefly come from Catholic Ireland.[99]

It is unlikely that the countless young men who continued to enrol in the Queen's Colleges, and who travelled to England or Scotland for university, shared this opinion. They did not see themselves as soldiers of Catholic Ireland; rather, they seemed to have identified as Irishmen and/ or as Britons who were Catholic. They were committed to their faith, but not militantly so, and there is little evidence to suggest that they engaged with the notion of an Irish Catholic world in the same way that some of the clergy did.[100] Their understandings of Irishness were nuanced, and often linked with an inclusive vision of the empire, because they possessed multiple and shifting identities. What most, if not all, would have identified with, though, was the difficulty in accessing the professions. Careers in law, as mainstream military officers, senior civil servants, and even engineers were often out of reach for most Catholics, but Irish ones faced additional discrimination. Medicine became so popular because the empire needed doctors more than it needed lawyers, and the type of medicine practised in the Royal Navy, the army, the Indian Medical Service, and even generally in the tropical or frigid climates of the colonies, was dangerous and often deadly. Indeed, Richard McClement died of the malaria he contracted when working with the West African Squadron. If young Catholic doctors were prepared to take the risks, then opportunities for a professional career were waiting for them.

The importance of the empire, and Ireland's place within it, was a theme that featured strongly in the rhetoric of the Queen's Colleges. In 1864 the president of the Belfast college reported that the Queen's Colleges had exceeded expectations and were emerging as important centres of learning where students were "men of high professional distinction able to compete successfully in intellectual contests for the public service."[101] One of the college's mandates was to strengthen ties between mainland Britain and Ireland, but another was to build stronger links between Ulster and the empire and with medicine; this was relatively easy, since the majority of Irish doctors found jobs in England or the armed services as civilian medical officers.[102] Education, professionalization, and respectability preoccupied middle-class Ireland, and in 1885, Robert Esler, senior physician at Belfast's Ulster Hospital reported that the city's graduates were "occupying posts of honour and distinction in almost every University, and certainly in every country where her Majesty's Union Jack floats over a free and

Figure 12. Frederick McClement at Richard McClement's grave
(with permission of Chris McClement)

independent people."[103] Medicine in Ireland had come a long way since 1806, when Esler's Belfast Medical Society was founded and the number of physicians and surgeons serving a city of 22,000 was just nineteen.[104] Ireland's ability to feed the British Empire with physicians and surgeons improved the status of Catholics.

The medical training on offer in Britain and Ireland far exceeded anything available in the colonies, and so it was rather commonplace to find "colonials" training as doctors in the United Kingdom.[105] From the 1850s, however, the British North American colonies had growing provisions for university education, and, unlike in Britain and Ireland, where the only Catholic university was in Dublin, a growing number of these institutions were Catholic. The first type of Catholic educational

Figure 13. Richard McClement (with permission of Chris McClement)

institution proposed for a colony was usually a seminary or a motherhouse, but these often morphed into colleges before becoming full-fledged universities. Taking a broad survey of the western Atlantic world, the first Catholic institutions outside of Britain opened in the Maritime colonies and in Quebec, where colonial society was more established. Examples include Saint Mary's University in Nova Scotia (1839–40), Quebec's Université Laval (1852), St Michael's Academy (later St Thomas University) in New Brunswick (1860), and Mount Saint Vincent Academy (became Mount Saint Vincent University), which was run by the Sisters of Charity in Nova Scotia (1873). St. Francis Xavier University, which was founded in 1854 in Antigonish, Nova Scotia, began its life as a seminary for training English-speaking priests to serve Catholics living east of Quebec, but its mission expanded to include a broader educational program for lay students when it was granted degree-awarding powers in 1866 by the Nova Scotia legislature.[106]

The desperate need for priests and women religious in many of the colonies prompted the establishment of seminaries and colleges: recruiting from the United Kingdom and Europe was a major challenge, as numerous accounts of religious foundations testify.[107] John Cameron, a priest in search of religious personnel for the Maritimes, experienced significant difficulties when engaged in this task in Paris in 1854. Writing to his superiors in Rome, Cameron noted the trouble he encountered when attempting to recruit five women religious and two priests for Nova Scotia. In the end, he managed to get only one priest and was annoyed by the opposition he faced from an obstinate French establishment that had little time for the constant requests for help from the North Americans. His recollection of a meeting with Abbé Deluol, director of the city's Sulpician Seminary, was especially revealing:

> This venerable old man received me with quite a scowl and assured me that he is determined not to do the slightest service either to me or to anyone else, and that he had been greatly annoyed by the importunities of Americans – Bishops, Priests, lay people – since his return from America, and that he is not to be the slave of others any longer. "Let them mind their own business," he said, "and I'll mind mine." He would not even tell me where I could find a convenient place to stay without having to pay too much, but merely asserted – and quite emphatically: "There are plenty of good hotels in Paris"!!! "Give me patience, my God," I said to myself as I left, "and don't allow my pride to spoil the merit of your work which I am trying to do."[108]

Part of the aim of building St. Francis Xavier University was to centralize the training of priests and to assert a measure of Scottish Catholic authority over an expanding Catholic population in a colony where the tensions between Irish and Scottish Catholics were high. It might not be a coincidence that St. Francis Xavier University was founded in the same year as Ireland's Catholic University: although it was an attempt to circumvent the influence of Halifax's emerging and increasingly powerful Irish Catholic community, it also helped raise the aspirations of Scottish Highland Catholics. Moreover, it also eroded further the influence of francophone Catholicism.[109] Ethnic tensions in the Catholic world were never far from the surface.

Although Cameron himself was born in St. Andrews, Nova Scotia, his father had emigrated to the province from the Scottish Highlands. In 1841, Cameron was sent to Rome to study theology at Urban College, an institution focused exclusively on preparing priests for the missions. He was ordained in 1853 but, before returning to Canada in 1854, he served as secretary to Allesandro Cardinal Barnabo, the future cardinal-prefect and gate-keeper for the pope at *Propaganda Fide*, the arm of the church responsible for Catholic activities in non-Catholic countries and regions, such as the United Kingdom. This marked the start of a rather illustrious career for Cameron, which included appointments as rector of St. Francis Xavier University, vicar-general of Arichat, and bishop of Antigonish.[110]

Expanding the educational opportunities for young middle-class Catholics was a priority for the church leadership, and significant progress had been made by the late 1870s. The once limited education for Catholics that began in Britain in the late 1790s had expanded by leaps and bounds. The role of religious communities in this growth and culture shift cannot be underestimated, nor can the growing confidence instilled within an expanding Catholic middle class. They exploited the educational opportunities available to them in ways that enabled them to realize their professional ambition and enhance their reputations as respectable citizens. The religious life and medicine stood out as professions that encouraged a deeper engagement with education than had previously been imagined for anyone outside of the higher ranks of society. While opportunities at home were relatively limited, those in the empire, in colonial missions, and in the armed services were plentiful. The presence of well-educated young Catholic women and men dramatically improved the standing of an emerging Catholic middle class and put them within reach of additional opportunities.

Chapter Six

The Decline of Lay Authority: Ecclesiastical Reorganization and Imperial Power in Trinidad and Newfoundland

Previous chapters have focused on how Catholics negotiated relationships with the imperial state and how they used those relationships to extend their authority. They revealed aspects of the activity and activism of the laity and the ways in which members of this group fused their religious identities with the ambitions of the state and how that influenced socio-economic development in places they settled. In this final chapter, focus shifts from lay Catholics to bishops in Trinidad and Newfoundland. Bishops became powerful symbols of Catholic authority from the late 1820s, as their influence grew and as they were able to exert more authority over local populations. Supportive of Britain's colonial management strategies, they were social controllers, disciplinarians, and willing collaborators in the process of colonialism, in spite of colonial officials being uneasy with the bishops' authority deriving from the pope via the Sacred Congregation of *Propaganda Fide* in Rome.[1]

Trinidad and Newfoundland had three important commonalities: both had large Catholic populations; both were run by governors as opposed to elected assemblies until the early 1830s; and, at least up until 1830 (and in sharp contrast to the Maritime colonies), they were both classified by *Propaganda Fide* in the series *Congressi*, sub-series *America Antille* (West Indies), and not in the sub-series *America Settentrionale* (British North America).[2] These commonalities also accommodated differences. Each possessed distinctive administrative structures: Trinidad was a Crown colony, whereas Newfoundland was technically run from England as a seasonal migratory fishing station until 1825.[3] Moreover, their Catholic populations were very different: the Catholics of Trinidad were predominantly non-British – enslaved, free people of colour, French, and Spanish – and those in Newfoundland were almost exclusively Irish and concentrated in and around the Avalon Peninsula until the middle of the nineteenth century, when a mixed Catholic population of Acadian, Québécois, Scottish, Irish, and Mi'kmaq emerged on the southwestern coast.[4] Newfoundland was the only place in British North America where the Irish did not confront a pre-existing Catholic population. Nova Scotia, Prince Edward Island, Upper Canada, and Lower Canada (Quebec) had substantial French (including Acadian) and/or Scottish Highland Catholic communities that either dominated local Catholic culture or were proportionately significant in size and geographic distribution.[5] The influence of Quebec was omnipresent in Newfoundland, but it was actually the English Catholic Church that played a foundational role in managing Catholicism there and in Trinidad (once it was under British jurisdiction). Consequently, this chapter reflects a recognition of Newfoundland's alignment with a Hiberno-Roman world and Trinidad's firm encasement within a British imperial one. Outside Newfoundland, we cannot assume the existence of a "Hiberno-Catholic homogeneity" for Irish Catholics in what would become Canada, since the presence of other Catholic groups often prevented such uniformity.[6] Newfoundland was an outlier because of its geographic isolation.

Trinidad's free Catholics had more freedom than Catholics in Newfoundland because Britain recognized the Articles of Capitulation when it gained control of the Caribbean island with the Treaty of Amiens in 1802. First introduced in 1797, the articles were designed to preserve private property and recognize "the free coloureds ... in their liberty, person and property [upon] taking the oath of allegiance and behaving like peaceful citizens."[7] These protections enabled the French to retain their economic dominance and gave "a certain measure of independence" to the island's free people of colour.[8] The vibrant Catholic culture that was woven into the social fabric of Trinidad contrasted sharply with what existed in Newfoundland.

Since the middle of the eighteenth century, Britain had been acquiring valuable experience in dealing with its new Catholic subjects. Cooperation with Catholic authorities was often a necessity, and one of the Colonial Office's most effective strategies had been to offer them financial support. In many places, British money paid for priests' salaries, chapel and cathedral construction, furniture for bishops' houses, and even altar breads, which was astonishing given the intense Protestant opposition to the Catholic doctrine of transubstantiation. This support helped the church's ecclesiastical structures grow while cementing them to Britain's imperial program. Rome's understanding of colonial missions was limited, and its response to issues depended on location. It was less comfortable, for example, with Britain's authority in Trinidad than in Newfoundland. Ecclesiastical jurisdiction in the latter was held by the

vicar apostolic of the London District from 1756 until 1784, when Pope
Pius VI declared Newfoundland a separate jurisdiction after successful
lobbying by a contingent of English and Irish clergy.[9] In Trinidad's case,
Rome avoided transferring ecclesiastical jurisdiction from the bishop
of Guyana to the vicar apostolic of the London District for as long as
possible. Given the level of uncertainty in Europe on account of the Napoleonic Wars, and the papacy's own crises under Napoleon, this hes-
itation was understandable, but after a British victory was confirmed,
Pope Pius VII established the vicariate apostolic of the West Indies in
1817.[10] Anchored at Port of Spain, this new jurisdiction had responsibility for all of Britain's Caribbean assets, including Demerara, Essequibo,
and Berbice – the territories situated on the northeast coast of the South
American mainland that had been acquired from the Dutch in 1814.

Although Trinidad and Newfoundland experienced significant ecclesiastical change during the nineteenth century, each transforming from
missions to bishoprics to archdioceses, this chapter pays more attention
to Trinidad because it has received far less attention than Newfoundland in studies of the British Empire. Additionally, Trinidad's status as a
former Spanish colony, with a large and predominantly Black Catholic
population, makes it an invaluable location for exploring the complex
and multi-layered relationship between the church and the imperial
state. The diversity of Trinidad's Catholics, its transition from enslaved
to waged labour, and how perceptions of race shaped church development led to a much greater degree of cooperation between Catholic and
colonial officials there than in Newfoundland.

Establishing British Catholic Authority in Trinidad

An island measuring 4,800 square kilometres, Trinidad sits off the east
coast of Venezuela. Claimed as a colony of Spain in 1498, it remained
sparsely settled until the early 1780s. Around 18,000 people are thought
to have been living there in 1797, but when it was formally ceded to
Britain in 1802, the population ballooned to around 29,250, as planters
imported more and more slaves and as migrants from neighbouring islands arrived in search of safety and religious tolerance.[11] Its economy,
like most other Caribbean colonies, came to revolve around plantation
slavery, and over two-thirds of its people were enslaved. The Europeans, who numbered between 8,000 and 9,000, were mostly French and
Spanish, and, although the number of Protestant Britons rose significantly after 1802, Catholicism remained the dominant faith.[12]

When Britain gained control of Trinidad, colonial officials encountered a "three-tiered community of land-holding 'seigneurs' primarily

French in origin and culture," free people of colour, and a large enslaved population that was "economically impotent."[13] Despite its Spanish colonizers, the number of francophones (both European and free people of colour) had been rising since the early 1780s, due to article 1 of its Cedula of Population, which required newcomers to "profess the Roman Catholic religion."[14] Although Catholic culture in Trinidad had once been a blend of French and Spanish elements, French culture dominated after the French Revolution and turned the island into a "French colony in all but name."[15]

Notwithstanding the inevitable tensions that existed between the island's European Catholic groups, their relationship with British colonial officials was relatively good until the mid-1840s. A major reason for the relative harmony was Rome's willingness to accommodate Colonial Office requests for English- or English-born bishops. The first three appointments were Thomas Gillow, a Lancashire recusant; James Buckley, a Londoner, who served from 1819 to 1828; and Daniel McDonnell, another Londoner but one of Irish descent, who served from 1828 until 1837. It is likely that McDonnell came from London's "distinguished and prosperous" Irish Catholic community, which included some of the most politically connected, imperially networked, and wealthy Irish Catholics of the time.[16] The shortage of English clergy willing to go to Trinidad meant that the fourth appointment, Richard Patrick Smith, was an Irishman. Smith, who had trained at Maynooth and served in Trinidad from 1837 until his death in 1852, oversaw Catholicism during the island's transition from enslaved to waged labour and its church's transformation from a vicariate apostolic into an archdiocese.[17] The tenures of these ecclesiastics, notwithstanding their many controversies and conflicts, stabilized Catholicism in Trinidad during a period of significant change.

A pivotal figure in the development of Catholicism in Trinidad after 1802 was the vicar apostolic of the London District, and the most active, by far, was William Poynter, who had held the post from 1812 until 1827. Ordained in 1786, Poynter was an English recusant who had trained at the English College at Douai in France. While possessing the manners and temperament needed to win the confidence of government and church officials, he also had his share of enemies.[18] His alienation of sections of Ireland's Catholics following the veto crisis of the early nineteenth century, when there was an attempt by some in the church to give state officials the right to veto a prospective bishop in exchange for emancipation, resulted their declaring him, among other things, an "unhappy wretch," an "infamous hypocrite," and a "traytor."[19] Most of his brother bishops respected him, and, during his quarrels with John Milner, the hot-tempered vicar apostolic of England's

Western District, the Scottish bishops came to his defence as their agent and promised "any support [their] Scotch influence may afford."[20] As a rule, the British government recognized the vicar apostolic of the London District as its main point of contact for anything related to Catholic affairs or the Catholic Church in British territories. In the context of the four nations, Poynter's authority was occasionally unsettling, particularly if it was perceived to interfere with the independence of the Scottish and Irish Catholic churches, but the government's recognition of the London bishop as its primary contact meant that the communication channels between the United Kingdom's Catholic leaders were more open than they might have been otherwise. Yet, the dominance of Scottish and Irish Catholics in Britain's colonial world created a more effective awareness of the constituent traditions.

One of the most pressing issues for the vicar apostolic of the London District was the need to balance Rome's desire for control over church governance with London's desire to instil a British ethos in the colonies. In Trinidad, this responsibility included making clerical appointments that would satisfy the British government, and so, when Rome finally established the vicariate apostolic of the West Indies, the task of finding a suitable English candidate fell to Poynter.[21] Identifying someone willing to leave the comfort of England was a challenge, given the reputation of the Caribbean as having an oppressive climate, scarce resources, and exceedingly high rates of death and illness. Predictably, Poynter was able to properly appoint a vicar apostolic of the West Indies only in 1819 (despite approval of the position by Rome two years earlier), and even then it took another year before anyone was actually on the ground on the island.[22]

Although the first vicar apostolic of the West Indies was technically Thomas Gillow, the man never actually served there. Poynter's first choice, Gillow had studied at the English College in Douai before becoming private chaplain to a wealthy Northumberland family at Callaly Castle.[23] The problem was that, while he had been approved by officials in London and Rome, he had not wanted the appointment and had no intention of accepting it. He tried everything to convince Poynter to withdraw his name, even going so far as to claim that his deficiencies in "abilities, in learning, & in piety" rendered him unfit for the mission and that he was so unwell that he was "literally little better than a leper."[24] When all of his excuses failed, he simply delegated back to Poynter "all the power and jurisdiction conferred upon me by the Pope's Briefs in those islands" until another candidate was identified.[25]

The job was finally accepted by James Buckley, the former president of Lisbon's English College, though not without trepidation. Writing to the rector of Rome's English College, Buckley confessed that he had "received the congratulations of some; and the condolence of others upon [his] appointment, who consider it as an honourable exile," and he added that he looked "back to Lisbon with regret, & had [he foreseen] this mission to the West Indies would never have left it."[26] His decision to accept the post surprised many of his friends, who worried about how he would cope in the "climate of lightnings, hurricanes, black & yellow fevers." One even wrote that, "in such a climate, & amidst such strangers, he can have no happiness in life unless it be in promoting the honour of God & the good of his creatures."[27] As it turned out, Buckley was a good choice – he was competent, committed, and seemed to like the Caribbean and its people. His arrival at Port of Spain in 1820 was a major event, and, according to the *Trinidad Gazette*, it was marked by a procession followed by a Mass and a welcome reception at Government House that was attended by a number of dignitaries including the governor, chief judge, and members of the executive council, *cabildo*, and the *alcaldes* of barrios (municipal officials). The Royal Trinidad Artillery offered a "Royal Salute" on the occasion[28] The details of the event were reported back to officials at *Propaganda Fide*, who were also given a copy of the address, which highlighted Britain's authority and Buckley's British credentials: "We congratulate the colony and more particularly that great majority of it that belong to the Church of Rome in being withdrawn from a foreign jurisdiction and on having the advantage of an authority, that is known to themselves, and that had received the high sanction of our sovereign."[29]

As a Catholic, regardless of place of birth, Buckley was obliged to swear oaths of allegiance to the Crown, which he did without issue. As he settled into his role, he began a regular correspondence with Poynter about the state of his mission. His letters offer an interesting window on Trinidad in the 1820s. They detail the local church's struggles with scant resources and a governing body, far away in Rome, that knew practically nothing about the local conditions: in Buckley's opinion, these were the main issues impeding the progress of Catholicism in the Caribbean.[30] He was not the only bishop to complain about this: Upper Canada's Alexander Macdonell also criticized *Propaganda Fide* for throwing up "unnecessary difficulties" due to the failure of its officials to "understand the reality of life on the ground in the colonies."[31]

Buckley ingratiated himself to the local elites and, without a trace of modesty, informed Poynter that he was "thought a wonderfully clever fellow, and quite a favourite with the governor."[32] His "Englishness" comforted colonial officials, who saw him as someone who would safeguard Britain's interests. Trinidad's governor, Sir Ralph James

Woodford, depended on Buckley to recruit priests who were "English-men speaking French, but as they are not to be found, Scotch, Irish, French if recommended well."[33] The reasons for preferring English candidates are complex, but national preference was a major factor when it came to most church leadership posts.[34] In Trinidad, as elsewhere, cultivating a loyalty to the state among the new subjects was a priority, and all of Britain and Ireland's Christian missionaries, regardless of sect, were active participants in this process. Catholicism had a fixed presence on the island, and so the governors encouraged priests whom they deemed capable of building a national attachment:

> Nothing can contribute more to make the numerous Catholic inhabitants of our colonies happy and firmly attached to our government by principle and affection than supplying them with a sufficient number of enlightened, prudent, & pious Catholic clergymen … If these clergymen are natives of the British colonies or at least, British subjects & receive their ecclesiastical education in England our government will have greater security of their loyalty & a stronger ground of confidence in them.[35]

So committed was Woodford to securing English-born priests that he had even planned to travel to England at one point to help with recruitment. Aware of the challenge Woodford faced, Buckley suggested that, as an alternative, the Colonial Office consider funding the seminary training of young men from Trinidad in England or at an English college. Henry Bathurst, 3rd Earl Bathurst and secretary of state for war and the colonies, who had authorized funds to cover Buckley's salary and furnishings, agreed and was prepared to support seminarians at the English College in Rome.[36] Nothing came of this plan due to the limited educational foundation of most of the island's young men.[37]

A complicating factor for Buckley's ability to recruit priests was the inherently negative perceptions that many church and colonial officials had of the island's free people of colour, whose training and employment as religious personnel were actively discouraged. In 1822, for example, Woodford had refused Buckley's request to employ a Black priest, even though the need for clergy was desperate.[38] Church leaders rarely mentioned the race issue in their correspondence, and so it was especially revealing when Buckley, who had a Black servant (most likely an enslaved person), wrote of his frustration with the prejudice he encountered at every turn: "Coloured persons are never thought worthy to aspire to any liberal profession; they are treated as a secondary race & never admitted to the society of the whites. I hope in Demerara these prejudices do not exist; here I should not be permitted by the governor or people to give any employment to a coloured priest."[39]

The new "free coloured" priest whom Buckley wished to employ was Father Francis de Ridder, a young cleric born in 1800 to an enslaved mother and Dutch planter father in Dutch Demerary (Demerara) on the northeast coast of South America.[40] Somehow, the young man had managed to get permission to work under Buckley, but he faced an immediate backlash from the white congregants. His experience reveals how enslaved people and free people of colour narrated and defined their own Catholicity in spite of white opposition. An indication of de Ridder's significance to the island's free people of colour was noted by Buckley the year he arrived:

> A coloured priest in this country is dangerous, he was soon taken away from me by his class & taught to distrust me. They [people of colour] have been so exalted at his coming that they could not hide their extravagant pretensions. They have done all they could to keep him in town. I never had a harder task to perform. I wanted to show him all the attention possible. I have asked him to dine and breakfast with me, the coloured people are not contented because I did not present him to the all the White people.[41]

Connecting de Ridder with the island's formal church structure was virtually impossible, since the majority of the white congregants "refused to receive him in their houses."[42] Their resistance threw the island's deep racial divide into sharp relief and revealed a conflict with the church's broader ambition to secure conversions. According to Katherine Gerbner, Catholic missionaries were generally more successful than many of their Protestant counterparts because of their more uniform approach and because they were not divided into a range of sects.[43] The situation was more complicated when it came to promoting Catholicism among the enslaved people, and evidence from *Propaganda Fide* suggests that the church yielded to the wishes of British officials and reduced the opportunities open to them for formal worship. In 1820, Buckley had been directed to reduce the number of feast days celebrated by the island's Catholics and, as a concession to the planters, who were, "for the greatest part Protestants," to exclude enslaved people from all feasts and holidays.[44]

As a free person of colour, de Ridder technically fell into a different category than the excluded enslaved population, but such distinctions mattered little to the island's white Catholics. Ever the pragmatist, Buckley had a different view. He saw a man with the potential to bring "all of the coloured Protestants & even Methodists" into the Catholic fold.[45] Extremely popular among the free people of colour, de Ridder emerged as a kind of spokesman for their concerns. His rising star frustrated the Catholic leadership and worried the local colonial administrators, who saw him as a subversive figure who threatened public order. Exasperated by the prejudice he encountered in the form of suspensions, redeployments, and general isolation, de Ridder protested to Buckley's successor, Daniel McDonnell, that he could "no longer be silent; and I am deeply afflicted that it so happens, that I am the only priest here who dares to stand up in the cause of his creed – in the defence of the law of God, and of the discipline of his church. I cannot and never will submit to you, my lord, unless you retract your [racist] principles."[46] Unable to reconcile with his Trinidad superiors, de Ridder decided to take his case to Rome, but he died en route, at Bristol, in 1833. An issue for de Ridder and his superiors was that he straddled two worlds: the enslaved and the free. That no mention is made of him in the papers of Propaganda Fide's Scritture riferite nei Congressi, America Antille volumes, which comprise missionary letters and reports from across the region, is telling and suggests that the internalized racism of the Catholic Church and the "trade in [Black] flesh" enabled a culture of anti-Blackness to permeate Catholic culture.[47]

While many individual European Catholics were opposed to African enslavement and the slave trade, the Catholic Church's ambiguous position shaped how many clergy operated at local levels. Notwithstanding the limited (and unconvincing) argument that Rome opposed slavery from the early seventeenth century,[48] the competing priorities of Propaganda Fide and the various popes confounded any definitive condemnation of the enslavement of Black Africans. The Holy See's impotence was evidenced by its failure to invoke excommunication as a punishment for slave-ownership or for the physical abuse of enslaved people. What needs to be remembered (or understood) is that the Catholic Church was the "church of the privileged" as well as the "church of the poor and the oppressed," and many of its patrons were the beneficiaries of slave-based economies.[49] Only in 1839 did the Holy See take a clear position on the issue of African enslavement; up to that point, many religious communities, like the Maryland Jesuits, the founders of Georgetown University, owned slaves.[50] Previously, Rome had left the decision about whether or not to own slaves up to the individual religious communities. It was this culture of reticence that enabled Europe's two largest Catholic countries, France and Spain, to maintain their systems of slavery for as long as they did without consequence. France outlawed slavery only in 1848, and Spain allowed it to continue until 1876; even then, Cuba was an exception: it continued there until 1886.[51] One reason for France's delay in abolishing slavery may have been the lack of a Protestant Nonconformist anti-slavery lobby similar to that of Britain,[52] but its need for an economic boost following the Napoleonic Wars was another.

The growing number of coordinated rebellions by enslaved people across the Caribbean from the mid-1820s, coupled with intensifying public unrest and a rapidly deteriorating relationship between the planters and colonial officials, provoked concern over how the slave colonies would be managed in the post-emancipation era. Trinidad, like Quebec in the 1770s, required special consideration. The island's French character and the overwhelming presence of enslaved Catholics prompted a kind of informal collaboration between colonial and Catholic officials. In this and in other ways, Catholic religious personnel became part of the British missionary enterprise that aimed to extend Christianity, loyalty, and social order throughout the region and across the empire.[53]

Trinidad's Catholic population had reached 45,000 by the 1840s, dwarfing the 10,000 (mainly British) Protestants.[54] The vast majority were enslaved, and Sue Peabody has argued that many enslaved people found Catholicism's emphasis on spiritual powers and the sense of equality with their "masters" attractive.[55] Back in Britain, the notion of one human being owning another had become repugnant to many by the 1820s, and so when the Abolition of Slavery Act passed in 1833 and outlawed slavery in all of Britain's territories, there was a collective sigh of relief.[56] Yet the transitional system of apprenticeship, which required the enslaved to continue working without pay on the plantations as a way of helping the planters adjust to paid labour, meant that freedom was by no means complete or immediate.

Unsurprisingly, protests by enslaved people against their enslavers were commonplace in the run-up to 1833 and during the subsequent period of apprenticeship, and governors often turned to Catholic priests for support in suppressing such activity. For their cooperation, clergymen expected the protection of the rights and privileges that (non-enslaved) Catholics already possessed. When Henry MacLeod, governor between 1840 and 1846, threatened to reduce Bishop Richard Smith's salary, the cleric was quick to remind him of his role in suppressing the 1831 slave revolt:

> When the slaves of the very important quarters of North and South Naparima and Point a Pierre, containing 103 Sugar Estates were in an alarming state of disorder, when all the White people, the Ladies particularly were obliged to go on board the ships, off San Fernando for safety, when several Sugar Estates were set on fire; when the local magistrate had no influence

whatever with the slaves, I was sworn in as magistrate by the Governor, Sir Lewis Grant, at the request of the Planters of all religious denominations, as the surest means of inspiring the slaves with confidence and disabusing them of the misapprehensions under which they laboured, I did all the duty gratuitously for six months, and had the good fortune to receive the thanks of the Colonial Government, of the Planters and of the Slaves for my successful efforts on the occasion.[57]

Smith, like Buckley before him and McDonnell after him, wanted bishops to focus on promoting "peace and harmony amongst all classes & denominations in the community" and to avoid politics.[58] He even advised his Roman superiors that "a bishop who wants to do good in these colonies should not, I think, manifest any political opinion nor get involved nor mixed up in local discussions except to contribute to the maintenance of peace."[59] One important subtext to this was a desire to oppose political radicalism: being Irish himself, Smith was acutely aware of the possibility of serious reputational damage to Catholicism while all of Britain's Caribbean holdings were experiencing major socio-economic upheaval. Another equally important subtext was the antagonism between some of the French and Irish clergy. In a candid letter to the cardinal prefect of *Propaganda Fide*, Smith admitted that, if a small group of French priests got their way, they would "expel by all means in their power" himself, Bishop McDonnell "and all the Irish clergy."[60]

Tensions among the enslaved population and the planter class ran high throughout the 1830s and 1840s: enslaved and, then, newly free people were frustrated by their condition; free people of colour were exasperated by their lack of inclusion in civil society; and planters were angry because their businesses were falling apart – despite being generously compensated by the public purse for their losses.[61] Motivated in part by rising business costs, many planters complained bitterly to the government that, in their opinion, formerly enslaved people had too much money and no sense of financial responsibility.[62] Chronic labour shortages caused by the departure of newly free people from many estates pushed colonial officials to work with Catholic leaders to stem the exodus by opening chapels on the "edges of or near the estates," by establishing more schools, and by recruiting additional religious personnel.[63] In 1842, Father Samuel Power was enlisted by Grenadian planters to help with the "improvement" of the newly free labourers. He tried to "impress upon their minds the necessity of being more settled in their habits and more punctual in the discharge of their duties" with extended Masses aimed at promoting such habits.[64] This activity met with some success because it coincided with efforts from the "Black petite bourgeoisie" to

reframe their image as former enslaved people in ways that would enable them and their descendants to shake off the stigma of the past.[65]

William Wilberforce's 1823 *Appeal to the Religion, Justice, and Humanity
of the Inhabitants of the British Empire in Behalf of the Negro Slaves in the West
Indies* argued that the "extreme degradation" of the slave population was
due to their want of education and "moral improvement." Wilberforce
was a vociferous and influential abolitionist whose opinion carried tremendous weight, and, in the 1830s, schools for the children of enslaved
people were incorporated into the mission of the Christian churches, especially in the period between the abolition of slavery and the end of the
"apprenticeship" system in 1838.[66] Yet he was neither a Catholic ally nor
sympathizer. Indeed, in a statement to Parliament in 1839, he advised
that Trinidad should not be looked to for examples of "ameliorating
principles" because of the dominance of Catholicism. That religion, he
argued, was "unfavourable and inimical to the growth of ... moral and
social improvement."[67] Colonial officials blamed the insufficient "negro
education" on the island on the lack of English, the predominance of
Catholicism, and "the manner in which its motley population is found
scattered in distinct and often isolated groups."[68] Notwithstanding this
critique, and while reprimanding the church for its lack of attention to
education, Commissioner Charles LaTrobe also commended Bishop
Smith for refocusing his clergy on schooling, particularly in the island's
more remote districts.[69] As a general point, the progress of Catholic education was slow across Britain and the empire until the late 1830s when
the expansion of female teaching congregations enabled the deployment
of women in significant numbers throughout the colonial missions.

The pressures of controlling its Caribbean empire led the imperial
government to support Catholic institutions in the region. Schools were
a basic starting point for implanting societal governance, and so, as the
end of enslavement neared, a range of missionary-run schools, Catholic
ones included, received direct payments from the Colonial Office. Crucially, London's support for the Catholic Church expanded beyond education and included money for at least ten chapels and schools across
the island, the salaries of fifteen priests (including the vicar apostolic),
and £1,000 for Port of Spain's Catholic Cathedral.[70] In 1838, the year
apprenticeship ended, the Colonial Office spent a total of £2,952 on the
Catholic Church on the island, in contrast to the £1,350 allocated to the
Church of England. Despite the salaries of Catholic priests being less
than half of what their Anglican counterparts received, the £1,000 allocated to the Catholic bishop at Port of Spain, who was responsible for
Catholics across the whole of the West Indies, was £400 more than the
highest-ranking Anglican.[71]

Figure 14. Catholic Cathedral, Port of Spain

When it came to educating the children of newly free people, the Colonial Office had either badly underestimated the extent of the need and associated costs or had assumed, wrongly, that the churches would foot the bill. Most of the churches refused and wasted little time in telling the secretary of state, Lord Glenelg, that the budget, which amounted to a paltry £34,000 for the entire region, was insufficient.[72] While the Church of England's Church Missionary Society explained that it could not expand its work because of the "very large increase in the Society's expenditure in the West Indies,"[73] the Wesleyan Missionary Society noted that

> the salaries of the teachers and other incidental expenses will so very considerably exceed the calculations which were made in the first instance, and that so little is likely to be unused, for some time to come, by local exertions, to meet annual expenditures, that the committee dare not venture to increase their responsibilities by adding to the number of school houses on the principle that only one-third of the annual expenses shall be met out of the Parliamentary Grant for the year.[74]

Given its larger base of followers, the Catholic Church had a broad remit: in addition to small village schools that opened under its supervision, the St. Joseph's Boys' and Girls' schools were founded to build up a Black middle class, and the Arima Indian mission boys' school (funded by the "profits of the liquor-store of the settlement") was established to convert the Indigenous population.[75] In 1836, the Sisters of St. Joseph of Cluny opened a convent boarding school in Port of Spain for the daughters of affluent Europeans, and the resident clergymen established the College of St. George for boys of the same category three years later. These two schools offered a local alternative, but St. George's was mired in controversy because of infighting between Smith and a French priest by the name of René Bertin who did not like the Irish clergy and wanted control of the institution.[76]

The schools run by women religious were pivotal to extending the authority of both the Catholic Church and the British state. Established in France in the first decade of the nineteenth century by the Burgundy-born Anne-Marie Javouhey, the Sisters of St. Joseph of Cluny devoted themselves to the care and education of young women. Cluny communities emerged on the west coast of Africa in Sierra Leone and Gambia in the early 1820s. In 1824, one was established in Martinique, and it was from there, twelve years later, that the Port of Spain foundation was made at the request of Bishop Daniel McDonnell.[77] Like so many other communities of women religious at the time, growth was rapid: in less than a decade, the Port of Spain community had grown from six professed sisters to twenty, and together they taught over 200 pupils in their boarding, day, and poor schools. The *Irish Catholic Directory* reported that these women gave "the utmost satisfaction to parents, guardians, and the community at large."[78]

According to one researcher, the deep connection that many enslaved people had had with Catholicism, through "the reception of baptism, Sunday observance, the acquisition of an elementary knowledge of the Faith, the recitation of certain fixed prayers, and the celebration of the four great annual Holy days of Christmas, New Year, Good Friday and Corpus Christi," continued after their emancipation.[79] A significant proportion of free people of colour, those described as having been "partly French in their cultural orientation [and] Roman Catholic insofar as they adhered to any European religion," remained loyal to the church after emancipation, at least for a time.[80] Research on last wills and testaments reveals that, until the early 1840s, most of these people acknowledging a relationship with Catholicism bequeathed money to the church and left personal religious possessions, such as statues, pictures of saints, and rosaries, to loved ones.[81] The decline in donations after this point may have been influenced by a desire for a more formal break with the symbols of white European culture following the end of apprenticeship. The Catholic Church was, after all, ensconced within the white establishment and had shown little interest in helping the newly emancipated people and their children move beyond proscribed boundaries.

Mounting Tensions between Britain and Rome

Between 1840 and 1865, "a two-pronged secular and religious civilizing mission crystallized," giving way to "self-supporting, self-governing, and ultimately self-extending churches."[82] While Trinidad exemplified this process, it was also a colonial space that bore witness to major tensions between the Church of England, the British government, and Rome. In the 1840s, a dark cloud of religious antagonism settled over the island. Centuries of missionary enterprise had given the Catholic Church a decided advantage, allowing it to embed and consolidate its authority. Yet, the Church of England, as one of Britain's state churches, felt entitled to special status, and so Anglican missionaries embarked upon an aggressive expansion campaign from their base in Barbados.[83] It had been common for colonial officials to privilege Protestantism: Catholic lands in Grenada, for example, were turned over to Protestant petitioners in the 1780s. What complicated the situation in Trinidad was its diverse Catholic majority.[84]

A culture of reform in the Catholic Church saw Rome centralize and extend its authority throughout the empire, as it elevated numerous vicariates (mission territories with their own bishops) to metropolitans (archdioceses). Church of England missionaries feared these changes, and the governor, Henry MacLeod, worried that the Anglican population was too small and too scattered to attract "educated" clergymen or to even justify the construction of a church.[85] Nonetheless, in 1844, he established the Church of England in Trinidad. Although Thomas Parry, the Anglican bishop of Barbados, is widely reputed to have pressured him into it, the ecclesiastical ordinance that established the Church of England on the island (Ordinance 16) had ultimately been MacLeod's decision.[86] The island's other religious groups were incensed with this action, and the *Respectful Memorial of the undersigned Inhabitants of Trinidad* to the governor and council revealed their widespread frustration. Bearing the signatures or marks of more than 1,500 people, the memorial expressed "great apprehension and alarm" at the ordinance, which threatened "to destroy the religious peace, which now exists in this island."[87] Calculated to undermine Catholicism's influence, it was a definite blow to its status. Bishop McDonnell explained to Lord Stanley, the colonial secretary, that, although he had instructed his followers not to protest the ordinance, a few "Irish Roman Catholics; men who never attend Church" managed to attend the debate in council that had introduced the ordinance.[88] Six years later, the Holy See made Port of Spain an archdiocese and upgraded Roseau in neighbouring Dominica to a diocese. This move cemented ultramontane authority and introduced a more uniform religious culture that was guided by papal encyclicals such as *Ubi Primum* (1847), which imposed a stricter code of conduct for female and male religious.[89]

The wing of the church responsible for shepherding these changes was the Sacred Congregation *de Propaganda Fide*, which was notorious for overlooking (or ignoring) colonial realities and for its sluggish movement on all matters.[90] This modus operandi meant that conflicts were often managed poorly. A succession crisis that hit Port of Spain in the early 1850s exposed the tensions engulfing the church over the rise of ultramontanism and the animosity that plagued French and Irish relations on the island. The death in 1852 of the enormously respected bishop Richard Patrick Smith was a tumultuous event because he had not named a successor. Born in County Longford, Ireland, in 1802, Smith had trained at Maynooth before serving as bishop in Trinidad from 1837. During his tenure, he worked closely with colonial officials to manage the Catholic population during the transition from enslaved to waged labour, and he guided Port of Spain's transformation from a vicariate apostolic to an archdiocese in 1850.[91] He had (for the most part) contained or at least controlled internal frictions with the church in Trinidad's, but his death exposed the serious rift that existed between ultramontanists and those opposed to the growing authority of Rome. The first sign of trouble came when twenty-one of Trinidad's priests (mostly Irish, but some French) called upon London's Cardinal Wiseman to "use his influence with the Lord Primate of Ireland," the forceful Dublin-based ultramontane Paul Cardinal Cullen, to ensure the appointment of a "worthy successor."[92] They gave no indication as to whom they wanted, but in approaching Wiseman, arguably the most powerful ultramontane Catholic figure in Britain at the time, they were almost certainly seeking an English or Irish replacement with similar sympathies. Some of the island's French priests would later emphasize the need for "English bishops" as a way of subverting the influence of the Irish.[93]

Although Smith's relationship with his predecessor, Daniel McDonnell, was acrimonious, both men had shared a preference for British missionaries, and neither made any attempt to hide the fact that they wanted a Trinidad priesthood filled with men of "British birth and connexions." Smith had even complained to the governor that "persevering and unscrupulous ... lay and clerical foreigners" – that is, French Catholics – were undermining his efforts to build a united church on the island.[94] In fact, the situation was more complicated than this, but what is clear is that the island's leading French priests distinguished between British and Irish and had a strong preference for the former.

Nicholas Wiseman, who had become cardinal archbishop of Westminster in 1850, was too distracted with domestic matters to worry much about what was happening in the Caribbean. Focused on the internal strife engulfing his own district, and neglectful of the need to be careful in the handling of the Port of Spain appointment, it was only in 1855 when he made his first move to find a replacement, offering the post to George Errington, an English priest from Yorkshire who had trained at Rome's English College. Errington's problem was not a lack of experience – far from it, as he had served as bishop of Plymouth before becoming coadjutor bishop of Westminster under Wiseman. Rather, it was his involvement in the battle that raged between Wiseman and the high-profile convert John Henry Newman, a sceptic of rigid ultramontanism.[95] As a staunch Newman ally, Errington was forced out of the Westminster post and offered Port of Spain as a concession. His refusal of the post barely registered in England, but it caused a three-year leadership vacuum in the British Caribbean that disrupted the practical functioning of the church and provoked the Colonial Office.[96] The uncertainty also inflamed the tensions between the Irish and French to such an extent that *Propaganda Fide* dispatched Monsignor George Talbot, an Etonian- and Oxford-educated English convert who was chamberlain to Pope Pius IX, to mediate.[97] A Wiseman ally, Talbot was an unfortunate and ineffectual choice, as he was already involved with the English feud.[98] His ethnicity, as one Irish observer noted, was also tricky: "I suppose you have heard that monsr Talbot is about [to be] sent on a secret mission towards Trinidad; I suppose to see how stand the relations between the French & Irish in that quarter. Whoever heard of an Englishman making peace between Paddy & the French?"[99] This comment, from a gossipy letter written by Patrick Feltram of Rome's Irish College to Cullen, is indicative of the wider problems plaguing the church. While Cullen had significant influence in many places, it seems to have been more limited in the Caribbean, where the French presence overwhelmed the Irish and where the Colonial Office had demonstrated a strong preference for English Catholic leadership.[100]

A dramatic shake-up happened in 1855, when, seemingly out of the blue, the Holy See appointed Vincent Spaccapietra, an Italian papal diplomat, who had been travelling in the Caribbean, as archbishop of Port of Spain. His status as a religious (meaning that he belonged to a religious institute), rather than a secular priest (he was a Vincentian of the Congregation of the Mission) troubled locals and British colonial officials,[101] but more provocative was that neither the London clergy nor the Colonial Office appear to have been consulted about the appointment – a stark contrast to procedures for all previous appointments. The total exclusion of London from the process concerned Colonial Office officials, who perceived it as a challenge to British authority. The person most aggrieved was Charles Elliot, Trinidad's governor, who took exception to the cleric's "foreign" status. Elliot had been governor of Bermuda from 1846 to 1852 before moving on to Trinidad, and was experienced in dealing with a range of Catholics, from clergy and convicts to soldiers and sailors.[102] He first clashed with Spaccapietra when the latter sent Michael Monaghan, the Irish-born bishop of Roseau, who had been managing the archdiocese since Smith's death, back to Dominica.

Perceived as a man of liberal principles, Elliot was, above all, a British imperialist who opposed the assertion of authority by foreign power, including Rome, in a British territory. Elliot condemned the removal of Monaghan, whom he described as a "respected prelate" and British subject, as the work of a conniving "foreigner."[103] As a punishment, Elliot refused to admit Spaccapietra as a member of the Royal Patriotic Fund, an organization founded in 1854 to support the families of British military personnel fighting in the Crimea and to bring together the clergy "of all persuasions" as advocates of the cause.[104] This exclusion drew sharp criticism from the Colonial Office, not least because the archbishop had donated £207 to the fund. Nonetherless, a belligerent Elliot argued that "instincts of common sense and good breeding satisfied me that it was unsuitable to ask a foreign Ecclesiastic of rank, residing amongst us casually, to take part in a purely national object."[105] Following this, and with the support of the Protestant-dominated legislative council, Elliot cut the archbishop's salary from £1,000 to £500 before refusing to pay it altogether, since, he felt, British money should be reserved for British subjects. He also bombarded the Colonial Office with protest letters lambasting "foreign" influence:

Dispassionate persons of British origin, whether Roman Catholic or Protestant, would do well to consider that there is something far more important at the source of this agitation, than a question of £500 ... viz whether a Foreign Ecclesiastic, arriving here, as he states, with a general delegation from the Court of Rome, should by virtue of that instrument, insist upon official recognition by the government of a British colony and dismiss the respected Prelate being a British subject, in the due receipt of the official stipend, and claim it himself as a matter of strict right ... Roman Catholics and Protestants of British origin are alike concerned that the persons placed in spiritual or temporal authority over them should be their fellow subject.[106]

Some, but not all, of Trinidad's British Catholic subjects agreed with the governor. The chair of the island's Roman Catholic Committee, James Kavanagh, published an address of support for Spaccapietra in the *Port of Spain Gazette* and organized a petition criticizing Elliot's conduct. The ultramontane cohort of signatories, which included a range of ethnicities, with a preponderance of Irish, French, and Spanish, called upon the queen to "interfere on behalf of forty-five thousand of [her] dutiful subjects":

> The impartial and liberal treatment which the Catholics of Trinidad have always received from the British government to the present time, is only of those strong and indissoluble ties by which they are bound and directed, and which makes their attachment to the mother country a pleasure as well as a duty – that in case the government choose to tear asunder those bonds, Your Majesty's Catholic subjects will deeply deplore the measure as the greatest injury which they can be called on to suffer.[107]

Like many of his contemporaries, Elliot was almost certainly influenced by the papal aggression rhetoric swirling about in the wake of the 1850 restoration of England's Roman Catholic Hierarchy. This major development changed the shape of Catholic culture at home and in the colonies, as English, Irish, and Scottish Catholics became more confident, more secure, and much more outward looking. Conversely, publications like *Punch* were consumed with anti-Catholic commentary: pieces like "Beef from the Vatican," which joked about the "recent importations of foreign cattle, the most remarkable is that of the extraordinary Bull from Rome," were deliberately provocative. Such articles sat alongside cartoons such as "The Guy Fawkes of 1850. Preparing to Blow up All England," which depicted a masked Pope Pius IX preparing a pyre of Anglican mitres.[108] George Augustus Sala's *The Grand Procession*, a series of twenty-four fold-out plates of a colourful (and very long) anti-restoration procession, provided alternative and amusing perspectives on the deeply contentious issue.[109]

Elliot, who was not anti-Catholic, was quick to respond to accusations of prejudice, declining "to vindicate [himself] against imputations of intention to slight a minister of religion and persons professing the Roman Catholic or any other form of worship."[110] He stressed that in

THE GUY FAWKES OF 1850
PREPARING TO BLOW UP ALL ENGLAND!

Figure 15. *Punch* cartoon

Figure 16. Anti-restoration procession (with permission of Beinecke
Rare Book and Manuscript Library)

no way was he passing judgment on the island's British Catholic subjects. His past behaviour when confronted with another appointment on which he had not been consulted tends to support this. William Walsh, the disagreeable bishop of Halifax, who had ecclesiastical responsibility for Bermuda, had taken the liberty of appointing a priest to that colony without consulting Elliot, who was governor there at the time.[111] Elliot made no issue of the appointment. In fact, it was only two years later, after Elliott had gone to Trinidad, and when it looked like Walsh was going to make another unilateral appointment, that the colonial secretary, Henry Pelham Fiennes Pelham-Clinton, 5th Duke of Newcastle-under-Lyme, instructed Bermuda's acting governor, Montgomery Williams, to remind the bishop of Halifax "that any selection he may make for supplying this vacancy must be subject to the approval of the governor of Bermuda and the secretary of state."[112] However, there were two important differences between these examples and what happened in Trinidad: first, the Bermuda appointments involved Irish clergy; second, they were low level and did not involve Rome. In Trinidad, conversely, the new archbishop was a top-brass appointment made by Rome.

Private notes in the Colonial Office papers reveal that officials in London had lost patience with Elliot and were in no mood to pick a fight with Rome. Officials disagreed, for example, with Elliot's presumption that the salary allocated to the archbishop of Port of Spain could be paid only to a British subject. Publicly, the secretary of state for war and the colonies, Henry Labouchere, stood by Elliot, but only long enough to arrange the governor's reassignment to the Royal Navy as rear-admiral.[113] Once Elliot was safely "promoted" and away from Trinidad in the spring of 1856, Labouchere instructed the new governor, William Robert Keate, to administer the oaths of allegiance to Spaccapietra and release his salary. Intermediaries were then told to inform Rome of the "desirableness of appointing a British subject" to the post in the future and to stipulate that the Trinidad priesthood "should be generally British-born" and that "the funds of the colony ought not to be" spent on foreign ecclesiastics.[114] Under these difficult circumstances, Spaccapietra lasted only another three years and failed to unify the Catholic body. When he left in 1859, serious damage had been done: among other things, the clergy lacked motivation, and the rate of attrition was dangerously high. A letter from the principal of the normal college at St. Lucia to Cullen described the situation: "My Grace the Bishop of Roseau/Dominica [Monaghan] is dead; the archbishop of Trinidad is about to return to his native Italy; our pastors are not over industrious, many of them are so occupied with the care of acquiring the means of enabling them to return and live at ease in Europe that they have no time to combat proselytism."[115]

While Rome had spectacularly misjudged the situation with the appointment of Spaccapietra, the episode had the interesting effect of positioning the Irish clergy in the Caribbean as representatives of Britain. In Newfoundland, as the following section reveals, the lack of any non-British contingent meant that the position of the Irish Catholics was markedly different.

Newfoundland

Perched on the extreme northeastern edge of North America, Newfoundland was one of Britain's most sparsely populated colonies. Wars, a seasonal fishery, anti-settler government policy, and an unwelcoming climate conspired to keep people away.[116] In 1764, its population was around 16,000. The governor, Hugh Palliser, an English-born naval officer, reported that Catholics outnumbered Protestants by a ratio of three to one (a ratio that would remain intact throughout the century), with Irish Catholics from Waterford, in the southeastern part of the country, representing a steady two-thirds of the Catholic population.[117] Newfoundland experienced its highest rates of immigration between 1815 and 1831, when large numbers of Irish Catholics arrived. By the late 1820s, the number of residents was just shy of 60,000.[118] This influx was short lived: migration started to decline during the 1840s before slowing to little more than a trickle as migrants sought locations with more robust economies. Newfoundland's concentration on fishing prevented the emergence of other industries and restricted employment opportunities.[119] Thus, when Newfoundland's population topped 107,000 in the 1860s, it was mainly the result of natural increase as opposed to new migration from Ireland and England.[120] The majority of people were concentrated in and around St. John's, the sheltered capital on the Avalon Peninsula; beyond that, they were scattered among the tiny fishing outposts that punctuated the coastline. Anthony Fleming, Catholic bishop of St. John's from 1830 to 1850, described these settlements:

> In three … towns, 4,000, 3,000, 2,000. In two or three other places about 1,000; and in no other place more than 500, which, for the most part you find them scattered here 40, there, 30, at a distance of twenty miles 20, perhaps thirty miles further 4 or 5, and in isolated harbours two, sometimes one family cut off from all communication with man save the precarious highway of the ocean, a path that is closed against them for six or seven months of the year by precarious barriers of ice.[121]

Newfoundland's unforgiving climate tested the limits of even the hardiest of settlers. The ones who managed to tough it out were sustained by two fisheries – cod and seal. These dominated the economy and were overseen by an aggressive pack of merchants whose profits depended entirely on the strength of markets in Europe and the Caribbean. Newfoundland's salt fish put it at the "heart of a consumer economy," but this position came at a heavy price for its people, who were at the mercy of the open northern Atlantic.[122] Deaths at sea were so frequent that widows and orphans were a fact of community life.[123]

Although Scottish Highland, Acadian, and Mi'kmaq communities emerged in and around the Codroy Valley on the southern coast from the early 1840s, the Irish dominated in many areas of the more populated east, in spite of their exclusion from the British union before 1801.[124] The British government's discouragement of permanent settlement made their lives difficult, since the infrastructure normally set up to facilitate colonial development was absent. Moreover, "oppressive restrictions" had adversely affected Newfoundland's Catholics. Palliser's Act of 1775, which "prohibited labourers who were not indentured servants from remaining ... after the summer fishery had ended," was particularly detrimental to Catholics, the majority of whom were labourers.[125] Nevertheless, many found ways of remaining. Over time, the economic diversity of the colony increased, and the Catholic community expanded to include shopkeepers, merchants, and independent artisans, along with a small group of other professionals, all of whom who were all eager to build up their prospects while enhancing Catholicism's respectability.[126]

The loyalty of Newfoundland's Catholics, like others elsewhere, was "motivationally complex" and shaped as much by economic ambition, political will, and personal aspiration as by a desire for peace, security, and religious freedom.[127] These concerns shaped their colonial identities, but, unlike the Catholics of Trinidad, those in Newfoundland had no recourse to pre-existing legal protections for their religious status. Moreover, the denial of self-government and Britain's insistence on trying to "establish a viable Protestant state" in a colony where the number of Catholics was growing rapidly impeded stability and confined the majority to abject poverty. Unsurprisingly, a climate of socio-political restlessness emerged.[128]

Prior to the early 1830s, the only Catholics with any real authority in Newfoundland were the members of the merchant and professional classes. The extension of "a liberty of conscience to all persons" in 1779 encouraged local Catholic business leaders, specifically James Keating, Patrick Gaul, John Comins, and Luke Marshall, to seek the governor's permission to recruit a Catholic priest and build a chapel in St. John's.[129] With the governor's consent, they identified James O'Donel, a County Tipperary Franciscan, whose Irish superiors were eager to help secure the requisite permissions from London and Rome so that he might be installed in Newfoundland. William Egan, the bishop of Waterford, gave James Talbot, vicar apostolic of the London District, a glowing reference for O'Donel:

> His conduct has been exceptionally irreproachable & regular; He is well informed, & long experienced in the duties of his sacred ministry – a zealous and popular preacher in both the English & the Irish language; (& this latter I beg leave to observe to your lordship, is indispensably necessary, to render a missionary useful in Newfoundland, as most of those, upon whom his labours are to be employ'd speak nothing else).[130]

It was hoped that O'Donel's presence would ensure proper spiritual provision and help stabilize the Catholic mission by pushing out the itinerant Irish missionaries who had brought "great scandal & detriment to religion."[131] Not only had these enterprising missionaries set themselves up in various outposts without sanction from Talbot, but they also stoked intra-Irish tensions between Leinster and Munster factions.

O'Donel, who never fully settled in Newfoundland, was initially viewed with suspicion. One American observer, a Dr. Gardner, noted that the Roman Catholics have "been indulged with leave to erect a mass house at St John's, and the officiating priest is an Irish gentleman who was chaplain in the last war to a French regiment, and it is probable, he is now on half pay from that Crown."[132] Yet from his arrival in St. John's as prefect apostolic in 1784, O'Donel focused on building a stronger relationship with government officials. O'Donel, whose tenure lasted from 1784 until 1807, was described as a "product of the Catholic Enlightenment, tolerant, conciliatory, and deeply respectful of legitimate civil authority." Governor John Campbell welcomed O'Donel's collaborative manner and permitted the cleric to do what was needed (including officiating at Catholic marriages) to "improve" the colony's Catholics.[133] According to one report, he succeeded in chasing away the unattached Irish missionaries, improving law and order, and "reclaim[ing] many of the natives from a state of semi-barbarism."[134] The "excellent relations" that he appeared to have with the local governing elite helped mend fences following the 1800 mutiny at the St. John's garrison. While the risk of an actual rising was minimal, the fear of one was real, and the execution of eight mutineers sent a warning. In spite of O'Donel's efforts to calm anxieties, this episode convinced local

Protestants of the need to maintain a Royal Navy presence at St. John's and stoked the fires of anti-Irishness.[135]

When he had been in Newfoundland for about a decade, O'Donel's supporters began pushing for his elevation to vicar apostolic. Dublin's Dominican archbishop, John Thomas Troy, was especially proactive and secured support from John Douglass, Talbot's successor in London, and Charles Erskine, a papal diplomat of Scottish Jacobite descent. As papal diplomat to the Court of St. James's, Erskine took the temperature of the British officials with respect to O'Donel's elevation. Receiving no objections, Rome declared the mission a vicariate apostolic in 1796; O'Donel was consecrated bishop in a ceremony held in Quebec.[136]

O'Donel described Newfoundland as a "dreary" place, but he had a deep commitment to the mission and established a foundation for Catholicism that was built upon and expanded by his successors, Patrick Lambert and Thomas Scallan, and a growing body of (mostly Irish) priests.[137] A visitor to Newfoundland in 1814 recorded that six priests worked under Lambert – one each in St. John's, Placentia, Harbour Grace, Ferryland, Trinity, and Conception Bay.[138] Like O'Donel, Lambert and Scallan were Franciscans, and they worked with the laity to expand the church's influence by building chapels and schools and by supporting inter-denominational philanthropic initiatives such as the Benevolent Irish Society. They were so successful in building up "good will among people generally that Catholics and Protestants frequently attended each other's services."[139]

These developments and the relatively good relationships that existed between the bishops and governors did not change the fact that Newfoundland had no real system of local governance. In fact, Newfoundland was an anomaly, when compared to the other colonies examined here, because conditions discouraged the integration of the Irish as imperial partners and as Britons.[140] This was influenced significantly by the homogeneity of the Catholic population until the middle of the nineteenth century.[141] The challenges surrounding the establishment of a local legislative assembly in 1832 highlighted the tensions that existed between the "Protestant elite" and the "Catholic establishment," and the precarious position of the merchant class, which was struggling with a declining cod fishery. Additionally, it underscored the entrenched belief among colonial officials that Irish Catholics were incapable of distinguishing between "spiritual and temporal authority."[142]

When naval rule came to an end in 1824, the post of governor became a civil appointment. The following year, when a Royal Charter was issued to "revamp" the Supreme Court in Newfoundland and introduce circuit courts, Newfoundland was "nominally recognised as an official colony," and the governor was permitted to establish a council to help him govern locally.[143] Antagonism from London coupled with local opposition saw Catholics confront a more pronounced culture of institutional prejudice in Newfoundland than elsewhere. The Colonial Office, for example, blocked Governor Thomas Cochrane's attempts to nominate three Catholics for the executive council, citing the lack of "oaths of allegiance and supremacy" as the reason.[144] Their exclusion pushed the bourgeois laity to exploit any opportunity available so that they might carve out a space in the emerging society.[145] Such ambitions faced increased scrutiny from the mid-1820s as a new and increasingly powerful current of ultramontane ecclesiastical authority took hold. The tensions that emerged between the laity and the bishops as a consequence of this were counterproductive and divisive and led to a protracted period of conflict and instability upon the wider Catholic community.[146]

The Rise of Ultramontanism

Newfoundland's first three bishops (O'Donel, Lambert, and Scallan) were known for respecting the authority of government and for giving the laity a wide berth; their collaborative approach had stabilized the church in the colony.[147] Michael Anthony Fleming, Scallan's successor, was not like them. A native of County Kilkenny, Fleming was also a Franciscan but one who lacked the diplomatic tact of his predecessors. He despised the authority of the laity, frowned upon religious mixing, and sought control of all Catholic-related institutions. Terry Murphy's description of Fleming as "the first clear example in Atlantic Canada of an ultramontane bishop, uncompromising in religion, but progressive in politics, whose popular clericalism signalled a new alliance between prelates, priests, middle-class reformers, and the Catholic rank and file" seems appropriate.[148] His divisive and unaccommodating manner led to a major clash with the Benevolent Irish Society (BIS).

The BIS had been established in 1806 by five Protestants and one Catholic, Thomas Meagher; its aim was to emphasize the Irish population's "own distinctive ethnicity and at the same time to prove their loyalty to the Protestant political establishment."[149] The BIS resembled Halifax's Charitable Irish Society (CIS) with its aims and non-denominationalism, but the early membership of the BIS was much larger than that of its Nova Scotia counterpart, with somewhere between 100 and 120 people. Women also appear to have been more involved in the BIS than in the CIS, since the former's rule offered membership to "Natives of Ireland, Sons of Irishmen, or women descendants of any present or future member."[150] The BIS privileged the elite, and, while "the poorest

Irish" accepted its support, they felt alienated from the group. It was this sense of alienation that gave Fleming a base from which to challenge the influence and ecumenism of the BIS.[151]

The Benevolent Irish Society was still firmly non-denominational in the 1820s, despite the bulk of its membership being Catholic. Although this infuriated Fleming, he was powerless to do anything while Scallan was alive. Fleming took particular issue with the BIS's Orphan Asylum School and the fact that its governing board refused to permit religious instruction during normal school hours.[152] Wanting to teach the tenets of Catholicism alongside the normal curriculum (reading, writing, arithmetic, bookkeeping, and navigation) to the roughly 250 boys and 215 girls attending the school by 1830, Fleming launched a campaign to discredit those in charge.[153] As numerous scholars testify, Fleming eventually gained control of the school and forced those not amenable to his wishes off the governing board, but the episode split the town's middle-class Catholics and marked the beginning of a protracted battle for control of education in Newfoundland.[154]

Fleming transformed Catholic culture in Newfoundland in two ways. First, he won over the fishers, who felt exploited and neglected by the Catholic merchants, and, second, he exploited the deeply entrenched spirit of reform that had already infused a cross-section of society.[155] In criticizing the lack of Catholic representation in the colony's political institutions, he tapped into a pre-existing vein of discontent surrounding Parliament's failure to deliver genuine constitutional reform for Newfoundland and the Colonial Office's unwillingness to see Newfoundland as a colony capable of running its own affairs.[156] Frustration existed across the denominational spectrum along with widespread incredulity at the prospect of London imposing import duties without offering political representation in exchange.[157] Additionally, the delay over the introduction of equitable treatment of Catholics created an acrimonious political climate. This mounting pile of grievances created the platform for Fleming's ecclesiastical authoritarianism.

Providing a cradle-to-grave menu of Catholic-run services characterized Fleming's plan for the reorganization of Newfoundland Catholicism along ultramontane lines. To get the ball rolling, he recruited two communities of women religious to St. John's, the Presentation Nuns and the Sisters of Mercy, and increased the number of clergy so that, by 1844, Newfoundland had twenty-seven priests.[158] There was also significant building activity: in less than fifteen years, a convent for the Sisters of Mercy was up, in addition to four new churches, and a cathedral in St. John's was underway.[159] Fleming made every effort to demonstrate just how invested Newfoundland's Catholic Church was in maintaining colonial stability. During a speech in Dublin (on one of his many trips to Ireland), he described Newfoundland as "one of the most useful of the British colonies" because of the value of its fisheries and its ability to train sailors for the Royal Navy. He added that James Louis O'Donel's appointment had been approved because of the government's need to find a way of controlling the "lowest order of English, Irish and Scottish" resident there. Like many other colonial bishops, Fleming made a concerted effort to connect the Catholic Church with colonial management, emphasizing that the "extraordinary influence of the Catholic priesthood over a congregation of Irish Catholics" was a solution to the "public disorder, arguments, and drunkenness, and debauchery, and violence, and tumult [that had] reigned triumphant."[160] Seeing Fleming as a "constitutional nationalist" who prioritized an Irish identity within a British imperial framework, as opposed to an anti-British Irishman, offers a more constructive understanding of Catholicism in Newfoundland at the time.[161] As noted in the first two chapters, Irishness and Britishness did not have to be mutually exclusive: more often than not, people from the four nations possessed at least dual, and often multiple, identities.

Above all, Fleming was an ultramontane autocrat. In this, he was by no means unique, though he did have a special talent for alienating people: while church and government officials in Newfoundland, London, and Rome found him insufferable, the laity thought him obstinate. As Newfoundland's first ultramontane bishop, Fleming challenged almost everything about how the church had been operating in the colony. His willingness to engage in politics, his criticism of the local assembly for its lack of Catholic representation, his complaints about the delay in allocating land for a cathedral, and his challenge to the anti-Catholic culture of St. John's earned him frequent reprimands from Rome.[162] He was even reproached in 1838 for his political meddling by Pope Gregory XVI, who wrote: "For since it is necessary that all types of men come to know more clearly the light of day, Catholic priests should seek and will nothing other than the glory of Jesus Christ and the spread of religion; something that, without pious behaviour and the study of fraternal charity we never achieve."[163] Even this reminder failed to bring him in line. Subsequently, the British government made representations to Rome about the bishop's conduct and requested his removal (the failure to do so resulted in London's refusal to permit a Catholic mission at Corfu). *Propaganda Fide* issued yet another stern warning:

> Now ... you will easily grasp how much is to be feared from Your Grace's behaviour, not listening to the repeated admonitions of this Sacred

Congregation, nor indeed of the Holy Father himself, when indeed you may see from this that both the dignity of the Holy See and the good of the Catholic religion are brought into disrepute.[164]

It was only after Fleming received a letter from Antonio De Luca, his Roman agent, who pleaded with him "not to live in a state of open hostility with the English government in political affairs," that he finally reined in his behaviour.[165]

Relations between Fleming and colonial officials improved a little after 1841, but things remained tense until 1846, when a devastating fire swept through St. John's and destroyed much of the Catholic infrastructure that had begun to emerge, including the Presentation Convent, which was a devastating loss. Although upwards of 1,000 children were taught at the convent before the fire, accommodation for just 400 was possible afterwards, and most of the books were destroyed.[166] Fortunately, help arrived from many sources:

> The British Government have subscribed £3,000 – Canada has poured in about £6,000, Nova Scotia which led the way in the march of charity sent us nearly £3,000. Prince Edward's Island and New Brunswick too have given their ___ and London, Liverpool and Manchester in England – and in Scotland, Glasgow has not forgotten the claims of this old and faithful and profitable British colony.[167]

In 1847, the rebuilding of St. John's coincided with the darkest year of Ireland's Famine. The governor increased Fleming's annual stipend to £300 and expected him to use the money "to repress religious differences in Newfoundland and promote peace and contentment happily now subsisting amongst all classes in the colony."[168] He spent it on Catholic education.

The real drivers of education in Newfoundland, like elsewhere, were women religious. The Presentation Nuns, who were the dominant teaching community, were instrumental in helping authorities manage the growth of the church in Newfoundland.[169] Despite arriving from Ireland in 1833 as an enclosed community, the mission's demands, which included sick visitations, necessitated its transformation into a mixed one.[170] This meant that, although the nuns still took solemn vows, they were no longer confined to their convent and able to be more involved in external activities. The nuns' relocation to Newfoundland was difficult, and they were unprepared for the harsh life that awaited them. Basics such as cream, butter, and eggs that were easily procured in Ireland were expensive luxuries in Newfoundland, and their accommodations left much to be desired. Their first convent was a former tavern, known locally as the Rising Sun, and their first school was in a (probably poorly) converted slaughterhouse.[171] Insufficient heating made the harsh winters almost unbearable, and the convent's food and water froze regularly.[172]

The Sisters of Mercy were Newfoundland's other religious community. In 1842, the Dublin motherhouse sent three professed sisters and one postulant to St. John's. Sisters M. Francis Creedon, M. Ursula Frayne, M. Rose Lynch, and Maria Supple left Ireland on the *Sir Walter Scott* on 2 May and arrived on 4 June.[173] Creedon was an important figure for the Newfoundland foundation. Orphaned at a young age in Ireland, she had been adopted by the Nugents, an affluent County Waterford family, and had moved with them to St. John's when Bishop Fleming, their family friend, invited them. When Creedon came of age, Fleming sent her to Dublin to undertake her novitiate with the Sisters of Mercy. He had intended her to return to Newfoundland and lead the new Mercy community, but the Dublin leadership had other ideas and intended the more experienced Sister M. Ursula for the role of superior.[174] Not surprisingly, the relationship between Fleming and Frayne became so tense that the latter left Newfoundland the following year.[175] Like many religious congregations, the Mercies regularly and effectively opposed the intervention of male clerics, sometimes by leaving, when they tried to set courses for community direction that diverged from the aims of the congregation or community's leadership.[176]

An important part of the Mercy mission was nursing work, and so, in addition to teaching, the sisters made sick calls and provided care to the sick poor.[177] An outbreak of measles within a month of their arrival meant that their nursing work began before their teaching did. Their efforts won them early praise from the sympathetic editor of the *Patriot and Terra Nova Herald*, who described them as "Angels of Mercy – flitting from one scene of misery to another, administering to the wants of those who otherwise might suffer without assistance and die for want of it."[178] Yet, it was teaching that shaped their identity in Newfoundland. The Sisters of Mercy concentrated on the daughters of the "wealthier classes," leaving the Presentation Nuns to corral the rest and teach "an average of 800 girls annually."[179] Across the British world, women religious emerged as agents of education and as entrepreneurs who built up the foundations for other projects.

Over the course of the 1840s and 1850s, Newfoundland's bishops built relationships with their colleagues in Canada West, Canada East, and the Maritimes, as well as with officials in Rome and London.[180] Despite such relationships Fleming and his counterparts in Nova Scotia and Prince Edward Island opposed attempts by Quebec to make itself the centre of an ecclesiastical province in the early 1840s. According to Mark McGowan, Fleming saw the Catholics of Newfoundland as having much more in common with those of Ireland and Europe than of Quebec. Moreover, the historic ties of the coastal communities of these three colonies to the Atlantic world meant that any ecclesiastical union that put them under the jurisdiction of Quebec was unlikely to gain traction.[181] Rome's unwelcomed intervention in 1847 in elevating Newfoundland to a bishopric attached to the archdiocese of Quebec incited protest from Fleming, who was ultimately successful in lobbying to have Newfoundland's ecclesiastical independence restored.[182] As with the appointment of Spaccapietra to Port of Spain a few years later, this kind of top-down intervention by Rome revealed its inability to appreciate colonial realities.

In some ways, Newfoundland's resistance to a formal ecclesiastical connection with Quebec demonstrated its connection to an emerging British Catholic world, shaped by a four-nations reality, but in other ways the colony showed a clear connection to a broader Hiberno-Roman world.[183] In any case, because of its homogeneous Irish Catholic population, Newfoundland was an outlier in the empire. Colonies such as Trinidad and Newfoundland are useful cases for exploring some of the ways in which the empire's more peripheral and coastal populations contributed to its development. Each case reveals interesting contrasts to the other colonies. The presence of such a large population of enslaved and free persons of colour in Trinidad shaped how colonial and church officials interacted and was a major factor in the strong preference for English vicars apostolic. Loyalty and concerns about its conditionality connected both colonies. In Newfoundland, where disloyalty was never really an issue, despite being a genuine fear, and where the Catholic population was almost entirely Irish, the government extended few concessions.

Conclusion

We must ... confess that, without Catholic blood or Catholic valour, no victory could ever have been obtained, and the first military talents in Europe might have been exerted in vain at the head of an army.

"The Duke of Wellington on Catholic Loyalty"

Tucked away in the Charles Kent papers at Yale's Beinecke Library, a small newspaper clipping entitled "The Duke of Wellington on Catholic Loyalty" bears these words. The clipping is from a late 1870s reprint of the speech delivered by the prime minister, Arthur Wellesley, 1st Duke of Wellington, to the House of Commons in 1829. In making a case for Catholic emancipation, he acknowledged the contribution made by Catholic soldiers in Britain's most recent war with France. Wellington declared it was "well known to your Lordships that the troops which our gracious Sovereign did me the honour to entrust to my command at various periods during the war – a war undertaken expressly for the purpose of securing the happy institutions and independence of the country – that at least one-half were Roman Catholics."[1] Charles Kent, a London-born Catholic journalist, was the editor of the *Sun*, "a liberal evening newspaper," from 1845 until 1871, and then the *Weekly Register*, a Catholic journal, between 1874 and 1881,[2] and he may have saved this particular clipping because his family had a personal connection with that conflict. His father, William, had served as an officer in the Royal Navy and would have been among the service's first batch of Catholic officers. Convincing this family, and countless others like them, that they were not Britons would have been impossible.

This and the other examples of Catholic identity highlighted in the preceding chapters have raised new and important questions about the kind of image that needs to be projected of the British Empire. The

evidence presented here demonstrates that it was not exclusively Protestant – far from it – and that there was considerable diversity, which
began with people from the four home nations who were active in negotiating new local and colonial roles for themselves, their families,
and the various communities to which they belonged. Neither Britain
nor its empire belonged to any one nation or group, and long before
the home country's population became one-quarter Catholic, with the
union that created the United Kingdom of Great Britain and Ireland,
Catholics from Ireland, Scotland, England, and Wales had collaborated
with their fellow Britons in advancing the imperial program. The empire offered Catholics the opportunity to reframe their image as loyal
subjects and to redefine their futures as respectable citizens. It was a
rapidly expanding space, pregnant with possibilities, and it was never
the case that anyone from the four nations had to stop being Catholic
to start being British.

  Empire and Emancipation was a project that enabled me to begin exploring this diversity by considering the experience of Catholics at the
fringe of Britain's north Atlantic empire and as a way of reflecting on
the agency of minority groups in an imperial state. In focusing on the
mix of Catholic experiences in places like Nova Scotia, Newfoundland,
Cape Breton, Trinidad, and Bermuda, I have given significant consideration to the decentred nature of the British maritime world, which
has opened up exciting new perspectives on the sea-based approach
to the British Empire. In these places, Catholics were either the majority population or a very large minority; in all cases, they were active
in expanding the boundaries of their citizenship by using what rights
they possessed to acquire more. It is in these places, the ones often overlooked because of their coastal locations, that we encounter some of the
empire's earliest, largest, and most diverse Catholic populations and
where we can view the myriad ways in which they learned how to
exert social, economic, and political influence within the communities
they helped to establish. All of the colonies and territories considered
here were central to Britain's Atlantic empire, and it is obvious that, in
such an empire, the people and places at the ocean's fringe were among
the most central to its success. It is unsurprising, then, that these Catholic populations were important to the imperial government and took
a major part in the emancipative process. After all, the Atlantic world
was an area of exchanges and processes that went in many directions,
not least from west to east.

  I have paid particular attention to the experiences of the Irish and
the Scots, and, in casting light on some of the creative strategies that
they adopted to expand their sense of belonging, I have offered a new

argument about how understandings of Britain and Britishness began to unfold. This work is not finished, but, in showing how these parts of the British Empire functioned as main outlets for Catholic ambition, an important case has been made for including minority perspectives in studies of British imperialism. The objective of *Empire and Emancipation* is to start a conversation about some of the missing components of the British imperial context by highlighting the roles that Catholics played in expanding the reach of the state. In concentrating, in part, on a selection of colonies and territories in northeastern British North America, more details about Catholicism's entanglement with empire emerges. Place anchors this book, and the choices were deliberate. None of the colonies and territories selected were glamorous, and many were places that Scottish and Irish migrants went to because they had few alternatives. Yet each one has substantial value in helping us to understand, in more precise terms, the ways in which Catholics and the Catholic Church engaged with and contributed to the progress of British imperialism.

The book's overarching themes are empire and emancipation, but three sub-themes of imperial security, minority agency, and national identity are essential components. I have interrogated these themes from the perspective of a four-nations analysis – my decision to do this was also deliberate, because the bulk of the colonizing Catholic Britons came from Scotland and Ireland, not from England and Wales. Analysing these themes in this way has helped me to complicate perspectives on what the imperial state meant. In focusing on Catholics, we can see the influence that ethno-religious collaboration between the United Kingdom's constituent nations played in the emergence of this state. This approach has clarified that, in the context of empire (and within Britain for that matter), *Catholic* was not synonymous with *Irish*, and has made room for Scottish and English Catholics and asked questions about their roles in and influence over the shaping of colonial Catholic identities. At the same time, the approach I have taken has enabled the integration of the Irish Catholics in a way that did not compromise their national integrity. We need to understand the depth, complexity, and diversity of the empire's Catholic story. This book makes an important contribution by drawing attention to the fact that, although numerically dominant in many places, the Irish were by no means the only Catholic group with some influence or authority operating abroad. Scottish Catholics had significant influence in many parts of British North America before 1850 and, during the eighteenth and early to mid-nineteenth centuries, the vicars apostolic of the London District and the rectors of a number of the Continental English colleges played defining roles in how Catholics in the colonies were managed.

This book has shown that, although commonly associated with enslaved Africans, emancipation was a term that also held tremendous significance for Catholic Britons. Unlike the enslaved, who lacked the kind of access to parliamentary circles and pressure groups that Irish and Scottish Catholics had, many Catholics from across the four nations were active collaborators in the campaign to achieve social and economic equality. While the eventual emancipation of enslaved people was predicated upon a resolution of the financial concerns of their "owners," the cause of Catholic emancipation was advanced, first and foremost, by broader concerns about the security of the empire.

In engaging with imperial security, minority agency, and national identity, I have been able to start to test just how powerful and influential the British state and its overarching imperial identity actually became. I argue that the concepts of *Britain* and *British* actually survived and were strengthened because of the meaningful collaboration (in various forms) among the four nations and their constituent populations, Catholics included. This book will not stop *nation* from being a highly contested term in the British context – indeed, I had no intention of writing a book that would do that – but it has shown another dimension to the forging the British state. While the 1707 union between England and Wales and Scotland cast Britishness as an experience of national and imperial belonging, the empire enabled Britons from across the religious spectrum to claim a place in the nation, state, and empire and to influence the development of each as a consequence.

Ultimately, this book is intent on progressing understandings of Britain and Britishness by exploring how one religious minority, Catholics, used the opportunities of empire to expand the boundaries of citizenship. It represents a call to see Britain's imperial program as a constantly evolving process that depended on continuous negotiation and renegotiation between various collaborators – some of whom were British and some of whom were not. Considered in this way, it becomes easier to see how the British Empire's expansion happened. As Catholics gained access to new opportunities, they became more proactive in responding to the rapidly changing global dynamic and acquired authority as a result. Together, the book's chapters provide a cogent analysis of the various ways in which this was achieved and how it translated into greater civic and professional responsibility, which facilitated their socioeconomic mobility. Building an awareness of the Catholic experience is an important and necessary step in broadening understandings of just how complex the British Empire actually was and what it meant to those who engaged with its development. This area of research is full of possibilities, and much more work is needed to unpack the complexity of the British Catholic Atlantic. The next phase of my research will be taking a closer look at the Caribbean by moving beyond Trinidad. There is an urgent need to interrogate how the Catholicism of enslaved people, free people of colour, and other groups influenced the development of imperial policy and church development. There is a need to understand more about the archival landscape in this region so that researchers are in a better position to connect the dots and to understand more about Catholicism's integration with the processes of imperialism and colonization.

Abbreviations

AASJ	Archdiocese Archives of St. John's, St. John's, Canada
ADA	Archdiocese of Dublin Archives, Dublin, Ireland
AHA	Archdiocese of Halifax Archives, Halifax, Canada
APF	Archives of Propaganda Fide, Rome, Italy
ARCAT	Archives of the Catholic Archdiocese of Toronto, Toronto, Canada
AVCAU	Archivum Venerabilis Collegii Anglorum de Urbe, Rome, Italy
BICBU	Beaton Institute, Cape Breton University, Sydney, Canada
BL	British Library, London, England
BRBML	Beineke Rare Book and Manuscript Library, Yale University, New Haven, United States
CMA	Chestico Museum and Archives, Port Hood, Canada
DULASC	Durham University Library, Archives and Special Collections, Durham, England
LAC	Library and Archives Canada, Ottawa, Canada
NLS	National Library of Scotland, Edinburgh, Scotland
NSA	Nova Scotia Archives, Halifax, Canada
PACM	personal archives of Chris McClement, Oxfordshire, England
PAEB	private archives of the English Benedictines, England
PAMK	personal archives of Myles Kehoe, Margaree Forks, Canada
QUBA	Queen's University Belfast Archives, Belfast, Northern Ireland
SCA	Scottish Catholic Archives, Edinburgh, Scotland
SCRA	Scots College Rome Archives, Rome, Italy
TNA	The National Archives, London, England
UCLUD	Ushaw College Library and Special Collections, University of Durham, Durham, England
WDA	Westminster Diocesan Archives, London, England

Notes

Introduction

1 P.J. Marshall, *Remaking the British Atlantic: The United States and the British Empire after American Independence* (Oxford: Oxford University Press, 2012); Stephen Conway, "Christians, Catholics, Protestants: The Religious Links of Britain and Ireland with Continental Europe, c. 1689–1800," *English Historical Review* 124:509 (2009): 834.

2 J.M. Bumsted, "The Consolidation of British North American, 1783–1860," in *Canada and the British Empire*, ed. Phillip Buckner (Oxford: Oxford University Press, 2010), 44.

3 S. Karly Kehoe, "Catholic Highland Scots and the Colonization of Prince Edward Island and Cape Breton Island, 1772–1830," in *Reappraisals of British Colonization in Atlantic Canada, 1700–1900*, ed. S. Karly Kehoe and Michael E. Vance (Edinburgh: Edinburgh University Press, 2020); J.M. Bumsted, *Land, Settlement and Politics on Eighteenth-Century Prince Edward Island* (Montreal and Kingston: McGill-Queen's University Press, 1987).

4 L.W.B. Brockliss and David Eastwood, eds., *A Union of Multiple Identities: The British Isles, c. 1750–c. 1850* (Manchester: Manchester University Press, 1997).

5 Linda Colley, *Britons: Forging the Nation, 1707–1837* (New Haven, CT: Yale University Press, 1992); Jerry Bannister and Liam Riordan, "Loyalism and the British Atlantic, 1660–1840," in *The Loyal Atlantic: Remaking the British Atlantic in the Revolutionary Era*, ed. Bannister and Riordan (Toronto: University of Toronto Press, 2012), 8–11.

6 Conway, "Christians, Catholics, Protestants," 858.

7 J.G.A. Pocock, "Empire, State and Confederation: The War of American Independence as a Crisis in Multiple Monarchy," in *A Union for Empire: Political Thought and the British Unions of 1707*, ed. John Robertson (Cambridge: Cambridge University Press, 1995), 331.

8 Barry Crosbie, *Irish Imperial Networks: Migration, Social Communication and Exchange in Nineteenth-Century India* (Cambridge: Cambridge University Press, 2012), 19.

9 P.A. Buckner, "Making British North America British, 1815–1860," in *Kith and Kin: Canada, Britain and the United States from the Revolution to the Cold War*, ed. C.C. Eldridge (Cardiff: University of Wales Press, 1997), 27.

10 Joanna Innes, "'Reform' in English Public Life: The Fortunes of a Word," in *Rethinking the Age of Reform: Britain 1780–1850*, ed. Arthur Burns and Joanna Innes (Cambridge: Cambridge University Press, 2003), 71–2.

11 Mark McGowan, "The Maritimes Region and the Building of a Canadian Church: The Case of the Diocese of Antigonish after Confederation," *Canadian Catholic Historical Association Historical Studies* 70 (2004): 48–70.

12 Kehoe, "Catholic Highland Scots."

13 Adrian Hastings, *The Construction of Nationhood: Ethnicity, Religion and Nationalism* (Cambridge: Cambridge University Press, 1997), 17–18.

14 C.A. Bayly, "The Second British Empire," in *The Oxford History of the British Empire*, vol. 5, *Historiography*, ed. Roger Winks and Wm. Roger Louis (Oxford: Oxford University Press, 1999), 71. For an interesting perspective on Scotland, see Colin Kidd, "The Gaelic Dilemma in Early Modern Scottish Political Culture," chap. 6 in *British Identities before Nationalism: Ethnicity and Nationhood in the Atlantic World, 1600–1800* (Cambridge: Cambridge University Press, 1999), 123–45.

15 John M. MacKenzie, "Empire and Metropolitan Cultures," in *The Oxford History of the British Empire*, vol. 3, *The Nineteenth Century*, ed. W. Roger Louis (Oxford: Oxford University Press, 1999), 270–93; Jennifer Ridden, "Britishness as an Imperial and Diasporic Identity: Irish Elite Perspectives, c. 1820s–70s," in *Victoria's Ireland? Irishness and Britishness, 1837–1901*, ed. Peter Gray (Dublin: Four Courts Press, 2008), 88–9, 96; Andrew Mackillop, *"More Fruitful Than the Soil": Army, Empire and the Scottish Highlands, 1715–1815* (East Linton, SCT: Tuckwell Press, 2000); Catherine Hall, *Macaulay and Son: Architects of Imperial Britain* (New Haven, CT: Yale University Press, 2012); Barry Crosbie, *Irish Imperial Networks: Migration, Social Communication and Exchange in Nineteenth-Century India* (Cambridge: Cambridge University Press, 2012).

16 Martin Daunton and Rick Halpern, "Introduction: British Identities, Indigenous Peoples, and the Empire," in *Empire and Others: British Encounters with Indigenous People, 1600–1850*, ed. Daunton and Halpern (Philadelphia: University of Pennsylvania Press, 1999), 5–6.

17 Catherine Hall, "Culture and Identity in Imperial Britain," in *The British Empire: Themes and Perspectives*, ed. Sarah Stockwell (Oxford: Blackwell Published, 2008), 200–2.

18 *An Act for Making More Effectual Provision for the Governance of the Province of Quebec in North America* (*The Quebec Act*, 7 October 1774), http://avalon.law.yale.edu/18th_century/quebec_act_1774.asp.

19 Michael Gauvreau, "Covenanter Democracy: Scottish Popular Religion, Ethnicity, and Varieties of Politico-religious Dissent in Upper Canada, 1815–1841," *Histoire sociale/Social History* 35:71 (2003): 55–84; Stewart J. Brown, *Thomas Chalmers and the Godly Commonwealth in Scotland* (Oxford: Oxford University Press, 1982).

20 C.A. Bayly, *Imperial Meridian: The British Empire and the World, 1780–1830* (Harlow, EN: Longman, 1989), 137.

21 Gabriel Glickman, "A British Catholic Community? Ethnicity, Identity and Recusant Politics, 1660–1750," in *Early Modern English Catholicism: Identity, Memory and Counter-Reformation*, ed. James E. Kelly and Susan Royal (Leiden: Brill, 2017), 62.

22 Marshall, *Remaking the British Atlantic*, 121. G.I.T. Machin, "Resistance to Repeal of the Test and Corporation Acts, 1828," *Historical Journal* 22:1 (1979): 115–39.

23 Christopher Tozzi, "Jews, Soldiering, and Citizenship in Revolutionary and Napoleonic France," *Journal of Modern History* 86 (2014): 233–57.

24 Ibid., 234–5.

25 An interesting perspective is provided by Matthew Dziennik, "Imperial Conflict and the Contractual Basis of Military Society in the Early Highland Regiments," in *Soldiering in Britain and Ireland, 1750–1850: Men at Arms*, ed. Catriona Kennedy and Matthew McCormack (London: Palgrave, 2013), 17–36.

26 Sarah Roddy, "Spiritual Imperialism and the Mission of the Irish Race: The Catholic Church and Emigration from Nineteenth-Century Ireland," *Irish Historical Studies* 38:152 (2013): 600–19; S. Karly Kehoe, "Accessing Empire: Irish Surgeons and the Royal Navy, 1850–1880," *Social History of Medicine* 26:2 (2013): 204–22; S. Karly Kehoe, "Catholic Relief and the Political Awakening of Irish Catholics in Nova Scotia, 1780–1830," *Journal of Imperial and Commonwealth History* 46:1 (2018), http://dx.doi.org/10.1080/03086534.2017.1390893.

27 Pamela Scully and Diana Paton, eds., *Gender and Slave Emancipation in the Atlantic World* (Durham, NC: Duke University Press, 2005), 5.

28 Debbie Lee, ed., *Slavery, Abolition and Emancipation: Writing in the British Romantic Period*, vol. 3, *The Emancipation Debate* (London: Pickering & Chatto, 1999), xvi.

29 Liam Hogan, Laura McAtackney, and Matthew C. Reilly, "The Irish in the Anglo-Caribbean: Servants or Slaves?" *History Ireland* 24:2 (2016): 18–22.

30 Stephen Lenik, "Mission Plantations, Space and Social Control: Jesuits as Planters in French Caribbean Colonies and Frontiers," *Journal of Social Archaeology* 12:1 (2011): 51–71.

31 Nini Rodgers, "Ireland and the Black Atlantic in the Eighteenth Century," *Irish Historical Studies* 32:126 (2000): 190; Howard A. Fergus, *Montserrat: History of a Caribbean Colony* (Oxford: Macmillan, 2004), 62–77. Fergus was knighted in 2001.

32 Rodgers, "Ireland and the Black Atlantic," 190.

33 Nini Rodgers, "Richard Robert Madden: An Irish Anti-Slavery Activist in the Americas," in *Ireland Abroad: Politics and Professions in the Nineteenth Century*, ed. Oonagh Walsh (Dublin: Four Courts Press, 2003), 130; Fergus, *Montserrat*, 63–5.

34 Sven Beckert, "Emancipation and Empire: Reconstructing the Worldwide Web of Cotton Production in the Age of the American Civil War," *American Historical Review* 109:5 (2004): 1405–38.

35 Colin Kidd, "Ethnicity in the British Atlantic World, 1688–1830," in *A New Imperial History: Culture, Identity and Modernity in Britain and the Empire, 1600–1840*, ed. Kathleen Wilson (Cambridge: Cambridge University Press, 2004), 260–77.

36 Hall, *Macaulay and Son*, chap. 4.

37 Ibid., 150.

38 Michael A. Schoeppner, "Status across Borders: Roger Taney, Black British Subjects, and a Diplomatic Antecedent to the Dred Scott Decision," *American Historical Review* 100:1 (2013): 46–67.

39 Quoted in Nini Rodgers, *Ireland, Slavery and Anti-Slavery, 1612–1865* (Basingstoke, EN: Palgrave Macmillan, 2007), 191–2.

40 Alvin Jackson, *The Two Unions: Ireland, Scotland and the Survival of the United Kingdom, 1707–2007* (Oxford: Oxford University Press, 2012), 143.

41 Richard A. Keogh, "'Nothing Is so Bad for the Irish as Ireland Alone': William Keogh and Catholic Loyalty," *Irish Historical Studies* 38:150 (2012): 232–3.

1 Catholics, Colonies, and the Imperial State

1 Cape Breton Island had been a French possession but was annexed to Nova Scotia when that colony was acquired by Britain during the Seven Years' War. It was separated and given its own lieutenant governor in 1784; it remained a separate colony until 1820, when it was re-annexed to Nova Scotia.

2 Kevin Whelan, "An Underground Gentry? Catholic Middlemen in Eighteenth-Century Ireland," in *The Tree of Liberty: Radicalism, Catholicism and the Construction of Irish Identity, 1760–1830* (Cork, IE: Cork University

Press, 2006), 3–58; Kevin Whelan, "The Catholic Community in Eighteenth-Century County Wexford," in *Endurance and Emergence: Catholic in Ireland in the Eighteenth Century*, ed. T.P. Power and Kevin Whelan (Dublin: Irish Academic Press, 1990), 137–44.

3   John Bergin, "Irish Catholics and Their Networks in Eighteenth-Century London," *Eighteenth-Century Life* 39:1 (2015): 75, 84–5, 91.

4   Kate Gibson, "Marriage Choice and Kinship among the English Catholic Elite, 1680–1730," *Journal of Family History* 41:2 (2016): 144–64; Geoffrey Scott, "The Throckmortons at Home and Abroad, 1680–1800," in *Catholic Gentry in English Society: The Throckmortons of Coughton from Reformation to Emancipation*, ed. Peter Marshall and Geoffrey Scott (Farnham, EN: Ashgate, 2009), 176–80.

5   Alasdair F.B. Roberts, "The Role of Women in Scottish Catholic Survival," *Innes Review* 70:2 (1991): 129–50; Gibson, "Marriage Choice"; S. Karly Kehoe, *Creating a Scottish Church: Catholicism, Gender and Ethnicity in Nineteenth-Century Scotland* (Manchester: Manchester University Press, 2010).

6   Richard A. Keogh, "'Nothing Is so Bad for the Irish as Ireland Alone': William Keogh and Catholic Loyalty," *Irish Historical Studies* 38:150 (2010): 230.

7   Catherine Hall, *Macaulay and Son: Architects of Imperial Britain* (New Haven, CT: Yale University Press, 2012), 157; Kevin Whelan, "The Other Within: Ireland, Britain and the Act of Union," in *Acts of Union: The Causes, Contexts and Consequences of the Act of Union*, ed. Dáire Keogh and Kevin Whelan (Dublin: Four Courts Press, 2001), 23.

8   Colin Kidd, "Wales, the Enlightenment and the New British History," *Welsh Review of History* 25:2 (2010): 212.

9   J.G.A. Pocock, "British History: A Plea for a New Subject," *Journal of Modern History* 4:4 (1975): 611–2.

10   James Kelly, "The Act of Union: Its Origins and Background," in Keogh and Whelan, *Acts of Union*, 49.

11   Richard Bourke, "Pocock and Presuppositions of the New British History," *Historical Journal* 53:3 (2010): 747–70.

12   Kidd, "Wales, the Enlightenment," 210; Laurence W.B. Brockliss and David Eastwood, eds., *A Union of Multiple Identities: The British Isles, c. 1750–c. 1850* (Manchester: Manchester University Press, 1997).

13   Linda Colley, *Britons: Forging the Nation, 1707–1837* (New Haven, CT: Yale University Press, 1992).

14   Thomas Bartlett, "Britishness, Irishness and the Act of Union," in Keogh and Whelan, *Acts of Union*, 255.

15   Andrew MacKillop, *"More Fruitful Than the Soil": Army, Empire and the Scottish Highlands, 1715–1815* (East Linton, SCT: Tuckwell Press, 2000), 207–8.

16 Tony Claydon and Ian McBride, "The Trails of the Chosen Peoples: Recent Interpretations of Protestantism and National Identity in Britain and Ireland," in *Protestantism and National Identity: Britain and Ireland, c. 1650–c. 1850*, ed. Tony Claydon and Ian McBride (Cambridge: Cambridge University Press, 1998), 14–15.

17 David Allan, "Protestantism, Presbyterianism and National Identity in Eighteenth-Century Scottish History," in Claydon and McBride, *Protestantism and National Identity*, 182–205.

18 Colin Kidd, *Unions and Unionisms: Political Thought in Scotland, 1500–2000* (Cambridge: Cambridge University Press, 2008), 51.

19 Claydon and McBride, "The Trails of the Chosen Peoples," 19.

20 John Bergin, "Irish Catholics and Their Networks in Eighteenth-Century London," *Eighteenth-Century Life* 39:1 (2015): 75 and 91.

21 Archives of Propaganda Fide (hereafter APF), *Scritture riferite nei Congressi, Fondo Irlanda* 15/70, clipping, unknown newspaper, February 1781.

22 James Kelly and Martyn J. Powell, eds., *Clubs and Societies in Eighteenth-Century Ireland* (Dublin: Four Courts Press, 2010); Bergin, "Irish Catholics," 70–1, 81; Vincent Morley, "The Idea of Britain in Eighteenth-Century Ireland and Scotland," *Studia Hibernica* 33 (2004–5): 116–17.

23 Colin Kidd, "Ethnicity in the British Atlantic World, 1688–1830," in *A New Imperial History: Culture, Identity and Modernity in Britain and the Empire, 1600–1840*, ed. Kathleen Wilson (Cambridge: Cambridge University Press, 2004), 276; Toby Barnard, "Protestantism, Ethnicity and Irish Identities, 1660–1760," in Claydon and McBride, *Protestantism and National Identity*, 221.

24 Barnard, "Protestantism, Ethnicity," 209–11.

25 Kidd, "Ethnicity," 276.

26 Barnard, "Protestantism, Ethnicity," 216.

27 Kidd, *Unions and Unionisms*, 41.

28 Craig Bailey, "'A Child of the Emerald Isle': Ireland and the Making of James Johnson, MD," *Eighteenth-Century Life* 39:1 (2015): 212–35; S. Karly Kehoe, "Accessing Empire: Irish Surgeons and the Royal Navy, 1850–1880," *Social History of Medicine* 26:2 (2013): 204–22.

29 Morley, "The Idea of Britain," 101–24.

30 Sheila M. Kidd, "Gaelic Books as Cultural Icons: The Maintenance of Cultural Links between the Highlands and the West Indies," in *Within and Without Empire: Scotland across the (Post)Colonial Borderline*, ed. Carla Sassi and Theo van Heijnsbergen (Newcastle: Cambridge Scholars Publishing, 2013), 56–8; S. Karly Kehoe, "From the Caribbean to the Scottish Highlands: Charitable Enterprise in the Age of Improvement, c. 1750 to c. 1820," *Rural History* 27:1 (2016): 37–59.

31 Derek J. Patrick, "The Kirk, Parliament and the Union, 1706–7," in
    Union of 1707: New Dimensions, ed. Stewart J. Brown and Christopher A.
    Whatley (Edinburgh: Edinburgh University Press, 2014), 94–115; Whelan,
    "The Other Within," 17–18.
32 Kehoe, *Creating a Scottish Church*, 2; Whelan, "The Other Within," 24.
33 Scottish examples include Marjory Harper and Michael E. Vance, eds.,
    *Myth, Migration and the Making of Memory: Scotia and Nova Scotia, c. 1700–
    1990* (Edinburgh: John Donald Publishers, 1999) and Tanja Bueltmann,
    Scottish Ethnicity and the Making of New Zealand Society, 1850 to 1930
    (Edinburgh: Edinburgh University Press, 2011).
34 P.A. Buckner, "Making British North America British, 1815–1860," in *Kith
    and Kin: Canada, Britain and the United States from the Revolution to the Cold
    War*, ed. C.C. Eldridge (Cardiff: University of Wales Press, 1997), 27.
35 John M. MacKenzie, "Empire and Metropolitan Cultures," in *The Oxford
    History of the British Empire*, vol. 3, *The Nineteenth Century*, ed. W. Roger
    Louis (Oxford: Oxford University Press, 1999), 273.
36 S. Karly Kehoe, "Accessing Empire: Irish Surgeons and the Royal Navy,
    1850–1880," *Social History of Medicine* 26:2 (2013): 204–22.
37 National Library of Scotland (hereafter NLS), *An Account of the
    Highland Society of London from its earliest establishment in May 1778 to the
    Commencement of the Year 1813* (London, 1813), 35 and 37.
38 See, for example, the work of Graeme Morton, *Unionist-Nationalism:
    Governing Urban Scotland, 1830–1860* (East Linton, SCT: Tuckwell Press,
    1999); James Livesey, *Civil Society and Empire: Ireland and Scotland in the
    Eighteenth-Century Atlantic World* (New Haven, CT: Yale University Press,
    2009), 16; and William Jenkins, "Ulster Transplanted: Irish Protestants,
    Everyday Life and Constructions of Identity in Late Victorian Toronto,"
    in *Irish Protestant Identities*, ed. Mervyn Busteed, Frank Neal, and
    Jonathan Tonge (Manchester: Manchester University Press, 2008), 211.
    Morton's work focuses on urban Scots and reveals how the middle class
    used civil society to preserve a sense of Scottishness while connecting
    with the centre state and validating their own authority. Livesey
    contends that, in the empire, national elites coped with the "tensions and
    difficulties" of the union by using civil society to engage with an imperial
    agenda that would reaffirm their authority.
39 Hall, *Macaulay and Son*, 142.
40 Kidd, "Ethnicity," 260–77.
41 James Belich, *Replenishing the Earth: The Settler Revolution and the Rise of
    the Anglo-World, 1783–1939* (Oxford: Oxford University Press, 2009), 42.
    MacKillop, *"More Fruitful Than the Soil,"* 10.
42 Jeffrey L. McNairn, "'Everything Was New, yet Familiar': British
    Travellers, Halifax and the Ambiguities of Empire," *Acadiensis* 36:2

(2007): 42–3; MacKenzie, "Empire and Metropolitan Cultures," 271, 274, and 289–90; Buckner, "Making British North America," 11–44. C.A. Bayly suggests that the empire enabled domestic British integration –see "The British and Indigenous Peoples, 1760–1860: Power, Perception and Identity," in *Empire and Others: British Encounters with Indigenous People, 1600–1850*, ed. Martin Daunton and Rick Halpern (Philadelphia: University of Pennsylvania Press, 1999), 19–21.

43 Michael Gauvreau, "Covenanter Democracy: Scottish Popular Religion, Ethnicity, and Varieties of Politico-religious Dissent in Upper Canada, 1815–1841," *Histoire sociale/Social History* 35:71 (2003): 55–84. See also J.M. Bumsted, "The Consolidation of British North America, 1783–1860" in *Canada and the British Empire*, ed. Phillip Buckner (Oxford: Oxford University Press, 2010); John G. Reid and Elizabeth Mancke, eds., *Britain's Oceanic Empire: Atlantic and Indian Ocean Worlds, c. 1550–1850* (Cambridge: Cambridge University Press, 2012), 45.

44 Gauvreau, "Covenanter Democracy," 59; Hilary Carey, *God's Empire: Religion and Colonialism in the British World, c. 1801–1908* (Cambridge: Cambridge University Press, 2011), 13. Carey points out that the lack of an established church in the colonies enhanced colonial loyalty to the British imperial state.

45 Phillip Buckner, "Introduction: Canada and the British Empire," in Buckner, *Canada and the British Empire*, 6; Mark McGowan, *The Waning of the Green: Catholics, the Irish, and Identity in Toronto, 1887–1922* (Montreal and Kingston: McGill-Queen's University Press, 1999).

46 Richard A. Keogh, "'From Education, from Duty, and from Principle": Irish Catholic Loyalty in Context, 1829–1874," *British Catholic History* 33:3 (2017): 421–50; Keogh, "'Nothing Is so Bad,'"; Kehoe, "Accessing Empire"; S. Karly Kehoe, "Unionism, Nationalism and the Scottish Catholic Periphery," *Britain and the World* 4:1 (2011); 65–83; Barry Crosbie, *Irish Imperial Networks: Migration, Social Communication and Exchange in Nineteenth-Century India* (Cambridge: Cambridge University Press, 2012); David Dickson, Justyna Pyz, and Christopher Shepard, eds., *Irish Classrooms and British Empire: Imperial Contexts in the Origins of Modern Education* (Dublin: Four Courts Press, 2012); MacKillop, *"More Fruitful Than the Soil,"* 8; Bernard Aspinwall, "The Formation of a British Identity within Scottish Catholicism, 1830–1914," in *Religion and National Identity: Wales and Scotland, c. 1700–2000*, ed. Robert Pope (Cardiff: University of Wales Press, 2001), 268–306; Carey, *God's Empire*.

47 Bumsted, "The Consolidation of British North America," 64.

48 Buckner, "Introduction," 18; Eric Richards, *Britannia's Children: Emigration from England, Scotland, Ireland and Wales* (London: Hambledon, 2004), 286.

49 "Power, Politics and Protest: The Growth of Political Rights in Britain in the 19th Century," on the National Archives website, https://www.nationalarchives.gov.uk/education/politics/g1/background.htm

50 Gabriel Glickman, *The English Catholic Community, 1688–1745: Politics, Culture and Ideology* (Woodbridge, EN: Boydell Press, 2009).

51 Kehoe, *Creating a Scottish Church.*

52 Gordon Millar, "Maynooth and Scottish Politics: The Rome of the Maynooth Grant Issues, 1845–1857," *Records of the Scottish Church History Society* 27 (1997): 220–79.

53 Oliver P. Rafferty, *Violence, Politics and Catholicism in Ireland* (Dublin: Four Courts Press, 2016), 60.

54 Willem Frijhoff, "Shifting Identities in Hostile Settings: Towards a Comparison of the Catholic Communities in Early Modern Britain and the Northern Netherlands," in *Catholic Communities in Protestant States: Britain and the Netherlands, c. 1570–1720*, ed. Benjamin Kaplan et al. (Manchester: Manchester University Press, 2009), 3.

55 John D. Gay, *The Geography of Religion in England* (London: Gerald Duckworth, 1971), 88–92; Desmond Keenan, *The Grail of Catholic Emancipation*, chap. 1, Des Keenan's Books on Irish History (website), http://www.deskeenan.com/1GrChap1.htm.

56 Susan Mitchell Sommers, "Sir John Coxe Hippisley: That '*Busy* Man' in the Cause of Catholic Emancipation," *Parliamentary History* 27:1 (2008): 86, 90; Alban Hood, "The Throckmortons Come of Age: Political and Social Alignments, 1826–1862," in Marshall and Scott, *Catholic Gentry*, 247–68.

57 Paul O'Leary, "When Was Anti-Catholicism? The Case of Nineteenth- and Twentieth-Century Wales," *Journal of Ecclesiastical History* 56:2 (2005): 311; Kehoe, *Creating a Scottish Church*, 48–74.

58 A.D.M. Barrell, "The Background to *Cum universi*: Scoto-Papal Relations, 1159–1192," *Innes Review* 46:2 (1995): 116–38.

59 Michael E. Williams, "A British College in Rome?" in *The Scots College, Rome, 1600–2000*, ed. Raymond McCluskey (Edinburgh: John Donald Publishers, 2000), 148.

60 Fiona MacDonald, *Missions to the Gaels: Reformation and Counter-Reformation in Ulster and the Highlands and Islands of Scotland, 1560–1760* (Edinburgh: John Donald Publishers, 2006).

61 Peter Phillips, ed., *The Diaries of Bishop William Poynter, V.A. (1815–1824)* (London: Catholic Record Society, 2006), 30, 35.

62 Archivum Venerabilis Collegii Anglorum de Urbe (hereafter AVCAU), Scr. 55/9/9, letter from An Irishman, Dublin, (signature completely illegible) to William Poynter, London, 18 May 1814, and Scr. 55/9/10, letter from An Irish Catholic Layman (no other signature), Armagh, to William Poynter, London, 1814.

63 Amy McKinney, "An Efficacious Irish Triumvirate: Paul Cullen, Tobias Kirby and Joseph Dixon," in *The Irish College, Rome and Its World*, ed. Dáire Keogh and Albert McDonnell (Dublin: Four Courts Press, 2008), 165.

64 Ushaw College Library and Special Collections, University of Durham (hereafter UCLUD), Ushaw College Papers, UC/PA/R11, letter from Robert Gradwell, Rome, to Thomas Sherburne, Ushaw College, 31 March 1818.

65 Joseph P. Chinnici, *The English Catholic Enlightenment: John Lingard and the Cisalpine Movement, 1780–1850* (Shepherdstown, WV: Patmos Press, 1980); Frank M. Turner, *John Henry Newman: The Challenge to Evangelical Religion* (New Haven, CT: Yale University Press, 2002).

66 McKinney, "An Efficacious Irish Triumvirate," 163.

67 Westminster Diocesan Archives, London (hereafter WDA), A.42/32, letter from George Hay, Aberdeen, to Talbot, London, 23 March 1783. Letters A.42/39–43 are a continuation of the discussion in England. See also A.42/15.

68 Joan Connell, *The Roman Catholic Church in England, 1780–1850: A Study in Internal Politics* (Philadelphia: American Philosophical Society, 1984), 95.

69 Ibid.

70 Paul Christopher Manuel, Lawrence C. Reardon, and Clyde Wilcox, eds., *The Catholic Church and the Nation State: Comparative Perspectives* (Washington, DC: Georgetown University Press, 2006); Kaplan et al., eds., *Catholic Communities in Protestant States*, provides examples from the early modern period, and most of its chapters note the tension over the issue of citizenship.

71 McGowan, *The Waning of the Green*.

72 Luca Codignola, "Roman Catholic Conservatism in a New North Atlantic World, 1760–1829," *William and Mary Quarterly* 64:4 (2007): 717, 721; Roberto Perin, *Rome in Canada: The Vatican and Canadian Affairs in the Late Victorian Age* (Toronto: University of Toronto Press, 1990), 5.

73 John Martin Robinson, *Cardinal Consalvi, 1757–1824* (London: Bodley Head, 1987), 100–4, 117; Margaret M. O'Dwyer, *The Papacy in the Age of Napoleon and the Restoration: Pius VII, 1800–1823* (Lanham, MD: University Press of America, 1985), 189–96.

74 Keenan, *The Grail of Catholic Emancipation*.

75 Hilda Neatby, *The Quebec Act: Protest and Policy* (Scarborough, ON: Prentice-Hall, 1972), 33–45.

76 See, for example, Jeffrey O. von Arx, "Manning's Ultramontanism and the Catholic Church in British Politics," *Recusant History* 19:1 (1989): 343.

77 Oliver P. Rafferty, "The Catholic Church, Ireland and the British Empire, 1800–1921," *Historical Research* 84:224 (2011): 297–8.

78 APF, *Scritture riferite nei Congressi, Fondo America Settentrionale*, 2/206,
    letter from Prince Edward, Kensington Palace, to unknown bishop,
    likely in the United States, 21 March 1814. For more on *praemunire*, see
    Jacquline Rose, *Godly Kingship in Restoration England: The Politics of The
    Royal Supremacy, 1660–1688* (Cambridge: Cambridge University Press,
    2011), 237; Perin, *Rome in Canada*, 7; and Luca Codignola, "Conflict or
    Consensus? Catholics in Canada and the United States, 1780–1820,"
    Canadian Catholic Historical Association Historical Studies 55 (1988): 53.
    The National Archives (hereafter TNA), CO 880/1, f.13, correspondence
    showing what passed during the period Lord Stanley was secretary of
    state for the colonies, respecting the Division of the Roman Catholic
    Diocese of Kingston, Canada, and the creation of a Roman Catholic
    Archbishopric for the North American colonies (1851). See also S. Karly
    Kehoe and Darren Tierney, "'Like a Kind Mother': Imperial Concerns and
    Britain's Changing Perceptions of Rome, 1783–1815," *Historical Studies* 81
    (2015): 11–31.
79 "Sir John Coxe Hippisley," *Oxford Dictionary of National Biography Online*,
    https://doi.org/10.1093/ref:odnb/13361 W. Maziere Brady, *Anglo-
    Roman Papers: The English Palace in Rome; II: The eldest natural son of
    Charles II; III: Memoirs of Cardinal Erskine, papal envoy to the court of George
    III* (London, 1890), 125, 128–9, 144–5; William James Anderson, "Abbe
    Paul MacPherson's History of the Scots College, Rome," *Innes Review* 12
    (1961): 155–6.
80 WDA, A.41.111, Richard Challoner, *Pastoral Letter Addressed to the
    Catholicks of the British Islands in the West-Indies*, 19 December 1770;
    A. 41.33, statement from Propaganda Fide confirming Challoner's
    responsibility for the American possessions that had been acquired by
    Britain following the Seven Years War, 9 July 1763.
81 APF, *Scritture riferite nei Congressi, Fondo Irlanda* 15/70, untitled
    newspaper clipping, Dublin, February 1781.
82 Scottish Catholic Archives (hereafter SCA), SM 15/2/13, *A pastoral address
    to the Roman Catholics of Scotland by George Hay, Daulien, V.A.* (Edinburgh,
    1798), 3.
83 Rafferty, *Violence, Politics*, 45.
84 Andrew R. Holmes, "Professor James Thompson Sr. and Lord Kelvin:
    Religion, Science, and Liberal Unionism in Ulster and Scotland," *Journal
    of British Studies* 50 (2011): 100–24. The delay of this legislation on account
    of the powerful Protestant Ascendency lobby ensured that this would not
    be the case.
85 Keogh, "From Education," 428–31; L. Perry Curtis, *Apes and Angels: The
    Irishman in Victorian Caricature*, rev. ed. (Washington, DC: Smithsonian
    Institution Press, 1997); Roy Douglas, Liam Harte, and Jim O'Hara,

Drawing Conclusions: A Cartoon History of Anglo-Irish Relations, 1798–1998 (Belfast: Blackstaff Press, 1998); Michael de Nie, *The Eternal Paddy: Irish Identity and the British Press, 1798–1882* (Madison: University of Wisconsin Press, 2004).

86 Daniel Szechi, "Negotiating Catholic Kingship for a Protestant People: 'Private' Letters, Royal Declarations and the Achievement of Religious Détente in the Jacobite Underground, 1702–1718," in *Debating the Faith: Religion and Letter Writing in Great Britain, 1550–1880*, ed. Anne Dunan-Page and Clotilde Prunier (London: Springer, 2013), 113–16.

87 Colin M. Coates and Cecilia Morgan, *Heroines and History: Representations of Madeleine de Verchères and Laura Secord* (Toronto: University of Toronto Press, 2002), 121.

88 Keogh, "From Education," 421–50; Keogh, "'Nothing Is so Bad,'" 230. Francis Young, *The Gages of Hengrave and Suffolk Catholicism, 1640–1767* (Suffolk, EN: Boydell Press, 2015), xxiii.

89 "Catholic Loyalty," *The Casket* (Antigonish, Nova Scotia), 17 December 1857. See also "Catholic and Protestant Loyalty" and "Catholic Loyalty," *The Casket*, 12 November 1857 and 30 September 1860, respectively.

90 Mary Hickman, "Catholicism and the Nation-State in Nineteenth-Century Britain," in *Commitment to Diversity: Catholics and Education in a Changing World*, ed. Mary Eaton, Jane Longmore, and Arthur Naylor (London: Cassell, 2000), 53.

91 See, for example, Nini Rodgers, *Ireland, Slavery and Anti-Slavery, 1612–1865* (London: Palgrave Macmillan, 2007); Douglas Hamilton, *Scotland, the Caribbean and the Atlantic World, 1750–1820* (Manchester: Manchester University Press, 2005); and Kehoe, "From the Caribbean."

92 Perin, *Rome in Canada*, 13; S. Karly Kehoe, "Catholic Identity in the Diaspora: Nineteenth-Century Ontario," in *Bluid, Kin and Countrie: Scottish Associational Culture in the Diaspora*, ed. Tanja Bueltmann, Andrew Hinson, and Graeme Morton (Toronto: Stewart Publishing, 2009), 83–100; Peter Ludlow, "A 'Primitive Germ of Discord' in the North Atlantic World: Newfoundland-Irish Roman Catholics in Scottish Cape Breton," *Journal of Irish and Scottish Studies* 3:1 (2009): 175–92. The personal memoir of Susanna Moodie, a nineteenth-century English Anglican immigrant to Upper Canada, includes a number of references to this: see *Roughing It in the Bush* (Toronto: McClelland Stewart, 1989).

2 Imperial Security and Catholic Relief

1 John Langton, "The Continuity of Regional Culture: Lancashire Catholicism from the Late Sixteenth to the Early Nineteenth Century," in *Issues of Regional Identity*, ed. Edward Royle (Manchester: Manchester University

Press, 1998), 91; Alban Hood, "The Throckmortons Come of Age: Political and Social Alignments, 1826–1862," in *Catholic Gentry in English Society: The Throckmortons of Coughton from Reformation to Emancipation*, ed. Peter Marshall and Geoffrey Scott (Farnham, EN: Ashgate, 2009), 247–68.

2 Joan Connell, *The Roman Catholic Church in England, 1780–1850: A Study in Internal Politics* (Philadelphia: American Philosophical Society, 1984), 58–9; Langton, "The Continuity of Regional Culture." Mary Heimann points out that the practices of many, if not most, Irish, Scottish, and English Catholics were "hardly Roman, let alone orthodox." See "Devotional Stereotypes in English Catholicism, 1850–1940," in *Catholicism in Britain and France since 1789*, ed. Frank Tallett and Nicholas Atkin (London: Hambledon Press, 1996), 15.

3 Patrick J. Corish, *The Irish Catholic Community in the Seventeenth and Eighteenth Centuries* (Dublin: Helicon, 1981), 19–20.

4 Brad Gregory, "Situating Early Modern English Catholicism," in *Early Modern English Catholicism: Identity, Memory and Counter-Reformation*, ed. James E. Kelly and Susan Royal (Leiden: Brill, 2017), 30.

5 Hilda Neatby, *The Quebec Act: Protest and Policy* (Scarborough, ON: Prentice-Hall, 1972), 17–21.

6 Jenny Shaw, *Everyday Life in the Early English Caribbean: Irish, Africans and the Construction of Difference* (Athens: University of Georgia Press, 2013), 156–84; Thomas M. Truxes, "Dutch-Irish Cooperation in the Mid-Eighteenth-Century Wartime Atlantic," *Early American Studies* 10:2 (2012): 302–34.

7 Joanna Innes, "'Reform' in English Public Life: The Fortunes of a Word," in *Rethinking the Age of Reform: Britain 1780–1850*, ed. Arthur Burns and Joanna Innes (Cambridge: Cambridge University Press, 2003), 72–3.

8 Carys Brown, "Catholic Politics and Creating Trust in Eighteenth-Century England," *British Catholic History* 33:4 (2017): 622–44; Gregory, "Situating Early Modern English Catholicism," 22; Gabriel Glickman, "A British Catholic Community? Ethnicity, Identity and Recusant Politics, 1660–1750," in Kelly and Royal, *Early Modern English Catholicism*, 68–9.

9 Langton, "The Continuity of Regional Culture"; Margaret H. Turnham, *Catholic Faith and Practice in England, 1779–1992: The Role of Revivalism and Renewal* (Woodbridge, EN: Boydell Press, 2015), 24–7; Susan Mitchell Sommers, "Sir John Coxe Hippisley: That '*Busy* Man' in the Cause of Catholic Emancipation," *Parliamentary History* 27:1 (2008): 83; Trystan O. Hughes, "Roman Catholicism," in *The Religious History of Wales: Religious Life and Practice in Wales from the Seventeenth Century to the Present Day*, ed. Richard C. Allen and David Ceri Jones (Cardiff: Welsh Academic Press, 2014), 69–70; Paul O'Leary, "When Was Anti-Catholicism? The Case of Nineteenth- and Twentieth-Century Wales," *Journal of Ecclesiastical History* 56:2 (2005): 308–25.

10 S. Karly Kehoe, *Creating a Scottish Church: Catholicism, Gender and Identity in Nineteenth-Century Scotland* (Manchester: Manchester University Press, 2010).

11 Mary Peckham Magray, *The Transforming Power of the Nuns: Women, Religion and Cultural Change in Ireland, 1750–1900* (New York: Oxford University Press, 1998); Thomas Bartlett, *The Fall and Rise of the Catholic Nation: The Catholic Question, 1690–1830* (Dublin: Gill and Macmillan, 1992); S.J. Connolly, *Divided Kingdom: Ireland, 1630–1800* (Oxford: Oxford University Press, 2008).

12 David Dickson, *Old World Colony: Cork and South Munster, 1630–1830* (Cork, IE: Cork University Press, 2005), 135–48, 166–9.

13 Edward Norman, *Roman Catholicism in England from the Elizabethan Settlements to the Second Vatican Council* (Oxford: Oxford University Press, 1985), 57; Glickman, "A British Catholic Community."

14 Patrick Allitt, *Catholic Converts: British and American Intellectuals Turn to Rome* (Ithaca, NY: Cornell University Press, 1997), 27.

15 For examples, see Patricia O'Connell, *The Irish College at Lisbon, 1590–1834* (Dublin: Four Courts Press, 2001); Simon Johnson, *The English College at Lisbon*, vol. 1, *From Reformation to Toleration* (Somerset, EN: Downside Abbey Press, 2015); Raymond McCluskey, ed. *The Scots College, Rome, 1600–2000* (Edinburgh: John Donald Publishers, 2000).

16 Patrick Fagan, *Divided Loyalties: The Question of the Oath for Irish Catholics in the Eighteenth Century* (Dublin: Four Courts Press, 1997), 17–18. Hood, "The Throckmortons," 249.

17 Desmond Keenan, *The Grail of Catholic Emancipation*, chap. 1, Des Keenan's Books on Irish History, http://www.deskeenan.com/1GrChap1.htm.

18 BRBML, Sheridan Papers, letter from John Milner to Richard Brinsley Sheridan, 15 June 1800.

19 An excellent collection of letters detailing the plight of the religious exists within the Lisbon College Papers at the Ushaw College Library and Special Collections at the University of Durham.

20 Patrick Griffin, "The Birth, Death and Resurrection of the Provincial Dilemma," *History Compass* 9:2 (2011): 134–46.

21 Philip Lawson, "'The Irishman's Prize': Views of Canada from the British Press, 1760–1774," *Historical Journal* 28:3 (1985): 583. The population was "above sixty-five thousand Persons" in 1774. *An Act for Making More effectual Provision for the Governance of the Province of Quebec in North America* (*The Quebec Act*, 7 October 1774), http://avalon.law.yale.edu/18th_century/quebec_act_1774.asp.

22 David Milobar, "Quebec Reform, the British Constitution and the Atlantic Empire: 1774–1775," in *Parliament and the Atlantic Empire*, ed. Philip Lawson (Edinburgh: Edinburgh University Press, 1995), 71.

23 C.E. Carrington, *The British Overseas: Exploits of a Nation of Shopkeepers*, Part 1, *Making of the Empire*, 2nd ed. (Cambridge: Cambridge University Press, 1968), 35–6.

24 Edward L. Cox, "Fedon's Rebellion, 1795–96: Causes and Consequences," *Journal of Negro History* 67:1 (1982): 7–19; Mark Quintanilla, "The World of Alexander Campbell: An Eighteenth-Century Grenadian Planter," *Albion* 35:2 (2003): 229–56; Philip Lawson, *The Imperial Challenge: Quebec and Britain in the Age of the American Revolution* (Montreal and Kingston: McGill-Queen's University Press, 1989), 4–15.

25 Neatby, *The Quebec Act*, 21, 26.

26 Quoted in Kristen Block and Jenny Shaw, "Subjects without an Empire: The Irish in the Early Modern Caribbean," *Past and Present* 210 (2011): 57–8. See "Regime of the Gentry," chap. 3 in Dickson's *Old World Colony*, for a discussion about forfeited estates.

27 Cox, "Fedon's Rebellion," 9–10. See also Aaron Willis, "The Standing of New Subjects: Grenada and the Protestant Constitution after the Treaty of Paris (1763)," *Journal of Imperial and Commonwealth History* 42:1 (2014): 1–21.

28 Quintanilla, "The World of Alexander Campbell," 242.

29 Lawson, "The Irishman's Prize," 583.

30 Neatby, *The Quebec Act*, 33–46.

31 Milobar, "Quebec Reform," 67.

32 Lawson, *The Imperial Challenge*, 44–5.

33 Ibid., 45.

34 Milobar, "Quebec Reform," 65; Jessica L. Harland-Jacobs, "Incorporating the King's New Subjects: Accommodation and Anti-Catholicism in the British Empire, 1763–1815," *Journal of Religious History* 39:2 (2015): 203–23; Hannah Weiss-Muller, *Subjects and Sovereign: Bonds of Belonging in the Eighteenth-Century British Empire* (New York: Oxford University Press, 2017); Philip Lawson, *Imperial Challenge*; *The Quebec Act*.

35 Maurice J. Bric, "Catholicism and Empire: Ireland and Lower Canada, 1760–1830," in *Ireland and Quebec: Multidisciplinary Perspectives on History, Culture and Society*, ed. Margaret Kelleher and Michael Kenneally (Dublin: Four Courts Press, 2016), 33.

36 Milobar, "Quebec Reform," 73–81; Martin J. Powell, "The Aldermen of Skinner's Alley: Ultra-Protestantism before the Orange Order," in *Clubs and Societies in Eighteenth-Century Ireland*, ed. James Kelly and Martin J. Powell (Dublin: Four Courts Press, 2010), 204–6; Colin Haydon, "'I Love My King and My Country, but a Roman Catholic I Hate': Anti-Catholicism, Xenophobia and National Identity in Eighteenth-Century England," in *Protestantism and National Identity: Britain and Ireland, c. 1650–c. 1850*, ed. Tony Claydon and Ian McBride (Cambridge: Cambridge University Press, 1998), 35–6.

37 Lawson, "The Irishman's Prize," 596.

38 Haydon, "'I Love My King,'" 38–43.

39 Griffin, "The Birth."

40 Padraig Higgins, *A Nation of Politicians: Gender, Patriotism and Political Culture in Late Eighteenth-Century Ireland* (Madison: University of Wisconsin Press, 2010), 37–47.

41 BRBML, *A letter from Thomas Lord Lyttleton, to William Pitt, Earl of Chatham on the Quebec Bill* (New York, 1774).

42 Peter Marshall, "The Political Persistence of British North America, 1763–1815," in *Kith and Kin: Canada, Britain and the United States from the Revolution to the Cold War*, ed. C.C. Eldridge (Cardiff: University of Wales Press, 1997), 5.

43 Oliver P. Rafferty, "The Catholic Church, Ireland and the British Empire, 1800–1921," *Historical Research*, 84:224 (2011): 294.

44 Wayne J. Hankey, "From Augustine and St. Denys to Olier and Bérulle's Spiritual Revolution: Patristic and Seventeenth-Century Foundations of the Relations between Church and State in Quebec," *Laval théologique et philosophique* 63:3 (2007): 531.

45 Ibid., 535.

46 John Garner, "The Enfranchisement of Roman Catholics in the Maritimes," *Canadian Historical Review* 34:3 (1953): 204. In 1758, the legislative assembly was established for Nova Scotia. See also Frederick Madden, ed., *Imperial Reconstruction, 1763–1840: Evolution of Alternative Systems of Colonial Government*, vol. 3 (New York: Greenwood Press, 1983), 363.

47 Nova Scotia Archives (hereafter NSA), RG1, vol. 443, no. 1, General Return of the Several Townships in the Province of Nova Scotia the First Day of January 1767; A.A. Johnston, *A History of the Catholic Church in Eastern Nova Scotia*, vol. 1 (Antigonish, NS: St Francis Xavier University, 1960), 103–4.

48 NSA, Cape Breton Island Petitions, 1787–1843, https://novascotia.ca /archives/land/.

49 Neatby, *The Quebec Act*, 23–6.

50 Orla Power, "Irish Planters, Atlantic Merchants: The Development of St Croix, Danish West Indies, 1750–1766" (PhD diss., National University of Ireland, Galway, 2011).

51 TNA, CO 106/9, letter to the Lords of the Treasury, entry for 24 April 1765, Dominica; House of Commons Sessional Papers, *Select Committee appointed for the purpose of taking the examination of such witnesses as shall be produced on the part of several petitioners who have petitioned the House of Commons against the abolition of the Slave Trade*, testimony of Alexander Campbell, 13 February 1790, 135.

52 David Beck Ryden, "'One of the Finest and Most Fruitful Spots in America': An Analysis of Eighteenth-Century Carriacou," *Journal of*

Interdisciplinary History 43:4 (2013): 549, 554, 556. His study suggests that, in 1776, the heads of farming households were broken down as follows: "Of-colour," 11%; white French, 44%; white British, 43% (26% Scottish, 17% English); unknown, 2%. In 1790, there was a slight change: "Of-colour," 19%; white French, 33%; white British, 48% (23% Scottish, 25% English); unknown, 0%. By 1790, the majority of the absentee owners were either Scottish or English; the French absentees had all but disappeared, despite a significant, though declining, number remaining on the island.

53 Michael Duffy, "War, Revolution, and the Crisis of the British Empire," in *The French Revolution and British Popular Politics*, ed. Mark Philp (Cambridge: Cambridge University Press, 1991), 127–8. For a useful overview, see K.J. Kesselring. "'Negroes of the Crown': The Management of Slaves Forfeited by Grenadian Rebels, 1796–1831," *Journal of the Canadian Historical Association* 22:2 (2011): 1–29.

54 TNA, PC1/62, f.19, At the Council Chambers, Whitehall, By a Committee of the Lords of His Majesty's most honourable Privy Council, 18 February 1790.

55 SCA, BL 4/33/11, letter from Angus MacEachern to John Geddes, 14 November 1791.

56 Alpheus Todd, *Parliamentary Government in the British Colonies* (Boston: Little, Brown, 1880), 316.

57 Connolly, *Divided Kingdom*, 388–9.

58 James Kelly, "The Act of Union: Its Origins and Background," in *Acts of Union: The Causes, Contexts and Consequences of the Act of Union*, ed. Dáire Keogh and Kevin Whelan (Dublin: Four Courts Press, 2001), 62.

59 Thomas Bartlett, "Britishness, Irishness and the Act of Union," in Keogh and Whelan, *Acts of Union*, 247–55.

60 Patrick M. Geoghegan, "The Catholics and the Union," *Transactions of the Royal Historical Society* 10 (2000): 244–7; Kevin Whelan, "The Other Within: Ireland, Britain and the Act of Union," in Keogh and Whelan, *Acts of Union*, 15.

61 Innes, "Reform," 87–92; Higgins, *A Nation of Politicians*, 210–23.

62 John Bergin, "Irish Catholics and Their Networks in Eighteenth-Century London," *Eighteenth-Century Life* 39:1 (2015): 68, 80–1.

63 Bartlett, *The Fall and Rise*, 82–102, 121–45.

64 Robert E. Burns, "The Catholic Relief Act in Ireland, 1778," *Church History* 32:2 (1968): 181; Robert Kent Donovan, "The Military Origins of the Roman Catholic Relief Programme of 1778," *Historical Journal* 28:1 (1985): 79–102. In the meticulously researched *A History of the Catholic Church*, Johnston notes a "definite connection between England's political difficulties and the indulgence she showed towards her Catholic subjects" (101).

65 Alvin Jackson, "Ireland, the Union and the Empire, 1800–1960," and
    Kevin Kenny, "The Irish in Empire," both in *Ireland and the British Empire*,
    ed. K. Kenny (Oxford: Oxford University Press, 2004), 125–53 and 90–124,
    respectively; Bartlett, *The Fall and Rise*, 287.
66 Michael Tamko, *British Romanticism and the Catholic Question: Religion,
    History and National Identity, 1778–1829* (Basingstoke, EN: Palgrave
    Macmillan, 2011), 4–5.
67 Ibid., 119–47; Richard Allen, "Mary Shelley as Editor of the Poems
    of Percy Shelley," in *Women, Scholarship and Criticism: Gender and
    Knowledge, c. 1790–1900*, ed. Joan Bellamy, Anne Laurence, and Gill Perry
    (Manchester: Manchester University Press, 2000), 77–90.
68 Arthur Burns, "English 'Church Reform' Revisited, 1780–1850," in Burns
    and Innes, *Rethinking the Age of Reform*, 145–7.
69 SCA, BL4/65/9, letter from MacPherson to Hay, 26 November 1782
    (emphasis in original).
70 Keenan provides a very useful overview of the continued relationship
    between London and Rome in *The Grail of Catholic Emancipation*, chap. 1;
    Sommers, "Sir John Coxe Hippisley."
71 Scots College Rome Archives (hereafter SCRA), 28/3, Memorandum on
    the Colleges, January 1800; UCLUD, Ushaw College Papers, UC/PA/
    R11, letter from John Gradwell, Rome, to Thomas Sherburne, Ushaw
    College, 31 March 1818.
72 W. Maziere Brady, *Anglo-Roman Papers: The English Palace in Rome; II: The
    eldest natural son of Charles II; III: Memoirs of Cardinal Erskine, papal envoy to
    the court of George III* (London, 1890).
73 S. Karly Kehoe and Darren Tierney, "'Like a Kind Mother': Imperial
    Concerns and Britain's Changing Perceptions of Rome, 1783–1815,"
    Historical Studies 81 (2015): 11–31; Michael E. Williams, *The Venerable
    English College Rome: A History, 1579–1979* (London: Associated Catholic
    Publications, 1979), 74–5.
74 Allitt, *Catholic Converts*, 25–6. The Catholic middle class in England and
    Scotland remained relatively small until the 1830s.
75 WDA, A.41/115, Challoner Papers, The Humble Address, and Petition
    of the Roman Catholics of Ireland, which is presented to his Excellency,
    the Earl of Buckinghamshire, Lord Lieutenant of Ireland on the 27th Day
    of October by the Earl of Fingal, the Hon. James Preston and Anthony
    Dermot, Esq., 27 October 1771.
76 UCLUD, MC/M4/315 c., the Memorial of the Right Honourable Charles
    Lord Stourton, Robert Edward Lord Petre, John Courtenay Throckmorton
    Esq., Thomas Stapleton Esq. and Thomas Hornyold Esq for themselves
    and others of his Majesty's Subjects professing the Roman Catholic
    Religion, n.d., but ca. 1778/79.

77 Ibid.

78 Bric, "Catholicism and Empire," 34, 43.

79 Fagan, *Divided Loyalties*, 19.

80 Connolly, *Divided Kingdom*, 393, 394.

81 Marianne Elliott, *The Catholics of Ulster: A History* (New York: Basic Books, 2001), 187–90.

82 Connolly, *Divided Kingdom*, 444–5. Keenan, *The Grail of Catholic Emancipation*.

83 Connell, *The Roman Catholic Church*, 57.

84 Sommers, "Sir John Coxe Hippisley," 83–4.

85 WDA, A.42/132, Talbot Papers, note relating to a meeting of the Catholic Committee, 20 May 1788.

86 Bartlett, *The Fall and Rise*, 306. He offers a useful discussion about the difference associated with the proposed state veto over the appointment of Catholic bishops.

87 James Livesay, *Civil Society and Empire: Ireland and Scotland in the Eighteenth-Century Atlantic World* (New Haven, CT: Yale University Press, 2009), 12.

88 David Craig, "Burke and the Constitution," in *The Cambridge Companion to Edmund Burke*, ed. David Dwan and Christopher J. Insole (Cambridge: Cambridge University Press, 2012), 104–16.

89 C.A. Bayly, *Imperial Meridian: The British Empire and the World, 1780–1830* (Harlow, EN: Longman, 1989), 189.

90 Kevin Whelan, *The Tree of Liberty: Radicalism, Catholicism and the Construction of Irish Identity, 1760–1830* (Cork, IE: Cork University Press, 1996), 25–37; Andrew R. Holmes, "Professor James Thompson Sr. and Lord Kelvin: Religion, Science, and Liberal Unionism in Ulster and Scotland," *Journal of British Studies* 50 (2011): 100–24.

91 Dáire Keogh, "Catholic Responses to the Act of Union," in Keogh and Whelan, *Acts of Unions*, 95–105.

92 BRBML, General Committee of Roman Catholics of Ireland, *An Address from the general committee of Roman Catholics, to their Protestant fellow subjects, and to the public in general, respecting the calumnies and misrepresentations … circulated with regard to their principles and conduct* (Dublin, 1792), 21–2.

93 Ibid., 30.

94 BRBML, Edmund Burke, *A letter from the Right Hon. Edmund Burke in the Kingdom of Great Britain to Sir Hercules Langrishe, Bart. M.P. on the subject of Roman Catholics of Ireland, and the propriety of admitting them to the elective franchise, consistently with the principles of the constitution, as established at the Revolution* (Dublin, P. Byrne, 1792), 51.

95 Ian Harris, "Burke and Religion," in Dwan and Insole, *Cambridge Companion to Edmund Burke*, 98–9.

96 BRBML Burke, *A Letter*, 82–3. The "he" to whom Burke is referring in the quote is thought to be either Archbishop Secker of Canterbury or Archbishop John Ryder of Tuam. Bartlett, *The Fall and Rise*, 101.

97 Innes, "Reform," 88.

98 Harris, "Burke and Religion," 98–9.

99 Bartlett, *The Fall and Rise*, 289. My thanks to Daniel Szechi for his advice on this facet of the argument.

100 Murray G.H. Pittock, *Celtic Identity and the British Image* (Manchester: Manchester University Press, 1999), 26–7; Whelan, *The Tree of Liberty*, 33. Rowan Strong explains that it was a similar situation with Episcopalians; see "Reconstructions of Episcopalian Identity," *Scottish Church History Records* 33 (2003): 143–64.

101 An example would be the Statues of Iona in 1609. See Julian Goodare, "The Statutes of Iona in Context," *Scottish Historical Review* 77:1 (1998): 31–57; M.D. MacGregor, "The Statutes of Iona: Text and Context," *Innes Review* 57:2 (2006): 111–81; and Alison Cathcart, "The Statutes of Iona: The Archipelagic Context," *Journal of British Studies* 49:1 (2010): 4–27.

102 SCA, BL/4/85/10, letter from George Hay to John Geddes, 7 April 1794.

103 SCA, BL 4/85/7 and 4/8/10, letters from George Hay to John Geddes, 15 March and 7 April 1794.

104 James Livesey, "Acts of Union and Disunion: Ireland in Atlantic and European Contexts," in Keogh and Whelan, *Acts of Unions*, 95–105; Geoghegan, "The Catholics," 244.

105 I am grateful to Ciaran O'Neill for his advice on interpretations of the union.

106 K. Theodore Hoppen, *Governing Hibernia: British Politicians and Ireland, 1800–1921* (Oxford: Oxford University Press, 2016), 31–64.

107 Ibid., 25.

108 Alvin Jackson, *The Two Unions: Ireland, Scotland and the Survival of the United Kingdom, 1707–2007* (Oxford: Oxford University Press, 2012), 4.

109 Whelan, "The Other Within," 23. For an interesting discussion on this, see Richard W. Davis, "Wellington, the Constitution and Catholic Emancipation," *Parliamentary History* 15:2 (1996): 209–14, and G.I.T. Machin, "The Catholic Question and the Monarchy, 1827–1829," *Parliamentary History* 16:2 (1997): 213–20.

110 Keenan, *The Grail of Catholic Emancipation*.

111 Keogh, "Catholic Responses," 162–3; Bartlett, *The Fall and Rise*, 243.

112 Bartlett, *The Fall and Rise*, 270–1.

113 Brady, *Anglo-Roman Papers*, 125; Peter Phillips, ed., *The Diaries of Bishop William Poynter, V.A. (1815–1824)* (London: Catholic Record Society, 2006), 30–45.

114 Coronation Oath Act, 1688, http://legislation.gov.uk/aep/WillandMar /1/6/section/III.

115 BRBML, A Foe to Bigotry, *The patriot King: appropriately dedicated to His Royal Highness, the Duke of Cumberland, in which the claims of the Catholics are legally, equitably, and liberally considered, and, the talents and virtues of the present ministers contrasted with those of the last* (London: C. Chapple, 1807), 8–9.

116 BRBML, John Milner, *A short view of the chief arguments against the Catholic petition now before Parliament, and of the answers to them: in a letter to a member of the House of Commons* (London, 1805), pp. 14, 20–1, 34, 43–5.

117 Jackson, *The Two Unions*, 81–2.

118 Whelan, "The Other Within," 17. For a succinct overview of the divisions within the anti-union camp, see James Kelly, "The Failure of Opposition," in *The Irish Act of Union, 1800: Bicentennial Essays*, ed. Michael Brown, Patrick M. Geoghegan, and James Kelly (Dublin: Irish Academic Press, 2003), 108–28.

119 Keogh, "Catholic Responses," 161, 164; Geoghegan, "The Catholics," 246.

120 Livesay, "Acts of Union and Disunion," 100.

121 Allan I. MacInnes, "Commercial Landlordism and Clearance in the Scottish Highlands: The Case of Arichonan" in *Communities in European History*, ed. Juan Pan-Montojo and Frederik. Pedersen (Pisa: Pisa University Press, 2007), 47–64; Stephen Mullen, "A Glasgow–West India Merchant House and the Imperial Dividend, 1779–1867," *Journal of Scottish Historical Studies* 33 (2013): 196–233; S. Karly Kehoe, "From the Scottish Highlands to the Caribbean: Charitable Enterprise in the Age of Improvement, c. 1750–1820," *Rural History* 27:1 (2016): 37–59.

122 Hoppen, *Governing Hibernia*, 11.

123 Ibid., 20, 34.

124 BRBML, Sir John Joseph Dillon, *The question as to the admission of Catholics to Parliament, considered upon the principles of existing laws: with supplemental observations on the coronation oath: to which is annexed a further supplement, occasioned by the second edition of Mr. Reeve's considerations, on the same subject* (London: E. Booker and J. Debrett, 1801), 47.

125 Ibid., 85–6, 119–22.

126 BRBML, Henry Augustus Dillon-Lee, Viscount, *Short view of the catholic question, in a letter to a counsellor at law in Dublin* (London: J. Debrett, 1801), 6, 11–13. Educated in England at Christ Church Oxford, Dillon-Lee became an MP first for Harwich and then for County Mayo.

127 BRBML, Milner, *A Short View*, 4–5.

128 Patrick Geoghegan makes the same point in "The Catholics."

129 Andrew MacKillop, *"More Fruitful Than the Soil": Army Empire and the Scottish Highlands, 1715–1815* (East Linton, SCT: Tuckwell Press, 2000);

Kevin Kenny, "The Irish in Empire," in *Ireland and the British Empire* ed. Kenny (Oxford: Oxford University Press, 2004).

130 BRBML, Rev. J. Milner, *The case of conscience solved: or, the Catholic claims proved to be compatible with the coronation oath/in a letter from a divine in the country to his friend in town; with a supplement in answer to Considerations on the coronation oath, by J. Reeves, Esq. Case of conscience solved Catholic claims proved to be compatible with the coronation oath* (London: Keating, Brown, 1807), 23.

131 BRBML, Denys Scully, *An Irish Catholic's advice to his brethren, how to estimate their present situation, and repel French invasion, civil wars, and slavery*, new ed. (Dublin: M.N. Mahon, 1803), 15.

132 BRBML, Dillon, *The Question as to the admission of Catholics*, 76; Scully, *An Irish Catholic's advice*, 17. This edition was printed as an anti-emancipation tract. It was copied in full, but commentary footnotes were added.

133 BRBML, Milner, *The case of conscience solved*, 21.

134 James Kelly, "'Era of Liberty': The Politics of Civil and Political Rights in Eighteenth-Century Ireland," in *Exclusionary Empire: English Liberty Overseas, 1600–1900*, ed. Jack P. Greene (Cambridge: Cambridge University Press, 2010), 77–112; Holmes, "Professor James Thomson," 100–1.

135 Marianne Elliott, "The Defenders in Ulster," in *The United Irishmen: Republicanism, Radicalism and Rebellion*, ed. David Dickson, Dáire Keogh and Kevin Whelan (Dublin: Lilliput Press, 1993), 222–33; Keenan, *The Grail of Catholic Emancipation*.

136 UCLUD, Lisbon College Papers, LC/C841, letter from J. Douglass, Holborn, to William Fryer, English College, Lisbon, 28 March 1805.

137 BRBML, *The Patriot King*, 23.

138 Willem Frijhoff, "Shifting Identities in Hostile Settings: Towards a Comparison of the Catholic Communities in Early Modern Britain and the Northern Netherlands," in *Catholic Communities in Protestant States: Britain and the Netherlands, c. 1570–1720*, ed. Benjamin Kaplan, et al. (Manchester: Manchester University Press, 2009), 3–5. Fagan notes the tension between France and Rome, in *Divided Loyalties*, 13–14. See also S. Karly Kehoe, "Unionism, Nationalism and the Scottish Catholic Periphery, 1850–1930," *Britain and the World* 4:1 (2011): 65–83.

139 Connell, *The Roman Catholic Church*, 95.

140 BRBML, *An appeal against the Roman Catholic claims* (London: J.J. Stockdale, 1812), 7.

141 Bric, "Catholicism and Empire," 36–8.

142 Bartlett, *The Fall and Rise*, 305.

143 BRBML, *The Substance of the speech of the Right Hon. Henry Grattan, upon his motion, "That the petition of the Catholics of Ireland be referred to a*

committee to consider the state of the laws imposing civil disabilities on His Majesty's subjects professing the Roman Catholic religion": containing the general petition of the Catholics of Ireland, and the names of the minority, in support of the motion (London, 1812).

144 Scott Reynolds Nelson highlights the on-going trade relationship on the ground in *A Nation of Deadbeats: An Uncommon History of America's Financial Disasters* (New York: Alfred Knopf, 2012), 45–7.

145 Lawrence A. Peskin, "Conspiratorial Anglophobia and the War of 1812," *Journal of American History* 98:3 (2011): 647–69.

146 Michael E. Vance, *Imperial Immigrants: Scottish Settlers in the Upper Ottawa Valley, 1815–1840* (Toronto: Dundurn, 2012), 50–4.

147 BRBML, *The Substance of the speech.*

148 BRBML, *The Patriot King*, 20–1; William Hunter, *A letter to His Royal Highness the Prince Regent: on the ultimate tendency of the Roman Catholic claims* (London, 1812); John Walter Howard, *The alarm sounded; or, An address to the Protestants of Great Britain* (London, 1812); Beilby Porteus, *Reasons against emancipating the Roman Catholics* (London, 1812); *A Traitor, A letter to the Right Honourable the Earl of Liverpool, on the claims of the Roman Catholics* (London, 1813).

149 *The Scotsman*, 7 February 1829; see also 18 March 1829 and 9 July 1829.

150 BRBML, Osborn Collection, Catholic Emancipation Poetry (1830s), Josiah Spode, "On the Catholic Emancipation," in a medium-sized, hard-covered notebook.

3 Colonial Catholics and Constitutional Change

1 Thomas Bartlett, *The Fall and Rise of the Catholic Nation: The Catholic Question, 1690–1830* (Dublin: Gill and Macmillan, 1992), 268–9, 272, 295.

2 Terrence Murphy, "The Emergence of Maritime Catholicism, 1781–1830," *Acadiensis* 13:2 (1984): 29.

3 For information on the region's population, see Luca Codignola, "The Policy of Rome towards English-Speaking Catholics," in *Creed and Culture: The Place of English-Speaking Catholics in Canadian Society, 1750–1930*, ed. Terry Murphy and Gerald Stortz (Montreal and Kingston: McGill-Queen's University Press, 1993), 104; Heidi MacDonald, "Developing a Strong Roman Catholic Social Order in Late Nineteenth-Century Prince Edward Island," *Canadian Catholic Historical Association Historical Studies* 69 (2003): 36; Murphy, "The Emergence of Maritime Catholicism," 29; Statistics Canada, Censuses of Canada 1665–1871, https://www150.statcan.gc.ca/n1/pub/98–187-x/4064809-eng.htm#part2.

4 J.R. Miller, "Anti-Catholicism in Canada: From the British Conquest to the Great War," in Murphy and Stortz, *Creed and Culture*, 27.

5 B.A. Balcom and A.J.B Johnston, "Missions to the Mi'kmaq: Malagawatch and Chapel Island in the 18th Century," *Journal of the Royal Nova Scotia Historical Society* 9 (2006): 115–41; Ruma Chopra, "Maroons and Mi'kmaw in Nova Scotia, 1796–1800," *Acadiensis* 46:1 (2017): 14.

6 Murphy, "The Emergence of Maritime Catholicism," 31.

7 S. Karly Kehoe, "Catholic Highlands Scots and the Colonisation of Prince Edward Island and Cape Breton Island, 1772–1830," in *British Colonisation in Atlantic Canada, 1700–1930: A Reappraisal*, ed. S. Karly Kehoe and Michael Vance (Edinburgh: Edinburgh University Press, 2020), 77–92.

8 John G. Reid, *Six Crucial Decades: Times of Change in the History of the Maritimes* (Halifax: Nimbus Publishing, 1987), 76.

9 Ibid., 64.

10 A database I'm working on for all 3,340 petitions for land in Cape Breton is showing an extremely high proportion of Catholic settlement across the island. NSA, Cape Breton Island Petitions, 1787–1843, https://novascotia.ca/archives/land/.

11 SCRA, 12/111, letter from Aeneas MacEachern to Aeneas Macdonald, 6 May 1828. See also Murphy, "The Emergence of Maritime Catholicism," 32, and Heidi MacDonald, "Developing a Strong Roman Catholic Social Order in Late Nineteenth-Century Prince Edward Island," *Canadian Catholic Historical Association Historical Studies* 69 (2003): 36.

12 S. Karly Kehoe, "Catholic Relief and the Political Awakening of Irish Catholics in Nova Scotia, 1780–1830," *Journal of Imperial and Commonwealth History* 46:1 (2018): 1–20; Mark G. McGowan, "The Maritimes Region and the Building of a Canadian Church: The Case of the Diocese of Antigonish after Confederation," *Canadian Catholic Historical Association Historical Studies* 70 (2004): 48–70.

13 Shannon Ryan, "Fishery to Colony: A Newfoundland Watershed, 1793–1815," *Acadiensis* 12:2 (1983): 34–52; Sean T. Cadigan, *Newfoundland and Labrador: A History* (Toronto: University of Toronto Press, 2009), 45–71.

14 For more on Newfoundland, see Jerry Bannister, *The Rule of the Admirals: Law, Custom and Naval Government in Newfoundland, 1699–1832* (Toronto: University of Toronto Press, 2003).

15 John P. Greene, *Between Damnation and Starvation: Priests and Merchants in Newfoundland Politics, 1745–1855* (Montreal and Kingston: McGill-Queen's University Press, 1999), 13. There are conflicting population statistics, as John G. Reid and Elizabeth Mancke propose a population of 3,000 in 1720: "From Global Processes to Continental Strategies: The Emergence of British North America to 1783," in *Canada and the British Empire*, ed. Phillip Buckner (Oxford: Oxford University Press, 2008), 30. See also Maryanne Kowaleski, "The Expansion of the South-Western Fisheries in Late Medieval England," *Economic History Review* 53:3 (2000): 452.

16 Reid, *Six Crucial Decades*, 62.

17 Reid and Mancke, "From Global Processes," 30–1.

18 WDA, Talbot Papers, A.42/53, notification of appointment sent from Propaganda Fide, Rome, to Bishop Talbot, London, 5 June 1784.

19 Raymond Devas, *Conception Island or the Troubled Story of the Catholic Church in Grenada, British West Indies* (Edinburgh: Sands & Co., 1932), 34 and 418.

20 Greene, *Between Damnation*, 15, 18, 21.

21 WDA, Talbot Papers, A.42/44 and A.42/47, letter from the Bishop of Waterford, Ireland, to Bishop Talbot, London, 14 January 1784, and letter from Dr Egan, Bishop of Clonmel, Ireland, to Bishop Talbot, London, 4 February 1784.

22 Terence J. Fay, *A History of Canadian Catholics* (Montreal and Kingston: McGill-Queen's University Press, 2002), 45.

23 Ibid., 37 and 43.

24 S. Karly Kehoe, *Creating a Scottish Church: Catholicism, Gender and Ethnicity in Nineteenth-Century Scotland* (Manchester: Manchester University Press, 2010); Carmen M. Mangion, *Contested Identities: Catholic Women Religious in Nineteenth-Century England and Wales* (Manchester: Manchester University Press, 2008); Fiona A. MacDonald, *Missions to the Gaels: Reformation and Counter-Reformation in Ulster and the Highlands and Islands of Scotland, 1560–1760* (Edinburgh: John Donald, 2006).

25 SCRA, Papers of Aeneas MacEachern, folder 12. See also Codignola, "The Policy of Rome," 103.

26 R.A. MacLean, "Burke (Bourke), Edmund (1753–1820)," *Dictionary of Canadian Biography*, vol. 5 (University of Toronto/Université Laval, 2003), http://www.biographi.ca/en/bio/burke_edmund_1753_1820_5E.html.

27 Archdiocese of Halifax Archives (hereafter AHA), letter from Father Burke to Cardinal Antonelli, n.d., quoted in Burke Papers, vol. 1; P.W. Browne, "Bishop Edmund Burke – First Vicar-Apostolic of Nova Scotia," *Studies: An Irish Quarterly Review* 22 (1933): 658.

28 "Edmund Burke," *Dictionary of Canadian Biography Online*, http://www .biographi.ca/EN/009004–119.01-e.php?id_nbr=2297.

29 Library and Archives Canada (hereafter LAC), MG24.J.13, letters of the Rt. Rev. Alexander Macdonell, first bishop of Upper Canada, copies from the originals in the Bishop's Palace, Kingston, 1836–38. See also Teresa Gourlay, "Subject to Authority: Bishop Alexander MacDonnel and His Scottish Religious Superiors, 1788–1804," *Innes Review* 61:2 (2010): 150–68.

30 "Joseph-Octave Plessis," *Dictionary of Canadian Biography Online*, http:// www.biographi.ca/009004–119.01-e.php?id_nbr=3076.

31 Beaton Institute, Cape Breton University (hereafter BICBU), MG 13/43, English translation of "The Plessis Diary of 1811 and 1812," 77, 78.

32　UCLUD, Ushaw College Papers, UC/PA/J37, letter from Andrew Scott, Glasgow, to Thomas Sherburne, Ushaw College, 13 February 1835.

33　BICBU, MG 13/43, "The Plessis Diary," 97.

34　Sarah Roddy, "Spiritual Imperialism and the Mission of the Irish Race: The Catholic Church and Emigration from Nineteenth-Century Ireland," *Irish Historical Studies* 38:152 (2013): 600–19.

35　Katherine Crooks, "The Quest for Respectability: The Charitable Irish Society in Victorian Halifax," *Historical Studies* 81 (2015): 167–94.

36　James Kelly, "Charitable Societies: Their Genesis and Development, 1720–1800," in *Clubs and Societies in Eighteenth-Century Ireland*, ed. James Kelly and Martyn J. Powell (Dublin: Four Courts Press, 2010), 89–91.

37　NSA, MG20, vol. 65, *Articles agreed upon by the Charitable Irish Society, in Halifax Nova Scotia, for the better management of their charity* (1786); *The Rules and Constitutions of the Charitable Irish Society established at Halifax Nova Scotia* (1795); emphasis in original.

38　Archdiocese of Dublin Archives (hereafter ADA), Troy Papers, letter from Father Phelan, Halifax, to Archbishop Troy, Dublin, c. 1785.

39　NSA, MG20, vol. 66, minute book of the Charitable Irish Society, entry around St Patrick's Day, 1819.

40　NSA, MG20, vol. 68, minute book of the Charitable Irish Society, entries for August 1864 (day illegible) and 18 August 1873.

41　NSA, MG20, vol. 65, minute book of the Charitable Irish Society, 1786–1808, entry for 17 May 1798.

42　Fay, *A History of Canadian Catholics*, 48. Colin Kidd offers an interesting perspective on the Scottish context in "Sentiment, Race and Revival: Scottish Identities in the Aftermath of Enlightenment," in *A Union of Multiple Identities: The British Isles, c. 1750–1850*, ed. Laurence Brockliss and David Eastwood (Manchester: Manchester University Press, 1997), 110–26.

43　Michael Gauvreau, "Covenanter Democracy: Scottish Popular Religion, Ethnicity, and Varieties of Politico-Religious Dissent in Upper Canada, 1815–1841," *Histoire sociale/Social History* 35:71 (2003): 59, 61.

44　Mark G. McGowan, *The Waning of the Green: Catholics, the Irish and Identity in Toronto, 1887–1920* (Montreal and Kingston: McGill-Queen's University Press, 1999), 7.

45　Greene, *Between Damnation*, 10; Murphy, "The Emergence of Maritime Catholicism," 29–30.

46　Oliver P. Rafferty, "The Catholic Church, Ireland and the British Empire, 1800–1921," *Historical Research* 84:224 (2011): 299.

47　A special thank you to Matthew Cook and Anne Marie Lane Jonah of Parks Canada's Fortress of Louisbourg for supplying these population statistics. They also suggest that the soldier numbers are actually an underestimate. Robert J. Morgan, "Orphan Outpost: Cape Breton Colony, 1784–1820" (PhD diss., University of Ottawa, 1972), 9.

48 Stephen J. Hornsby, *Nineteenth-Century Cape Breton: A Historical Geography* (Montreal and Kingston: McGill-Queen's University Press, 1992), 19–23, 48; Reid, *Six Crucial Decades*, 68.

49 Julian Gwyn, *Excessive Expectations: Maritime Commerce and the Economic Development of Nova Scotia, 1740–1870* (Montreal and Kingston: McGill-Queen's University Press, 1998), 151; Hornsby, *Nineteenth-Century Cape Breton*, 85–93.

50 Gwyn, *Excessive Expectations*, 46. See also Michael E. Vance, *Imperial Immigrants: Scottish Settlers in the Upper Ottawa Valley, 1815–1840* (Toronto: Dundurn, 2012), 33–4.

51 Phyllis MacInnes Wagg, "Laurence Kavanagh I: An Eighteenth-Century Cape Breton Entrepreneur," *Nova Scotia Historical Review* 10 (1990): 128.

52 Ibid., 126. For a good study of another Irish family, see Orla Power, "Stateless and Destitute: O'Rourke Family at Saint Domingue, Nantes and Wexford," in *Irish Imperial Connections, 1775–1947*, ed. Danile Sanjiv Roberts and Jonathan Jeffrey Wright (London: Palgrave Macmillan, 2019), 233–50.

53 NSA, RG1, vol. 44, no. 61, Dartmouth, Halifax, 24 April 1775.

54 Many of the Irish merchants were linked to the West Indian trade networks. Personal communication between S. Karly Kehoe and Robert Dunphy, genealogist and independent historian, January and February 2013.

55 A.A. Johnston, *A History of the Catholic Church in Eastern Nova Scotia*, vol. 1 (Antigonish, NS: St. Francis Xavier University, 1960), 102–4; Frederick Madden, ed., *Imperial Reconstruction, 1763–1840: The Evolution of Alternative Systems of Colonial Government. Select Documents on the Constitutional History of the British Empire and Commonwealth*, vol. 3 (New York: Greenwood Press, 1987), 363–4; Murphy, "The Emergence of Maritime Catholicism," 31.

56 NSA, RG1, vol. 222, doc. 91, letter to Richard Hughes, Lieutenant Governor of Nova Scotia, from Mullowny and John McDaniel, 5 July 1781.

57 Such an assertion was becoming the norm, as Martin Daunton and Rick Halpern point out. Previously, the "settlers' claims to the rights of Englishmen" had precipitated the loss of the thirteen American colonies. Martin Daunton and Rick Halpern, "Introduction: British Identities, Indigenous Peoples, and the Empire," in *Empire and Others: British Encounters with Indigenous People, 1600–1850* (Philadelphia: University of Pennsylvania Press, 1999), 9.

58 NSA, RG1, vol. 222, doc. 92, letter to Sir Andrew Snape Hamond, Lieutenant Governor of Nova Scotia, from John Cody, James Kavanagh, John Mullowny, and John Murphy, 1782.

59 NSA, RG1, vol. 301, doc. 49, copy of letter to the Nova Scotia House of Assembly from Sir Andrew Snape Hamond, Lieutenant Governor, 8 October 1783; Murphy, "The Emergence of Maritime Catholicism," 30–1, 41.

60 NSA, RG1, vol. 222, doc. 93; WDA, Talbot Papers, A.42.25, letter to Sir Andrew Snape Hamond, Lieutenant Governor of Nova Scotia, from John Cody, John Murphy, John Mullowny William Meany, and James Kavanagh, 1782.

61 Wagg, "Laurence Kavanagh," 130.

62 Personal archives of Myles Kehoe (hereafter PAMK), letter from Laurence Kavanagh at St Peter's to Lieut. Col. Armstrong, Adjutant General, Cape Breton Militia, 22 April 1813.

63 Morgan, "Orphan Outpost," 216.

64 PAMK, letter from Miles McDaniel of Margaree to Laurence Kavanagh of St Peter's, spring 1825, and draft of public notice from Laurence Kavanagh to Miles McDaniel, 19 May 1825.

65 Alban Hood, "The Throckmortons Come of Age: Political and Social Alignments, 1826–1862," in *Catholic Gentry in English Society: The Throckmortons of Coughton from Reformation to Emancipation*, ed. Peter Marshall and Geoffrey Scott (Farnham, EN: Ashgate, 2009), 255–8.

66 Morgan, "The County of Nova Scotia, 1816–1820," chap. 7 of "Orphan Outpost."

67 Herbert Leslie Stewart, *The Irish in Nova Scotia: Annals of the Charitable Irish Society of Halifax, 1786–1836* (Kentville, NS: Kentville Publishing, 1949), 131.

68 See Bartlett, *The Fall and Rise*, 321.

69 Maurice J. Bric, "Catholicism and Empire: Ireland and Lower Canada, 1760–1830," in *Ireland and Quebec: Multidisciplinary Perspectives on History, Culture and Society*, ed. Margaret Kelleher and Michael Kenneally (Dublin: Four Courts Press, 2016), 36–7.

70 "Sir James Kempt," *Dictionary of Canadian Biography Online*, http://www.biographi.ca/009004–119.01-e.php?id_nbr=4004.

71 LAC, MG24.J7, letter from Aeneas MacDonald, Rome, to unspecified recipient in Montreal, 14 November 1823.

72 SCRA, 12/111, letter from Aeneas MacEachern to Aeneas McDonald, 6 May 1828, and 12/112, letter from William Fraser to Angus MacDonald, 8 October 1828. Charles J. McMillan provides a biographical sketch of MacEachern in *Eminent Islanders: Prince Edward Island, from French Colony to the Cradle of Confederation* (Bloomington, IN: Authorhouse, 2009), 62–109.

73 NSA, MG20, vol. 66, minute book of the Charitable Irish Society of Halifax, entry for 19 February 1822.

74 "Sir James Kempt."

75 Beamish Murdoch, *A History of Nova Scotia, or Acadie* (Halifax: James Barnes, 1867), 478–9

76 Ibid., 479; Jerry Bannister and Liam Riordan, "Loyalism and the British Atlantic, 1660–1840," in *The Loyal Atlantic: Remaking the British Atlantic in the Revolutionary Era*, ed. Bannister and Riordan (Toronto: University of Toronto Press, 2012), 22.

77 Bannister and Riordan, "Loyalism and the British Atlantic," 22; Bric, "Catholicism and Empire," 37.

78 Vance, *Imperial Immigrants*, 34–5.

79 NSA, RG 1, vol. 230, doc. 154, copy of letter from James Kempt to the Earl of Bathurst, 20 March 1822.

80 NSA, RG 1, vol. 230, doc. 164, copy of letter from the Earl of Bathurst to James Kempt, 8 May 1822; see also vol. 231, doc. 13, Statement on Province of Nova Scotia.

81 NSA, *Journal and Proceedings of the House of Assembly, 1823*, entry for 3 April 1823. See also *Acadian Recorder*, 5 April 1823.

82 NSA, *Journal and Proceedings of the House of Assembly, 1823*, entry for 3 April 1823.

83 NSA, RG 1, vol. 222, no. 91, Petition of Roman Catholics, 5 July 1781.

84 NSA, *Acadian Recorder*, 8 February 1823 and 15 February 1823.

85 Andrew R. Holmes, "Professor James Thompson Sr. and Lord Kelvin: Religion, Science, and Liberal Unionism in Ulster and Scotland," *Journal of British Studies* 50 (2011): 100–24.

86 NSA, *Acadian Recorder*, 28 August 1830.

87 AHA, Burke Papers, 3/6, *State of the Catholics in Nova Scotia*, prepared for circulation by Edward Blout (May 1827), 4; Murdoch, *A History of Nova Scotia*, 571.

88 "Sir Brenton Halliburton," *Dictionary of Canadian Biography Online*, http://biographi.ca/009004–119.01-e.php?id_nbr=3949.

89 AHA, Burke Papers, *State of the Catholics in Nova Scotia*, 5.

90 Ibid., 7. He was first elected in 1826 and re-elected in 1830.

91 NSA, *Journal and Proceedings of the House of Assembly, 1827*, entry for 6 March 1827, "To The King's Most Excellent Majesty: The Humble Address of the House of Representatives in the General Assembly," 65–6. See also Appendix 3 in Murdoch, *A History of Nova Scotia*, 589.

92 Letter from T.C. Haliburton to Abbé Jean-Mande Sigogne, 10 March 1827, in *The Letters of Thomas Chandler Haliburton*, ed. Richard A. Davies (Toronto: University of Toronto Press, 1988), 37.

93 AHA, Burke Papers, *State of the Catholics in Nova Scotia*, 6.

94 NSA, *Journal and Proceedings of the House of Assembly, 1827*, entries for 30 March and 17 April 1827.

95 AHA, Burke Papers, *State of the Catholics in Nova Scotia*.

96 Richard W. Davis, "Wellington, the Constitution and Catholic Emancipation," *Parliamentary History* 15:2 (1996): 209–14; G.I.T. Machin, "The Catholic Question and the Monarchy, 1827–1829," *Parliamentary History* 16:2 (1997): 213–20.

97 Nicholas Meagher, *The Religious Warfare in Nova Scotia, 1855–1860: Its Political Aspect, the Honourable Joseph Howe's Part in It and the Attitudes of Catholics* (Halifax, 1927), 15; NSA, RG5, GP, vol. 11, no. 12, Petition of Laurence O'Connor Doyle, April 1828. His presidencies were 1826, 1829–31, and 1843–44.

98 By this time, Uniacke was also the province's attorney general. Stewart, *The Irish*, 133–5. The dates for Doyle's presence at Stonyhurst were provided by its archivist, David Knight, on 24 January 2013. He was sent to England from Nova Scotia by his parents due to the lack of suitable institution in the province.

99 NSA, Virtual Archives, Charitable Irish Society, Lawrence O'Connor Doyle, http://gov.ns.ca/nsarm/virtual/CIS/archives.asp?ID=63.

100 NSA, RG5, series P, vol. 10, no. 11, Petition of Adam Esson against the election and return of Laurence Doyle for the Township of Halifax, 26 January 1848.

101 NSA, *Nova Scotian*, 7 November 1864; NSA, MG100, vol. 136, no. 8, Biographical pamphlet of Laurence O'Connor Doyle.

102 Chestico Museum and Archives (hereafter CMA), warrant for the appointment of Peter Smyth, as a Member of the Legislative Council of the Province of Nova Scotia, 29 November 1867, and letter from the Secretary of State for the Provinces to Peter Smyth, 26 December 1867.

103 CMA, notice of appointment to Captain of the 1st Battalion, 3rd Regiment Cape Breton Militia, 2 October 1854, and notice of appointment to Lieutenant Colonel unattached, 4 April 1864.

104 CMA, binder entitled Killarney Manor, Port Hood, Nova Scotia, newspaper clipping, "The Story of 'Peter Smyth's' Song. Written by Alasdair MacLean, c. 1870s, after his brother lost his property to Smyth, the song continues for five more verses and gets increasingly negative. The "Sam" referred to in the song was his lawyer, and the reference to drink refers to the accusation that he would offer people drinks when they came into his shop, and they would then buy more on credit than they could actually afford.

105 SCRA, 12/117, letter from Aeneas MacEachern to Aeneas McDonald, 14 October 1830.

106 SCRA, 12/117, letter from Aeneas MacEachern to Aeneas McDonald, 8 July 1831.

107 Roberto Perin, *Rome in Canada: The Vatican and Canadian Affairs in the Late Victorian Age* (Toronto: University of Toronto Press, 1990), 16–17, 27.

108 NSA, *Acadian Recorder*, 16 May 1829; *Nova Scotian*, 3 April 1829 and 23 April 1829.

4 Engaging with Imperial Traditions

1 Gavin Daly, *The British Soldier in the Peninsular War: Encounters with Spain and Portugal, 1808–1814* (Basingstoke, EN: Palgrave Macmillan, 2013), 156–85.

2 Catherine Hall et al., *Legacies of British Slave-Ownership: Colonial Slavery and the Formation of Victorian Britain* (Cambridge: Cambridge University Press, 2014); Kenneth Donovan, "Slaves and Their Owners in Ile Royale, 1713–1760," *Acadiensis* 25:1 (1995): 3–32; Harvey Amani Whitfield, "Slave Life and Slave Law in Colonial Prince Edward Island, 1769–1825," *Acadiensis* 38:2 (2009): 29–51; Afua Cooper, *The Hanging of Angelique: The Untold Story of Canadian Slavery and the Burning of Old Montreal* (Toronto: Harper Perennial, 2006).

3 Jenny Shaw, *Everyday Life in the Early English Caribbean: Irish, Africans and the Construction of Difference* (Athens: University of Georgia Press, 2013); Lydia M. Pulsipher and Conrad "Mac" Goodwin, "'Getting the Essence of It': Galways Plantation, Montserrat, West Indies," in *Island Lives: Historical Archaeology of the Caribbean*, ed. Paul Farnsworth (Tuscaloosa: University of Alabama Press, 2001), 165–206.

4 Thomas Bartlett, "'A Weapon of War Yet Untried': Irish Catholics and the Armed Forces of the Crown, 1760–1830," in *Men, Women and War*, ed. T.G. Fraser and Keith Jeffrey (Dublin: Lilliput Press, 1993), 67.

5 Richard Keogh and James McConnel, "The Esmonde Family of Co. Wexford and Catholic Loyalty," in *Irish Catholic Identities*, ed. Oliver Rafferty (Manchester: Manchester University Press, 2013), 274–91; John Bergin, "Irish Catholics and Their Networks in Eighteenth-Century London," *Eighteenth-Century Life* 39:1 (2015): 70; Charles Ivar McGrath, "Waging War: The Irish Military Establishment and the British Empire, 1688–1763," in *The Primacy of Foreign Policy in British History, 1660–2000: How Strategic Concerns Shaped Modern Britain*, ed. William Mulligan and Brendan Simms (Basingstoke, EN: Palgrave Macmillan, 2010), 108–9.

6 In the early eighteenth century, the number had been just 30,000: personal correspondence with Michael Snape – many thanks to him for this number.

7 My thanks to Michael Snape for these figures.

8 C.A. Bayly, "Ireland, India and the Empire: 1780–1914," *Transactions of the Royal Historical Society* 10 (2000): 389.

9 TNA, CO 101/35/27, letter from Alexander Houston, lieutenant governor of Grenada, to the Duke of Portland, 22 February 1797.

10 Jeremy D. Popkin, "Thermidor, Slavery, and the 'Affaire des Colonies,'" *French Historical Studies* 38:1 (2015): 61–82; Christopher L. Brown, "From Slaves to Subjects: Envisioning an Empire without Slavery, 1772–1834," in *Black Experience and the Empire*, ed. Philip D. Morgan and Sean Hawkins (Oxford: Oxford University Press, 2004), 133.

11 Karsten, "Irish Soldiers in the British Army, 1792–1922: Suborned or Subordinate?" *Journal of Social History* 17:1 (1983): 38–9; Catriona Kennedy, *Narratives of the Revolutionary and Napoleonic Wars: Military and Civilian Experience in Britain and Ireland* (Basingstoke, EN: Palgrave Macmillan, 2013), 43–5. The young Charles O'Neil remarked that "Ireland has charming and beautiful girls [but they] were scarcely willing to regard any young man as honourable or brave, who did not enlist, and aim to deserve well of his country." Charles O'Neil, *The military adventurers of Charles O'Neil, who was a soldier in the army of Lord Wellington during the memorable Peninsular War and the Continental Campaigns from 1811 to 1815* (Worcester, 1851), 9.

12 LAC, MG24.J.13, letters of the Rt. Rev. Alexander MacDonnel, first bishop of Upper Canada, copies from the originals in the Bishop's Palace, Kingston, 1836–38.

13 James Hagerty and Tom Johnstone, "Catholic Military Chaplains in the Crimean War," *Recusant History* 27:3 (2005): 416. Peter Karsten shows the same figures, in "Irish Soldiers in the British Army," 36, 39. For a useful overview of the politics of Scotland's militarism at the end of the eighteenth century, see J.E. Cookson, *The British Armed Nation, 1793–1815* (Oxford: Clarendon Press, 1997), especially chap. 5, "Scotland's Fame."

14 Hagerty and Johnstone, "Catholic Military Chaplains," 416.

15 Christopher Tozzi, "Jews, Soldiering, and Citizenship in Revolutionary and Napoleonic France," *Journal of Modern History* 86 (2014): 243–7.

16 Kennedy, *Narratives*, 43–5; Alvin Jackson, *The Two Unions: Ireland, Scotland and the Survival of the United Kingdom, 1707–2007* (Oxford: Oxford University Press, 2012), 80–1.

17 S. Karly Kehoe, "Accessing Empire: Irish Surgeons and the Royal Navy, 1840–1880," *Social History of Medicine* 26:2 (2013); Barry Crosbie, *Irish Imperial Networks: Migration, Social Communication and Exchange in Nineteenth-Century India* (Cambridge: Cambridge University Press, 2012), 204–24; Alvin Jackson, "Ireland, the Union and the Empire, 1800–1960," and Kevin Kenny, "The Irish in Empire," both in *Ireland and the British Empire*, ed. Kevin Kenny (Oxford: Oxford University Press, 2004), 125–53 and 90–124, respectively; Jenny Shaw, *Everyday Life in the Early English Caribbean* (Athens: University of Georgia Press, 2013), 172–4.

18 Karl Schweizer, "Jacobitism and the Historian: Some Neglected Sources on the Jacobite Insurrections of 1715 and 1745," *Canadian Journal of*

History 48 (2013): 447; Allan I. Macinnes, "Union, Empire and Global Adventuring with a Jacobite Twist, 1707–53," in *Jacobitism, Enlightenment and Empire, 1680–1820*, ed. D.J. Hamilton and A.I. Macinnes (London: Pickering & Chatto, 2014), 123–40.

19 Keogh and McConnel, "The Esmonde Family."

20 Thomas O'Connor, "Ireland and Europe, 1580–1815: Some Historiographical Remarks," and Mary Ann Lyons, "The Emergence of an Irish Community in Saint-Malo, 1550–1710," in *The Irish in Europe, 1580–1815*, ed. Thomas O'Connor (Dublin: Four Courts Press, 2001), 107–26; J.G. Simms, "Connacht in the Eighteenth Century," *Irish Historical Studies* 11:42 (1958): 120.

21 Bartlett, "'A Weapon of War,'" 69–70; S.J. Connolly, *Divided Kingdom: Ireland, 1630–1800* (Oxford: Oxford University Press, 2008), 297–8.

22 WDA, A.42/132, Talbot Papers, Statement from the Catholic Committee, 20 May 1788.

23 SCA, BL 4/85/7 and 4/8/10, letters from George Hay to John Geddes, 15 March and 7 April 1794.

24 Bartlett, "'A Weapon of War,'" 78.

25 Kennedy, *Narratives*, 36; Daly, *The British Soldier*, 159–61; Charles Butler, *Historical Memoirs of the English, Irish and Scottish Catholics, since the Reformation*, vol. 4 (London, 1822), 257–60; Stephen Conway, "Christians, Catholics, Protestants: The Religious Links of Britain and Ireland with Continental Europe, c. 1689–1800," *English Historical Review* 124:509 (2009): 844, 858; Markus Ackroyd et al., *Advancing with the Army: Medicine, the Professions and Social Mobility in the British Isles, 1790–1850* (Oxford: Oxford University Press), 90–1.

26 Butler, *Historical Memoirs*, 259.

27 Bayly, "Ireland, India and the Empire," 181.

28 British Library (hereafter BL), MS.38737, f.191–214, series of correspondence, dated 4 February to 18 March 1807, between Lord Grenville, the cabinet, and King George III about Catholic relief and the possibility of Irish Catholics serving as officers in the British Army and the Royal Navy, letter dated 9 February 1807.

29 Ibid., letters dated 15 and 18 March 1807.

30 Kennedy, *Narratives*, 62.

31 J.E. Rea, "Alexander McDonell," *Dictionary of Canadian Biography Online*, http://www.biographi.ca/en/bio/mcdonell_alexander_7E.html.

32 For more on the tensions, see S. Karly Kehoe, *Creating a Scottish Church: Catholicism, Gender and Ethnicity in Nineteenth-Century Scotland* (Manchester: Manchester University Press, 2010) and Martin J. Mitchell, *The Irish in the West of Scotland, 1797–1848: Trade Unions, Strikes and Political Movements* (Edinburgh: John Donald, 1998).

33 SCRA, 12/119, letter from William Fraser to Aeneas Macdonald, 28 December 1831, and 12/120, letter from Alexander Macdonell to Aeneas Macdonald, 31 July 1831; Crosbie, *Irish Imperial Networks*, 134.

34 AVCAU, Scr. 55/9/12, letter from Thomas Weld, layman, London, to Rev. Dr. Wiseman, English College, Rome, 19 May 1829.

35 SCRA, 12/126, letter from William P. MacDonald to Aeneas Macdonald, 29 September 1832; LAC, MG 24.J.13, letter from Alexander Macdonell to Lord Durham, 14 June 1838.

36 SCRA, 12/123, letter from Alexander Macdonell to Aeneas Macdonald, 1 September 1832. Crosbie's research reveals that this was a fear that extended to many colonies: see *Irish Imperial Networks*, 135.

37 Kehoe, *Creating a Scottish Church*; S. Karly Kehoe, "Irish Migrants and the Recruitment of Catholic Sisters to Glasgow, 1847–1878," in *Ireland and Scotland in the Nineteenth Century*, ed. Frank Ferguson and James McConnell (Dublin: Four Courts Press, 2009), 35–47; Mitchell, *The Irish in the West of Scotland*.

38 SCRA, 12/122, letter from Alexander Macdonell, York, to Aeneas Macdonald, Rome, 20 August 1832.

39 APF, *Scritture riferite nei Congressi, Fondo America Settentrionale* 3/144br-144bv, Alexander Macdonell to Sir John Colborne, February 1833, and 3/141vb-144, Alexander Macdonell to Sir John Colborne, 8 January 1833.

40 LAC, MG24.J.13, *The Address of Bishop McDonell to the Inhabitants of the County of Glengarry* (1839).

41 ADA, Troy Papers, letter from Father Phelan, Halifax, to Archbishop Troy, Dublin, c. 1785; Terrence Murphy, "The Emergence of Maritime Catholicism, 1781–1830," *Acadiensis* 13:2 (1984): 35–7.

42 TNA, CO 101/78/56–9 and 81–92, series of correspondence relating to Father A. O'Hannan, c. 1829–5; Bernard Ince, "Rebel with a Cause: The Fall and Rise of Abbé Samuel Power," *Journal of Caribbean History* 41:1 (2013): 29–31.

43 Olive Anderson, "The Growth of Christian Militarism in Mid-Victorian Britain," *English Historical Review* 86:338 (1971): 60.

44 AHA, Burke Papers, vol. II/105, letter from Edmund Burke to Joseph-Octave Plessis, Quebec, 13 September 1798.

45 J.E. Cookson, *The British Armed Nation, 1793–1815* (Oxford: Clarendon Press, 1997), 123–4; AHA, Burke Papers, vol. II/129, letter from Edmund Burke to Joseph-Octave Plessis, Quebec, 10 August 1805, and vol. II/141, letter from Edmund Burke to Joseph-Octave Plessis, Quebec, 1 May 1805.

46 AHA, Burke Papers, vol. II/141, letter from Edmund Burke to Leveque, Quebec, 1 May 1807, and letter from Edmund Burke to Joseph-Octave Plessis, Quebec, 1 May 1807.

47 Michael Snape, *The Redcoat and Religion: The Forgotten History of the British Soldier from the Age of Marlborough to the Eve of the First World War* (London: Routledge, 2005), 189, 195; Kennedy, *Narratives*, chaps 2 and 6.

48 ADA, folder 325/194, Catholic Soldiers & Sailors, 1853–54, Allowances to Officiating Clergymen at home (1854). Catholics received half the pay of Anglican chaplains who served between fifty and a hundred men. BL, IOR E/4/817, f. 1139–1158, India Ecclesiastical Department (notes the replies to various letters, few specifics noted), replies to letters from 1851 (10 November 1852). After going blind in India, one priest asked for support to return to Britain, but officials dragged their feet and agreed only after he had left. See also Maria Luddy, ed., *The Crimean Journals of the Sisters of Mercy, 1854–56* (Dublin: Four Courts Press, 2004) for difficulties faced by women religious.

49 Anderson, "The Growth," 61; Archdiocese Archives of St. John's (hereafter AASJ), Mullock Papers, 104/1/39, letter from Secretary at War to Mullock, 24 October 1851.

50 TNA, HO 44/11/389–96, letter from T. O'Mealy, Sheerness, Kent, to Robert Peel, Whitehall, March 1822.

51 *Irish Catholic Directory* (1844), 478.

52 AASJ, Mullock Papers, 104/1/39, letter from Thomas Mullock, St. John's, to Downing Street, 1 October 1851.

53 AASJ, Mullock Papers, 104/1/39, letter from Secretary at War, London, to Thomas Mullock, St. John's, 24 October 1851.

54 John Handby Thompson, "The Free Church Army Chaplains, 1830–1930" (PhD diss., University of Sheffield, 1990); *Irish Catholic Directory* (1861), 336.

55 ADA, AB/40/3/I/19, John O'Rourke, *State of Catholics in the Navy*, 20 June 1859.

56 ADA, AB/321/6/I/11, W.L. Woollett, *Catholics in the British Navy*, 23 March 1870.

57 Dom Aidan Henry Germain, "Catholic Military and Naval Chaplains," *Catholic Historical Review* 15:2 (1929): 171–8.

58 AHA, Burke Papers, vol. II/168, letter from Edmund Burke to Joseph-Octave, Bishop of Quebec, 18 November 1812. At Penetanguishene in Upper Canada, another priest, John Bell, complained that the number of Catholics under his care, which included a growing number of soldiers, made it impossible to provide adequate spiritual guidance, let alone any proper grounding in the faith. Archives of the Catholic Archdiocese of Toronto (hereafter ARCAT), McDonell Papers, AC 14.06, letter from John Bell, Penetanguishene, to Alexander Macdonell, York, 18 June 1833.

59 Anderson, "The Growth," 62; Daly, *The British Soldier*, 172.

60 Durham University Library, Archives and Special Collections (hereafter DULASC), 3rd Earl Grey Papers, GRE/B95/1/115 and GRE/B95/1/116,

letters from Henry George, 3rd Earl Grey, to General Charles Grey, December 1836 and 31 December 1836.

61 O'Rourke, *State of Catholics*; Woollett, *Catholics in the British Navy*. See also Kevin Lynch, *Britain and Wellington's Army: Recruitment, Society and Tradition, 1807–15* (Basingstoke, EN: Palgrave Macmillan, 2011), 114; Snape, *The Redcoat*, 230.

62 O'Neil, *The military adventurers*, 44.

63 Ibid., 47. The "cat" was an instrument approximately eighteen inches long and "composed of nine small cords, twisted very hard, and having three knots in each cord."

64 Ibid., 48.

65 Woollett, *Catholics in the British Navy*.

66 Private Archives of the English Benedictines (hereafter PAEB), diary of Richard Carr McClement, 1857–69; personal archives of Chris McClement (hereafter PACM), journal of Frederick McClement, vol. 1, entry for 27 July 1869.

67 PACM, McClement journal, 19 November 1865.

68 Lynch, *Britain and Wellington's Army*, 146; H.M. Chichester, "Calvert, Sir Harry, first baronet (*bap.* 1763, *d.* 1826)," revised by John Sweetman, *Oxford Dictionary of National Biography Online*, http://www.oxforddnb.com/view/article/4422.

69 Lynch, *Britain and Wellington's Army*, 116; Bartlett, "'A Weapon of War,'" 76–7.

70 O'Rourke, *State of Catholics*; Woollett, *Catholics in the British Navy*.

71 Jean de Chantal Kennedy, *Biography of a Colonial Town: Hamilton, Bermuda, 1790–1897* (Hamilton: Bermuda Book Stores, 1961), 274–6; J.K. Laughton, "Elliot, Sir Charles (1801–1875)," revised by Andrew Lambert, *Oxford Dictionary of National Biography Online*, http://www.oxforddnb.com/view/article/8656.

72 AHA, Walsh Papers, vol. 1, copies of letters, 1/72, letter from Thomas Lyons, St George's, Bermuda, to William Walsh, Halifax, 6 December 1850. Emphasis in original.

73 Kennedy, *Biography*, 276.

74 AASJ, Mullock Papers, 103/13, letter from E. Marwick Harvey, Government House, St John's, to unknown, St John's, 9 November 1843. See also Phillip Buckner, "Harvey, Sir John," *Dictionary of Canadian Biography*, vol. 8, University of Toronto/Université Laval, 2003, http://www.biographi.ca/en/bio/harvey_john_8E.html.

75 Phillip McCann, *Island in an Empire: Education, Religion and Social Life in Newfoundland, 1800–1855* (Portugal Cove, NL: Bolder Books, 2016), 211–19; John P. Greene, *Between Damnation and Starvation: Priests and Merchants, Newfoundland Politics, 1745–1855* (Montreal and Kingston: McGill-Queen's University Press, 1999), 37–8.

76 TNA, CO 37/134/51–2, letter from Charles Elliot, Bermuda, to Vice-Admiral, the Earl of Dundonald, 11 July 1850. See also TNA, CO 37/134/31A-31B, CO 37/134/42, CO 37/134/44, CO 37/134/48 and CO 37/134/51–2 for a full commentary on the dispute about non-Anglican burials.

77 AHA, Walsh Papers, vol. 1, 1/65, letter from William Clancy, vicar apostolic of British Guiana, to William Walsh, 1 November 1842. Extremely unflattering descriptions of him come from APF, *Scritture riferite nei Congressi, America Antille*, vol. 7, f. 303, letter to Rev. Rogers, Barbados, from Richard Smith, Trinidad, 6 September 1842.

78 AHA, Walsh Papers, vol. 1, 67, letter from Robert Higgs, St George's, Bermuda, to William Walsh, Halifax, 20 November 1843.

79 P.J. Marshall, *Remaking the British Atlantic: The United States and the British Empire after American Independence* (Oxford: Oxford University Press, 2012), 261.

80 John M. McCarthy, *Bermuda's Priests: The History of the Establishment and Growth of the Catholic Church in Bermuda* (Halifax: Archdiocese of Halifax, 1954), 12, 15; Robert Berard, "The Roman Catholic Archdiocese of Halifax and the Colony of Bermuda, 1832–1953," *Collections of the Royal Nova Scotia Historical Society* 42 (1986): 121–38.

81 AHA, Walsh Papers, vol. 1, 85, letter from James Rogers, Bermuda, to Archbishop William Walsh, Halifax, 5 June 1858. See also Jerome Devitt, "Fenianism's Bermuda Footprint: Revolutionary Nationalism in the Victorian Empire," *Eire-Ireland* 51:1/2 (2016): 141–70

82 TNA, CO37/146/103, letter from Governor Elliot, Bermuda, to Duke of Newcastle, Secretary of State, 20 January 1854; Kennedy, *Biography*, 275.

83 Thomas Bartlett, *The Fall and Rise of the Irish Nation: The Catholic Question, 1690–1830* (Dublin: Gill and Macmillan, 1992), 324–6.

84 *Reports on the Schemes of the Church of Scotland with overtures or draft acts sent to Presbyteries for their opinion and legislative acts passed by the general assembly* (1915), 545–53 and (1917), 392–415.

85 Snape, *The Redcoat*, 229 and 231; Anderson, "The Growth," 62–3; Steven Schwamenfeld, "The Foundation of British: National Identity and the British Common Soldier" (PhD diss., Florida State University, 2006), 12, 187–8.

86 Hagerty and Johnstone, "Catholic Military Chaplains," 438; Daly, *The British Soldier*, 156–85.

87 Anderson, "The Growth," 46–53.

88 Brown, "'Like a Devoted Army,'" 607–8.

89 Hagerty and Johnstone, "Catholic Military Chaplains," 438; Hansard, House of Commons, Debates, "Religious Wants of Roman Catholic Soldiers and Sailors," 3 March 1854, vol. 131.

90 Hansard, House of Commons, Debates, Frederick Lucas, "Religious Wants of Roman Catholic Soldiers," 3 December 1854, vol. 131, cc. 314–30,

http://hansard.millbanksystems.com/commons/1854/mar/03 /religious-wants-of-roman-catholic.

91 Michael Brown, "'Like a Devoted Army': Medicine, Heroic Masculinity, and the Military Paradigm in Victorian Britain," *Journal of British Studies* 49:3 (2010): 596. A note on this is included in the *Port of Spain Gazette*, 23 January 1855.

92 Ackroyd et al., *Advancing with the Army*, 91.

93 Sisters of Mercy, Limerick, Annals, 1849, Mother Mary Vincent, poem about Limerick's cholera epidemic, 106–9.

94 Luddy, *The Crimean Journals*, 247; "The Sisters of Mercy at Crimea," *The Tablet*, 13 April 1895.

95 Sisters of Mercy, Limerick, Annals, 1849, Mother Mary Vincent, poem, 177. For the actual poem, see Luddy, *The Crimean Journals*, 6–7, 65. See also Mary Ellen Doona, "Sister Mary Joseph Croke: Another Voice from the Crimean War, 1854–1856," *Nursing History Review* 3 (1995): 3–41.

96 Luddy, *The Crimean Journals*, 142.

97 J.J.W. Murphy, "An Irish Sister of Mercy in the Crimean War," *Irish Sword* 5:21 (1962): 251.

98 Luddy, *The Crimean Journals*, 24. For biographical detail on Doyle, see M. de Lourdes Fahy, "Mother M. Aloysius Doyle (1820–1908)," *Journal of the Galway Archaeological and Historical Society* 36 (1977–78): 70–7.

99 Murphy, "An Irish Sister," 256.

100 Maria Luddy, "'Angels of Mercy': Nuns as Workhouse Nurses, 1861–1898," in *Medicine, Disease and the State in Ireland, 1650–1940*, ed. Greta Jones and Elizabeth Malcolm (Cork, IE: Cork University Press, 1999), 102–17; S. Karly Kehoe, "Nursing the Mission: The Franciscan Sisters of the Immaculate Conception and the Sisters of Mercy in Glasgow, 1847–1860," *Innes Review* 56 (2005): 46–60.

101 Maria Monk, *The Awful Disclosures of Maria Monk, as exhibited in a narrative of her suffering during a residence of five years as a novice and two years as a black nun in the Hotel Dieu Nunnery at Montreal* (Edinburgh: A. M'Kerracher, 1836); Rebecca Reed and Maria Monk, *Veil of Fear: Nineteenth-Century Convent Tales*, ed. Nancy Lusignan Schultz (Purdue, IN: Purdue University Press, 1999); Daly, *The British Soldier*, 165.

102 Seámus Enright, "Women and Catholic Life in Dublin 1766–1852," in *History of the Catholic Diocese in Dublin*, ed. James Kelly and Dáire Keogh (Dublin: Four Courts Press, 2000), 287–8.

103 PACM, Journal of Frederick McClement, vol. 1, entry for 27 July 1869.

104 Quoted in Hagerty and Johnstone, "Catholic Military Chaplains," 439.

105 Crosbie, *Irish Imperial Networks*, 201.

106 Kehoe, "Accessing Empire," 221.

107 TNA, ADM101/227, Journal of Her Majesty's Floating Battery, North American & West Indian Station, Alexander Crosbie, Asst-Surgeon, 1 January to 31 December 1864, Case Entry 36.

108 PAEB, Diary of Richard Carr McClement, 1857–69, entries for 31 July 1860 and 28 April 1861.

109 Ibid., entries for 6 March 1865, 12 April 1865.

110 TNA, WO 334/32, Annual Report of the Sick and Wounded 39th Regiment of Foot Stationed in Bermuda from 1 January 1861 to 31 December 1861.

111 TNA, WO 334/32, Annual Report of the Sick and Wounded of Royal Artillery Stationed in Halifax from 1 January 1861 to 31 December 1861.

112 Devitt, "Fenianism's Bermuda Footprint," 149–54.

113 William Dillon, *The Life of John Mitchel* (London, 1888), 257.

114 TNA, WO 334/32, Annual Report of the Sick and Wounded 39th Regiment of Foot Stationed in Bermuda from 1 January 1861 to 31 December 1861.

115 Kehoe, "Accessing Empire." For a collection of useful essays on this, see David Boyd Haycock and Sally Archer, eds., *Health and Medicine at Sea, 1700–1900* (Woodbridge, EN: Boydell Press, 2009)

116 Snape, *The Redcoat*, 225.

117 Sue Peabody, "'A Dangerous Zeal': Catholic Missions to Slaves in the French Antilles, 1635–1800," *French Historical Studies* 25:1 (2002): 66–7.

118 Vincent Brown, "History Attends to the Dead," *Small Axe* 14:1 (2010): 219–27; Vincent Brown, "Spiritual Terror and Scared Authority in Jamaican Slave Society," *Slavery and Abolition* 24:1 (2003): 24–53.

119 Peabody, "'A Dangerous Zeal,'" 60. For a useful overview of the Jesuits' organization, see J. Gabriel Martínez-Serna, "Procurators and the Making of the Jesuits' Atlantic Network," in *Soundings in Atlantic History: Latent Structures and Intellectual Currents, 1500–1830*, ed. Bernard Bailyn and Patricia L. Denault (Cambridge, MA: Harvard University Press, 2011), 181–209.

120 TNA, CO 106/9, Sale of Lands in the Ceded Islands, Saint Vincent, Resolutions of the Board, 24 April 1765, 65 and 82.

121 Peabody, "'A Dangerous Zeal,'" 78, 80, 83; Fiona A. Macdonald, *Missions to the Gaels: Reformation and Counter-Reformation in Ulster and the Highlands and Islands of Scotland, 1560–1760* (Edinburgh: John Donald, 2006); B.A. Balcom and A.J.B. Johnston, "Missions to the Mi'kmaq: Malagawatch and Chapel Island in the 18th Century," *Journal of the Royal Nova Scotia Historical Society* 9 (2006): 131–3.

122 David R. Watters, "Historical Archaeology in the British Caribbean," in Farnsworth, *Island Lives*.

123 Vincent Brown, "Spiritual Terror and Sacred Authority in Jamaican Slave Society," *Slavery and Abolition* 24:1 (2003): 24–53; "History Attends to the Dead," *Small Axe* 14:1 (2010): 219–27.

124 Luis Martinez-Fernández, *Frontiers, Plantations and Walled Cities: Essays on Society, Culture and Politics in the Hispanic Caribbean, 1800–1945* (Princeton, NJ: Markus Wiener Publishers, 2011), 57–63.

125 Ibid., 63–7.

126 Quote from *Sublimus Dei*, apostolic letter of Pope Paul III, 29 May 1537, http://www.papalencyclicals.net/Paul03/p3subli.htm; *Sicut Dudum*, Apostolic Letter of Pope Eugene IV, 13 January 1435, http://www.papalencyclicals.net/Eugene04/eugene04sicut.htm.

127 *In Supremo Apostolatus*, apostolic letter of Pope Gregory XVI, 3 December 1839, http://www.papalencyclicals.net/Greg16/g16sup.htm. See also Joel S. Panzer, *The Popes and Slavery* (New York: Alba House, 1996).

128 TNA, CO 138/30, Précis of Correspondence, Jamaica, entries for 14 July 1780 and 15 February, 10 August, 23 October, 18 November, and 9 December 1790.

129 Nini Rodgers, "Richard Robert Madden: An Irish anti-Slavery Activist in the Americas" in *Ireland Abroad: Politics and Professions in the Nineteenth Century*, ed. Oonagh Walsh (Dublin: Four Courts Press, 2003), 127. For another influential Irish Catholic figure, see H.M. Chichester, "M'Carthy, Sir Charles (1764–1824)," revised by Lynn Milne, *Oxford Dictionary of National Biography Online*, http://www.oxforddnb.com/view/article/17375.

130 Nini Rodgers, "Ireland and the Black Atlantic in the Eighteenth Century," *Irish Historical Studies* 32:126 (2000): 174–92; Hilary Beckles, "A 'Riotous and Unruly Lot': Irish Indentured Servants and Freemen in the English West Indies, 1644–1713," *William and Mary Quarterly* 47:4 (1990): 503–22; Howard A. Fergus, *Montserrat: History of a Caribbean Colony* (Oxford: Macmillan, 2004).

131 R.C. Nash, "Irish Atlantic Trade in the Seventeenth and Eighteenth Centuries," *William and Mary Quarterly* 42:3 (1985): 329–56; David J. Pope, "Liverpool's Catholic Ships' Captains, c. 1745–1807," *Recusant History* 29:1 (2008): 48–76.

132 Lyons, "The Emergence," 107–26; Simms, "Connacht," 124; Thomas M. Truxes, "Dutch-Irish Cooperation in the Mid-Eighteenth-Century Wartime Atlantic," *Early American Studies* 10:2 (2012): 302–34.

133 Caroline Quarrier Spence, "Ameliorating Empire: Slavery and Protection in the British Colonies, 1783–1865" (PhD diss., Harvard University, 2014), 37. For more on the Code Noir, see Sally Hadden, "The Fragmented Laws of Slavery in the Colonial and Revolutionary Era," in *The Cambridge History of Law in America*, vol. 1, ed. Michael Grossberg and Christopher Tomlins (New York: Cambridge University Press, 2007), 253–87.

134 Lyons, "The Emergence," 109.

135 Bertie Mandelblatt, "A Transatlantic Commodity: Irish Salt Beef in the French Atlantic World," *History Workshop Journal* 63 (2007): 35; David

Dickson, *Old World Colony: Cork and South Munster, 1630–1830* (Cork, IE: Cork University Press, 2005), 135–48, 166–9; Kristen Block and Jenny Shaw, "Subjects without an Empire: The Irish in the Early Modern Caribbean," *Past and Present* 210 (2011): 33–60.

136 Cynthia M. Kennedy, "The Other White Gold: Salt, Slaves, the Turks and Caicos Islands, and British Colonialism," *The Historian* 69:2 (2000): 219 and 229; Marshall, *Remaking the British Atlantic*, 120–1.

137 Mandelblatt, "A Transatlantic Commodity," 32; Fergus, *Montserrat*; Nini Rodgers, "Ireland and the Black Atlantic," 174–192; Nini Rodgers, *Ireland, Slavery and Anti-Slavery: 1625–1865* (Hampshire, EN: Palgrave Macmillan, 2007); Catherine Hall et al., *Legacies of British Slave-Ownership: Colonial Slavery and the Formation of Victorian Britain* (Cambridge: Cambridge University Press, 2014). See also the Legacies of British Slave-Ownership project website, at https://www.ucl.ac.uk/lbs/.

138 UCLUD, Lisbon College Papers, LC/C869, letter from William Fryer, London, to Edmund Winstanley, Lisbon, 23 February 1819.

139 WDA, A.42/9, Talbot Papers, Faculties given by Cardinal Borgia, Propaganda Fide, to Richard Talbot, London, 4 March 1781.

140 John T. Harricharan, *Church and Society in Trinidad, Part I and II: The Catholic Church in Trinidad, 1498–1863* (Bloomington, IN: Author House, 2006), 46.

141 S. Karly Kehoe, "Colonial Collaborators: Britain and the Catholic Church in Trinidad, c. 1820–1840," *Slavery and Abolition* 40:1 (2018): 130–46; Butler, *Historical Memoirs*, 553.

142 BRBML, Nicholas Patrick Wiseman, *An Appeal to the reason and good feeling of the English people on the subject of the Catholic hierarchy* (London, 1850), 4.

143 Harricharan, *Church and Society*, 54–9. Beckles notes that this preference was also dominant in the seventeenth century: see "A 'Riotous and Unruly Lot,'" 509–10.

144 Frederick Madden, ed., *Imperial Reconsiderations, 1763–1840: The Evolution of Alternative Systems of Colonial Government. Selected Documents on the Constitutional History of the British Empire and Commonwealth*, vol. 3 (New York: Greenwood Press, 1987), 732.

145 Eric Williams, *History of the People of Trinidad and Tobago* (New York: Frederick A. Praeger, 1964), 67.

5 Enabling Ambition through Education

1 The Medical Missionaries of Mary are a twentieth-century example. See John Manton, "Administering Leprosy Control in Ogoja Province, Nigeria, 1945–67: A Case Study in Government-Mission Relations," in *Healing Bodies, Saving Souls: Medical Missionaries in Asia and Africa*, ed.

David Hardinman (Amsterdam: Wellcome Trust Series in the History of Medicine, 2006), 307–32.

2 Stephen Conway, *Britain, Ireland, and Continental Europe in the Eighteenth Century: Similarities, Connections, Identities* (Oxford: Oxford University Press, 2011); Barry Crosbie, *Irish Imperial Networks: Migration, Social Communication and Exchange in Nineteenth-Century India* (Cambridge: Cambridge University Press, 2012); S. Karly Kehoe, "Accessing Empire: Irish Surgeons and the Royal Navy, 1840–1880," *Social History of Medicine* 26:2 (2013): 204–24.

3 S. Karly Kehoe and Darren Tierney, "'Like a Kind Mother': Imperial Concerns and Britain's Changing Perceptions of Rome, 1783–1815," *Historical Studies* 81 (2015): 11–31; Mary Hickman, "Catholicism and the Nation-State in Nineteenth-Century Britain," in *Commitment to Diversity: Catholics and Education in a Changing World*, ed. Mary Eaton, Jane Longmore, and Arthur Naylor (London: Cassell, 2000), 48–66; Kevin Lougheed, "National Education and Empire: Ireland and the Geography of the National Education System," in *Irish Classrooms and British Empire: Imperial Contexts in the Origins of Modern Education*, ed. David Dickson, Justyna Pyz, and Christopher Shepard (Dublin: Four Courts Press, 2012), 5–18; Greta Jones and Elizabeth Malcolm, "Introduction: An Anatomy of Irish Medical History," in *Medicine, Disease and the State in Ireland, 1650–1940* , ed. Jones and Malcolm (Cork: Cork University Press, 1999), 6.

4 Donald H. Akenson, *The Irish Education Experiment: The National System of Education in Nineteenth-Century Ireland* (Toronto: University of Toronto Press, 1970), 92–102.

5 Peter Froggart, "Competing Philosophies: The 'Preparatory' Medical Schools of the Royal Belfast Academical Institution and the Catholic University of Ireland, 1835–1909," in Jones and Malcolm, *Medicine, Disease and the State*, 65.

6 Ciaran O'Neill, *Catholics of Consequence: Transnational Education, Social Mobility, and the Irish Catholic Elite, 1850–1900* (Oxford: Oxford University Press, 2014).

7 Ibid., 3.

8 Eric G. Tenbus, "'We Fight for the Cause of God': English Catholics and Education of the Poor, and the Transformation of Catholic Identity in Victorian Britain," *Journal of British Studies* 46 (2007): 861–83; James C. Albisetti, Joyce Goodman, and Rebecca Rogers, eds., *Girls Secondary Education in the Western World, from the 18th to the 20th Century* (New York: Palgrave Macmillan, 2010).

9 Deidre Raftery, "'Je Suis d'aucune Nation': The Recruitment and Identity of Irish Women Religious in the International Mission Field,

c. 1840–1940," *Paedagogica Historica* 49:4 (2013): 513–30; Susan O'Brien, "French Nuns in Nineteenth-Century England," *Past and Present* 154 (1997): 142–80; Hilary Carey, *God's Empire: Religion and Colonialism in the British World, c. 1801–1908* (Cambridge: Cambridge University Press, 2012), 78, 155.

10 Alison Prentice, "The Feminization of Teaching in British North America and Canada, 1845-75," in *The Neglected Majority: Essays in Canadian Women's History*, vol. 1, ed. Susan Mann Trofimenkoff and Alison Prentice (Toronto: McClelland and Stewart, 1977), 49–69.

11 Joyce Goodman, "Class and Religion: Great Britain and Ireland," and Rebecca Rogers, "Culture and Catholicism in France," both in Albisetti, Goodman, and Rogers, *Girls Secondary Education*, 11 and 30.

12 O'Brien, "French Nuns"; S. Karly Kehoe, "Border Crossings: *Being* Irish in Nineteenth-Century Scotland and Canada," in *Irish Women in the Diaspora: Theories, Concepts and New Perspectives*, ed. Mary Hickman and Jim MacPherson (Manchester: Manchester University Press, 2014), 152–67.

13 O'Neill, *Catholics of Consequence*, 6.

14 Patricia Simpson, *Marguerite Bourgeoys and Montreal, 1640–1665* (Montreal and Kingston: McGill-Queen's University Press, 1997); Terence J. Fay, *A History of Canadian Catholics* (Montreal and Kingston: McGill-Queen's University Press, 2002), 17–18. Canonized on 31 October 1982, Bourgeoys became Canada's first female saint. See Vatican Digital Resources, "Marguerite Bourgeoys (1620–1700), foundress of the Sisters of the Congregation of Notre-Dame," http://www.vatican.va/news_services /liturgy/saints/ns_lit_doc_19821031_bourgeoys_en.html. Wayne J. Hankey, "From Augustine and St. Denys to Olier and Bérulle's Spiritual Revolution: Patristic and Seventeenth-Century Foundations of the Relations between Church and State in Quebec," *Laval théologique et philosophique* 63:3 (2007): 518–19.

15 AHA, Burke Papers, vol. 1; P.W. Browne, "Bishop Edmund Burke, First Vicar-Apostolic of Nova Scotia," *Studies: An Irish Quarterly Review* 22:88 (1933): 665; Ruma Chopra, "Maroons and Mi'kmaq in Nova Scotia, 1796–1800," *Acadiensis* 46:1 (2017): 17–21. For biographical information on Wentworth, see "Sir John Wentworth," *Dictionary of Canadian Biography Online*, http://www.biographi.ca/en/bio.php?id_nbr=2710.

16 National Records of Scotland, RD: 685/05, ED 100/000, 1861 Census; RD: 685/05, ED 113/000, 1871 Census; RD: 685/05, ED 110/000, 1891 Census; RD: 685/05, ED 108/000, 1901 Census.

17 O'Neill, *Catholics of Consequence*, 77.

18 Timothy G. McMahon, "Irish Jesuit Education and Imperial Ideals" in Dickson, Pyz, and Shepard, *Irish Classrooms*, 114. For more information

on the Jesuits, see Maurice Whitehead, *English Jesuit Education: Expulsion, Suppression, Survival and Restoration, 1762–1803* (Farnham: Ashgate, 2013).

19 McMahon, "Irish Jesuit Education," 112. See also Senia Paseta, *Before the Revolution: Nationalism, Social Change and Ireland's Catholic Elite, 1879–1922* (Cork, IE: Cork University Press, 1999).

20 William James Anderson, "Some Notes on Catholic Education for Scottish Children in Pre-Emancipation days," *Innes Review* 14:1 (1963): 39–41.

21 Mary Peckham Magray, *The Transforming Power of the Nuns: Women, Religious and Cultural Change in Ireland, 1750–1900* (Oxford: Oxford University Press, 1998), 19.

22 Susan O'Brien, "Women of the 'English Catholic Community': Nuns and Pupils at the Bar Convent, York, 1680–1790," in *Monastic Studies: The Continuity of Tradition*, ed. Judith Loades (Bangor, WS: Headstart History, 1990), 270; Anderson, "Some Notes on Catholic Education."

23 O'Brien, "Women of the 'English Catholic Community,'" 277.

24 Carmen Mangion, *Contested Identities: Catholic Women Religious in Nineteenth-Century England and Wales* (Manchester: Manchester University Press, 2008), 35.

25 Susan O'Brien, "A Survey of Research and Writing about Roman Catholic Women's Congregations in Great Britain and Ireland," in *Religious Institutes in Western Europe in the 19th and 20th Centuries*, ed. Jan de Maeyer, Sophie Leplae, and Joachim Schmiedl (Leuven, BE: Leuven University Press, 2004), 93; Mangion, *Contested Identities*, 34–5, 37, 42. See also Susan O'Brien's excellent *Leaving God for God: The Daughters of Charity of St Vincent de Paul in Britain, 1847–2017* (London: Darton, Longman and Todd, 2017).

26 John Watts, *A Canticle of Love: The Story of the Franciscan Sisters of the Immaculate Conception* (Edinburgh: John Donald Publishers, 2006), 250–60.

27 S. Karly Kehoe, "From the Caribbean to the Scottish Highlands: Charitable Enterprise in the Age of Improvement, c. 1750 to c. 1820," *Rural History* 27:1 (2016): 37–59; Kehoe, *Creating a Scottish Church: Catholicism, Gender and Ethnicity in Nineteenth-Century Scotland* (Manchester: Manchester University Press, 2010), 94–5; David Alston, "A Forgotten Diaspora: The Children of Enslaved and 'Free Coloured' Women and Highland Scots in Guyana before Emancipation," *Northern Scotland* 6:1 (2015): 49–69.

28 Institute of the Blessed Virgin Mary Archives, Toronto, CAB 1137, letter to Archbishop of Toronto from Mother Teresa Dease, 23 November 1855. The Toronto community uses the spelling *Loretto*, whereas the Irish one uses *Loreto*.

29 TNA, CO 318 138, copy of a report from C.J. LaTrobe, Esq., to Lord Glenelg on Negro Education in British Guiana and Trinidad (London, 1839) (hereafter LaTrobe report), 84.

30 Nuns from a mixed order, like Scotland's Franciscan Sisters of the Immaculate Conception, took solemn vows but worked outside the convent.

31 Carmen Mangion, "'To Console, to Nurse, to Prepare for Eternity': The Catholic Sickroom in Late Nineteenth-Century England," *Women's History Review* 21:4 (2012): 657–78.

32 Karly Kehoe, "Nursing the Mission: The Franciscan Sisters of the Immaculate Conception and the Sisters of Mercy in Glasgow, 1847–1866," *Innes Review* 56:1 (2005): 46–59.

33 Jane McDermid, *The Schooling of Girls in Britain and Ireland, 1800–1900* (New York: Routledge, 2012), 126–7.

34 O'Neill, *Catholics of Consequence*, 88; Kehoe, *Creating a Scottish Church*, 110–48.

35 Sara Karly Kehoe, "Special Daughters of Rome: Glasgow and Its Roman Catholic Sisters, 1847–1913" (PhD diss., University of Glasgow, 2005), 161–2.

36 Latrobe Report, 84.

37 Watts, *A Canticle of Love*, 55.

38 C. Dorothy M. Little, *"You Did It Unto Me": The Story of the ALPHA and the Sisters of Mercy in Jamaica* (Cincinnati, OH: Beyond the Trees, 2013), 29–30, 61–3.

39 Quoted in ibid., 49.

40 Quoted in ibid., 28.

41 Mary Eileen Scott, "The Congregation of Notre Dame in Early Nova Scotia," *Canadian Catholic Historical Association Report* 20 (1953): 67–80.

42 Ibid., 79.

43 Ibid., 74–80.

44 James D. Cameron, *For the People: A History of St Francis Xavier University* (Montreal and Kingston: McGill-Queen's University Press, 1996), 96–7.

45 Municipality of the County of Inverness, Nova Scotia, Registry of Deeds Office, Port Hood, Nova Scotia, Probate, Will Book B, 502. The probate documents originally held at the Municipality of the County of Inverness have been transferred to the Nova Scotia Department of Justice in Port Hawkesbury, NS.

46 Carmen Mangion, "'Good Teacher' or 'Good Religious'? The Professional Identity of Catholic Women Religious in Nineteenth-Century England and Wales'" *Women's History Review* 14:2 (2005), 224.

47 Ibid., 230.

48 McDermid, *The Schooling*, 128.

49 Kim Lowden, "Women Religious and Teacher Education: A Case Study of the Sisters of Notre Dame in the Nineteenth Century," in *Commitment to Diversity: Catholics and Education in a Changing World*, ed. Mary Eaton, Jane Longmore, and Arthur Naylor (London: Cassell, 2000), 69.

50 Goodman, "Class and Religion," 15.

51 The "Past Students' Pages" of the *Dowanhill Training College Magazine* mention numerous students who received bachelor's and master's degrees from the University of Glasgow and then entered religious life. The sample used here was from issues between 1909 and 1913. Kehoe, "Special Daughters," chap. 5.

52 Based on *Dowanhill Training College Magazine*, 1909–13.

53 O'Brien, "French Nuns," 142.

54 Susan O'Brien suggests the ability to "overcome" feelings of nationalism, ibid., 159, but the work of others suggests the opposite. See Kehoe, *Creating a Scottish Church*, and Mangion, *Contested Identities*, 186, 190–2.

55 For a broader and integrated discussion of this, see Kehoe's *Creating a Scottish Church*, and O'Brien's *Leaving God for God*.

56 Christopher Shepard, "Cramming, Instrumentality and the Education of Irish Imperial Elites" in Dickson et al., *Irish Classrooms*, 172. See also John A. Murphy, *The College: A History of Queen's/University College, Cork, 1845–1995* (Cork, IE: Cork University Press, 1995), and Tadhg Foley and Thomas A. Boylan, eds., *From Queen's College to National University: Essays towards an Academic History of QUC/UCG/NUI, Galway* (Dublin: Four Courts Press, 1999).

57 F.O.C. Meenan, *Cecilia Street: The Catholic University School of Medicine, 1855–1931* (Dublin: Gill and Macmillan, 1987), 2.

58 Froggart, "Competing Philosophies," 60–1.

59 UCLUD, Lisbon College Papers, LC/C682, letter from Simon Bordley, Liverpool, to William Fryer, Lisbon, 2 September 1790.

60 O'Neill, *Catholics of Consequence*, 114, 120.

61 Shepard, "Cramming," 175–7. For the Royal Navy, see Kehoe, "Accessing Empire."

62 J.E. Cairnes, *University Education in Ireland* (London: Macmillan, 1866), 71.

63 Meenan, *Cecilia Street*, 2. Trinity College had opened to Catholics in 1794 but, by refusing them access to scholarships and fellowships, had done little to ingratiate itself to prospective Catholic students.

64 Queen's University Belfast Archives (hereafter QUBA), QUB/B/2/2/1, *The Report of the President of Queen's College, Belfast, for the Session 1850–51*, 2.

65 Kehoe, "Accessing Empire," 214; Shepard, "Cramming," 173.

66 QUBA, *The Report of the President*; Froggart, "Competing Philosophies," 64.

67 Froggart, "Competing Philosophies," 59–84, 83. He lists twenty-nine in the army and thirteen in the navy. C.A. Cameron, *History of the Royal College of Surgeons in Ireland and of the Irish Schools of Medicine Including a Medical Bibliography and a Medical Biography* (Dublin: Fannin & Company, 1916), 359.

68 Kehoe, "Accessing Empire," 213–14. See also Crosbie's section on difficulty in accessing various fields, in *Irish Imperial Networks*, 177–85.

69 QUBA, *Report of the President of the Queen's College, Belfast, for the Academic Year of 1864*.

70 Carey, *God's Empire*, 290. Thanks to Ciaran O'Neill for advice on the point about oversupply.

71 Ultramontanism prioritized the prerogative of the pope above that of the national bishops.

72 Cairnes, *University Education*, 66; Amy McKinney, "An Efficacious Irish Triumvirate: Paul Cullen, Tobias Kirby and Joseph Dixon," in *The Irish College, Rome and Its World*, ed. Dáire Keogh and Albert McDonnell (Dublin: Four Courts Press, 2008), 149.

73 T.W. Moody and J.C. Beckett, *Queen's, Belfast 1845–1949: The History of a University*, vol. 1 (London: Faber & Faber, 1959), 277–89; SCA, *Irish Catholic Directory*, 1864, 27. Queen's University was condemned by the controversial Synod at Thurles. For an idea of Cullen's influence, see Colin Barr's, "'Imperium in Imperio': Irish Episcopal Imperialism in the Nineteenth Century," *English Historical Review* 123:502 (2008): 611–50.

74 McKinney, "An Efficacious Irish Triumvirate," 160. Joseph Doyle discusses Cullen's approach to education in "Cardinal Cullen and the System of National Education in Ireland," in *Cardinal Paul Cullen and His World*, ed. Dáire Keogh and Albert McDonnell (Dublin: Four Courts Press, 2011), 190–204.

75 Cairnes, *University Education*, 9 and 11.

76 *Optime Noscitis, On the proposed Catholic University of Ireland*, Encyclical of Pope Pius IX, 20 March 1854, http://www.papalencyclicals.net/Pius09/p9optim1.htm. For a detailed examination of this institution, see Colin Barr, *Paul Cullen, John Henry Newman and the Catholic University of Ireland, 1845–1865* (Notre Dame, IN: University of Notre Dame Press, 2003).

77 AHA, Walsh Papers, vol. 2, letter from T. Kirby to William Walsh, Halifax, 18 October 1857; Michael Olden, "Kirby (1804–1895): The Man Who Kept the Papers," in Keogh and McDonnell, *The Irish College*, 137.

78 J.M. Bumsted, "Scottish Catholicism in Canada, 1770–1845," in *Creed and Culture: The Place of English-Speaking Catholics in Canadian Society, 1750–1930*, ed. Terence Murphy and Gerald Stortz (Montreal and Kingston: McGill-Queen's University Press, 1993), 82, 93.

79 St. Francis Xavier University Archives, Antigonish, Nova Scotia, MG45/2/108, Rev. William Xavier Edwards Papers, letter from William Chisholm to Bishop Cameron, 12 April 1879. Similar Irish-English tensions existed in Australia: see Anne Cunningham, *The Rome Connection: Australia, Ireland and the Empire, 1865–1885* (Sydney, AU: Crossing Press, 2002).

80 Vatican Library, Rome, Cui Bono, Rev. H.A. Rawes, *A Letter to a Catholic Layman* (London, 1864), 2–3.

81 Quoted in Meenan, *Cecilia Street*, 5–6. Newman was rector between 1854 and 1860.

82 SCA, *Irish Catholic Directory*, 1861, 219 and 233. The Diocese of Killaloe, for example, subscribed £516. Meenan, *Cecilia Street*, 8. See also William Rigney, "Bartholomew Woodlock and the Catholic University, 1861–1879" (PhD diss., University College Dublin, 1994).

83 Cairnes, *University Education*, 18.

84 *Irish Catholic Directory* (1864), 27.

85 Patrick M. Geoghegan, "The Catholics and the Union," *Transactions of the Royal Historical Society* 10 (2000): 253.

86 QUBA, *The Report of the President of Queen's College Belfast, for the session ending 21st July 1870*, 6 and *The Report of the President of Queen's College Belfast, for the session ending 21st July 1881*, 4 and 11 (Appendix A).

87 Based on denominational notes made in the margins of the archive's copy of the *Belfast Queen's College Calendar, 1856*, which were cross-checked with names and denominations listed in the *Register Book*, Queen's College, Belfast (November 1849–October 1877), QUBA, QUB/B/2/4/B3.

88 QUBA, Queen's College Council Minute Book, various correspondence, 7 February–16 May 1857.

89 Kehoe, "Accessing Empire."

90 Archives of the Catholic Archdiocese of Toronto (hereafter ARCAT), LAE 08.05, letter from John Joseph Lynch to the archbishops and bishops of Canada, 24 October 1878.

91 Hankey, "From Augustine," 522.

92 ARCAT, LAE 08.18, letter from Sir M.E. Hicks, Downing Street, to the Marquis of Lorne, Sir John Douglas Sutherland Campbell, Governor General of Canada, 4 March 1879.

93 ARCAT, LAE 08.02, copy of Petition from the Roman Catholic Archbishops and Bishops of Her Majesty's Dominions in North America, Archbishopric of Toronto, 1878.

94 Ibid.

95 Ibid.

96 Numerous letters between Lynch and MacDonald and Dufferin are in ARCAT, fonds LAF.

97 Cairnes, *University Education*; Greta Jones, "'Strike Out Boldly for the Prizes That Are Available to You': Medical Emigration from Ireland, 1860–1905," *Medical History* 54 (2010): 68. The Catholic University's survival depended on medical student fees.

98 There were 1,082 Irish medical students in Belfast, 827 at Cork, and 416 at Galway. Trinity College had 1,185 medical students during this period – less than half of the number at Queen's University. Cairnes, *University Education*, 69.

99 SCA, *Irish Catholic Directory*, 1864, 298.

100 For a useful discussion about the efforts of the clergy to promote an Irish Catholic world, see Barr, "'Imperium in Imperio.'"

101 QUBA, *Report of the President of the Queen's College, Belfast, for the Academic Year of 1864*, 3.

102 Jones, "Strike Out Boldly," pp. 57 and 60. The reliance that Ireland had on medical personnel exports came under serious scrutiny in the middle of the twentieth century. See Greta Jones, "'A Mysterious Discrimination': Irish Medical Emigration to the United States in the 1950s," *Social History of Medicine* 24:1 (2011).

103 *Transactions of the Ulster Medical Society*, session 1884–85, transcribed for the *Dublin Journal of Medical Science* 79 (January–June 1885): 169. Jones's concluding quote shows that this rhetoric continued beyond 1900. "Strike Out Boldly," 74.

104 QUBA, B/2/2/1, *The Report of the President of Queen's College Belfast for the Session 1880–81*, 4.

105 Colin Howell, "Scottish Influences in Nineteenth-Century Nova Scotia Medicine: A Study of Professional, Class and Ethnic Identity," in *Myth, Migration and the Making of Memory: Scotia and Nova Scotia, c. 1700–1990*, ed. Marjory Harper and Michael E. Vance (Edinburgh: John Donald Publishers, 1999), 202–17.

106 *An Act to Amend and Consolidate the Acts relating to St Francis Xavier University* (2014), http://nslegislature.ca/legc/bills/62nd_1st/3rd _read/b050.htm; Cameron, *For the People*, 47–9. Terrence J. Fay discusses the push for an English-speaking Catholic university in Ontario in "The Jesuits and the Catholic University of Canada at Kingston," *Canadian Catholic Historical Association Historical Studies* 58 (1991): 57–77.

107 For an example about the Sisters of Mercy in Jamaica, see Little, *"You Did It Unto Me."*

108 BICBU, John Cameron Papers, MG 13.10, letter to unknown at Propaganda Fide, Rome, from John Cameron, Arichat, Nova Scotia, 16 October 1854, translated from Italian.

109 Ibid.

110 "John Cameron," *Dictionary of Canadian Biography Online*, http://www .biographi.ca/en/bio/cameron_john_1827_1910_13E.html.

6 The Decline of Lay Authority

1 TNA, CO 295/185 f.189–91, letter from Nicolas Wiseman to Benjamin Hawes, 12 May 1849.

2 Luca Codignola, *Guide to Documents Relating to French and British North America in the Archives of the Sacred Congregation "de Propaganda Fide" in Rome, 1622–1799* (Ottawa: National Archives of Canada, 1991).

3 Jerry Bannister, *The Rule of the Admirals: Law, Custom, and Naval Government in Newfoundland, 1699–1832* (Toronto: University of Toronto Press, 2003), 4.

4 WDA, Poynter Papers, box 64, letter from James Buckley to Earl Bathurst, 5 August 1821; Mark McGowan, "'Pregnant with Perils': Canadian Catholicism and Its Relation to the Catholic Churches of Newfoundland, 1840–1949," *Newfoundland and Labrador Studies* 28:2 (2013): 202.

5 Mark McGowan, "The Tales and Trials of a 'Double Minority': The Irish and French Catholic Engagement for the Soul of the Canadian Catholic Church," in *Religion and Greater Ireland: Christianity and Irish Global Networks, 1750–1900*, ed. Colin Barr and Hilary M. Carey (Montreal and Kingston: McGill-Queen's University Press, 2015), 97.

6 McGowan, "The Tales and Trials," 98.

7 Carl C. Campbell, *Cedulants and Capitulants: The Politics of Coloured Opposition in the Slave Society of Trinidad, 1783–1838* (Port of Spain, TT: Paria Publishing, 1992), 228.

8 H.O.B. Wood, "The Constitutional History of Trinidad and Tobago," *Caribbean Quarterly* 6:2 (1960): 146.

9 WDA, Talbot Papers, A.42/53, notification of appointment sent from Propaganda Fide, Rome, to Bishop Talbot, London, 5 June 1784.

10 Robin Anderson, *Pope Pius VII, 1800–1823: His Life, Times and Struggle with Napoleon in the Aftermath of the French Revolution* (Charlotte, NC: TAN Books, 2001); John T. Harricharan, *Church and Society in Trinidad, Part I and II: The Catholic Church in Trinidad, 1498–1863* (Bloomington, IN: Authorhouse, 2006), 64.

11 Ennis B. Edmonds and Michelle A. Gonzalez, eds., *Caribbean Religious History: An Introduction* (New York: New York University Press, 2010), 138. Wood, "The Constitutional History," 144; Harricharan, *Church and Society*, 46.

12 Wood, "The Constitutional History," 146.

13 Ibid., 145.

14 Quoted in ibid., 144; Harricharan, *Church and Society*, 46

15 Harricharan, *Church and Society*, 48.

16 John Bergin, "Irish Catholics and Their Networks in Eighteenth-Century London," *Eighteenth-Century Life* 39:1 (2015): 66–102.

17 Kevin Condon, *The Missionary College of All Hallows, 1842–1891* (Dublin: Irish Press, 1987), 119–21; Raymond Devas, *Conception Island or the Troubled Story of the Catholic Church in Grenada, British West Indies* (Edinburgh: Sands & Co., 1932), 418.

18 J.P. Chinnici, "Poynter, William (1762–1827)," *Oxford Dictionary of Canadian Biography*, http://www.oxforddnb.com/view/article/22688.

19 AVCAU, Scr. 55/9/9, letter from An Irishman, Dublin (signature illegible), to William Poynter, London, 18 May 1814.

20 AVCAU, Scr. 55/1/3, letter from Eneas (John) Chisholm, Inverness, to William Poynter, London, 28 December 1818.

21 APF, *Scritture riferite nei Congressi, America Antille*, vol. 3, f. 365, summary document drawn up by officials at *Propaganda Fide* outlining the jurisdiction of the vicar apostolic of the London district, n.d. (c. 1800–10).

22 Harricharan, *Church and Society*, 64.

23 Rosemary Mitchell, "Gillow, Thomas (1769–1857)," *Oxford Dictionary of National Biography*, http://www.oxforddnb.com/view/article/10753.

24 WDA, Poynter Papers, box 64, letters from Thomas Gillow to William Poynter, 24 June 1817, 23 August 1817, 19 April 1818.

25 WDA, Poynter Papers, box 64, letter from Thomas Gillow to William Poynter, 27 September 1818.

26 AVCAU, Scr. 63/6/275, letter from James Buckley to Monsignor Gradwell, rector, English College, Rome, 19 April 1819.

27 UCLUD, Lisbon College Papers, LC/C869, letter from William Fryer, probably London, to Edmund Winstanley, Lisbon, 23 February 1819, and LC /A1/6/37, letter from William Fryer, probably London, to Edmund Winstanley, Lisbon, 10 July 1818.

28 *Trinidad Gazette*, 10 January 1821.

29 WDA, Poynter Papers, box 64, Address of John Carter, Government House, Port-of-Spain, 29 March 1820. A copy of the address is also found in APF, *Scritture riferite nei Congressi, America Antille*, vol. 4, f. 23–4, Colonial office dispatches.

30 APF, *Scritture riferite nei Congressi, America Antille*, vol. 4. f. 207–8, letter from James Buckley, Trinidad, to William Poynter, London, 31 October 1824.

31 AVCAU, Scr. 67/12/8, letter from Alexander Macdonell, Glengarry, to Robert Gradwell, English College, Rome, 18 August 1826.

32 WDA, Poynter Papers, box 64, letter from James Buckley to William Poynter, 16 April 1820.

33 WDA, Poynter Papers, box 64, letter from James Buckley to William Poynter, 30 July 1820.

34 S. Karly Kehoe, *Creating a Scottish Church: Catholicism, Gender and Ethnicity in Nineteenth-Century Scotland* (Manchester: Manchester University Press, 2010).

35 WDA, Poynter Papers, box 64, copy of letter to R. Wilmot, Colonial Office, from unknown, 18 November 1822.

36 WDA, Poynter Papers, Trinidad Folder, letter from Downing Street to William Poynter, 25 January 1825; Harricharan, *Church and Society*, p. 86.

37 WDA, Poynter Papers, box 64, letters from James Buckley to William Poynter, 12 February 1821 and 3 June 1824; Harricharan, *Church and Society*, 58.

38 WDA, Poynter Papers, box 64, letter from Buckley to Poynter, July 1822.
39 WDA, Poynter Papers, box 64, letter from James Buckley to William Poynter, 8 November 1821.
40 S. Karly Kehoe, "Colonial Collaborators: Britain and the Catholic Church in Trinidad, c. 1820–1840," *Slavery and Abolition* 40:1 (2018): 130–46; Campbell, *Cedulants*, 280.
41 WDA, Poynter Papers, box 64, letter from Buckley to Poynter, 25 July 1825.
42 Ibid.
43 Katherine Gerbner, "Theorizing Conversion: Christianity, Colonization, and Consciousness in the Early Modern Atlantic World," *History Compass* 13:3 (2015): 134–47.
44 APF, *Scritture riferite nei Congressi, America Antille*, vol. 4, f. 63, letter from William Poynter, London, to Robert Gradwell, English College Rome, 12 December 1820.
45 WDA, Poynter Papers, box 64, letter from Buckley to Poynter, 25 July 1825.
46 Quoted in Campbell, *Cedulants*, 275; in chapter 7, Campbell also includes a useful discussion of this episode. Selwyn R. Cudjoe, *Beyond Boundaries: The Intellectual Tradition of Trinidad and Tobago in the Nineteenth Century* (Wellesley, MA: Calaloux Publications, 2003), 30. *Trinidad and Tobago Guardian*, 8 April 2012, http://www.guardian.co.tt/news/2012-04-08/church-our-lady-rosary.
47 M. Shawn Copeland, "Anti-Blackness and White Supremacy in the Making of American Catholicism," *American Catholic Studies* 127:3 (2016): 6–8.
48 Richard Gray, *Black Christians and White Missionaries* (New Haven, CT: Yale University Press, 1990), 11–34.
49 Ibid., 25.
50 The Georgetown slaves were the "property" of this Jesuit community. When Georgetown University was at risk of folding due to mounting debts, the community sold 272 enslaved people to raise funds to save it. They were sold one year before Rome issued *In Supremo Apostolatus*, which finally condemned what the apostolic letter called the "shameful" practice of African enslavement, *In Supremo Apostolatus*, apostolic letter of Pope Gregory XVI, 3 December 1839, http://www.papalencyclicals.net/Greg16/g16sup.htm.
51 Bridget Brereton and Kevin A. Yelvington, "Introduction: The Promise of Emancipation," in *The Colonial Caribbean in Transition: Essays on Post Emancipation Social and Cultural History*, ed. Brereton and Yelvington (Barbados: University of West Indies Press, 1999), 4.
52 Ibid.; Lawrence C. Jennings, *French Reaction to British Slave Emancipation* (Baton Rouge: Louisiana State University Press, 1988), 13–14.

53 Andrew Porter, "An Overview, 1700–1914," in *Missions and Empire*, ed. Norman Etherington (Oxford: Oxford University Press, 2005), 40.

54 TNA, CO295/136 f.274–82, letter to Lord Stanley from Governor MacLeod, 9 June 1842, and CO295/144 f.341, letter to Governor MacLeod from Daniel McDonnell, 1 August 1844.

55 Sue Peabody, "'A Dangerous Zeal': Catholic Missions to Slaves in the French Antilles, 1635–1800," *French Historical Studies* 25:1 (2002): 66–7.

56 Debbie Lee, ed., *Slavery, Abolition and Emancipation: Writings in the British Romantic Period*, vol. 3, *The Emancipation Debate* (London: Pickering & Chatto, 1999), xvi.

57 TNA, CO 295/144 f. 233, letter from Richard P. Smith to Sir Henry MacLeod, 30 October 1844.

58 Ibid.

59 Quoted in John M. Feheney, "Catholic Education in Trinidad in the Twentieth Century: Shaking Off British Protestant Influence," *Recusant History* 29:4 (2009): 555.

60 APF, *Scritture riferite nei Congressi, America Antille*, vol. 7, f. 207, letter from Richard Smith, Trinidad, to Cardinal Fransoni, Rome, 26 March 1842.

61 Caree Banton, "Barbadians' Struggle against Whig Emancipation and Its Afterlife," and Christienna Fryar, "Imperial Ideologies of Ruin and Promise in Late-Nineteenth-Century Jamaica," papers presented at the North American Conference on British Studies Annual Meeting, November 2017; Nicholas Draper, *The Price of Emancipation: Slave-Ownership, Compensation and British Society at the End of Slavery* (Cambridge: Cambridge University Press, 2009), 2; Hilary Beckles, *Britain's Black Debt: Reparations for Caribbean Slavery and Native Genocide* (Jamaica: University of the West Indies Press, 2013), 143–59.

62 TNA, CO 295/127 f. 268–9, letter to Lord John Russell from James Cadett, 1839.

63 Harricharan, *Church and Society*, 82; Brereton and Yelvington, "Introduction," 7.

64 APF, *Scritture riferite nei Congressi, America Antille*, vol. 7, f. 59–62, letter from Samuel Power, St. George's Parish, Grenada, to Daniel McDonnell, Port of Spain, 25 February 1842.

65 Stephen Scott, "Through the Diameter of Respectability: The Politics of Historical Representation in Post-Emancipation Colonial Trinidad," *New West Indian Guide* 76 (2002): 280.

66 Wm. Wilberforce, *An Appeal to the Religion, Justice and Humanity of the Inhabitants of the British Empire in behalf of the Negro Slaves in the West Indies* (London, 1823), 9; Lee, *Slavery, Abolition*, 20, 23; Pamela Scully and Diana Paton, eds., *Gender and Slave Emancipation in the Atlantic World* (Durham, NC: Duke University Press, 2005), 4.

67 Parliamentary Debates, n.s., vol. 2, 30 March–5 June 1824, c. 1408. Many thanks to Krista Kesselring for sharing this source with me.

68 TNA, CO 318/137 f. 16, letter from Charles LaTrobe to Lord Glenelg, 14 August 1838.

69 Ibid.

70 TNA, CO 318/137 f. 88–9, *Negro Education: British Guyana and Trinidad. Return to an Address of the Honourable House of Commons*, 14 February 1839; APF, *Scritture riferite nei Congressi, America Antille*, vol. 6, letter from Daniel McDonnell, Trinidad, to Cardinal Prefect of Propaganda Fide, Rome, 26 October 1840.

71 TNA, CO 318/137 f. 88–9, *Negro Education*.

72 TNA, CO.318/137 f. 16–37, preface to report compiled by Charles LaTrobe for Lord Glenelg, 14 August 1838.

73 TNA, CO.318/139 f. 135–6, letter from D. Cotes, Church Missionary Society, to Sir George Grey, Colonial Office, 26 May 1838.

74 TNA, CO.318/139 f. 147–8, letter from John Beecham, Wesleyan Missionary House, to Sir George Grey, Colonial Office, 7 June 1838.

75 TNA, CO 318/137 f. 80–2, *Negro Education: British Guyana and Trinidad. Return to an Address of the Honourable House of Commons*, 14 February 1839; Carl C. Campbell, *The Young Colonials: A Social History of Education in Trinidad and Tobago, 1834–1939* (Kingston: University of the West Indies Press, 1996), 14–28.

76 APF, *Scritture riferite nei Congressi, America Antille*, vol. 7, f. 230, letter from Richard Smith, Trinidad, to Cardinal Acton, Propaganda Fide, 26 October 1842.

77 Sisters of St Joseph of Cluny, "Our History in the Caribbean," http://www.clunycarib.org/ourhistory.html.

78 *Irish Catholic Directory* (1844), 477. For context, see James Patterson Smith, "Empire and Social Reform: British Liberals and the 'Civilizing Mission' in the Sugar Colonies, 1868–1874," *Albion* 27:2 (1995): 263–5.

79 Harricharan, *Church and Society*, 90.

80 Carl Campbell, "Black Testators: Fragments of Lives of Free Africans and Free Creole Blacks in Trinidad, 1813–1877," in Brereton and Yelvington, *The Colonial Caribbean in Transition*, 53.

81 Ibid., 45, 53–4.

82 Porter, "An Overview," 53.

83 Hilary Carey, *God's Empire: Religion and Colonialism in the British World, c. 1801–1908* (Cambridge: Cambridge University Press, 2011), 84–90.

84 TNA, CO 101/126 f.131–5, report transmitted from Edward Mathew, Governor of Grenada, 7 April 1785.

85 TNA, CO 295/136 f. 274–82, letter from Sir Henry MacLeod to Lord Stanley, 9 June 1842.

86 TNA, CO 295/144 f. 300, Report and Summary of *An Ordinance No. 16*, 1844; Joseph Hardwick, *The Anglican British World: The Church of England and the Expansion of the Settler Empire, c. 1790–1860* (Manchester: Manchester University Press, 2014), 116; C.A. Harris, "Parry, Thomas (1795–1870)," revised by H.C.G. Matthew, *Oxford Dictionary of National Biography*, http://www.oxforddnb.com/view/article/21435.

87 TNA, CO 295/144, *The Respectful Memorial of the undersigned Inhabitants of Trinidad to His Excellency the Governor, Colonel Sir Henry G. MacLeod, and the Honorable the Members of Her Majesty's Council of Government of Trinidad*, 3 August 1844; Harricharan, *Church and Society*, 136; Donald Wood, *Trinidad in Transition: The Years after Slavery* (Oxford: Oxford University Press, 1968), 194.

88 TNA, CO 295/144 f. 335, letter from Bishop McDonnell to Lord Stanley, 20 December 1844.

89 Pope Pius IX, *Ubi Primum, On Discipline for Religious*, 17 June 1847, http://www.papalencyclicals.net/pius09/p9ubipr1.htm

90 Codignola, *Guide to Documents*, 9.

91 Kevin Condon, *The Missionary College of All Hallows, 1842–1891* (Dublin: Irish Press, 1987), 119–21; Raymond Devas, *Conception Island or the Troubled Story of the Catholic Church in Grenada, British West Indies* (Edinburgh: Sands & Co., 1932), 418.

92 ADA, Hamilton Papers, 325/I/II/166, letter to Cardinal Wiseman from the priests on that Island, Port of Spain, 10 May 1852.

93 AVCAU, doc. 218, letter from L.A.A. de Verteuil, French priest in Trinidad, to George Talbot, papal diplomat, 16 February 1858.

94 TNA, CO 295/144 f. 255–6, letter from Richard P. Smith to Sir Henry MacLeod, 1 May 1845; APF, *Scritture riferite nei Congressi, America Antille*, vol 7, f. 59–62, 100–5, 207. Various letters and testimonies about their falling out are in APF, 1842.

95 *The Tablet*, 30 January 1886; Edward Norman, *The English Catholic Church in the Nineteenth Century* (Oxford: Clarendon Press, 1984), 111–57.

96 Denis Gywnn, *Cardinal Wiseman* (London: Burns Oates & Washbourne, 1929), 253–5; Wilfrid Philip Ward, *The Life and Times of Cardinal Wiseman* (London: Longmans, Green, 1898), 332.

97 W. Gordon Gorman, *Converts to Rome: A Biographical List of the More Notable Nonverts to the Catholic Church in the United Kingdom during the Last Sixty Years* (London: Sands & Co., 1910), 265.

98 Patrick Allitt, *Catholic Converts: British and American Intellectuals Turn to Rome* (Ithaca, NY: Cornell University Press, 1997), 98; Gywnn, *Cardinal Wiseman*, 253–5.

99 ADA, Hamilton Papers, 42/3/VII/10, letter from Patrick Feltram, St Agatha, Irish College, Rome, to Paul Cullen, Dublin, 13 November 1855.

100 Dàire Keogh and Albert McDonnell, eds., *Cardinal Paul Cullen and His World* (Dublin: Four Courts Press, 2011).

101 The Congregation of the Mission had been founded by St Vincent de Paul in 1624. Congregation of the Mission, http://cmglobal.org/en/about/.

102 Feheney, "Catholic Education in Trinidad," 556.

103 TNA, CO 295/187 f. 109–21, letter from Charles Elliot to Henry Grey, 24 February 1855, and CO 295/189/f.219–227, letter from William Robert Keate to Henry Labouchere, 17 December 1856.

104 *Port of Spain Gazette*, 23 January 1855.

105 *Accounts and Papers of the House of Commons: Colonies. Emigration*, vol. 7, Session 31 January–29 July 1856, dispatch from the Secretary of State, no. 70, 35; TNA, CO 295/187 f.143, letter from Charles Elliot to Henry Grey, late winter 1856.

106 TNA, CO 295/87 f. 222–6, letter from Charles Elliot to Henry Grey, 24 February 1855.

107 TNA, CO 295/185, "Humble Petition of the Undersigned Roman Catholic inhabitants of the island of Trinidad," March 1855, clipping from the *Port of Spain Gazette*, n.d. (c. early January 1856).

108 *Punch* 19 (July–December 1850), 187–9.

109 BRBML, George Augustus Sala, *Grand Processions against Papal Aggression to Present the Address and Obtain Redress in order that we may hear less of his holiness*, Published by the Society for the Confusion of Popish Knowledge, London, 1850. Descended from Italian and West Indian–born parents, Sala had worked as a journalist after moving to London as a young man; he converted to Catholicism on his deathbed in 1895; *The Mercury*, 15 November 1895, http://trove.nla.gov.au/newspaper/article /9316174. For more on the illustrator, see Peter Blake, *George Augustus Sala and the Nineteenth-Century Periodical Press: The Personal Style of a Public Writer* (Farnham, EN: Ashgate, 2015).

110 TNA, CO 295/187 f. 109–21, letter from Charles Elliot to Henry Grey, 7 February 1855.

111 Rev. William Walsh, *A Pastoral Letter for the Lent of MDCCCLIII addressed to the clergy and laity of the Archdiocese of Halifax* (Halifax, 1853), 48–9; TNA, CO37/146 f.327, letter from Mont Williams to the Duke of Newcastle, 28 June 1854.

112 TNA, CO 295/187, letter from the Duke of Newcastle to the governor of Bermuda, 8 August 1854.

113 TNA, CO 295/87 f. 222–6, letter from Charles Elliot to Henry Grey (with comments on reverse), 10 and 25 October 1855.

114 TNA, CO 295/219 f. 219–27, letter from Charles Elliot to Henry Grey, 24 February 1855.

115 ADA, Hamilton Papers, 3/9/4/I/14, letter from W.R. Sulton, principal, Col. W.M. Schools, St Lucia, to Paul Cullen, Dublin, 27 July 1858.

116 John P. Greene, *Between Damnation and Starvation: Priests and Merchants in Newfoundland Politics, 1745–1855* (Montreal and Kingston: McGill-Queen's University Press, 1999), 18–21.

117 Ibid., 22; Michael Staveley, "Population Dynamics in Newfoundland: The Regional Patterns," in *The Peopling of Newfoundland: Essays in Historical Geography*, ed. John Mannion (St John's: Memorial University of Newfoundland, 1977), 53; Bannister, *The Rule of the Admirals*, 215.

118 Carolyn Lambert, "No Choice but to Look Elsewhere: Attracting Immigrants to Newfoundland, 1840–1890," *Acadiensis* 41:2 (2012): 92.

119 Ibid., 92–4.

120 Staveley, "Population Dynamics," 54–5.

121 Archdiocese Archives of Saint John's (hereafter AASJ), Fleming Papers, 103/27, "State of Religion in Newfoundland," by Anthony Fleming, printed in the *Newfoundland Indicator*, 16 July 1847.

122 Jerry Bannister, "Atlantic Canada in an Atlantic World? Northeastern North America in the Long 18th Century," *Acadiensis* 43:2 (2014): 11.

123 Phillip McCann, *Island in an Empire: Education, Religion, and Social Life in Newfoundland, 1800–1855* (Portugal Cove, NL: Boulder Publications, 2016), 58.

124 McGowan, "'Pregnant with Perils,'" 194, 202; Rosemary E. Ommer, "Highland Scots Migration to Southwestern Newfoundland: A Study of Kinship," in *The Peopling of Newfoundland: Essays in Historical Geography*, ed. John Mannion (St John's: Memorial University of Newfoundland, 1977), 212–33.

125 Jerry Bannister, *The Rule of the Admirals: Law, Custom and Naval Government in Newfoundland, 1699–1832* (Toronto: University of Toronto Press, 2003), 237–8. For more details, see John Reeves, *History of the Government of the Island of Newfoundland with an Appendix containing the Acts of Parliament made respecting the Trade and Fishery* (London, 1793), 135–8.

126 Terrence Murphy, "Trusteeism in Atlantic Canada: The Struggle for Leadership among the Irish Catholics of Halifax, St John's and Saint John, 1780–1850," in *Creed and Culture: The Place of English-Speaking Catholics in Canadian Society, 1750–1930*, ed. Terrence Murphy and Gerald Stortz (Montreal and Kingston: McGill-Queen's University Press, 1993), 127.

127 Richard A. Keogh, "'Nothing Is so Bad for the Irish as Ireland Alone': William Keogh and Catholic Loyalty," *Irish Historical Studies* 38:150 (2010): 230.

128 McCann, *Island in an Empire*, 53.

129 J.R. Miller, "Anti-Catholicism in Canada: From the British Conquest to the Great War," in Murphy and Stortz, *Creed and Culture*, 30.

130 WDA, Talbot Papers, A42/47, letter from William Egan to James Talbot, London, 4 February 1784. The need for Irish translators was also noted by Bannister, *The Rule of the Admirals*, 215.

131 WDA, Talbot Papers, A42/47, letter from Egan to Talbot, 4 February 1784.

132 Quoted in Bannister, *The Rule of the Admirals*, 219.

133 Murphy, "Trusteeism in Atlantic Canada," 135.

134 *The Annual Register or a View of the History, Politics, and Literature for the Year 1811* (London, 1812), 159.

135 Bannister, *The Rule of the Admirals*, 219–20; Willeen Keough, "Contested Terrains: Ethnic and Gendered Spaces in the Harbour Grace Affray," *Canadian Historical Review* 90:1 (2009): 54–5. See also Bannister, "Atlantic Canada," 15 and 28. I am grateful to Jerry Bannister for his thoughts on the significance of the fear that existed in St John's.

136 Greene, *Between Damnation and Salvation*, 17; S. Karly Kehoe and Darren Tierney, "'Like a Kind Mother': Imperial Concerns and Britain's Changing Perception of Rome, 1783–1815," *Historical Studies* 83 (2015): 11–31.

137 Quoted in McCann, *Island in an Empire*, 64.

138 AVCAU, Scr. 55/9/12, letter from Francis Delarue to William Poynter, 27 November 1814.

139 Greene, *Between Damnation and Starvation*, 36–7.

140 Jennifer Ridden, "Britishness as an Imperial and Diasporic Identity: Irish Elite Perspectives, c. 1820–70s," in *Victoria's Ireland? Irishness and Britishness, 1837–1901*, ed. Peter Gray (Dublin: Four Courts Press, 2004), 88–9.

141 McGowan, "'Pregnant with Perils,'" 202.

142 Greene, *Between Damnation and Starvation*, 47–50; Bannister, *The Rule of the Admirals*, 220.

143 Bannister, *The Rule of the Admirals*, 263–4.

144 Terence J. Fay, *A History of Canadian Catholics* (Montreal and Kingston: McGill-Queen's University Press, 2002), 54.

145 J.B. Darcy, *Fire upon the Earth: The Life and Times of Bp. Michael Anthony Fleming, OSF* (St John's, NL: Creative Publishers, 2003), 30.

146 Murphy, "Trusteeism in Atlantic Canada," 127.

147 McCann, *Island in an Empire*, 68.

148 Murphy, "Trusteeism in Atlantic Canada," 140.

149 McCann, *Island in an Empire*, 55; John Mannion, "Migration and Upward Mobility: The Meagher Family in Ireland and Newfoundland, 1780–1830," *Irish Economic and Social History* 40 (1988): 56.

150 McCann, *Island in an Empire*, 55.

151 Ibid., 57.

152 John Edward Fitzgerald, "Michael Anthony Fleming and Ultramontanism in Irish-Newfoundland Roman Catholicism, 1829–1850," *Canadian Catholic Historical Association Historical Studies* 64 (1998): 31; Greene, *Between Damnation and Starvation*, 42–3.

153 McCann, *Island in an Empire*, 73.

154 For a useful overview, see chapter 4 in Greene's *Between Damnation and Starvation*; McCann, *Island in an Empire*, 73–9; and Murphy, "Trusteeism in Atlantic Canada," 136–40.

155 Mark McGowan, *Michael Power: The Struggle to Build the Catholic Church on the Canadian Frontier* (Montreal and Kingston: McGill-Queen's University Press, 2005), 183.

156 Bannister, *The Rule of the Admirals*, 273.

157 Bannister offers a very useful discussion of London's import duties without representation, ibid., 263–279.

158 AASJ, Fleming Papers, 103/3/1, Statement about the Cathedral Lands; 103/4/1, letter to Lord Gray from Fleming, 7 April 1838; and 103/2/13, letter to Frederick Lucas from Fleming, 19 December 1842.

159 *Irish Catholic Directory* (1844), 479.

160 AASJ, Fleming Papers, 103/37, speech delivered at a dinner given in Fleming's honour by the Catholic Book Society, Dublin, October 1836.

161 Daniel Murphy, *A History of Irish Emigrant and Missionary Education* (Dublin: Four Courts Press, 2000), 286.

162 AASJ, Fleming Papers, 103/22/2, Fleming's Address to the House of Assembly, 1838.

163 AASJ, Fleming Papers, 103/16, letter to Fleming from Pope Gregory XVI, 7 October 1838 (translated from Latin).

164 AASJ, Fleming Papers, 103/30/5, letter to Fleming from the Holy See, 24 November 1840. See also John Edward Fitzgerald, "Conflict and Culture in Irish-Newfoundland Roman Catholicism, 1829–1850" (PhD diss., University of Ottawa, 1997).

165 AASJ, Fleming Papers, 103/7/1, letter to Fleming from Archbishop Ant. De Luca, Rome, n.d.

166 AASJ, Fleming Papers, 103/7/3, letter to James Crowdy from Fleming, 12 December 1848, and 103/7/1, clipping about the Presentation Nuns from an unnamed newspaper, 19 December 1842.

167 AASJ, Fleming Papers, 103/9/1, letter to Rev. Dr. O'Connell from Fleming, 1846.

168 AASJ, Fleming Papers, 103/7, letter to Governor Sir J.G. Le Marchant from Downing Street, 16 July 1847.

169 Murphy, *A History of Irish Emigrant and Missionary Education*, 286–7.

170 The Franciscan Sisters of the Immaculate Conception experienced the same kind of transition when they went to Glasgow in 1847. See S. Karly

Kehoe, *Creating a Scottish Church Catholicism, Gender and Ethnicity in Nineteenth-Century Scotland* (Manchester: Manchester University Press, 2010), pp. 81–5.

171 AASJ, Fleming Papers, 103/7/1, clipping about the Presentation Nuns from an unnamed newspaper. 19 December 1842.

172 Darcy, *Fire Upon the Earth*, 48.

173 Katherine E. Bellamy, *Weavers of the Tapestry* (St John's, NL: Flanker Press, 2006), 40–1.

174 Ibid., 45–6.

175 Ibid., 73.

176 Kehoe, *Creating a Scottish Church*, 91–104.

177 "Of the Visitation of the Sick," chap. 8 of *Customs, Observances and Devotional Practices of the Religious Called the Sisters of Mercy* (Dublin, 1886), 123–34. See also John Nicholas Murphy, *Terra Incognita or the Convents of the United Kingdom* (London, 1878), 153–79.

178 S.M. Pettengill, *Pettengill's Newspaper Directory and Advertiser's Handbook* (1872), 254, quoted in Bellamy, *Weavers of the Tapestry*, 60.

179 AASJ, Fleming Papers, 103/28/1, letter to the secretary of the Bishop of Quebec from Fleming, November 1845. For a brief discussion on education in Newfoundland, see Murphy, *A History of Irish Emigrant and Missionary Education*, 285–7.

180 The papers of bishops Alexander Macdonnel, Armand-Francois-Marie De Charbonnel, and John Joseph Lynch in ARCAT (collections AB, C, and AF) show significant interaction between the church and high-level British officials. In the National Archives, material is scattered throughout the papers of the Colonial Office, but, for starters, see CO 295.

181 McGowan, *Michael Power*, 112–13.

182 AASJ, Fleming Papers, 103/28/2, letter to Cardinal Prefect from Fleming, 25 November 1847.

183 The latter position has been advanced in Barr and Carey, eds., *Religion and Greater Ireland*.

Conclusion

1 BRBML, Charles Kent Papers, box 3, folder 127, untitled newspaper clipping, n.d.; article is republished from the *Weekly Register and Catholic Standard.*; Richard W. Davis, "Wellington and the 'Open Question': The Issue of Catholic Emancipation, 1821–1829," *Albion* 29:1 (1997): 39–56.

2 BRBML, Charles Kent Papers, http://hdl.handle.net/10079/fa/beinecke.wkent.

Bibliography

Primary Sources

Archives

Archdiocese Archives of St. John's, St. John's, Canada
    Fleming Papers
Archdiocese of Dublin Archives, Dublin, Ireland
    Hamilton Papers
    Troy Papers
Archdiocese of Halifax Archives, Halifax, Canada
    Burke Papers
Archives of the Catholic Archdiocese of Toronto, Toronto, Canada
    LAE 08
    LAF
    Macdonell Papers
Archives of *Propaganda Fide*, Rome, Italy
Beaton Institute, Cape Breton University, Sydney, Canada
    John Cameron Papers
Beineke Rare Book and Manuscript Library, Yale University, New Haven, United States
    Sheridan Papers
Chestico Museum and Archives, Port Hood, Canada
Durham University Library Archives and Special Collections, Durham, England
Ushaw College Library
    Lisbon College Papers
    Ushaw College Papers
Palace Green Library
    3rd Earl Grey Papers

Institute of the Blessed Virgin Mary Archives, Toronto, Canada
Library and Archives Canada, Ottawa, Canada
    MG 24 J.13 – Letters of the Rt. Rev. Alexander MacDonell
Municipality of the County of Inverness, Nova Scotia, Canada
    Registry of Deeds Office, Port Hood, Nova Scotia
National Archives, Kew, England
    Colonial Office papers
    Privy Council papers
National Library of Scotland, Edinburgh, Scotland
National Records of Scotland, Edinburgh, Scotland
Nova Scotia Archives, Halifax, Canada
    MG 20
    MG 100, Vol. 122
    MG 100, Vol. 136
    RG 1, Vol. 44
    RG 1, Vol. 222
    RG 1, Vol. 230
    RG 1, Vol. 301
    RG 5, Series P
    Clara Dennis Collection, 1981-541 no. 321 CB
    W.R. MacAskill Collection, 1978-453 no. 3606
    Journal and Proceedings of the House of Assembly, 1823, 1827
Personal Archives of Myles Kehoe, Margaree Forks, Canada
Queen's University Belfast Archives, Belfast, Northern Ireland
St Francis Xavier University Archives, Antigonish, Canada
Scots College Rome Archives, Rome, Italy
    Papers of Aeneas MacEachern
Westminster Diocesan Archives, London, England
    Challoner Papers
    Poynter Papers
    Talbot Papers

Newspapers

Acadian Recorder
The Casket
Dowanhill Training College Magazine
The Mercury
Nova Scotian
Punch
The Scotsman
The Tablet

Trinidad Gazette
Trinidad and Tobago Guardian

Published Primary Sources

Accounts and Papers of the House of Commons. Colonies. Emigration. Vol. 7. 31 January–29 July 1856. Despatch from the Secretary of State, No. 70.

The Annual Register or a View of the History, Politics, and Literature for the Year 1811. London, 1812.

Brady, W. Maziere. *Anglo-Roman Papers: The English Palace in Rome; II: The eldest natural son of Charles II; III: Memoirs of Cardinal Erskine, Papal Envoy to the Court of George III.* London, 1890.

Butler, Charles. *Historical Memoirs of the English, Irish and Scottish Catholics, since the Reformation.* Vol. 4. London, 1822.

Customs, Observances and Devotional Practices of the Religious Called the Sisters of Mercy. Dublin, 1886.

Hansard. House of Commons. Debates. "Religious Wants of Roman Catholic Soldiers and Sailors." Vol. 131. 3 March 1854.

Murphy, John Nicholas. *Terra Incognita or the Convents of the United Kingdom.* London, 1878.

Monk, Maria. *The Awful Disclosures of Maria Monk, as exhibited in a narrative of her suffering during a residence of five years as a novice and two years as a black nun in the Hotel Dieu nunnery at Montreal.* Edinburgh: A. M'Kerracher, 1836.

O'Neil, Charles. *The military adventurers of Charles O'Neil, who was a soldier in the army of Lord Wellington during the memorable Peninsular War and the Continental Campaigns from 1811 to 1815.* Worcester, 1851.

Parliamentary Debates. New series, vol. 2. 30 March–5 June 1824.

Pettengill, S.M. *Pettengill's Newspaper Directory and Advertiser's Handbook.* 1872.

Reeves, John. *History of the Government of the Island of Newfoundland with an Appendix containing the Acts of Parliament made respecting the Trade and Fishery.* London, 1793.

Reports on the schemes of the Church of Scotland with overtures or draft acts sent to Presbyteries for their opinion and legislative acts passed by the general assembly. 1915.

Walsh, Rev. William. *A Pastoral Letter for the Lent of MDCCCLIII addressed to the clergy and laity of the Archdiocese of Halifax.* Halifax, 1853.

Ward, Wilfrid Philip. *The Life and Times of Cardinal Wiseman.* London: Longmans, Green, 1898.

Wilberforce, Wm. *An appeal to the Religion, Justice and Humanity of the Inhabitants of the British Empire in behalf of the Negro Slaves in the West Indies.* London, 1823.

Secondary Sources

Books

Ackroyd, Marcus, Laurence Brockliss, Michael Moss, Kate Retford, and John Stevenson. *Advancing with the Army: Medicine, the Professions and Social Mobility in the British Isles, 1790–1850*. Oxford: Oxford University Press, 2006.

Akenson, Donald H. *The Irish Education Experiment: The National System of Education in Nineteenth-Century Ireland*. Toronto: University of Toronto Press, 1970.

Albisetti, James C., Joyce Goodman, and Rebecca Rogers, eds. *Girls Secondary Education in the Western World, from the 18th to the 20th Century*. New York: Palgrave Macmillan, 2010.

Allen, Richard C., and David Ceri Jones, eds. *The Religious History of Wales: Religious Life and Practice in Wales from the Seventeenth Century to the Present Day*. Cardiff: Welsh Academic Press, 2014.

Allitt, Patrick. *Catholic Converts: British and American Intellectuals Turn to Rome*. Ithaca, NY: Cornell University Press, 1997.

Anderson, Robin. *Pope Pius VII, 1800–1823: His Life, Times and Struggle with Napoleon in the Aftermath of the French Revolution*. Charlotte, NC: TAN Books, 2001.

Bailyn, Bernard, and Patricia L. Denault, eds. *Soundings in Atlantic History: Latent Structures and Intellectual Currents, 1500–1830*. Cambridge, MA: Harvard University Press, 2011.

Bannister, Jerry. *The Rule of the Admirals: Law, Custom, and Naval Government in Newfoundland, 1699–1832*. Toronto: University of Toronto Press, 2003.

Bannister, Jerry, and Liam Riordan, eds. *The Loyal Atlantic: Remaking the British Atlantic in the Revolutionary Era*. Toronto: University of Toronto Press, 2012.

Barr, Colin. *Paul Cullen, John Henry Newman and the Catholic University of Ireland, 1845–1865*. Notre Dame, IN: University of Notre Dame Press, 2003.

Barr, Colin, and Hilary M. Carey, eds. *Religion and Greater Ireland: Christianity and Irish Global Networks, 1750–1900*. Montreal and Kingston: McGill-Queen's University Press, 2015.

Bartlett, Thomas. *The Fall and Rise of the Catholic Nation: The Catholic Question, 1690–1830*. Dublin: Gill and Macmillan, 1992.

Bayly, C.A. *Imperial Meridian: The British Empire and the World, 1780–1830*. Harlow, EN: Longman, 1989.

Beckles, Hilary. *Britain's Black Debt: Reparations for Caribbean Slavery and Native Genocide*. Kingston, JM: University of the West Indies Press, 2013.

Belich, James. *Replenishing the Earth: The Settler Revolution and the Rise of the Anglo-World, 1783–1939*. Oxford: Oxford University Press, 2009.

Bellamy, Joan, Anne Laurence, and Gill Perry, eds. *Women, Scholarship and Criticism: Gender and Knowledge, c. 1790–1900*. Manchester: Manchester University Press, 2000.

Bellamy, Katherine E. *Weavers of the Tapestry*. St John's, NL: Flanker Press, 2006.

Blake, Peter. *George Augustus Sala and the Nineteenth-Century Periodical Press: The Personal Style of a Public Writer*. Farnham, EN: Ashgate, 2015.

Brereton, Bridget, and Kevin A. Yelvington, eds. *The Colonial Caribbean in Transition: Essays on Post-Emancipation Social and Cultural History*. Kingston, JM: University of West Indies Press, 1999.

Brockliss, Laurence W.B., and David Eastwood, eds. *A Union of Multiple Identities: The British Isles, c. 1750-c. 1850*. Manchester: Manchester University Press, 1997.

Brown, Michael, Patrick M. Geoghegan, and James Kelly, eds. *The Irish Act of Union, 1800: Bicentennial Essays*. Dublin: Irish Academic Press, 2003.

Brown, Stewart J. *Thomas Chalmers and the Godly Commonwealth in Scotland*. Oxford: Oxford University Press, 1982.

Brown, Stewart J., and Christopher A. Whatley, eds. *Union of 1707: New Dimensions*. Edinburgh: Edinburgh University Press, 2014.

Buckner, Phillip, ed. *Canada and the British Empire*. Oxford: Oxford University Press, 2008.

Bueltmann, Tanja. *Scottish Ethnicity and the Making of New Zealand Society, 1850 to 1930*. Edinburgh: Edinburgh University Press, 2011.

Bueltmann, Tanja, Andrew Hinson, and Graeme Morton, eds. *Bluid, Kin and Countrie: Scottish Associational Culture in the Diaspora*. Toronto: Stewart Publishing, 2009.

Bumsted, J.M., ed. *Interpreting Canada's Past*. Volume 1: *Before Confederation*. Toronto: Oxford University Press, 1986.

Burns, Arthur, and Joanna Innes, eds. *Rethinking the Age of Reform: Britain 1780–1850*. Cambridge: Cambridge University Press, 2003.

Busteed, Mervyn, Frank Neal, and Jonathan Tonge, eds. *Irish Protestant Identities*. Manchester: Manchester University Press, 2008.

Cadigan, Sean T. *Newfoundland and Labrador: A History*. Toronto: University of Toronto Press, 2009.

Cairnes, J.E. *University Education in Ireland*. London: Macmillan, 1866.

Cameron, C.A. *History of the Royal College of Surgeons in Ireland and of the Irish Schools of Medicine Including a Medical Bibliography and a Medical Biography*. Dublin: Fannin, 1916.

Cameron, James D. *For the People: A History of St Francis Xavier University*. Montreal and Kingston: McGill-Queen's University Press, 1996.

Campbell, Carl C. *Cedulants and Capitulants: The Politics of Coloured Opposition in the Slave Society of Trinidad, 1783–1838*. Port of Spain, TT: Paria Publishing, 1992.

– *The Young Colonials: A Social History of Education in Trinidad and Tobago, 1834–1939*. Kingston, JM: University of the West Indies Press, 1996.

Carey, Hilary. *God's Empire: Religion and Colonialism in the British World, c. 1801–1908*. Cambridge: Cambridge University Press, 2011.

Carrington, C.E. *The British Overseas: Exploits of a Nation of Shopkeepers*. Part 1: *Making of the Empire*. 2nd ed. Cambridge: Cambridge University Press, 1968

Chinnici, Joseph P. *The English Catholic Enlightenment: John Lingard and the Cisalpine Movement, 1780–1850*. Shepherdstown, WV: Patmos Press, 1980.

Claydon, Tony, and Ian McBride, eds. *Protestantism and National Identity: Britain and Ireland, c. 1650–c.1850*. Cambridge: Cambridge University Press, 1998.

Coates, Colin M., and Cecilia Morgan. *Heroines and History: Representations of Madeleine de Verchères and Laura Secord*. Toronto: University of Toronto Press, 2002.

Colley, Linda. *Britons: Forging the Nation, 1707–1837*. New Haven, CT: Yale University Press, 1992.

Condon, Kevin. *The Missionary College of All Hallows, 1842–1891*. Dublin: Irish Press, 1987.

Connell, Joan. *The Roman Catholic Church in England, 1780–1850: A Study in Internal Politics*. Philadelphia: American Philosophical Society, 1984.

Connolly, S.J. *Divided Kingdom: Ireland, 1630–1800*. Oxford: Oxford University Press, 2008.

Conway, Stephen. *Britain, Ireland, and Continental Europe in the Eighteenth Century: Similarities, Connections, Identities*. Oxford: Oxford University Press, 2011.

Cookson, J.E. *The British Armed Nation, 1793–1815*. Oxford: Clarendon Press, 1997.

Cooper, Afua. *The Hanging of Angelique: The Untold Story of Canadian Slavery and the Burning of Old Montreal*. Toronto: Harper Perennial, 2006.

Corish, Patrick J. *The Irish Catholic Community in the Seventeenth and Eighteenth Centuries*. Dublin: Helicon, 1981.

Crerar, Duff. *Padres in No Man's land: Canadian Chaplains and the Great War*. Montreal and Kingston: McGill-Queen's University Press, 1995.

Crosbie, Barry. *Irish Imperial Networks: Migration, Social Communication and Exchange in Nineteenth-Century India*. Cambridge: Cambridge University Press, 2012.

Cudjoe, Selwyn R. *Beyond Boundaries: The Intellectual Tradition of Trinidad and Tobago in the Nineteenth Century*. Wellesley, MA: Calaloux Publications, 2003.

Cunningham, Anne. *The Rome Connection: Australia, Ireland and the Empire, 1865–1885*. Sydney: Crossing Press, 2002.

Curtis, L. Perry. *Apes and Angels: The Irishman in Victorian Caricature*. Rev. ed. Washington, DC: Smithsonian Institution Press, 1997.

Daly, Gavin. *The British Soldier in the Peninsular War: Encounters with Spain and Portugal, 1808–1814*. Basingstoke, EN: Palgrave Macmillan, 2013.

Darcy, J.B. *Fire upon the Earth: The Life and Times of Bp. Michael Anthony Fleming, OSF*. St John's, NL: Creative Publishers, 2003.

Daunton, Martin, and Rick Halpern, eds. *Empire and Others: British Encounters with Indigenous People, 1600–1850*. Philadelphia: University of Pennsylvania Press, 1999.

Davies, Richard A., ed. *The Letters of Thomas Chandler Haliburton*. Toronto: University of Toronto Press, 1988.

de Maeyer, Jan, Sophie Leplae, and Joachim Schmiedl, eds. *Religious Institutes in Western Europe in the 19th and 20th Centuries*. Leuven, BE: Leuven University Press, 2004.

de Nie, Michael. *The Eternal Paddy: Irish Identity and the British Press, 1798–1882*. Madison: University of Wisconsin Press, 2004.

Devas, Raymond. *Conception Island or the Troubled Story of the Catholic Church in Grenada, British West Indies*. Edinburgh: Sands & Co., 1932.

Dickson, David. *Old World Colony: Cork and South Munster, 1630–1830*. Cork, IE: Cork University Press, 2005.

Dickson, David, Dáire Keogh, and Kevin Whelan, eds. *The United Irishmen: Republicanism, Radicalism and Rebellion*. Dublin: Lilliput Press, 1993.

Dickson, David, Justyna Pyz, and Christopher Shepard, eds. *Irish Classrooms and British Empire: Imperial Contexts in the Origins of Modern Education*. Dublin: Four Courts Press, 2012.

Dillon, William. *The Life of John Mitchell*. London, 1888.

Douglas, Roy, Liam Harte, and Jim O'Hara. *Drawing Conclusions: A Cartoon History of Anglo-Irish Relations, 1798–1998*. Belfast: Blackstaff Press, 1998.

Draper, Nicholas. *The Price of Emancipation: Slave-ownership, Compensation and British Society at the End of Slavery*. Cambridge: Cambridge University Press, 2009.

Dunan-Page, Anne, and Clotilde Prunier, eds. *Debating the Faith: Religion and Letter Writing in Great Britain, 1550–1880*. London: Springer, 2013

Dwan, David, and Christopher J. Insole, eds. *The Cambridge Companion to Edmund Burke*. Cambridge: Cambridge University Press, 2012.

Eaton, Mary, Jane Longmore, and Arthur Naylor, eds. *Commitment to Diversity: Catholics and Education in a Changing World*. London: Cassell, 2000.

Edmonds, Ennis B., and Michelle A. Gonzalez, eds. *Caribbean Religious History: An Introduction*. New York: New York University Press, 2010.

Eldridge, C.C., ed. *Kith and Kin: Canada, Britain and the United States from the Revolution to the Cold War*. Cardiff: University of Wales Press, 1997.

Elliott, Marianne. *The Catholics of Ulster: A History*. New York: Basic Books, 2001.

Etherington, Norman, ed. *Missions and Empire*. Oxford: Oxford University Press, 2005.

Fagan, Patrick. *Divided Loyalties: The Question of the Oath for Irish Catholics in the Eighteenth Century*. Dublin: Four Courts Press, 1997.

Farnsworth, Paul, ed. *Island Lives: Historical Archaeology of the Caribbean*. Tuscaloosa: University of Alabama Press, 2001.

Fay, Terence J. *A History of Canadian Catholics*. Montreal and Kingston: McGill-Queen's University Press, 2002.

Fergus, Howard A. *Montserrat: History of a Caribbean Colony*. Oxford: Macmillan, 2004.

Ferguson, Frank, and James McConnell, eds. *Ireland and Scotland in the Nineteenth Century*. Dublin: Four Courts Press, 2009.

Foley, Tadhg, and Thomas A. Boylan, eds. *From Queen's College to National University: Essays towards an Academic History of QUC/UCG/NUI, Galway*. Dublin: Four Courts Press, 1999.

Fraser, T.G., and Keith Jeffrey, eds. *Men, Women and War*. Dublin: Lilliput Press, 1993.

Gay, John D. *The Geography of Religion in England*. London: Gerald Duckworth, 1971.

Glickman, Gabriel. *The English Catholic Community, 1688–1745: Politics, Culture and Ideology*. Woodbridge, EN: Boydell Press, 2009.

Gorman, W. Gordon. *Converts to Rome: A Biographical List of the More Notable Converts to the Catholic Church in the United Kingdom during the Last Sixty Years*. London: Sands & Co., 1910.

Gray, Peter, ed. *Victoria's Ireland? Irishness and Britishness, 1837–1901*. Dublin: Four Courts Press, 2004.

Gray, Richard. *Black Christians and White Missionaries*. New Haven, CT: Yale University Press, 1990.

Greene, Jack P., ed. *Exclusionary Empire: English Liberty Overseas, 1600–1900*. Cambridge: Cambridge University Press, 2010.

Greene, John P. *Between Damnation and Starvation: Priests and Merchants in Newfoundland Politics, 1745–1855*. Montreal and Kingston: McGill-Queen's University Press, 1999.

Grossberg, Michael, and Christopher Tomlins, eds. *The Cambridge History of Law in America*. Vol. 1. New York: Cambridge University Press, 2007.

Gwyn, Julian. *Excessive Expectations: Maritime Commerce and the Economic Development of Nova Scotia, 1740–1870*. Montreal and Kingston: McGill-Queen's University Press, 1998.

Gywnn, Denis. *Cardinal Wiseman*. London: Burns Oates & Washbourne, 1929.

Hall, Catherine. *Macaulay and Son: Architects of Imperial Britain*. New Haven, CT: Yale University Press, 2012.

Hall, Catherine, Keith McClelland, Nick Draper, and Kate Donington, and Rachel Lang. *Legacies of British Slave-Ownership: Colonial Slavery and the Formation of Victorian Britain*. Cambridge: Cambridge University Press, 2014.

Hamilton, Douglas. *Scotland, the Caribbean and the Atlantic World, 1750–1820*. Manchester: Manchester University Press, 2005.

Hamilton, D.J., and A.I. Macinnes, eds. *Jacobitism, Enlightenment and Empire, 1680–1820*. London: Pickering & Chatto, 2014.

Hardinman, David, ed. *Healing Bodies, Saving Souls: Medical Missionaries in Asia and Africa*. Amsterdam: Wellcome Trust Series in the History of Medicine, 2006.

Hardwick, Joseph. *The Anglican British World: The Church of England and the Expansion of the Settler Empire, c. 1790–1860*. Manchester: Manchester University Press, 2014.

Harper, Marjory, and Michael E. Vance, eds. *Myth, Migration and the Making of Memory: Scotia and Nova Scotia, c. 1700–1990*. Edinburgh: John Donald Publishers, 1999.

Harricharan, John T. *Church and Society in Trinidad*. Part I and II. *The Catholic Church in Trinidad, 1498–1863*. Bloomington: Authorhouse, 2006.

Hastings, Adrian. *The Construction of Nationhood: Ethnicity, Religion and Nationalism*. Cambridge: Cambridge University Press, 1997.

Haycock, David Boyd, and Sally Archer, eds. *Health and Medicine at Sea, 1700–1900*. Woodbridge, EN: Boydell Press, 2009.

Hickman, Mary, and Jim MacPherson, eds. *Irish Women in the Diaspora: Theories, Concepts and New Perspectives*. Manchester: Manchester University Press, 2014.

Higgins, Padraig. *A Nation of Politicians: Gender, Patriotism and Political Culture in Late Eighteenth-Century Ireland*. Madison: University of Wisconsin Press, 2010.

Hornsby, Stephen J. *Nineteenth-Century Cape Breton: A Historical Geography*. Montreal and Kingston: McGill-Queen's University Press, 1992.

Jackson, Alvin. *The Two Unions: Ireland, Scotland and the Survival of the United Kingdom, 1707–2007*. Oxford: Oxford University Press, 2012.

Jennings, Lawrence C. *French Reaction to British Slave Emancipation*. Baton Rouge: Louisiana State University Press, 1988.

Johnson, Simon. *The English College at Lisbon*. Volume 1: *From Reformation to Toleration*. Somerset, EN: Downside Abbey Press, 2015.

Johnston, A.A. *A History of the Catholic Church in Eastern Nova Scotia*. Vol. 1. Antigonish, NS: St. Francis Xavier University, 1960.

Jones, Greta, and Elizabeth Malcolm, eds. *Medicine, Disease and the State in Ireland, 1650–1940*. Cork, IE: Cork University Press, 1999.

Juhász-Ormsby, Ágnes, and Nancy Earle, eds. *The Finest Room in the Colony: The Library of John Thomas Mullock*. St John's, NL: Memorial University Library, 2016.

Kaplan, Benjamin, Bob Moore, Henk van Nierop, and Judith Pollmann, eds. *Catholic Communities in Protestant States: Britain and the Netherlands, c. 1570–1720*. Manchester: Manchester University Press, 2009.

Kehoe, S. Karly. *Creating a Scottish Church: Catholicism, Gender and Ethnicity in Nineteenth-Century Scotland*. Manchester: Manchester University Press, 2010.

Kehoe, S. Karly, and Michael E. Vance, eds. *Reappraisals of British Colonisation in Atlantic Canada, 1700–1930*. Edinburgh: Edinburgh University Press, 2020.

Kelleher, Margaret, and Michael Kinneally, eds. *Ireland and Quebec: Multidisciplinary Perspectives on History, Culture and Society*. Dublin: Four Courts Press, 2016.

Kelly, James, and Dáire Keogh, eds. *History of the Catholic Diocese in Dublin*. Dublin: Four Courts Press, 2000.

Kelly, James, and Martyn J. Powell, eds. *Clubs and Societies in Eighteenth-Century Ireland*. Dublin: Four Courts Press, 2010.

Kelly, James E., and Susan Royal, eds. *Early Modern English Catholicism: Identity, Memory and Counter-Reformation*. Leiden: Brill, 2017.

Kennedy, Catriona. *Narratives of the Revolutionary and Napoleonic Wars: Military and Civilian Experience in Britain and* Ireland. Basingstoke, EN: Palgrave Macmillan, 2013.

Kennedy, Catriona, and Matthew McCormack, eds. *Soldiering in Britain and Ireland, 1750–1850: Men at Arms*. London: Palgrave, 2013.

Kennedy, Jean de Chantal. *Biography of a Colonial Town: Hamilton, Bermuda, 1790–1897*. Hamilton: Bermuda Book Stores, 1961.

Kenny, Kevin, ed. *Ireland and the British Empire*. Oxford: Oxford University Press, 2004.

Keogh, Dáire, and Albert McDonnell, eds. *Cardinal Paul Cullen and His World*. Dublin: Four Courts Press, 2011.

Keogh, Dáire and Albert McDonnell, eds. *The Irish College, Rome and Its World*. Dublin: Four Courts Press, 2008.

Keogh, Dáire, and Kevin Whelan, eds. *Acts of Union: The Causes, Contexts and Consequences of the Act of Union*. Dublin: Four Courts Press, 2001.

Kidd, Colin. *British Identities before Nationalism: Ethnicity and Nationhood in the Atlantic World, 1600–1800*. Cambridge: Cambridge University Press, 1999.

– *Unions and Unionisms: Political Thought in Scotland, 1500–2000*. Cambridge: Cambridge University Press, 2008.

Lawson, Philip. *Imperial Challenge: Quebec and Britain in the Age of the American Revolution*. Montreal and Kingston: McGill-Queen's University Press, 1989.

–, ed. *Parliament and the Atlantic Empire*. Edinburgh: Edinburgh University Press, 1995.

Lee, Debbie, ed. *Slavery, Abolition and Emancipation: Writing in the British Romantic Period*. Volume 3: *The Emancipation Debate*. London: Pickering & Chatto, 1999.

Lennon, Joseph. *Irish Orientalism: A Literary and Intellectual History*. Syracuse, NY: Syracuse University Press, 2004.

Little, Sister Mary Bernadette. *"You Did It Unto Me": The Story of the ALPHA and the Sisters of Mercy in Jamaica*. Cincinnati, OH: Beyond the Trees, 2013.

Livesay, James. *Civil Society and Empire: Ireland and Scotland in the Eighteenth-Century Atlantic World*. New Haven, CT: Yale University Press, 2009.

Loades, Judith, ed. *Monastic Studies: The Continuity of Tradition*. Bangor, WS: Headstart History, 1990.

Louis, W. Roger, ed. *The Oxford History of the British Empire*. Volume 3: *The Nineteenth Century*. Oxford: Oxford University Press, 1999.

Luddy, Maria, ed. *The Crimean Journals of the Sisters of Mercy, 1854–56*. Dublin: Four Courts Press, 2004

Macdonald, Fiona A. *Missions to the Gaels: Reformation and Counter-Reformation in Ulster and the Highlands and Islands of Scotland, 1560–1760*. Edinburgh: John Donald, 2006.

MacKillop, Andrew. *"More Fruitful Than the Soil": Army, Empire and the Scottish Highlands, 1715–1815*. East Linton, SCT: Tuckwell Press, 2000.

Madden, Frederick, ed. *Imperial Reconstruction, 1763–1840: The Evolution of Alternative Systems of Colonial Government. Select Documents on the Constitutional History of the British Empire and Commonwealth*. Vol. 3. New York: Greenwood Press, 1987.

Magray, Mary Peckham. *The Transforming Power of the Nuns: Women, Religion and Cultural Change in Ireland, 1750–1900*. New York: Oxford University Press, 1998.

Mangion, Carmen M. *Contested Identities: Catholic Women Religious in Nineteenth-century England and Wales*. Manchester: Manchester University Press, 2008.

Mannion, John, ed. *The Peopling of Newfoundland: Essays in Historical Geography*. St John's: Memorial University of Newfoundland, 1977.

Manuel, Paul Christopher, Lawrence C. Reardon, and Clyde Wilcox, eds. *The Catholic Church and the Nation State: Comparative Perspectives*. Washington, DC: Georgetown University Press, 2006.

Marshall, P.J. *Remaking the British Atlantic: The United States and the British Empire after American Independence*. Oxford: Oxford University Press, 2012.

Marshall, Peter, and Scott, Geoffrey, eds. *Catholic Gentry in English Society: The Throckmortons of Coughton from Reformation to Emancipation*. Farnham, EN: Ashgate, 2009.

Martinez-Fernández, Luis. *Frontiers, Plantations and Walled Cities: Essays on Society, Culture and Politics in the Hispanic Caribbean, 1800–1945*. Princeton, NJ: Markus Wiener Publishers, 2011.

McCann, Phillip. *Island in an Empire: Education, Religion, and Social Life in Newfoundland, 1800–1855*. Portugal Cove, NL: Boulder Publications, 2016.

McCarthy, John M. *Bermuda's Priests: The History of the Establishment and Growth of the Catholic Church in Bermuda*. Halifax: Archdiocese of Halifax, 1954.

McCluksey, Raymond, ed. *The Scots College, Rome, 1600–2000*. Edinburgh: John Donald Publishers, 2000.

McDermid, Jane. *The Schooling of Girls in Britain and Ireland, 1800–1900*. New York: Routledge, 2012.

McGowan, Mark. *Michael Power: The Struggle to Build the Catholic Church on the Canadian Frontier*. Montreal and Kingston: McGill-Queen's University Press, 2005.

– *The Waning of the Green: Catholics, the Irish, and Identity in Toronto, 1887–1922*. Montreal and Kingston: McGill-Queen's University Press, 1999.

Meagher, Nicholas. *The Religious Warfare in Nova Scotia, 1855–1860: Its Political Aspect, the Honourable Joseph Howe's Part in It and the Attitudes of Catholics*. Halifax, 1927.

Meenan, F.O.C. *Cecilia Street: The Catholic University School of Medicine, 1855–1931*. Dublin: Gill and Macmillan, 1987.

Mitchell, Martin J. *The Irish in the West of Scotland, 1797–1848: Trade Unions, Strikes and Political Movements*. Edinburgh: John Donald, 1998.

Morgan, Philip D., and Sean Hawkins, eds. *Black Experience and the Empire*. Oxford: Oxford University Press, 2004.

Moodie, Susanna. *Roughing It in the Bush*. 1852; Toronto: McClelland and Stewart, 1989.

Moody, T.W., and J.C. Beckett. *Queen's, Belfast 1845–1949: The History of a University*. Vol. 1. London: Faber & Faber, 1959.

Morton, Graeme. *Unionist-Nationalism: Governing Urban Scotland, 1830–1860*. East Linton, SCT: Tuckwell Press, 1999.

Mulligan, William, and Brendan Simms, eds. *The Primacy of Foreign Policy in British History, 1660–2000: How Strategic Concerns Shaped Modern Britain*. Basingstoke, EN: Palgrave Macmillan, 2010.

Murdoch, Beamish. *A History of Nova Scotia, or Acadie*. Halifax: James Barnes, 1867.

Murphy, Daniel. *A History of Irish Emigrant and Missionary Education*. Dublin: Four Courts Press, 2000.

Murphy, John A. *The College: A History of Queen's/University College, Cork, 1845–1995*. Cork, IE: Cork University Press, 1995.

Murphy, Terry, and Gerald Stortz, eds. *Creed and Culture: The Place of English-Speaking Catholics in Canadian Society, 1750–1930*. Montreal and Kingston: McGill-Queen's University Press, 1993.

Neatby, Hilda. *The Quebec Act: Protest and Policy*. Scarborough, ON: Prentice-Hall, 1972.

Nelson, Scott Reynolds. *A Nation of Deadbeats: An Uncommon History of America's Financial Disasters*. New York: Alfred Knopf, 2012.

Norman, Edward. *Roman Catholicism in England from the Elizabethan Settlements to the Second Vatican Council*. Oxford: Oxford University Press, 1985.

O'Brien, Susan. *Leaving God for God: The Daughters of Charity of St Vincent de Paul in Britain, 1847–2017*. London: Darton, Longman and Todd, 2017.

O'Connell, Patricia. *The Irish College at Lisbon, 1590–1834*. Dublin: Four Courts Press, 2001.

O'Connor, Thomas, ed., *The Irish in Europe, 1580–1815*. Dublin: Four Courts Press, 2001.

O'Neill, Ciaran. *Catholics of Consequence: Transnational Education, Social Mobility, and the Irish Catholic Elite, 1850–1900*. Oxford: Oxford University Press, 2014.

Pan-Montojo, Juan, and Frederik Pedersen, K., eds. *Communities in European History: Representations, Jurisdictions, Conflicts*. Pisa: Pisa University Press, 2007.

Paseta, Senia. *Before the Revolution: Nationalism, Social Change and Ireland's Catholic Elite, 1879–1922*. Cork, IE: Cork University Press, 1999.

Perin, Roberto. *Rome in Canada: The Vatican and Canadian Affairs in the Late Victorian Age*. Toronto: University of Toronto Press, 1990.

Phillips, Peter, ed. *The Diaries of Bishop William Poynter, V.A. (1815–1824)*. London: Catholic Record Society, 2006.

Philp, Mark, ed. *The French Revolution and British Popular Politics*. Cambridge: Cambridge University Press, 1991.

Pittock, Murray G.H. *Celtic Identity and the British Image*. Manchester: Manchester University Press, 1999.

Pope, Robert, ed. *Religion and National Identity: Wales and Scotland, c. 1700–2000*. Cardiff: University of Wales Press, 2001.

Power, T.P., and Kevin Whelan, eds. *Endurance and Emergence: Catholics in Ireland in the Eighteenth Century*. Dublin: Irish Academic Press, 1990.

Rafferty, Oliver, eds. *Irish Catholic Identities*. Manchester: Manchester University Press, 2013.

– *Violence, Politics and Catholicism in Ireland*. Dublin: Four Courts Press, 2016.

Reed, Rebecca, and Maria Monk. *Veil of Fear: Nineteenth-Century Convent Tales*. Edited by Nancy Lusignan Schultz. Purdue, IN: Purdue University Press, 1999.

Reid, John G. *Six Crucial Decades: Times of Change in the History of the Maritimes*. Halifax: Nimbus Publishing, 1987.

Reid, John G., and Elizabeth Mancke, eds. *Britain's Oceanic Empire: Atlantic and Indian Ocean Worlds, c. 1550–1850*. Cambridge: Cambridge University Press, 2012.

Richards, Eric. *Britannia's Children: Emigration from England, Scotland, Ireland and Wales*. London: Hambledon, 2004.

Roberts, Daniel, and Jonathan Jeffrey Wright, eds. *Irish Imperial Connections, 1775–1947*. London: Palgrave Macmillan, 2019.

Robertson, John, ed. *A Union for Empire: Political Thought and the British Union of 1707*. Cambridge: Cambridge University Press, 1995.

Robinson, John Martin. *Cardinal Consalvi, 1757–1824*. London: Bodley Head, 1987.

Rodgers, Nini. *Ireland, Slavery and Anti-Slavery, 1612–1865*. London: Palgrave Macmillan, 2007.

Rose, Jacqueline. *Godly Kingship in Restoration England: The Politics of the Royal Supremacy, 1660–1688*. Cambridge: Cambridge University Press, 2011.

Royle, Edward, ed. *Issues of Regional Identity*. Manchester: Manchester University Press, 1998.

Scully, Pamela, and Diana Paton, eds. *Gender and Slave Emancipation in the Atlantic World*. Durham, NC: Duke University Press, 2005.

Silvestri, Michael. *Ireland and India: Nationalism, Empire and Memory*. London: Palgrave Macmillan, 2009.

Simpson, Patricia. *Marguerite Bourgeoys and Montreal, 1640–1665*. Montreal and Kingston: McGill-Queen's University Press, 1997.

Snape, Michael. *The Redcoat and Religion: The Forgotten History of the British Soldier from the Age of Marlborough to the Eve of the First World War*. London: Routledge, 2005.

Stewart, Herbert Leslie. *The Irish in Nova Scotia: Annals of the Charitable Irish Society of Halifax, 1786–1836*. Kentville, NS: Kentville Publishing, 1949.

Stockwell, Sarah, ed. *The British Empire: Themes and Perspectives*. Oxford: Blackwell, 2008.

Tallett, Frank, and Nicholas Atkin, eds. *Catholicism in Britain and France since 1789*. London: Hambledon Press, 1996.

Tamko, Michael. *British Romanticism and the Catholic Question: Religion, History and National Identity, 1778–1829*. Basingstoke, EN: Palgrave Macmillan, 2011.

Todd, Alpheus. *Parliamentary Government in the British Colonies*. Boston: Little, Brown, 1880.

Turner, Frank M. *John Henry Newman: The Challenge to Evangelical Religion*. New Haven, CT: Yale University Press, 2002.

Turnham, Margaret H. *Catholic Faith and Practice in England, 1779–1992: The Role of Revivalism and Renewal*. Woodbridge, EN: Boydell Press, 2015.

Vance, Michael E. *Imperial Immigrants: Scottish Settlers in the Upper Ottawa Valley, 1815–1840*. Toronto: Dundurn, 2012.

Vargas, Bernarda. *Sister Bernard, Would You Like to Go to Chile?* Santiago: Sisters of Providence, 1982.

Walsh, Oonagh, ed. *Ireland Abroad: Politics and Professions in the Nineteenth Century*. Dublin: Four Courts Press, 2003.

Watts, John. *A Canticle of Love: The Story of the Franciscan Sisters of the Immaculate Conception*. Edinburgh: John Donald Publishers, 2006.

Weiss-Muller, Hannah. *Subjects and Sovereign: Bonds of Belonging in the Eighteenth-Century British Empire*. New York: Oxford University Press, 2017.

Whelan, Kevin. *The Tree of Liberty: Radicalism, Catholicism and the Construction of Irish Identity, 1760–1830*. Cork, IE: Cork University Press, 2006.

Whitehead, Maurice. *English Jesuit Education: Expulsion, Suppression, Survival and Restoration, 1762–1803*. Farnham, EN: Ashgate, 2013.

Wilson, Kathleen, ed. *A New Imperial History: Culture, Identity and Modernity in Britain and the Empire, 1600–1840*. Cambridge: Cambridge University Press, 2004.

Winks, Roger, and Wm. Roger Louis, eds. *The Oxford History of the British Empire*. Volume 5: *Historiography*. Oxford: Oxford University Press, 1999.

Wood, Donald. *Trinidad in Transition: The Years after Slavery*. Oxford: Oxford University Press, 1968.

Young, Francis. *The Gages of Hengrave and Suffolk Catholicism, 1640–1767*. Suffolk, EN: Boydell Press, 2015.

Journal Articles

Alston, David. "A Forgotten Diaspora: The Children of Enslaved and 'Free Coloured' Women and Highland Scots in Guyana before Emancipation." *Northern Scotland* 6:1 (2015): 49–69.

Anderson, Olive. "The Growth of Christian Militarism in Mid-Victorian Britain." *English Historical Review* 86:338 (1971): 46–72.

Anderson, William James. "Abbe Paul MacPherson's History of the Scots College, Rome." *Innes Review* 12 (1961): 3–172.

– "Some Notes on Catholic Education for Scottish Children in Pre-Emancipation Days." *Innes Review* 14:1 (1963): 38–45.

Bailey, Craig. "'A Child of the Emerald Isle': Ireland and the Making of James Johnson, MD." *Eighteenth-Century Life* 39:1 (2015): 212–35.

Balcom, B.A., and A.J.B. Johnston. "Missions to the Mi'kmaq: Malagawatch and Chapel Island in the 18th Century." *Journal of the Royal Nova Scotia Historical Society* 9 (2006): 115–41.

Bannister, Jerry. "Atlantic Canada in an Atlantic World? Northeastern North America in the Long 18th Century." *Acadiensis* 43:2 (2014): 3–30.

Barr, Colin. "'Imperium in Imperio': Irish Episcopal Imperialism in the Nineteenth Century." *English Historical Review* 123:502 (2008): 611–50.

Barrell, A.D.M. "The Background to *Cum universi*: Scoto-Papal Relations, 1159–1192." *Innes Review* 46:2 (1995): 116–38.

Bayly, C.A. "Ireland, India and the Empire: 1780–1914." *Transactions of the Royal Historical Society* 10 (2000): 377–97.

Beckert, Sven. "Emancipation and Empire: Reconstructing the Worldwide Web of Cotton Production in the Age of the American Civil War." *American Historical Review* 109:5 (2004): 1405–38.

Beckles, Hilary. "A 'Riotous and Unruly Lot': Irish Indentured Servants and Freemen in the English West Indies, 1644–1713." *William and Mary Quarterly* 47:4 (1990): 503–22.

Benton, Lauren, and Ford, Lisa. "Island Despotism: Trinidad, the British Imperial Constitution and Global Legal Order." *Journal of Imperial and Commonwealth Studies* (2017): 1–26.

Berard, Robert. "The Roman Catholic Archdiocese of Halifax and the Colony of Bermuda, 1832–1953." *Collections of the Royal Nova Scotia Historical Society* 42 (1986): 121–38.

Bergin, John, "Irish Catholics and Their Networks in Eighteenth-Century London." *Eighteenth-Century Life* 39:1 (2015): 66–102.

Block, Kristen, and Jenny Shaw. "Subjects without an Empire: The Irish in the Early Modern Caribbean." *Past and Present* 210 (2011): 33–60.

Bourke, Richard. "Pocock and Presuppositions of the New British History." *Historical Journal* 53:3 (2010): 747–70.

Brown, Carys. "Catholic Politics and Creating Trust in Eighteenth-Century England." *British Catholic History* 33:4 (2017): 622–44.

Brown, Michael. "'Like a Devoted Army': Medicine, Heroic Masculinity, and the Military Paradigm in Victorian Britain." *Journal of British Studies* 49:3 (2010): 592–622.

Brown, Vincent. "History Attends to the Dead." *Small Axe* 14:1 (2010): 219–27.

– "Spiritual Terror and Scared Authority in Jamaican Slave Society." *Slavery and Abolition* 24:1 (2003): 24–53.

Buckner, Phillip. "Defining Identities in Canada: Regional, Imperial, National." *Canadian Historical Review* 94:2 (2013): 289–311.

Burns, Robert E. "The Catholic Relief Act in Ireland, 1778." *Church History* 32:2 (1968): 181–206.

Cathcart, Alison. "The Statutes of Iona: The Archipelagic Context." *Journal of British Studies* 49:1 (2010): 4–27.

Chopra, Ruma. "Maroons and Mi'kmaw in Nova Scotia, 1796–1800." *Acadiensis* 46:1 (2017): 14.

Codignola, Luca. "Conflict or Consensus? Catholics in Canada and the United States, 1780–1820." *Canadian Catholic Historical Association Historical Studies* 55 (1988): 43–59.

– "Roman Catholic Conservatism in a New North Atlantic World, 1760–1829." *William and Mary Quarterly* 64:4 (2007): 717–56.

Conway, Stephen. "Christians, Catholics, Protestants: The Religious Links of Britain and Ireland with Continental Europe, c. 1689–1800." *English Historical Review* 124:509 (2009): 833–62.

Cox, Edward L. "Fedon's Rebellion 1795–96: Causes and Consequences." *Journal of Negro History* 67:1 (1982): 7–19.

Crooks, Katherine. "The Quest for Respectability: The Charitable Irish Society in Victorian Halifax." *Historical Studies* 81 (2015): 167–94.

Davis, Richard W. "Wellington, the Constitution and Catholic Emancipation." *Parliamentary History* 15:2 (1996): 209–14.

de Lourdes Fahy, M. "Mother M. Aloysius Doyle (1820–1908)." *Journal of the Galway Archaeological and Historical Society* 36 (1977–78): 70–7.

Devitt, Jerome. "Fenianism's Bermuda Footprint: Revolutionary Nationalism in the Victorian Empire." *Eire-Ireland* 51:1/2 (2016): 141–70.

Donovan, Kenneth. "Slaves and Their Owners in Ile Royale, 1713–1760." *Acadiensis* 25:1 (1995): 3–32.

Donovan, Robert Kent. "The Military Origins of the Roman Catholic Relief Programme of 1778." *Historical Journal* 28:1 (1985): 79–102.

Doona, Mary Ellen. "Sister Mary Joseph Croke: Another Voice from the Crimean War, 1854–1856." *Nursing History Review* 3 (1995): 3–41.

Fawcett, Louise. "Exploring Regional Domains: A Comparative History of Regionalism." *International Affairs* 80:3 (2004): 429–46.

Fay, Terrence J. "The Jesuits and the Catholic University of Canada at Kingston." *Canadian Catholic Historical Association Historical Studies* 58 (1991): 57–77.

Feheney, John M. "Catholic Education in Trinidad in the Twentieth Century: Shaking Off British Protestant Influence." *Recusant History* 29:4 (2009): 553–69.

Fitzgerald, John Edward. "Michael Anthony Fleming and Ultramontanism in Irish-Newfoundland Roman Catholicism, 1829–1850." *Canadian Catholic Historical Association Historical Studies* 64 (1998): 27–44.

Garner, John. "The Enfranchisement of Roman Catholics in the Maritimes." *Canadian Historical Review* 34:3 (1953): 203–18.

Gauvreau, Michael. "Covenanter Democracy: Scottish Popular Religion, Ethnicity, and Varieties of Politico-religious Dissent in Upper Canada, 1815–1841." *Histoire sociale/Social History* 35:71 (2003): 55–84.

Geoghegan, Patrick M. "The Catholics and the Union." *Transactions of the Royal Historical Society* 10 (2000): 243–58.

Gerbner, Katherine. "Theorizing Conversion: Christianity, Colonization, and Consciousness in the Early Modern Atlantic World." *History Compass* 13:3 (2015): 134–147.

Germain, Dom Aidan Henry. "Catholic Military and Naval Chaplains." *Catholic Historical Review* 15:2 (1929): 171–8.

Gibson, Kate. "Marriage Choice and Kinship among the English Catholic Elite, 1680–1730." *Journal of Family History* 41:2 (2016): 144–64.

Goodare, Julian. "The Statutes of Iona in Context." *Scottish Historical Review* 77:1 (1998): 31–57.

Gourlay, Teresa. "Subject to Authority: Bishop Alexander MacDonnel and His Scottish Religious Superiors, 1788–1804." *Innes Review* 61:2 (2010): 150–68.

Hagerty, James, and Tom Johnstone. "Catholic Military Chaplains in the Crimean War." *Recusant History* 27:3 (2005): 415–46.

Hankey, Wayne J. "From Augustine and St. Denys to Olier and Bérulle's Spiritual Revolution: Patristic and Seventeenth-Century Foundations of the Relations between Church and State in Quebec." *Laval théologique et philosophique* 63:3 (2007): 515–59.

Harland-Jacobs, Jessica L. "Incorporating the King's New Subjects: Accommodation and Anti-Catholicism in the British Empire, 1763–1815." *Journal of Religious History* 39:2 (2015): 203–23.

Hogan, Liam, Laura McAtackney, and Matthew C. Reilly. "The Irish in the Anglo-Caribbean: Servants or Slaves?" *History Ireland* 24:2 (2016): 18–22.

Holmes, Andrew R. "Professor James Thompson Sr. and Lord Kelvin: Religion, Science, and Liberal Unionism in Ulster and Scotland." *Journal of British Studies* 50 (2011): 100–24.

Ince, Bernard. "Rebel with a Cause: The Fall and Rise of Abbe Samuel Power." *Journal of Caribbean History* 41 (2013): 28–48.

Jones, Greta. "'A Mysterious Discrimination': Irish Medical Emigration to the United States in the 1950s." *Social History of Medicine* 24:1 (2011): 139–56.

– "'Strike Out Boldly for the Prizes That Are Available to You': Medical Emigration from Ireland, 1860–1905." *Medical History* 54 (2010): 55–74.

Karsten, Peter. "Irish Soldiers in the British Army, 1792–1922: Suborned or Subordinate?" *Journal of Social History* 17:1 (1983): 31–64.

Kehoe, S. Karly. "Accessing Empire: Irish Surgeons and the Royal Navy, 1850–1880." *Social History of Medicine* 26:2 (2013): 204–22.

– "Catholic Relief and the Political Awakening of Irish Catholics in Nova Scotia, 1780–1830." *Journal of Imperial and Commonwealth History* 46:1 (2018): 1–20.

– "From the Caribbean to the Scottish Highlands: Charitable Enterprise in the Age of Improvement, c. 1750 to c. 1820." *Rural History* 27:1 (2016): 37–59.

– "Nursing the Mission: The Franciscan Sisters of the Immaculate Conception and the Sisters of Mercy in Glasgow, 1847–1866." *Innes Review* 56:1 (2005): 46–60.

– "Unionism, Nationalism and the Scottish Catholic Periphery." *Britain and the World* 4:1 (2011): 65–83.

Kehoe, S. Karly, and Darren Tierney. "'Like a Kind Mother': Imperial Concerns and Britain's Changing Perception of Rome, 1783–1815." *Historical Studies* 83 (2015): 11–31.

Kennedy, Cynthia M. "The Other White Gold: Salt, Slaves, the Turks and Caicos Islands, and British Colonialism." *The Historian* 69:2 (2000): 215–30.

Keogh, Richard A., "'From Education, from Duty and from Principle': Irish Catholic Loyalty in Context." *British Catholic History* 33:3 (2017): 421–50.

– "'Nothing Is so Bad for the Irish as Ireland Alone': William Keogh and Catholic Loyalty." *Irish Historical Studies* 38:150 (2012): 230–48.

Keough, Willeen. "Contested Terrains: Ethnic and Gendered Spaces in the Harbour Grace Affray." *Canadian Historical Review* 90:1 (2009): 29–70.

Kesselring, K.J. "'Negroes of the Crown': The Management of Slaves Forfeited by Grenadian Rebels." *Journal of the Canadian Historical Association* 22:2 (2011): 1–29.

Kidd, Colin. "Wales, the Enlightenment and the New British History." *Welsh Review of History* 25:2 (2010): 209–30.

Kowaleski, Maryanne. "The Expansion of the South-Western Fisheries in Late Medieval England." *Economic History Review* 53:3 (2000): 429–54.

Lambert, Carolyn. "No Choice but to Look Elsewhere: Attracting Immigrants to Newfoundland, 1840–1890." *Acadiensis* 41:2 (2012): 89–108.

Lawson, Philip. "'The Irishman's Prize': Views of Canada from the British Press, 1760–1774." *Historical Journal* 28:3 (1985): 575–96.

Lenik, Stephen. "Mission Plantations, Space and Social Control: Jesuits as Planters in French Caribbean Colonies and Frontiers." *Journal of Social Archaeology* 12:1 (2011): 51–71.

Ludlow, Peter. "A 'Primitive Germ of Discord' in the North Atlantic World: Newfoundland-Irish Roman Catholics in Scottish Cape Breton." *Journal of Irish and Scottish Studies* 3:1 (2009): 175–92.

MacDonald, Heidi. "Developing a Strong Roman Catholic Social Order in late Nineteenth-Century Prince Edward Island." *Canadian Catholic Historical Association Historical Studies* 69 (2003): 34–51.

MacGregor, M.D. "The Statutes of Iona: Text and Context." *Innes Review* 57:2 (2006): 111–81.

Machin, G.I.T. "The Catholic Question and the Monarchy, 1827–1829." *Parliamentary History* 16:2 (1997): 213–20.

– "Resistance to Repeal of the Test and Corporation Acts, 1828." *Historical Journal* 22:1 (1979): 115–39.

MacKenzie, John. "Irish, Scottish, Welsh and English Worlds? A Four-Nation Approach to the History of the British Empire." *History Compass* 6:5 (2008): 1244–63.

Mandelblatt, Bertie. "A Transatlantic Commodity: Irish Salt Beef in the French Atlantic World." *History Workshop Journal* 63 (2007): 18–47.

Mangion, Carmen. "'Good Teacher' or 'Good Religious'? The Professional Identity of Catholic Women Religious in Nineteenth-Century England and Wales." *Women's History Review* 14:2 (2005): 223–42.

– "'To Console, to Nurse, to Prepare for Eternity': The Catholic Sickroom in Late Nineteenth-Century England." *Women's History Review* 21:4 (2012): 657–72.

Mannion, John. "Migration and Upward Mobility: The Meagher Family in Ireland and Newfoundland, 1780–1830." *Irish Economic and Social History* 40 (1988): 54–70.

McGowan, Mark G. "The Maritimes Region and the Building of a Canadian Church: The Case of the Diocese of Antigonish after Confederation." *Canadian Catholic Historical Association Historical Studies* 70 (2004): 48–70.

– "'Pregnant with Perils': Canadian Catholicism and Its Relation to the Catholic Churches of Newfoundland, 1840–1949." *Newfoundland and Labrador Studies* 28:2 (2013): 193–218.

McNairn, Jeffrey L. "'Everything Was New, yet Familiar': British Travellers, Halifax and the Ambiguities of Empire." *Acadiensis* 36:2 (2007): 28–54.

Millar, Gordon. "Maynooth and Scottish Politics: The Rome of the Maynooth Grant Issues, 1845–1857." *Records of the Scottish Church History Society* 27 (1997): 220–79.

Morley, Vincent. "The Idea of Britain in Eighteenth-Century Ireland and Scotland." *Studia Hibernica* 33 (2004–5): 101–24.

Mullen, Stephen. "A Glasgow–West India Merchant House and the Imperial Dividend, 1779–1867." *Journal of Scottish Historical Studies* 33 (2013): 196–233.

Murphy, J.J.W. "An Irish Sister of Mercy in the Crimean War." *Irish Sword* 5:21 (1962): 251–61.

Murphy, Terrence. "The Emergence of Maritime Catholicism, 1781–1830." *Acadiensis* 13:2 (1984): 29–49.

Nash, R.C. "Irish Atlantic Trade in the Seventeenth and Eighteenth Centuries." *William and Mary Quarterly* 42:3 (1985): 329–56.

O'Brien, Susan. "French Nuns in Nineteenth-Century England." *Past and Present* 154 (1997): 142–80.

O'Leary, Paul. "When Was Anti-Catholicism? The Case of Nineteenth- and Twentieth-Century Wales." *Journal of Ecclesiastical History* 56:2 (2005): 307–25.

Peabody, Sue. "'A Dangerous Zeal': Catholic Missions to Slaves in the French Antilles, 1635–1800." *French Historical Studies* 25:1 (2002): 53–90.

Peskin, Lawrence A. "Conspiratorial Anglophobia and the War of 1812." *Journal of American History* 98:3 (2011): 647–69.

Pocock, J.G.A. "British History: A Plea for a New Subject." *Journal of Modern History* 4:4 (1975): 601–21.

Pope, David J. "Liverpool's Catholic Ships' Captains, c. 1745–1807." *Recusant History* 29:1 (2008): 48–76.

Popkin, Jeremy D. "Thermidor, Slavery, and the 'Affaire des Colonies'." *French Historical Studies* 38:1 (2015): 61–82.

Quintanilla, Mark. "The World of Alexander Campbell: An Eighteenth-Century Grenadian Planter." *Albion* 35:2 (2003): 229–56.

Rafferty, Oliver P. "The Catholic Church, Ireland and the British Empire, 1800–1921." *Historical Research* 84:224 (2011): 288–309.

Raftery, Deidre. "'Je Suis d'aucune Nation': The Recruitment and Identity of Irish Women Religious in the International Mission Field, c. 1840–1940." *Paedagogica Historica* 49:4 (2013): 513–30.

Roberts, Alasdair F.B. "The Role of Women in Scottish Catholic Survival." *Innes Review* 70:2 (1991): 129–50.

Roddy, Sarah. "Spiritual Imperialism and the Mission of the Irish Race: The Catholic Church and Emigration from Nineteenth-Century Ireland." *Irish Historical Studies* 38:152 (2013): 600–19.

Rodgers, Nini. "Ireland and the Black Atlantic in the Eighteenth Century." *Irish Historical Studies* 32:126 (2000): 174–92.

Ryden, David Beck. "'One of the Finest and Most Fruitful Spots in America': An Analysis of Eighteenth-Century Carriacou." *Journal of Interdisciplinary History* 43:4 (2013): 539–70.

Schoeppner, Michael A. "Status across Borders: Roger Taney, Black British Subjects, and a Diplomatic Antecedent to the Dred Scott Decision." *American Historical Review* 100:1 (2013): 46–67.

Schweizer, Karl. "Jacobitism and the Historian: Some Neglected Sources on the Jacobite Insurrections of 1715 and 1745." *Canadian Journal of History* 48 (2013): 441–57.

Scott, Mary Eileen. "The Congregation of Notre Dame in Early Nova Scotia." *Canadian Catholic Historical Association Report* 20 (1953): 67–80.

Scott, Stephen. "Through the Diameter of Respectability: The Politics of Historical Representation in Post-Emancipation Colonial Trinidad." *New West Indian Guide* 76 (2002): 271–304.

Simms, J.G. "Connacht in the Eighteenth Century." *Irish Historical Studies* 11:42 (1958): 116–33.

Smith, James Patterson. "Empire and Social Reform: British Liberals and the 'Civilizing Mission' in the Sugar Colonies, 1868–1874." *Albion* 27:2 (1995): 253–77.

Sommers, Susan Mitchell. "Sir John Coxe Hippisley: That '*Busy* Man' in the Cause of Catholic Emancipation." *Parliamentary History* 27:1 (2008): 82–95.

Tenbus, Eric G. "'We Fight for the Cause of God': English Catholics and Education of the Poor, and the Transformation of Catholic Identity in Victorian Britain." *Journal of British Studies* 46 (2007): 861–83.

Tozzi, Christopher. "Jews, Soldiering, and Citizenship in Revolutionary and Napoleonic France." *Journal of Modern History* 86 (2014): 233–57.

Truxes, Thomas M. "Dutch-Irish Cooperation in the Mid-Eighteenth-Century Wartime Atlantic." *Early American Studies* 10 (2012): 302–34.

von Arx, Jeffrey O. "Manning's Ultramontanism and the Catholic Church in British Politics." *Recusant History* 19:1 (1989): 332–47.

Wagg, Phyllis MacInnes. "Laurence Kavanagh I: An Eighteenth-Century Cape Breton Entrepreneur." *Nova Scotia Historical Review* 10 (1990): 124–32.

Whitfield, Harvey Amani. "Slave Life and Slave Law in Colonial Prince Edward Island, 1769–1825." *Acadiensis* 38:2 (2009), 29–51.

Willis, Aaron. "The Standing of New Subjects: Grenada and the Protestant Constitution after the Treaty of Paris (1763)." *Journal of Imperial and Commonwealth History* 42:1 (2014): 1–21.

Wood, H.O.B. "The Constitutional History of Trinidad and Tobago." *Caribbean Quarterly* 6:2 (1960): 143–59.

Dissertations

Fitzgerald, John Edward. "Conflict and Culture in Irish-Newfoundland Roman Catholicism, 1829–1850." PhD diss., University of Ottawa, 1997.

Kehoe, Sara Karly. "Special Daughters of Rome: Glasgow and Its Roman Catholic Sisters, 1847–1913." PhD diss., University of Glasgow, 2005.

Morgan, Robert J. "Orphan Outpost: Cape Breton Colony, 1784–1820." PhD diss., University of Ottawa, 1972.

Rigney, William. "Bartholomew Woodlock and the Catholic University, 1861–1879." PhD diss., University College Dublin, 1994.

Schwamenfeld, Steven. "The Foundation of British: National Identity and the British Common Soldier." PhD diss., Florida State University, 2006.

Spence, Caroline Quarrier. "Ameliorating Empire: Slavery and Protection in the British Colonies, 1783–1865." PhD diss., Harvard University, 2014.

Thompson, John Handby. "The Free Church Army Chaplains, 1830–1930." PhD diss., University of Sheffield, 1990.

Web Sources

"Biography of John Keogh." *Library of Ireland Online*. http://www.libraryireland.com/biography/JohnKeogh.php.

Buckner, Phillip. "Harvey, Sir John." *Dictionary of Canadian Biography*, vol. 8. University of Toronto/Université Laval, 2003. http://www.biographi.ca/en/bio/harvey_john_8E.html.

"Charitable Irish Society, Lawrence O'Connor Doyle." Nova Scotia Archives, Virtual Archives. http://gov.ns.ca/nsarm/virtual/CIS/archives.asp?ID=63.

Chichester, H.M. "Calvert, Sir Harry, first baronet (*bap.* 1763, *d.* 1826)." Revised by John Sweetman. *Oxford Dictionary of National Biography Online*. http://www.oxforddnb.com/view/article/4422.

– "M'Carthy, Sir Charles (1764–1824)." Revised by Lynn Milne. *Oxford Dictionary of National Biography Online*. http://www.oxforddnb.com/view/article/17375.

Chinnici, J.P. "Poynter, William (1762–1827)." *Oxford Dictionary of Canadian Biography*. http://www.oxforddnb.com/view/article/22688.

Hansard. House of Commons. Debates. Frederick Lucas, "Religious Wants of Roman Catholic Soldiers." 3 December 1854. Vol. 131, cc. 314–30. http://hansard.millbanksystems.com/commons/1854/mar/03/religious-wants-of-roman-catholic.

Harris, C.A. "Parry, Thomas (1795–1870)." Revised by H.C.G. Matthew. *Oxford Dictionary of National Biography*. http://www.oxforddnb.com/view/article/21435.

In Supremo Apostolatus. Apostolic Letter of Pope Gregory XVI, December 3, 1839. http://www.papalencyclicals.net/Greg16/g16sup.htm.

"John Cameron." *Dictionary of Canadian Biography Online*. http://www
.biographi.ca/en/bio/cameron_john_1827_1910_13E.html.

"Joseph-Octave Plessis." *Dictionary of Canadian Biography Online*. http://www
.biographi.ca/009004–119.01-e.php?id_nbr=3076.

Keenan, Desmond. "The Grail of Catholic Emancipation." Des Keenan's Books
on Irish History. http://www.deskeenan.com/1GrChap1.htm.

Laughton, J.K. "Elliot, Sir Charles (1801–1875)." Revised by Andrew Lambert.
Oxford Dictionary of National Biography Online. http://www.oxforddnb.com
/view/article/8656.

"Marguerite Bourgeoys (1620–1700), Foundress of the Sisters of the
Congregation of Notre-Dame." Vatican Digital Resources. http://www
.vatican.va/news_services/liturgy/saints/ns_lit_doc_19821031_bourgeoys
_en.html.

MacLean, R.A. "Burke (Bourke), Edmund (1753–1820)," *Dictionary of Canadian
Biography*. Vol. 5. University of Toronto/Université Laval, 2003, http://
www.biographi.ca/en/bio/burke_edmund_1753_1820_5E.html.

Mitchell, Rosemary. "Gillow, Thomas." *Oxford Dictionary of National Biography
Online*. http://www.oxforddnb.com/view/article/10753.

Monkhouse, William Cosmo. "Representative Poetry Online." http://rpo
.library.utoronto.ca/poets/monkhouse-william-cosmo.

Optime Noscitis. On the Proposed Catholic University of Ireland. Encyclical of
Pope Pius IX. 20 March 1854. ?http://www.papalencyclicals.net/Pius09
/p9optim1.htm.

Rea, J.E. "Alexander McDonell." *Dictionary of Canadian Biography Online*.
http://www.biographi.ca/en/bio/mcdonell_alexander_7E.html.

Sicut Dudum. Apostolic Letter of Pope Eugene IV, 13 January 1435. http://
www.papalencyclicals.net/Eugene04/eugene04sicut.htm.

"Sir Brenton Halliburton." *Dictionary of Canadian Biography Online*. http://
biographi.ca/009004–119.01-e.php?id_nbr=3949.

"Sir James Kempt." *Dictionary of Canadian Biography Online*. http://www
.biographi.ca/009004–119.01-e.php?id_nbr=4004.

"Sir John Coxe Hippisley." *Oxford Dictionary of National Biography Online*.
https://doi.org/10.1093/ref:odnb/13361.

"Sir John Wentworth." *Dictionary of Canadian Biography Online*. http://www
.biographi.ca/en/bio.php?id_nbr=2710.

Sisters of St Joseph of Cluny. "Our History in the Caribbean." http://www
.clunycarib.org/castory.htm.

Sublimus Dei. Apostolic Letter of Pope Paul III, 29 May 1537. http://www
.papalencyclicals.net/Paul03/p3subli.htm.

Wolffe, John. "Charles Newdigate (1816–1887)." *Oxford Dictionary of National
Biography Online*. http://www.oxforddnb.com/view/article/20000.

Index

Page numbers in italics denote figures.

STUDIES IN ATLANTIC CANADA HISTORY

Editors: John G. Reid and Peter L. Twohig

Meaghan Elizabeth Beaton, *The Centennial Cure: Commemoration, Identity, and Cultural Capital in Nova Scotia during Canada's 1967 Centennial Celebrations*

Jeffers Lennox, *Homelands and Empires: Indigenous Spaces, Imperial Fictions, and Competition for Territory in Northeastern North America, 1690–1763*

Lachlan MacKinnon, *Closing Sysco: Industrial Decline in Atlantic Canada's Steel City*

Margaret Conrad, *At the Ocean's Edge: A History of Nova Scotia to Confederation*

S. Karly Kehoe, *Empire and Emancipation: Scottish and Irish Catholics at the Atlantic Fringe, 1780–1850*